THE DEVELOPMENT OF THE LAW OF THE SEA BY UNCLOS DISPUTE SETTLEMENT BODIES

This is the first study to provide both a systematic assessment of the ways by which the dispute settlement bodies of the United Nations Convention on the Law of the Sea (UNCLOS) contribute to the development of the law of the sea and an exposition of the factors that explain such contribution. The book analyses UNCLOS dispute settlement bodies' decisions and the legal reasoning in key areas of the law of the sea. It further examines the factors that impact the decision-making process of UNCLOS tribunals to explain the parameters within which UNCLOS tribunals operate and how this impacts their ability and willingness to develop the law. The book provides a unique reference point for lecturers, researchers and students of international law, particularly law of the sea, as well as practitioners and government advisors who wish to gain comprehensive insights into the functioning and the role of the UNCLOS dispute settlement system.

LAN NGOC NGUYEN is an assistant professor at Utrecht University School of Law. She obtained her BA (*summa cum laude*) from the Diplomatic Academy of Vietnam, her LLM in International Law (First Class Honours and awarded the Clive Parry (Overseas) Prize for International Law) and her PhD from the University of Cambridge. She has previously worked at the Diplomatic Academy of Vietnam and interned at the International Tribunal for the Law of the Sea.

The Development of the Law of the Sea by UNCLOS Dispute Settlement Bodies

LAN NGOC NGUYEN
Utrecht University

CAMBRIDGE
UNIVERSITY PRESS

CAMBRIDGE
UNIVERSITY PRESS

Shaftesbury Road, Cambridge CB2 8EA, United Kingdom

One Liberty Plaza, 20th Floor, New York, NY 10006, USA

477 Williamstown Road, Port Melbourne, VIC 3207, Australia

314–321, 3rd Floor, Plot 3, Splendor Forum, Jasola District Centre, New Delhi – 110025, India

103 Penang Road, #05–06/07, Visioncrest Commercial, Singapore 238467

Cambridge University Press is part of Cambridge University Press & Assessment, a department of the University of Cambridge.

We share the University's mission to contribute to society through the pursuit of education, learning and research at the highest international levels of excellence.

www.cambridge.org
Information on this title: www.cambridge.org/9781108845632

DOI: 10.1017/9781108980296

First published 2023

A catalogue record for this publication is available from the British Library

Library of Congress Cataloging-in-Publication Data
Names: Ngoc Nguyen, Lan, author.
TITLE: The development of the law of the sea by UNCLOS dispute settlement bodies / Lan Ngoc Nguyen, Utrecht University.
DESCRIPTION: Cambridge, United Kingdom ; New York, NY : Cambridge University Press, 2022. | Includes bibliographical references and index.
IDENTIFIERS: LCCN 2022025809 (print) | LCCN 2022025810 (ebook) | ISBN 9781108845632 (hardback) | ISBN 9781108980296 (paperback) | ISBN 9781108970105 (epub)
SUBJECTS: LCSH: Law of the sea. | Maritime law. | Marine resources conservation–Law and legislation. | Arbitration (International law) | International courts. | United Nations Convention on the Law of the Sea (1982 December 10)
CLASSIFICATION: LCC KZA1145 .N49 2022 (print) | LCC KZA1145 (ebook) | DDC 341.4/5–DC23/eng/20220801
LC record available at https://lccn.loc.gov/2022025809
LC ebook record available at https://lccn.loc.gov/2022025810

ISBN 978-1-108-84563-2 Hardback

Contents

Acknowledgements

This book is a revised version of my doctoral thesis, which was submitted to the University of Cambridge in 2018. I would first like to thank Professor Christine Gray for her guidance and support throughout my doctoral research. I am also indebted to my thesis examiners Dr Michael Waibel and Professor Robin Churchill, whose insightful comments and suggestions during my viva have been greatly helpful in the preparation of this book.

I would like to acknowledge the support that I have received from my colleagues at the International and European Law Department of Utrecht University. I would particularly like to thank my colleagues at the Netherlands Institute for the Law of the Sea (Utrecht University Centre for Water, Oceans and Sustainability Law) not only for their encouragement and advice at different stages in the preparation of this book but also for being a constant source of inspiration for my academic career. I would also like to thank Rosalie Wesselink and Lou McDonough Monroy for their assistance in preparing this book. I am grateful for the constant support that I have received from my former colleagues at the Diplomatic Academy of Vietnam, my former PhD companions at the Law Faculty of the University of Cambridge and my close friends from Vietnam.

I must also express my gratitude to Tom Randall and other staff members of Cambridge University Press, who were always very patient with my requests and who always promptly answered any questions that I had to guide me through the production of this book.

Finally, my family has been the backbone of all my academic endeavours. I thank my parents, Nguyen Thanh Binh and Trinh Thi Dinh, my brother, Nguyen Trinh Minh Anh, and my nephew, Nguyen Khang Nguyen, for their unflinching love and belief in me; and my in-laws the Pronkers and

Bosman for being a second loving family to me in the Netherlands. The most special thanks are for my husband, Matti Pronker, for being my shoulder to lean on, and for my children, Vi and Daan, for all the cuddles, kisses and the unconditional love that keep me going as a mother in academia. This book is dedicated to them.

Table of Cases

International Tribunal for the Law of the Sea

Camouco (Panama *v* France) (Prompt Release, Judgment) ITLOS Reports 2000, 10.

Case concerning the Detention of Three Ukrainian Naval Vessels (Ukraine *v* Russian Federation) (Provisional Measures, Order of 25 May 2019) ITLOS Reports 2019, 283.

Delimitation of the Maritime Boundary in the Atlantic Ocean (Ghana/Côte d'Ivoire) ITLOS Reports 2017, 4.

Delimitation of the Maritime Boundary in the Bay of Bengal (Bangladesh/Myanmar) (Judgment) ITLOS Reports 2012, 4.

Dispute Concerning Delimitation of the Maritime Boundary between Mauritius and Maldives in the Indian Ocean (Mauritius/Maldives) (Preliminary Objections, Order of 28 January 2021) ITLOS Reports 2021, 28.

Enrica Lexie (Italy *v* India) (Provisional Measures, Order of 24 July 2015) ITLOS Reports 2015, 176.

Grand Prince (Belize *v* France) (Prompt Release, Judgment) ITLOS Reports 2001, 17.

Hoshinmaru (Japan *v* Russian Federation) (Prompt Release, Judgment) ITLOS Reports 2005–2007, 18.

Juno Trader (Saint Vincent and the Grenadines *v* Guinea-Bissau) (Prompt Release, Judgment) ITLOS Reports 2004, 17.

Land Reclamation in and Around the Straits of Johor (Malaysia *v* Singapore) (Provisional Measures, Order of 8 October 2003) ITLOS Reports 2003, 10.

M/V 'Louisa' (Saint Vincent and the Grenadines *v* Kingdom of Spain) (Judgment) ITLOS Reports 2013, 4.

M/V 'Norstar' Case (Panama *v* Italy) (Preliminary Objections) ITLOS Reports 2016, 44.

M/V 'SAIGA' (Saint Vincent and the Grenadines *v* Guinea) (Prompt Release, Judgment) ITLOS Reports 1997, 6.

M/V 'SAIGA' (No. 2) (Saint Vincent and the Grenadines *v* Guinea) (Judgment) ITLOS Reports 1999, 10.

M/V 'Virginia G' (Panama/Guinea-Bissau) (Judgment) ITLOS Reports 2014, 4.

Monte Confurco (Seychelles *v* France) (Prompt Release, Judgment) ITLOS Reports 2000, 86.

MOX Plant (Ireland *v* United Kingdom) (Provisional Measures, Order of 3 December 2001) ITLOS Reports 2001, 95.

Request for Advisory Opinion Submitted by the Sub-Regional Fisheries Commission (Advisory Opinion, 2 April 2015) ITLOS Reports 2015, 4.

Responsibilities and Obligations of States with Respect to Activities in the area (Advisory Opinion, 1 February 2011) ITLOS Reports 2011, 10.

Southern Bluefin Tuna (New Zealand *v* Japan; Australia *v* Japan) (Provisional Measures, Order of 27 August 1999) ITLOS Reports 1999, 280.

Tomimaru (Japan *v* Russian Federation) (Prompt Release, Judgment) ITLOS Reports 2005–2007, 74.

Volga (Russian Federation *v* Australia) (Prompt Release, Judgment) ITLOS Reports 2002, 10.

UNCLOS Annex VII Arbitral Tribunals

Arbitration between Barbados and the Republic of Trinidad and Tobago, Relating to the Delimitation of the Exclusive Economic Zone and the Continental Shelf between them (11 April 2006) RIAA Volume XXVII 147.

Arbitration between Guyana and Suriname (Guyana *v* Suriname) (17 September 2007) RIAA Volume XXX 1.

Arbitration Regarding the Arctic Sunrise (Kingdom of the Netherlands *v* Russian Federation) (2014–2015) RIAA XXXII 183.

The Bay of Bengal Maritime Boundary Arbitration between the People's Republic of Bangladesh and the Republic of India (Bangladesh *v* India) (2014) RIAA XXXII 1.

Case Concerning Land Reclamation by Singapore in and around the Straits of Johor (Malaysia *v* Singapore) (2005) RIAA XVII 133.

Chagos Marine Protected Area Arbitration (Mauritius *v* United Kingdom) (2015) RIAA XXI 359.

Dispute Concerning Coastal State Rights in the Black Sea, Sea of Azov, and Kerch Strait (Ukraine *v* the Russian Federation) (Preliminary Objections) Award of 21 February 2020.

The Duzgit Integrity Arbitration (Malta *v* São Tomé and Príncipe), Arbitral Award of 5 September 2016.
The 'Enrica Lexie' Incident (Italy *v* India), Arbitral Award of 21 May 2021.
MOX Plant (Ireland *v* United Kingdom) Order N° 3 Suspension of Proceedings on Jurisdiction and Merits, and Request for Further Provisional Measures.
South China Sea Arbitration (Philippines *v* China), Award on Jurisdiction and Admissibility (2015) RIAA XXXIII 1.
The South China Sea Arbitration between the Republic of the Philippines and the People's Republic of China (Philippines *v* China) (2016) RIAA XXXIII 153.
Southern Bluefin Tuna Case (Australia and New Zealand *v* Japan), Award on Jurisdiction and Admissibility (4 August 2000) 39 ILM 1359.

International Court of Justice

Aegean Sea Continental Shelf (Greece *v* Turkey) [1978] ICJ Rep 3.
Armed Activities on the Territory of the Congo (Democratic Republic of the Congo *v* Uganda) [2005] ICJ Rep 168.
Case Concerning Rights of Nationals of the United States of American in Morocco (France *v* United States) [1952] ICJ Rep 176.
Case Concerning rights of nationals of the United States of America in Morocco (France *v* US) [1952] ICJ Rep 189.
Case Concerning the Northern Cameroons (Cameroon *v* United Kingdom) (Preliminary Objections) [1963] ICJ Rep 15.
Certain Activities Carried Out by Nicaragua in the Border Area (Costa Rica v Nicaragua) *and construction of a road in Costa Rica along the San Juan River* (Nicaragua *v* Costa Rica) [2015] ICJ Rep 665.
Certain Questions of Mutual Assistance in Criminal Matters (Djibouti *v* France) [2008] ICJ Rep 177.
Continental Shelf (Libyan Arab Jarnahiriya/Malta) [1985] ICJ Rep 13.
Continental Shelf (Tunisia/Libyan Arab Jamahiriya) [1982] ICJ Rep 18.
Delimitation of the Maritime Boundary in the Gulf of Maine area (Canada/ United States) [1984] ICJ Rep 246.
Dispute Regarding Navigational and Related Rights (Costa Rica *v* Nicaragua) [2009] ICJ Rep 243.
Fisheries case (United Kingdom *v* Norway) [1951] ICJ Rep 116.
Fisheries Jurisdiction (United Kingdom *v* Iceland) [1974] ICJ Rep 3.
Gabcikovo-Nagymaros Project (Hungary/Slovakia) [1997] ICJ Rep 7.
Interpretation of Peace Treaties, Advisory Opinion [1950] ICJ Rep 221.
Kasikili/Sedudu Island (Botswana/Namibia) [1999] ICJ Rep 1045.

Legal Consequences for States of the Continued Presence of South Africa in Namibia (South West Africa) Notwithstanding Security Council Resolution 276 (1970) [1971] ICJ Rep 16.

Legal Consequences for States of the Continued Presence of South Africa in Namibia (South West Africa) notwithstanding Security Council Resolution 276 (1970), Advisory Opinion [1971] ICJ Rep 16.

Legality of the Use or Threat of Nuclear Weapons, Advisory Opinion [1996] ICJ Rep 226.

Maritime Delimitation in the Indian Ocean (Somalia *v* Kenya), Judgment 12 October 2021.

Maritime Delimitation in the Indian Ocean (Somalia *v* Kenya), Preliminary Objections, [2017] ICJ Rep 3.

Oil Platforms (Islamic Republic of Iran *v* United States of America) [2003] ICJ Rep 161.

Pulp Mills on the River Uruguay (Argentina *v* Uruguay) [2010] ICJ Rep 14.

Question of the Delimitation of the Continental Shelf between Nicaragua and Colombia beyond 200 Nautical Miles from the Nicaraguan Coast (Nicaragua *v* Colombia), (Preliminary Objections) [2016] ICJ Rep 100.

South West Africa Cases (Ethiopia *v* South Africa, Liberia *v* South Africa) (Second Phase) [1966] ICJ Rep 6.

Territorial and Maritime Dispute (Nicaragua *v* Colombia) [2012] ICJ Rep 624.

Territorial and Maritime Dispute between Nicaragua and Honduras in the Caribbean Sea (Nicaragua *v* Honduras) [2007] ICJ Rep 659.

Whaling in the Antarctic (Australia *v* Japan: New Zealand intervening) [2014] ICJ Rep 226.

Ad hoc Arbitral Tribunals

Award of the Arbitral Tribunal in the Second Stage – Maritime Delimitation (Eritrea/Yemen) (1999) RIAA XXII 335.

Delimitation of Maritime Areas between Canada and France (10 June 1992) RIAA XXI 265.

Delimitation of the Anglo-French Continental Shelf Arbitration (UK/France), First Decision (30 June 1977) RIAA XVIII:3 63.

Iron Rhine Arbitration (Belgium *v* Netherlands), Award, ICGJ 373 (PCA 2005).

Proceedings Pursuant to the OSPAR Convention (Ireland/United Kingdom) (2003) RIAA XXIII 59.

Territorial Sovereignty and Scope of the Dispute (Eritrea and Yemen) (1998) RIAA XXII 209.

Other Courts and Tribunals

European Communities – Measures Affecting Asbestos and Asbestos-Containing Products, AB Report (12 March 2001) WT/DS135/AB/R.

European Communities – Measures Affecting the Approval and Marketing of Biotech Products, AB Report (29 September 2006) WT/DS291.

European Communities – Measures Concerning Meat and Meat Products (Hormones), AB Report (16 January 1998) WT/DS26/AB/R.

Korea – Measures Affecting Imports of Fresh, Chilled and Frozen Beef, AB Report (11 December 2000) WT/DS161,169/AB/R.

Marckx *v* Belgium, Application no. 6833/74, Judgment 13 June 1979.

Sunday Times (I) v UK 30 Eur. Ct. H.R. (ser. A), § 62

Tyrer *v* the United Kingdom, Application No. 5856/72, Judgment 25 April 1978.

United States – Import Prohibition of Certain Shrimp and Shrimp Products, AB Report (12 October 1998) WT/DS58/AB/R.

United States – Measures Affecting Cross-Border Supply of Gambling and Betting Services AB Report (7 April 2005) WT/DS285/AB/R.

Conciliation

Conciliation between the Democratic Republic of Timor-Leste and the Commonwealth of Australia, Decision on Australia's Objection to Competence (19 September 2016)

Table of Treaties and Documents

1945	Proclamation No. 2667 'Policy of the United States with Respect to the Natural Resources of the Subsoil of the Sea Bed and the Continental Shelf' (28 September 1945).
1945	Charter of the United Nations, 1 UNTS XVI (26 June 1945).
1946	International Convention for the Regulation of Whaling, 161 UNTS 361 (2 December 1946).
1958	Convention on the Continental Shelf, 499 UNTS 311 (29 April 1958).
1958	Convention on Fishing and Conservation of the Living Resources of the High Seas, 559 UNTS 285 (29 April 1958).
1958	Optional Protocol of Signature Concerning the Compulsory Settlement of Disputes, 450 UNTS 169 (29 April 1958)
1966	ILC, Yearbook of the International Law Commission, 1966, vol. II, A/CN.4/SER.A/1966/Add.l.
1969	Vienna Convention on the Law of Treaties, 1155 UNTS 331 (23 May 1969).
1972	Convention on the International Regulations for Preventing of Collisions at Sea, 1050 UNTS 16 (20 October 1972).
1972	Declaration of the United Nations Conference on the Human Environment, UN Doc. A/CONF 48/14/Rev.1, pp. 2ff. (16 June 1972).
1973	Convention on International Trade in Endangered Species of Wild Fauna and Flora 993 UNTS 243 (3 March 1973).
1975	Treaty Fixing the Maritime Boundaries between the Republic of the Gambia and the Republic of Senegal (4 June 1975).
1973–1982	Official Records of the Third United Nations Conference on the Law of the Sea, Volume II (Summary Records of Meetings of the

First, Second and Third Committees, Second Session), 16th Meeting A/CONF.62/C.2/SR.16.

1973–1982 Official Records of the Third United Nations Conference on the Law of the Sea, Volume II (Summary Records of Meetings of the First, Second and Third Committees, Second Session), 17th Meeting A/CONF.62/C.2/SR.17.

1973–1982 Official Records of the Third United Nations Conference on the Law of the Sea, Volume II (Summary Records of Meetings of the First, Second and Third Committees, Second Session), 18th Meeting A/CONF.62/C.2/SR.18.

1973–1982 Official Records of the Third United Nations Conference on the Law of the Sea, Volume II (Summary Records of Meetings of the First, Second and Third Committees, Second Session), 19th Meeting A/CONF.62/C.2/SR.19.

1982 United Nations Convention on the Law of the Sea, 1833 UNTS 396 (10 December 1982)

1982 Agreement on Marine Delimitation between the Government of Australia and the Government of the French Republic (New Caledonia, Chesterfield Islands) (4 January 1982).

1988 Agreement between the Government of the United Kingdom of Great Britain and Northern Ireland and the Government of the Republic of Ireland Concerning the Delimitation of Areas of the Continental Shelf between the Two Countries (7 November 1988).

1988 Agreement between the Government of Solomon Islands and the Government of Australia Establishing Certain Sea and Seabed Boundaries (13 September 1988).

1990 Treaty between the Republic of Trinidad and Tobago and the Republic of Venezuela on the Delimitation of Marine and Submarine Areas, 1654 UNTS 293 (18 April 1990).

1990 Bergen Declaration, Ministerial Declaration on Sustainable Development in the ECE Region, A/CONF/151/PC/10 (16 May 1990).

1992 UNGA, Law of the Sea: Report of the United Nations Secretary General, UN Doc. A/47/623 (24 November 1992).

1992 Rio Declaration on Environment and Development, UN Doc A/CONF.151/26.Rev.1 (13 June 1992).

1992 Convention for the Protection of the Marine Environment of the North-East Atlantic (OSPAR Convention), 2354 UNTS 67 (22 September 1992).

1992	Convention on the Protection of the Marine Environment of the Baltic Sea Area, 1507 UNTS 167 (9 April 1992).
1992	United Nations Framework Convention on Climate Change, 1771 UNTS 170 (9 May 1992).
1992	Convention on Biological Diversity 1760 UNTS 79 (5 June 1992).
1993	Agreement to Promote Compliance with International Conservation and Management Measures by Fishing Vessels on the High Seas, 2221 UNTS 91 (24 November 1993).
1993	Convention for the Conservation of Southern Bluefin Tuna, 819 UNTS 360 (10 May 1993).
1995	FAO, Code of Conduct for Responsible Fisheries (31 October 1995).
1995	The United Nations Agreement for the Implementation of the Provisions of the United Nations Convention on the Law of the Sea of 10 December 1982 Relating to the Conservation and Management of Straddling Fish Stocks and Highly Migratory Fish Stocks, 2167 UNTS 3 (4 August 1995).
1999	CLCS, 'Scientific and Technical Guidelines of the Commission on the Limits of the Continental Shelf' CLCS/11 (13 May 1999).
2000	Treaty between the Government of the United States of America and the Government of the United Mexican States on the Delimitation of the Continental Shelf in the Western Gulf of Mexico beyond 200 Nautical Miles UN Doc CLCS/78 (9 June 2000).
2000	Cartagena Protocol on Biosafety to the Convention on Biological Diversity, 39 ILM 1027 (29 January 2000).
2001	FAO, International Plan of Action to Prevent, Deter and Eliminate Illegal, Unreported and Unregulated Fishing (23 June 2001)
2004	Treaty between the Government of Australia and the Government of New Zealand Establishing Certain Exclusive Economic Zone and Continental Shelf Boundaries, 2441 UNTS 235 (25 July 2004).
2004	Treaty between the Government of Australia and the Government of the French Republic on Cooperation in the Maritime Areas Adjacent to the French Southern and Antarctic Territories (TAAF), Heard Island and the McDonald Islands (24 November 2003).
2005	Rules of Procedure for Meetings of States Parties (24 January 2005), SPLOS/2/Rev.4.

2009 FAO, Agreement on Port State Measures to Prevent, Deter and Eliminate Illegal, Unreported and Unregulated Fishing (22 November 2009).

2009 Rules of the International Tribunal for the Law of the Sea, ITLOS/8 (amended, 17 March 2009).

2010 Regulations on Prospecting and Exploration for Polymetallic Sulphides in the Area, ISBA/16/C/L.5 (6 May 2010).

2011 Draft Articles on Prevention of Transboundary Harm from Hazardous Activities, UN Doc A/RES/5683 (12 December 2011).

2012 The Future We Want, UNGA Res A/RES/66/288 (11 September 2012).

2012 Convention on the Determination of the Minimal Conditions for Access and Exploitation of Marine Resources within the Maritime Areas under the Jurisdiction of the SRFC's Member States (8 June 2012).

2013 Regulations on Prospecting and Exploration for Polymetallic Nodules in the Area, ISBA/19/C/17 (amended) (22 July 2013).

2015 Development of an International Legally Binding Instrument under the United Nations Convention on the Law of the Sea on the Conservation and Sustainable Use of Marine Biological Diversity of Areas Beyond National Jurisdiction, UN Doc A/RES/69/292 (19 June 2015).

Abbreviations

AJIL	American Journal of International Law
BYBIL	The British Yearbook of International Law
CBD	Convention on Biodiversity
CCAMLR	Convention for the Conservation of Antarctic Marine Living Resources
CCSBT	Convention for the Conservation of Southern Bluefin Tuna
CITES	Convention on International Trade in Endangered Species of Wild Fauna and Flora
CJIL	Chinese Journal of International Law
CLCS	Commission on the Limits of the Continental Shelf
COLREGS	Convention on the International Regulations for Preventing of Collisions at Sea
ECtHR	European Court of Human Rights
EEZ	exclusive economic zone
EIA	environmental impact assessment
EJIL	European Journal of International Law
FAO	Food and Agricultural Organization
ICJ	International Court of Justice
ICLQ	International and Comparative Law Quarterly
IJGLS	Indiana Journal of Global Legal Studies
IJIL	Indonesian Journal of International Law
IJMCL	The International Journal of Marine and Coastal Law
ILA	International Law Association
ILC	International Law Commission
ILM	International Legal Materials
IMO	International Maritime Organization

ISA	International Seabed Authority
ITLOS	International Tribunal for the Law of the Sea
IUU	illegal, unregulated and unreported
LJIL	Leiden Journal of International Law
MCA Convention	Convention on the Determination of the Minimal Conditions for Access and Exploitation of Marine Resources within the Maritime Areas under Jurisdiction of the Member States of the SRFC
MPA	marine protected area
MSY	maximum sustainable yield
nm	nautical miles
ODIL	Ocean Development & International Law
PCIJ	Permanent Court of International Justice
RECIEL	Review of European, Comparative & Environmental Law
RFMO	Regional Fisheries Management Organisation
RIAA	*Reports of International Arbitral Awards*
SBT	southern bluefin tuna
SDC	Seabed Disputes Chamber
SRFC	Sub-Regional Fisheries Commission
UNCLOS	United Nations Convention on the Law of the Sea
UNFSA	United Nations Fish Stocks Agreement
UNGA	United Nations General Assembly
VCLT	Vienna Convention on the Law of Treaties
WTO	World Trade Organization

1

Introduction and Theoretical Framework

1.1 BRIEF OVERVIEW OF THE UNCLOS DISPUTE SETTLEMENT SYSTEM

The dispute settlement system of the 1982 United Nations Convention on the Law of the Sea ('UNCLOS' or 'the Convention')[1] constitutes an integral part of the Convention. Unlike the 1958 Geneva Conventions for law of the sea, which relegate the settlement of disputes concerning the interpretation or application of these conventions to an optional protocol, Part XV of UNCLOS on Settlement of Disputes sets out compulsory dispute settlement procedures that are binding on States once they become a party to the Convention. It should be remembered that the Third Conference on the Law of the Sea (UNCLOS III) witnessed the participation of a large number of States with diverse backgrounds and legal traditions, and with different agendas and goals in mind. Thus, the mere fact that States were able to finally agree to establishing a compulsory dispute settlement system under UNCLOS was particularly remarkable.[2]

The dispute settlement system of UNCLOS is unique, in that Part XV combines an obligation to resort to some definite process to settle disputes with the maximum room for choice of procedure.[3] In other words, dispute settlement under UNCLOS is both compulsory and flexible.[4] Several features contribute to the flexibility of the system. The first is the freedom accorded to

[1] United Nations Convention on the Law of the Sea (10 December 1982) 1833 UNTS 396.

[2] John E Noyes, 'Compulsory Third-Party Adjudication and the 1982 United Nations Convention on the Law of the Sea' (1989) 4 Conn J Int'l L 675, 678.

[3] Christine Chinkin, 'Dispute Resolution and the Law of the Sea: Regional Problems and Prospects' in James Crawford and Donald Rothwell (eds), *The Law of the Sea in the Asian Pacific Region: Developments and Prospects* (Martinus Nijhoff 2012).

[4] Yoshifumi Tanaka, *The International Law of the Sea* (3rd ed, CUP 2019) 496.

States to settle their disputes by means of their own choice as stipulated by Article 279. This freedom is further demonstrated by the requirement under Section 1 of Part XV that compulsory procedure should be used only after States have exhausted their preferred means of settlement. This means that only when States cannot settle their disputes through the means of their own choice do the compulsory procedures in Section 2 of Part XV apply. Second, Article 287 in Section 2 allows States to choose one or more of the four following means for the settlement of disputes: the International Tribunal for the Law of the Sea (ITLOS); the International Court of Justice (ICJ); an arbitral tribunal constituted in accordance with Annex VII; and a special arbitral tribunal constituted in accordance with Annex VIII of the Convention.[5] Among these four bodies, the ICJ was at the time of negotiation the only existing institution; the other three were all new products of the Convention. UNCLOS remains until today one of the very few international conventions that provides States with such flexibility in choosing the forum for dispute settlement. Finally, when a court or tribunal is exercising compulsory jurisdiction under Section 2, States are still allowed under Section 3 of Part XV to exclude certain types of dispute from the jurisdiction of the court or tribunal in question. The flexibility accorded to States is thus evident not only in the choice of procedure offered but also in the scope of the issues that may be heard by an UNCLOS dispute settlement body.

The UNCLOS dispute settlement system has been in operation for nearly three decades. To date, some forty cases and two advisory requests have been initiated under the framework of Part XV. All these cases have been brought before either ITLOS or Annex VII arbitral tribunals – collectively referred to in this book as 'UNCLOS tribunals'. These tribunals have therefore had the opportunity to examine and shed light on a variety of legal issues pertaining to both the law of the sea and general international law. Despite the growing body of jurisprudence, comprehensive studies on the contribution of UNCLOS dispute settlement bodies to the development of the law of the sea or on the role of UNCLOS dispute settlement bodies in developing the law remain limited.[6] This book aims to undertake these tasks. The goal of this book is

[5] The choice of procedure contained in Article 287 is termed the Montreux formula. See: AO Adede, *The System for Settlement of Disputes under the United Nations Convention on the Law of the Sea: A Drafting History and a Commentary* (Martinus Nijhoff 1987) 54 (noting that the Montreux formula 'became an important aspect of the acceptance of multiplicity of jurisdictions as a permanent feature of the disputes settlement system being established under the Convention').

[6] See, for example, Angela Del Vecchio and Roberto Virzo (eds), *Interpretations of the United Nations Convention on the Law of the Sea by International Courts and Tribunals* (Springer 2019); Øystein Jensen (ed), *The Development of the Law of the Sea Convention* (Edward

two-fold: first, it examines the types and areas of contribution that UNCLOS tribunals have made to the development of the law of the sea. Second, it explores the factors that help to explain the role of UNCLOS tribunals in developing the law of the sea.

Before examining the contribution that UNCLOS tribunals have made to the development of the law of the sea, it is first necessary to provide a conceptual framework to understand the term 'development of law', to which this chapter now turns.

1.2 CONCEPTUAL FRAMEWORK FOR UNDERSTANDING 'DEVELOPMENT OF LAW' BY INTERNATIONAL COURTS AND TRIBUNALS

1.2.1 *'Development' of Law*

It goes without saying that international courts and tribunals are set up first and foremost to settle disputes. This function is clearly enshrined in the legal instruments setting up various courts and tribunals.[7] Faithful to their delegated task, international courts and tribunals often refuse to admit that their task comprises anything other than interpreting and applying existing rules of law to settle disputes or providing answers to legal questions presented before them. This is most clearly manifested in the well-known statement made by the ICJ in the *Advisory Opinion on the Legality of the Use or Threat of Nuclear Weapons*:

> It is clear that the Court cannot legislate . . . Rather its task is to engage in its normal judicial function of ascertaining the existence or otherwise of legal principles and rules applicable to the threat or use of nuclear weapons.[8]

Elgar 2020). While these collective works deal with how international courts and tribunals have examined different legal issues in the law of sea, their focus is not on the contribution of UNCLOS tribunals, nor do they examine in depth the role of UNCLOS tribunals in developing the law.

7 For example, Article 38(1) ICJ Statute: 'The Court, whose function is to decide in accordance with international law such disputes as are submitted to it . . .'; Understanding on Rules and Procedures Governing the Settlement of Disputes (15 April 1994) 1869 UNTS 401 www.wto.org/english/docs_e/legal_e/28-dsu.pdf accessed 25 January 2022.

8 *Legality of the Threat or Use of Nuclear Weapons* (Advisory Opinion) [1996] ICJ Rep 226, 237, [18]. See also, Understanding on Rules and Procedures Governing the Settlement of Disputes (n 7), Article 3(2), which states that 'the recommendations and rulings of the DSB cannot add to or diminish the rights and obligations provided in the covered agreements'. Andreas Zimmermann and others, *The Statute of the International Court of Justice: A Commentary* (2nd ed, OUP 2012) 1233.

However, portraying the task of international courts and tribunals as involving solely the settlement of disputes does not sufficiently cover the whole picture regarding the function of international courts. As Fitzmaurice pointed out,

> There are broadly two main possible approaches to the task of a judge .... There is the approach which conceives it to be the primary, if not the sole duty of a judge to decide the case in hand, with the minimum of verbiage necessary for this purpose, and to confine himself to that. The other approach conceives it to be the proper function of the judge, while duly deciding the case in hand, with the necessary supporting reasoning, and while not unduly straying outside the four corners of the case, to utilize those aspects of it which have a wider interest or connotation, in order to make general pronouncements of law and principle that may enrich and develop the law.[9]

The second task expounded in the above passage – that of developing the law – has not only been acknowledged by certain international judges themselves,[10] but also been studied with much interest by scholars.[11] Notwithstanding the rhetoric taken by international courts, 'the conception of international courts as actors in the development of the law has been a rather common theme in international legal thinking'.[12] As a result, the pertinent questions to be addressed no longer concern whether international courts and tribunals develop the law, but rather in what ways they have

9 Gerald Fitzmaurice, 'Hersch Lauterpacht: The Scholar as a Judge' (1961) 37 BYBIL 1, 14–15.

10 See, for example, Rosalyn Higgins, *Problems and Process: International Law and How We Use It* (OUP 1995) 202. For other examples, see: Opening lecture delivered by Judge Christopher G Weeramantry on the occasion of the opening of the LL.M. Public International Law Programme of the University of Leiden (2 October 1996).

11 See, for example, Armin von Bogdandy and Ingo Venzke, 'The Spell of Precedents: Lawmaking by International Courts and Tribunals' in Cesare Romano, Karen Alter and Yuval Shany (eds), *Oxford Handbook of International Adjudication* (OUP 2013); Rudiger Wolfrum, 'Enforcing Community Interests through International Dispute Settlement: Reality of Utopia' in Ulrich Fastenrath and others (eds), *From Bilateralism to Community Interest: Essays in Honour of Bruno Simma* (OUP 2011); Armin von Bogdandy and Ingo Venzke, *In Whose Name?: A Public Law Theory of International Adjudication* (OUP 2014); Tullio Scovazzi, 'Where the Judge Approaches the Legislator: Some Cases Relating to the Law of the Sea' in Nerina Boschiero and others (eds), *International Courts and the Development of International Law: Essays in Honour of Tullio Treves* (Springer 2013); Yuval Shany, *Assessing the Effectiveness of International Courts* (CUP 2014) (who does not consider law development as an indicator of effectiveness for most courts and tribunals); Karen Alter, *The New Terrain of International Law: Courts, Politics, Rights* (Princeton University Press 2014) (who focuses on the influence of international courts on international and domestic politics, rather than on the development of the law per se, but still acknowledging that the role of international courts goes beyond settling inter-state disputes).

12 Ingo Venzke, *How Interpretation Makes International Law: On Semantic Change and Normative Twists* (OUP 2012) 143–144.

brought about such developments,[13] and how to assess their performance in discharging this function.[14] In order to do so, it is pertinent to explore what is meant by 'development of law' and more specifically, what is 'development of law' by international courts and tribunals?

The plain meaning of the term 'development' is 'the process in which someone or something grows or changes and becomes more advanced'.[15] Thus development of law is a process in which the law changes, grows and becomes more advanced over time. As remarked by Messenger, 'the development of law contains within it an implicit acknowledgement of change. For something to develop, it must change from one or many things into another'.[16] Petersen echoes this focus on change when stating that '[a] development of the law occurs when the law is actually different in point t2 than it was in a prior point t1'.[17] To speak of development of the law by international courts and tribunals, thus, a causal link between the judicial decision and the change in the law should be established.

However, the development of law is a process that involves various actors, each of whom exerts a different kind of influence on and brings about changes to the law by different means. International courts and tribunals are but one actor in this process. As a result, in a decentralised system such as that of international law, as Tams and Tzanakopoulos argue in the context of the ICJ, 'the Court does not make or develop the law single-handedly, it operates within the broader context of legal development'.[18] Judicial decisions, therefore, 'are not per se relevant contributions to the process of legal development, but only to the extent that they are acceptable to the international legal community'.[19] When and if accepted, international courts 'exercise a normative pull that provides actors with incentives to adapt existing norms and

[13] Geert De Baere and Jan Wouters, *Contribution of International and Supranational Courts to the Rule of Law* (Edward Elgar 2015); John Merrills, 'The Place of International Litigation in International Law' in Natalie Klein (ed), *Litigating International Law Disputes: Weighing the Options* (CUP 2014) 15.

[14] See, for example, Armin von Bogdandy and Ingo Venzke (eds), *International Judicial Lawmaking on Public Authority and Democratic Legitimation in Global Governance* (Springer 2012); Nawab, 'Other Sources of International Law: Are Judicial Decisions of the International Court of Justice a Source of International Law?' (1979) 19 Indian JIL 526.

[15] Cambridge Dictionary https://dictionary.cambridge.org/dictionary/english/development accessed 25 January 2022.

[16] Gregory Messenger, *The Development of World Trade Organization Law* (OUP 2016) 3.

[17] Niels Petersen, 'Lawmaking by the International Court of Justice: Factors of Success' in von Bogdandy and Venzke (n 14) 413.

[18] Christian J Tams and Antonios Tzanakopoulos, 'Barcelona Traction at 40: The ICJ as an Agent of Legal Development' (2010) 23(4) LJIL 781, 784.

[19] Ibid 785.

adopt new ones'.[20] International courts and tribunals are thus not the sole driving force behind the creation of law; they are instead a stimulating element in the process of development of international law.[21] As a result, the role of international courts and international judges in the process of developing the law has been given various labels such as 'agency for developing the law',[22] 'agents of legal development'[23] or 'judicial entrepreneurs'.[24] The role of international courts in the development of the law is thus 'interstitial', meaning that the court 'stands between the past and the future'.[25]

It is therefore difficult, even impossible, to fully appreciate the contribution of a court or a tribunal's decision without the benefit of hindsight in light of subsequent developments, including the reception of the judgments by other actors.[26] Most of the assessment of the contributions of the Permanent Court of International Justice and the ICJ, for instance, is based on decades-old decisions, which allows the authors to track whether these courts' pronouncements on different legal issues have been accepted by States and other actors, subsequently resulting in changes in the law.[27] As the UNCLOS dispute settlement system has been in operation for a much shorter time, such an exercise may prove difficult.[28] This means that the impact of UNCLOS

[20] Theresa Squatrito and others (eds), *The Performance of International Courts and Tribunals* (CUP 2018) 23.

[21] See: Ingo Venzke, 'The Role of International Courts as Interpreters and Developers of the Law: Working Out the Jurisgenerative Practice of Interpretation' (2011) 34 Loy LA Int'l & Comp L J 99, 122; Gleider Hernandez, 'Interpretative Authority and the International Judiciary' in Andrea Bianchi, Daniel Peat and Matthew Windsor (eds), *Interpretation in International Law* (OUP 2015) 166.

[22] Hersch Lauterpacht, *The Development of International Law by the International Court* (Stevens & Sons 1958) 7.

[23] Franklin Berman, 'The International Court of Justice as an "Agent" of Legal Development?' in Christian J Tams and James Sloan (eds), *The Development of International Law by the International Court of Justice* (OUP 2013) 7

[24] Rosa Aloisi and James Meernik, *Judgment Day: Judicial Decision Making at the International Criminal Tribunals* (CUP 2017) 26.

[25] Venzke (n 21) 121.

[26] See Alan Boyle and Christine Chinkin, *The Making of International Law* (OUP 2007) 311 (arguing that 'the law-making effect of all judicial decisions, like all multilateral treaties, is contingent on the response of a broader international community and cannot be presumed in advance').

[27] See: Tams and Sloan (n 23).

[28] As Alter points out, 'Low levels of litigation are also to be expected in the first years of an IC's existence . . . The lesson: establishing international judicial authority takes time, even in the best of circumstances.' Karen J Alter, 'The Multiple Roles of International Courts and Tribunals: Enforcement, Dispute Settlement, Constitutional and Administrative Review' (2012) Faculty Working Papers 212, 349 https://scholarlycommons.law.northwestern.edu/cgi/viewcontent.cgi?article=1211&context=facultyworkingpapers accessed 25 January 2022.

dispute settlement bodies' decisions on the law in future remains largely a prediction. This does not mean, however, that an assessment of the contribution of international courts to the development of the law cannot be made based on an examination of the decisions rendered. While particular judicial decisions may only provide a snapshot of the law at a static point in time,[29] it is still possible to examine whether certain decisions or advisory opinions have shed new insights or cast new light on legal norms or principles which until then had been obscure or debated. Simply put, an assessment can still be made regarding whether and to what extent the judgment or award has made the law clearer at the point of issuance (point t2) as compared to before such a decision existed (point t1). Moreover, the growing body of jurisprudence produced by UNCLOS tribunals may also enable an examination of whether certain pronouncements or findings have been repeated and upheld by other actors.[30] As a result, while it is not possible to conclude with certainty whether UNCLOS tribunals' decisions will be accepted and thereby affect other actors' normative expectation, they still provide a useful starting point to identify the change brought about by UNCLOS tribunals to the law of the sea.

1.2.2 *How Do International Courts and Tribunals 'Develop' the Law?*

Judicial development is usually equated with clarification of the law.[31] Lauterpacht, in his seminal work on the development of international law by the International Court, argued that the wide recognition of the achievement of the ICJ was owed to the 'tangible contribution to the development and clarification of the rules and principles of law'.[32] Other scholars echo the understanding that clarification of the law is a form of development of the law by international courts, noting that 'the clarification of international law goes hand in hand with its development'.[33] Even when one accepts that

[29] See: Messenger (n 16) 6 (arguing that as 'law develops continually', 'snapshots . . . are not adequate to explain how law develops').

[30] von Bogdandy and Venzke, 'The Spell of Precedents: Lawmaking by International Court and Tribunals' (n 11) 508.

[31] Christopher Greenwood, 'The Development of International Humanitarian Law by the International Criminal Tribunal for the Former Yugoslavia' (1998) 2 Max Planck Yearbook of United Nations Law 97, 111.

[32] Lauterpacht (n 22) 5. Lauterpacht used the terms 'development' and 'clarification' side by side, which could at first glance suggest that they are separate concepts. However, a closer examination of his book shows that he used these terms interchangeably.

[33] Geert De Baere, Anna-Luise Chane and Jan Wouters, 'The Contributions of International and Supranational Courts to the Rule of Law: A Framework for Analysis' in De Baere and Wouters (n 13) 74.

international courts and tribunals develop the law through clarification of the law, it still seems pertinent to determine further what sort of clarification contributes to the development of the law.

In practice, States bring cases to international tribunals not only when they disagree on the facts, but also more often when they disagree on the applicable law and the application of the law to the facts. In dissecting the law and its application, international courts and tribunals contribute to the development of the law in several different ways, namely: (i) by clarifying whether a rule of a law exists within the corpus of international law; (ii) by articulating what the normative content of the rule is;[34] and (iii) by orienting the direction in which the rule of law develops.

More specifically, the identification and confirmation of the existence of a rule of law are apposite to customary international law. While the definition of customary international law is found in Article 38(1)(b) of the ICJ Statute, it is not at all easy in practice to ascertain whether the two constituent elements for the formation of a rule of customary law have been satisfied. The identification of international customary law has, thus, always been controversial and elusive.[35] Against such a backdrop, judicial decisions have widely been accepted as an authoritative and reliable source for identifying whether States' practice in implementing a certain rule of law has ripened to reach the status of customary law. Judicial pronouncement on the existence of a particular rule of customary law thus provides an authoritative point of reference, even, as some argue, 'the final proof of it'.[36] Such a confirmation then becomes a 'focal point' that inspires subsequent State practice and helps to harden a rule.[37]

Second, it is a truism to say that 'the legal rules need to be sufficiently clear in order to provide a reliable and predictable framework'.[38] However, as remarked by Crawford, 'all lawyers in all legal systems know that law is indeterminate, at least to some degree'.[39] International law is, of course, no exception. While customary law can be indeterminate in scope and content

34 Merrills (n 13) 17.

35 Scovazzi (n 11) 299. Jörg Kammerhofer, 'Uncertainty in the Formal Sources of International Law: Customary International Law and Some of Its Problems' (2004) 15 EJIL 523, 524.

36 Alain Pellet, 'Article 38' in Zimmermann and others (n 8) 864. See also: Christian J Tams, 'Meta-Custom and the Court: A Study in Judicial Law-Making' (2015) 14 The Law and Practice of International Courts and Tribunals 51.

37 Gleider Hernandez, *The International Court of Justice and the Judicial Function* (OUP 2014) 91.

38 De Baere, Chane and Wouters (n 33) 70.

39 James Crawford, *Chance, Order, Change: The Course of International Law, General Course on Public International Law* (Hague Academy of International Law, Martinus Nijhoff 2014) 147.

due to the informal and decentralised process in which customary law is formed, treaty law itself can be equally ambiguous. When concluding international treaties, States sometimes fail to anticipate or intentionally leave legal gaps or uncertainties in the final provisions – UNCLOS being a fine example, as will be analysed in the Chapters 2–7. When an international court or tribunal is requested to apply such provisions to settle the dispute, it would likely have to fill in these legal gaps and clarify the ambiguities. As argued by one commentator, 'judicial gap-filling seems an inescapable by-product of the application of any kind of law to fact'.[40] In such circumstances, by expounding the rule or principle of law invoked by the parties to the dispute, international courts and tribunals shed light on the meaning of the terms that are nebulous in the treaty and elucidate the scope of the rights and obligations that arise from the rule in question. Hence, through interpreting and applying the law to concrete cases, international courts 'channel it into a concrete form' and 'bestow it with meaning and authoritative weight'.[41] As described by Buergenthal, international courts' engagement with international law is a process of 'normative accretion', through which law is created in a modest, incremental fashion, clarifying ambiguities and resolving perceived gaps in the law.[42] In so doing, international courts develop the law by thickening the corpus of the law and adding substance to it. In the words of Lauterpacht, development means making law 'visible',[43] and the visibility of the law could be understood both in respect of its existence as well as its enriched content.

Third, as a corollary of the clarification of the law, international courts also 'provide systemization to a question of law where there might be conflicting practice or ambiguity',[44] thereby setting the direction for the rule subject to interpretation to develop. Due to the indeterminacy of international law as discussed above, 'all law (perhaps especially international law) is capable of supporting any claim, and that diametrically opposed views may, through the application of legal language be made equally justifiable'.[45] When hearing a case, a court or tribunal is frequently presented with competing views put

[40] See José E Álvarez, 'What Are International Judges for? The Main Functions of International Adjudication' in Romano, Alter and Shany (n 11) 158.

[41] Boyle and Chinkin (n 26) 272.

[42] Thomas Buergenthal, 'Lawmaking by the ICJ and Other International Courts' (2009) 103 Proceedings of the American Society of International Law 403, 403.

[43] Lauterpacht (n 22) 42–43.

[44] Gleider Hernadez, 'International Judicial Lawmaking' in Catherine Brolmann and Yannick Radi (eds), *Research Handbook on the Theory and Practice of International Lawmaking* (Edward Elgar 2016) 201.

[45] Crawford (n 39) 168.

forward by the parties, supported by references to relevant scholarly arguments which may also align themselves into opposing camps. In the process in which actors, including both the court and the parties, demand and give reasons for or against a particular interpretation of a provision, the law gains shape and develops.[46] The ICJ, while keen to portray its practice as just applying the existing law, accepted that 'in stating and applying the law, the Court necessarily has to specify its scope and sometimes note its general trend'.[47] Judge Waldock similarly contended that in determining and clarifying what is conceived to be the existing law, the ICJ 'threw fresh light on the considerations and the principles on which the law was based in a manner to suggest the path for future development'.[48] In other words, international courts and tribunals develop the law not only by clarifying its status and normative content, but also by suggesting a particular direction for the law to develop or 'orient' the development of the law.

In short, the premise of this book is that, while international courts and tribunals may not be given the explicit competence to develop international law, they do in practice contribute to the development of the law through the clarification of the law in the course of settling specific disputes. Judicial decisions confirm the existence of the rules pertinent to the case, identify their scope of application and shed light on their normative content. By virtue of such clarification, the law takes a more defined form, becomes more enriched and detailed, and so it develops. It is through the prism of development by clarification of the law that the contributions of UNCLOS tribunals to the development of the law of the sea will be examined in Chapters 2–7.

1.2.3 *Role of Legal Reasoning*

International courts and tribunals acknowledge the importance of legal reasoning, demonstrated by the fact that the procedural rules of most international courts and tribunals require them to provide reasons or justification for their decisions.[49] Such rules create the legitimate expectation that judicial

46 Venzke (n 21) 121; Tullio Scovazzi, 'The Contribution of the Tribunal to the Progressive Development of International Law' in Intl. Tribunal for the Law of the Sea (ed), *The Contribution of the International Tribunal for the Law of the Sea to the Rule of Law: 1996–2016* (Martinus Nijhoff 2017) 118.

47 *Legality of the Threat or Use of Nuclear Weapons* (n 8) [18].

48 Humphrey Waldock, 'The International Court of Justice as Seen from the Bar and the Bench' (1983) 54 BYBIL 1, 4.

49 Article 56(1) ICJ Statute, Article 30(1) ITLOS Statute and Article 10 Annex VII UNCLOS. The European Court of Human Rights (ECtHR) held that insufficient reasoning means the

decisions are grounded in sound and convincing reasoning.[50] However, opinions are divided to the role of legal reasoning in assessing the contribution of international courts and tribunals to the development of the law. On the one hand, if we accept, as discussed above, that the development of the law means clarification of the law, an assessment of judicial contribution to the development of the law cannot be based merely on what has been clarified but also on whether it has been clarified in a convincing and logical manner. The latter thus turns on an inquiry into the justification or reasoning provided by the court or the tribunal in question. It is the legal reasoning, by establishing connections between abstract legal principles and categorical statements about their status and meaning, which transcends individual fact-dependent cases. Similarly, if we accept that the change that international courts and tribunals bring about lies in the creation or shift of normative expectations, practice indicates that other actors more frequently use the reasoning and justification in subsequent legal discourses to argue about the meaning of the law rather than the outcome of the case itself. As a result, there is at least some recognition that the 'law-making effect depends not only on the voluntas of the judge, but also on the ratio of the reasons given'.[51] As argued by Rosenne, '[t]he Court's reasoning in law – its statement of what it regards as the correct legal position and why – enters into the general storehouse of public international law.'[52]

On the other hand, scholars have also expressed doubts about placing too much weight on the significance of legal reasoning. At the theoretical level, some stress the distinction between the outcome and the reasoning, arguing that, while related, the quality of the judgment can be assessed independently from the quality of judicial reasoning.[53] Further, there is also the question of how to assess the quality of reasoning. As Tams put it, '[c]ogency, much like beauty, is in the eye of the beholder'.[54] What matrix, if any, can be used to

violation of the fair trial principle. *Taxquet v Belgium* App no 926/05 (ECtHR, 16 November 2010) [90]. [92]. See also: Gleider Hernandez, *The International Court of Justice and the Judicial Function* (OUP 2014) 98–100.

[50] Mátyás Bencze and Gar Yein Ng, 'Measuring the Unmeasurable?' in Mátyás Bencze and Gar Yein Ng (eds), *How to Measure the Quality of Judicial Reasoning* (Springer 2018) 5.

[51] von Bogdandy and Venzke, *In Whose Name?* (n 11) 111. See also: Laurence R Helfer, 'The Effectiveness of International Adjudicators' in Romano, Alter and Shany (n 11) 479; Álvarez (n 40) 165.

[52] Shabtai Rosenne, *The World Court* (5th ed, Martinus Nijhoff 1995), 148.

[53] Mátyás Bencze, 'Obstacles and Opportunities – Measuring the Quality of Judicial Reasoning' in Bencze and Ng (n 50) 98.

[54] Christian J Tams, 'The ICJ as a 'Law-Formative Agency': Summary and Synthesis' in Tams and Sloan (n 23) 390.

determine whether the legal reasoning provided is 'good' or 'correct'? For the purposes of assessing the contribution of international courts and tribunals, scholars such as Petersen, having studied a number of landmark cases by the ICJ, argue that 'the concrete reasoning and the soundness of the legal argument are only of limited relevance in terms of impacting the legal discourse'.[55]

This book, however, does not purport to make predictions about the long-term impact of international judgments and awards based on the quality of reasoning. Rather, it focuses on the formal legal discourse by analysing the judgments themselves in order to determine whether and to what extent the rules and principles of law in question have become clearer as compared to before the judgment or award is rendered. The analysis takes the decisions rendered by UNCLOS tribunals as the departure point to assess their contribution to the development of the law. The answers as provided in the operative paragraphs of a judgment or award alone cannot provide a full picture of how the law has been clarified. The reasoning and justification play a crucial role in determining whether clarity and certainty has been provided on the legal issue in question. Accordingly, each chapter will examine both the outcome and the reasoning – or lack thereof – provided by UNCLOS dispute settlement bodies.

1.3 SCOPE AND STRUCTURE OF THE BOOK

This book does not claim to be exhaustive, its scope is limited in two aspects. First, as the central goal of this book is to examine the contribution of the dispute settlement system established under UNCLOS to the development of the law of the sea, it will focus only on the tribunals which (i) were established by UNCLOS, (ii) operate according to the rules and procedures of the Convention and (iii) have in practice heard cases brought to them under the auspices of the Convention. Based on these criteria, the book examines only the contributions made by ITLOS and the ad hoc arbitral tribunals established under Annex VII of the Convention. ITLOS and Annex VII arbitral tribunals are, of course, not the only dispute settlement bodies engaged in the interpretation and application of UNCLOS. However, even though ICJ has frequently received cases relating to the law of the sea – mostly maritime delimitation cases, none of the law of the sea disputes brought to the Court to date have been initiated within the framework of Part XV UNCLOS.

55 Petersen (n 17) 436.

Similarly, no cases have been brought to Annex VIII arbitral tribunals. That is not to say that ICJ judgments will be absent in the analysis. References will be made to ICJ decisions insofar as it is appropriate and relevant to the analysis of the role of UNCLOS tribunals.

Second, the book examines the contribution of UNCLOS tribunals in selected areas of the law of the sea. As argued by Boyle and Chinkin, '[t]he impact of international courts and tribunals on the evolution of international law largely depends upon how many cases are brought before them and the significance of those cases in terms of raising new and contested legal issues.'[56] The areas of law to which UNCLOS tribunals can make a contribution thus depend both on the topics which the tribunals have had the opportunity to examine most frequently as well as the novelty of the legal issues raised. In this respect, it is important to remember that while UNCLOS is built upon the four 1958 Geneva Conventions on the law of the sea, it contains remarkable novelties. The most important innovations include: the introduction of two new maritime zones, the EEZ and the Area; the concept of the continental shelf beyond 200 nm; the regime of islands and rocks, a dedicated Part XII on the protection and preservation of the marine environment and a compulsory dispute settlement system. Moreover, the distinction among coastal, flag and port States is also an important addition made by UNCLOS to the conceptual framework of the law of the sea.[57] The areas and topics chosen for analysis correspond to these novelties. It is acknowledged that an analysis of selected areas may limit the generality of the conclusions to be drawn. However, as the cases in these areas make up the bulk of UNCLOS tribunals' case law, they provide a rather clear indication of the ways the tribunals decide the cases and the kinds of contributions they have made.

The book is structured as follows. Chapter 2 examines the contributions that UNCLOS tribunals have made to the development of the law relating to coastal States' rights and obligations under the law of the sea, focusing on coastal States' sovereign rights and jurisdiction in the EEZ and historic fishing rights. Chapter 3 turns its attention flag States' rights and obligations under the law of the sea, examining the contribution of UNCLOS tribunals the development of the concept of 'flag States', flag States' freedom of navigation and exclusive jurisdiction as well as the corresponding obligations under UNCLOS, including the obligation to ensure safety at sea and obligations over vessels flying the flag of the State. The following three chapters

[56] Boyle and Chinkin (n 26) 269.

[57] Donald R Rothwell and Tim Stephens, *The International Law of the Sea* (2nd ed, Hart Publishing 2016) 17.

then move to a more thematic focus in terms of the legal issue addressed. Chapter 4 examines UNCLOS dispute settlement bodies' development of the law relating to maritime entitlement and maritime delimitation, including delimitation of maritime zones within and beyond 200 nautical miles (nm). Chapter 5 is then dedicated to exploring judicial development of the law concerning marine environmental protection, from the angle of development of key principles on this topic. Chapter 6 completes the discussion on contribution by focusing on the development of procedural rules by UNCLOS tribunals, particularly on the interpretation and application of the conditions for the establishment of compulsory jurisdiction and advisory jurisdiction under Part XV UNCLOS. Based on the findings of abovementioned chapters, Chapter 7 concludes by taking stock of the contributions and proving an answer to the main question raised, namely: in what ways have UNCLOS dispute settlement bodies contributed to the development of the law of the sea. This chapter also explores the factors that help to contextualise and understand the contribution of UNCLOS dispute settlement bodies and offers some concluding observations on the role of UNCLOS tribunals in the development of the law of the sea.

2

Coastal States' Rights and Obligations under the Law of the Sea

The key development brought about by the United Nations Convention on the Law of the Sea (UNCLOS) to coastal States' rights and obligations is found in the exclusive economic zone (EEZ).[1] In this new maritime zone, UNCLOS gives coastal States control in large swathes of what used to be the high seas, which includes not only exclusive sovereign rights and jurisdiction over natural resources but also jurisdiction in relation to artificial islands, installations and structure, as well as marine scientific research and environmental protection.[2] However, the scope of these rights and obligations is not always clearly set out in the relevant provisions, requiring further clarification and elaboration. Moreover, due to the power given to coastal States in the EEZ, questions have also arisen as to how coastal States' rights and obligations in this maritime zone interact with historic claims arising prior to the entry into force of UNCLOS. This chapter analyses the decisions rendered by UNCLOS tribunals that have dealt with coastal States' rights and obligations under the law of the sea and assesses the extent to which they have contributed to developing the relevant rules on this matter. Section 2.1 focuses on the decisions relating to coastal States' sovereign rights and jurisdiction in the EEZ. Section 2.2 examines the relationship between coastal States' rights and obligations under UNCLOS and historic rights.

1 The term 'coastal State' is not defined under UNCLOS despite being one of the most frequently used terms in the Convention. Scholars have defined coastal States as 'states with a coastline entitled to a territorial sea and the associated sovereign rights and jurisdiction over other maritime zones'. See: Donald R Rothwell and Tim Stephens, *The International Law of the Sea* (2nd ed, Bloomsbury Publishing Plc 2017) 17.

2 Article 56(1) UNCLOS.

2.1 COASTAL STATES' SOVEREIGN RIGHTS AND JURISDICTION IN THE EEZ

Article 56(1) grants coastal States 'sovereign rights for the purposes of exploring and exploiting, conserving and managing the natural resources, whether living or nonliving, in the waters superjacent to the sea-bed and of the sea-bed and its subsoil', as well as jurisdiction over three groups of issues, namely: (i) the establishment and use of artificial islands, installations and structures, (ii) marine scientific research and (iii) the protection and preservation of the marine environment. While coastal States seem to have been given vast power and control in the EEZ,[3] it is important to remember that the EEZ is a *sui generis* functional zone subject to a 'specific legal regime'.[4] The EEZ seeks to ensure a balance between the rights and the obligations of coastal States and those of flag States.[5] As a result, in the EEZ, there is no presumption in favour of coastal States, as with the territorial sea, or flag States, as with the high seas.[6] The balance that underlies the EEZ between coastal States' exclusive sovereign rights and jurisdiction and other States' freedom of the seas compatible with the Convention constitutes the essence of the EEZ legal regime. This balance is manifested through various provision in Part V, and perhaps most prominently in the obligation of due regard found in Articles 56 and 58.

Issues concerning the specific scope of coastal States' rights and obligations, as well as the balance between coastal States' and flag States' rights in the EEZ have arisen before UNCLOS tribunal in different forms. This section examines UNCLOS tribunals' decisions pertaining to coastal States' sovereign rights and jurisdiction over resources in the EEZ (Section 2.1.1), coastal States' jurisdiction over artificial islands, installations and structures (Section 2.1.2) and the interpretation of the obligation of due regard (Section 2.1.3).

3 The EEZ has been considered 'the most evident explication of individualism'. See: Umberto Leanza and Maria Cristina Caracciolo, 'The Exclusive Economic Zone' in David Attard, Malgosia Fitzmaurice and Norman A Martinez Gutierrez (eds), *The IMLI Manual on International Maritime Law*, Volume I: The Law of the Sea (OUP 2014) 177.

4 Article 55 UNCLOS.

5 David J Attard, *The Exclusive Economic Zone in International Law* (Clarendon Press 1987) 1; Francisco Orrego Vicuña, *The Exclusive Economic Zone* (CUP 1989) 3–15; Robert L Friedheim, 'Fishing Negotiations at the Third United Nations Conference on the Law of the Sea' (1991) 22 ODIL 209.

6 Leanza and Caracciolo (n 3) 191–192.

2.1.1 *Coastal States' Sovereign Rights and Jurisdiction over Resources in the EEZ*

As mentioned, coastal State have sovereign rights over living and non-living resources in the EEZ pursuant to Article 56(1)(a). In the exercise of these sovereign rights, coastal States are entitled to put in place laws and regulations pursuant to Article 62(4) and take measures to ensure compliance with these laws as per Article 73(1). In the exercise of its enforcement jurisdiction, coastal States have the right to arrest and detain vessels and crews; however Article 73(2) requires that the vessel should be promptly released upon the posting of a reasonable bond or security. The coastal State's failure to do so would enable the flag State to initiate prompt release proceedings. UNCLOS tribunals have had the opportunity to clarify coastal States' regulatory and enforcement competences both living and non-living resources, in the EEZ in cases such as *Virginia G*, *South China Sea* and *Arctic Sunrise*. In addition, many disputes relating to living resources in the EEZ brought before the International Tribunal for the Law of the Sea (ITLOS) have in fact been prompt release cases. This section examines the extent to which UNCLOS tribunals have clarified through these cases the scope of coastal States' regulatory power (Section 2.1.1.1), enforcement power (Section 2.1.1.2) and obligation of prompt release (Section 2.1.1.3) in the EEZ.

2.1.1.1 Scope of Coastal States' Regulatory Power in the EEZ

Unlike Article 77(2) concerning coastal States' sovereign rights in the continental shelf, Article 56 does not explicitly specify whether coastal States' sovereign rights in the EEZ are exclusive or not. The arbitral tribunal in *South China Sea*, however, has confirmed the exclusive nature of coastal States' sovereign rights despite the absence of the term 'exclusive' in Article 56(1). In this case, the tribunal was asked by the Philippines to find that China had violated its sovereign rights in the EEZ by, inter alias, imposing the 2012 moratorium on fishing in the area north of 12° N latitude.[7] The tribunal found that even though there was no evidence to show that China enforced the 2012 fishing moratorium against Philippine fishing vessel in the latter's EEZ,[8] 'the 2012 fishing moratorium constituted an assertion by China of jurisdiction in areas in which jurisdiction over fisheries is reserved to the

7 *The South China Sea Arbitration between the Republic of the Philippines and the People's Republic of China (Philippines v China)* (2016) RIAA XXXIII 153 [176].

8 Ibid [711].

Philippines'[9] and thus amounted to a breach of Article 56 UNCLOS. The tribunal did not only confirm the exclusivity of coastal States' sovereign rights in the EEZ, but also adopted a broad understanding of the scope of such exclusivity by rejecting any assertion of jurisdiction by a noncoastal State and any laws which have a deterring effect on the coastal States' exercise of sovereign rights in the EEZ, even when they are not enforced on the ground.

As part of the exercise of sovereign rights in the EEZ, Article 62(4) UNCLOS provides a list of activities which coastal States may regulate in order to conserve and manage their living resources. While this list is not exhaustive by virtue of the term 'inter alias', coastal States' laws and regulations under this article are all connected with fisheries issues. This has given rise to questions regarding the extent to which coastal State may regulate activities which are not strictly fishing-related in the EEZ. The bunkering of fishing vessels in the EEZ provides an example of such an activity. Under UNCLOS, bunkering activities in the EEZ are neither explicitly subjected to flag State jurisdiction nor do they explicitly fall under coastal States' regulatory power under Article 62(4).[10]

The question regarding whether bunkering of a fishing vessel in EEZ falls within the coastal State's regulatory jurisdiction was raised in three cases before ITLOS. In *M/V Saiga* prompt release, the very first case brought to ITLOS, ITLOS declined to offer a view on this question, deeming it unnecessary to resolve the case before it.[11] This notwithstanding, ITLOS still made a brief statement that 'laws or regulations on bunkering of fishing vessels may arguably be classified as laws or regulations on activities within the scope of the exercise by the coastal State of its sovereign rights to explore, exploit, conserve and manage the living resources in the EEZ'.[12] ITLOS again declined to make any findings on the question of bunkering of offshore

9 Ibid.

10 Rainer Lagoni, 'Offshore Bunkering in the Exclusive Economic Zone' in Tafsir Malick Ndiaye and Rüdiger Wolfrum (eds), *Law of the Sea, Environmental Law and Settlement of Disputes: Liber Amicorum Judge Thomas A. Mensah* (Martinus Nijhoff 2007) 614; *M/V 'SAIGA' (No. 2)* (*Saint Vincent and the Grenadines v Guinea*) (Judgment, Sep. Op. Anderson) ITLOS Reports 1999, 10 [137]; *M/V 'Virginia G'* (*Panama/Guinea-Bissau*) (Judgment, Dis. Op. Ndiaye) ITLOS Reports 2014, 4 [258]–[270].

11 *M/V 'SAIGA'* (*Saint Vincent and the Grenadines v Guinea*) (Prompt Release, Judgment) ITLOS Reports 1997, 6 [59].

12 Ibid [63]. Note, however, that this position was not supported by all the judges. See, for example, *M/V 'SAIGA'* (*Saint Vincent and the Grenadines v Guinea*) (Prompt Release, Dis. Op. Mensah) ITLOS Reports 1997, 6 [23]; Collective Dissenting Opinion by Judge Wolfrum and Yamamoto. *M/V 'SAIGA'* (*Saint Vincent and the Grenadines v Guinea*) ITLOS Reports 1997, 6 [22], [25].

activities in *M/V Saiga (No. 2)*, as it was able to settle the case without having to address the broader question of the rights of coastal States and other States with regard to bunkering in the EEZ.[13]

It was not until *Virginia G* in 2014 that ITLOS finally managed to provide a definitive answer to the long-standing question of whether coastal States can regulate the bunkering of fishing vessels under their fisheries laws and regulations.[14] The M/V Virginia G, which was flying the flag of Panama, was providing gas oil to foreign vessels fishing in the EEZ of Guinea-Bissau when it was arrested by the authorities of Guinea-Bissau. In examining whether Guinea-Bissau, in the exercise of its sovereign rights in respect of the exploration, exploitation, conservation and management of natural resources in its EEZ, had the competence to regulate bunkering of foreign vessels fishing,[15] ITLOS first identified that the legal basis for answering such question comprised Article 56 read together with Articles 61–68 of the Convention.[16] According to ITLOS, the term 'sovereign rights' in Article 56(1) encompassed all rights 'necessary for and connected with' the exploration, exploitation, conservation and management of the natural resources, 'including the right to take the necessary enforcement measures'.[17] The use of the terms 'conserving' and 'managing' in the same article, in the Tribunal's view, indicated that the rights of coastal States went beyond conservation in its strict sense.[18] On that basis, ITLOS found that Articles 56(1) and 62(4) were connected, in that the measures listed under Article 62(4) were indeed management measures within the meaning of Article 56(1).[19]

ITLOS further noted that while the list contained in Article 62(4) was not exhaustive,[20] in order for coastal States to regulate an activity as part of their fisheries laws, there must be a direct connection to fishing. ITLOS found that such a connection to fishing existed for the bunkering of foreign vessels fishing in the EEZ since this enabled them to continue their activities without interruption at sea.[21] To support its conclusion, ITLOS also referred to the fact that the definitions of 'fishing' and 'fishing-related' activities in

[13] *M/V 'SAIGA' (No. 2)* (*Saint Vincent and the Grenadines v Guinea*) (Judgment) ITLOS Reports 1999, 10 [138].
[14] *M/V 'Virginia G' (Panama/Guinea-Bissau)* (Judgment) ITLOS Reports 2014, 4 [207].
[15] Ibid [208].
[16] Ibid [209].
[17] Ibid [211].
[18] Ibid [212].
[19] Ibid.
[20] Ibid [213].
[21] Ibid [215].

international agreements 'establish a close connection between fishing and the various support activities, including bunkering'[22] and that the national legislation of several States regulated bunkering of foreign vessels in their EEZ as part of their fisheries law.[23]

Lastly, ITLOS had to establish whether the bunkering of foreign vessels was covered by the freedom of navigation provided for under Article 58.[24] ITLOS had already found the bunkering of fishing vessels to be closely related to fisheries and thus, coastal States' competence to regulate bunkering of fishing activities in the EEZ derives from their sovereign rights in the EEZ. Consequently, it concluded that Article 58 would not prevent coastal States from regulating, under Article 56, bunkering of foreign vessels fishing in their EEZs.[25] This meant that the coastal States' regulatory competence was limited only to the bunkering of fishing vessels; it did not extend to other bunkering activities.[26] For the above reasons, ITLOS held coastal States are entitled to regulate the bunkering of foreign vessels fishing in its EEZ to conserve and manage its living resources under Article 56 of the Convention read together with Article 62(4) of the Convention.[27]

ITLOS's decision in *Virginia G* was significant in that it not only settled the long-debated question of whether the bunkering of fishing vessels falls within the scope of Article 62(4) in favour of coastal States,[28] but also clarified the scope of coastal States' regulatory power in the EEZ more generally. It is now clear that in order for coastal States to regulate an activity under their fisheries laws and regulations, such an activity need not be specifically listed in Article 62(4). The key requirement is that there is a direct connection between fishing and the activity. ITLOS's interpretation of Article 62(4) stood in stark contrast with that of the arbitral tribunal in *Gulf of St. Lawrence*. In this case, the arbitral tribunal held that the coastal State's sovereign right to manage the living resources of the EEZ did not extend to the processing of fish caught in the EEZ.[29] Therefore, this arbitral tribunal concluded that Article 62(4) UNCLOS did not cover activities substantially different from

22 Ibid [216].
23 Ibid [217].
24 Ibid [220].
25 Ibid [222].
26 Ibid [223].
27 Ibid [217].
28 Judge ad hoc Sérvulo Correia called ITLOS's decision on regarding bunkering of fishing vessel a 'landmark decision'. See: *M/V 'Virginia G'* (*Panama/Guinea-Bissau*) (Judgment, Dis. Op. Sérvulo Correia) ITLOS Reports 2014, 4 [1].
29 *Case concerning filleting within the Gulf of St. Lawrence* (*Canada v France*) (17 July 1986) 19 RIAA 225 [50].

those listed therein. Arguably, ITLOS's approach is more reasonable for at least two reasons. First, it reflects the nature of the Convention as merely setting up a legal framework for activities at sea: it should not be interpreted in a narrow, rigid manner. Second, the fact that ITLOS interpreted Article 62(4) broadly in light of recently adopted international instruments as well as contemporary State practice ensures that State fishing practices are reflected under UNCLOS. This shows that ITLOS did not consider the Convention in a static mode but as an evolving instrument.

While ITLOS's conclusion is commendable, it should perhaps have been clearer regarding the method of interpretation that it employed. For example, ITLOS could have explained the basis on which it could resort to other international agreements or national legislation in interpreting Article 62(4). Within Part V UNCLOS itself, ITLOS also did not take notice of Article 59 which is designed to deal with situations in which UNCLOS does not attribute rights or jurisdiction to coastal States or to other States. A reasonable argument could be made that Article 59 was not applicable to this situation. This is because, as mentioned, the list under Article 62(4) is not exhaustive, thus it cannot be said that the bunkering of a fishing vessel is not regulated by the Convention. However, ITLOS could have acknowledged the existence of this article and explained why it was inapplicable. More transparent legal reasoning in general would have made their conclusion more nuanced and provided better guidance for future cases.

2.1.1.2 Scope of Coastal States' Enforcement Jurisdiction over Resources in the EEZ

To enable States to exercise their sovereign rights to explore, exploit, conserve and manage the living resources in the EEZ effectively, Article 73(1) allows coastal States to take measures 'as may be necessary to ensure compliance with the laws and regulations adopted by it in conformity with the Convention'. The phrase 'as may be necessary', however, does not provide clear guidance on the scope of enforcement measures that coastal States may take. Further, by virtue of the phrase 'to ensure compliance with the laws and regulations adopted ... in conformity with the Convention', UNCLOS establishes that the enforcement power of coastal States under Article 73(1) only extends to laws and regulations concerning fisheries-related activities prescribed under Article 62(4). This means that Article 73(1) only allows coastal States to take enforcement measures in the exercise of their sovereign rights with regards to living resources. No equivalent provision can be found for enforcement jurisdiction in relation to non-living resources in the EEZ. The question is then whether coastal States may also exercise enforcement jurisdiction with regard to non-living resources in the EEZ. This section analyses UNCLOS tribunals' decisions relating to the two above-mentioned issues.

ENFORCEMENT JURISDICTION OVER LIVING RESOURCES. Under Article 73(1), coastal States are permitted to take enforcement measures, such as boarding, inspection, arrest and judicial proceedings, to deal with foreign vessels illegally fishing in their EEZ. Article 73(3) only prohibits imprisonment and other forms of corporal punishment as penalties for violations of fisheries laws and regulations. This leaves open the question as to whether a coastal State is allowed to take a measure which is not only specified in Article 73(1) but is also not prohibited under Article 73(3). This question in essence revolves around the meaning of the term 'necessary' found in Article 73(1).

ITLOS has to date provided the most detailed examination of this question in *Virginia G* by examining the measure of vessel confiscation. It is worth noting that the issue of whether coastal State could legitimately confiscate foreign fishing vessels to ensure compliance with its fisheries law had come up in two earlier cases, namely: *Grand Prince* and *Tomimaru*. As these were both prompt release proceedings, ITLOS was not engaged in the interpretation of Article 73(1) per se. It found that it lacked jurisdiction in *Grand Prince* and thus did not deal with the issue. In *Tomimaru*, ITLOS only dealt with this topic in passing, noting that although Article 73 of the Convention made no reference to confiscation of vessels, it was aware that many States provided for the confiscation of fishing vessels in their legislation relating to the management and conservation of marine living resources.[30] ITLOS seemed to not have rejected the permissibility of confiscation per se, provided that it was to 'be used in such a manner as to upset the balance of the interests of the flag State and of the coastal State established in the Convention'.[31]

In *Virginia G*, the interpretation of Article 73(1) was key to examining the legality of confiscation as an enforcement measure under UNCLOS. ITLOS held that pursuant to this article, coastal States may take such measures 'as may be necessary to ensure compliance with the laws and regulations adopted by [them] in conformity with this Convention'.[32] Accordingly,

[30] *'Tomimaru' (Japan v Russian Federation)* (Prompt Release, Judgment) ITLOS Reports 2005–2007, 74 [72].

[31] Ibid [76].

[32] *M/V 'Virginia G'* (n 14) [252].

ITLOS had to establish whether (i) the legislation promulgated by Guinea-Bissau with regard to the confiscation of vessels in the EEZ was in conformity with the Convention and (ii) whether confiscation was necessary to ensure the compliance with the law and regulations adopted by the Coastal State.[33] With regards to the first question, ITLOS held that a law providing for the confiscation of a vessel offering bunkering services to foreign vessels fishing in the EEZ of Guinea-Bissau was not *per se* in violation of Article 73(1) of the Convention because the law did not require confiscation in all cases but allowed flexibility in sanctioning of violations.[34] Whether or not confiscation was justified depended on the facts and circumstances of a given case.[35] This seems to be the correct approach as the use of the phrase 'such measures as' in Article 73(1) indicates that the list of measures found therein is only illustrative and coastal States have the discretion to adopt other enforcement measures.[36] As for the second question, ITLOS determined that Panama had breached the obligation to obtain written authorisation for bunkering and to pay the prescribed fee, and that this was 'a serious violation'.[37] However, it held that this breach was the result of 'a misinterpretation of the correspondence' between the fishing vessels and the authorities of Guinea-Bissau.[38] Therefore, ITLOS found that the confiscation of the vessel and the gas oil on board 'was not necessary either to sanction the violation committed or to deter the vessels or their operators from repeating this violation',[39] and as a result Guinea-Bissau was not in compliance with Article 73(1). Arguably, the most crucial term in Article 73(1) that needed clarification was 'necessary' as this would determine whether confiscation was consistent with UNCLOS. ITLOS's application of this requirement in *Virginia G* was however, fact-based without setting out objective criteria to assess this requirement.

For ITLOS, the necessity test was performed through the balancing between the gravity of the offence and the gravity of the sanction. Compared with how the term 'necessary' has been interpreted by other international courts,[40] ITLOS's application of the requirement of 'necessary' seemed much more

33 Ibid [256].
34 Ibid [257].
35 Ibid.
36 James Harrison, 'Article 73' in Alexander Proelss (ed), *United Nations Convention on the Law of the Sea: A Commentary* (CH Beck, Hart, Nomos 2017) 558.
37 *M/V 'Virginia G'* (n 14) [267].
38 Ibid [269].
39 Ibid.
40 For example, WTO dispute settlement bodies, in examining whether a trade measure which would otherwise have violated WTO law was 'necessary' under Article XX(b) General Agreement on Tariffs and Trade or Article XIV(a) General Agreement on Trade in Services set

simplistic. ITLOS did not explain how or why the necessity test entailed the balancing between the gravity of the offence and that of the sanction. It did not engage in the interpretation of either the ordinary meaning of the term 'necessary' or the context of the provision in which Article 73(1) is found or the purpose of the provision. Enforcement measures under Article 73(1) are to be adopted in order to ensure compliance with coastal States' exercise of sovereign rights over marine living resources in the EEZ. At the same time, Article 73 also contains other safeguards to limit the exercise of coastal States' enforcement powers. As such, it seeks to 'ensure that coastal States do not misuse their enforcement powers and encroach on the rights of other States to access the living resources in the [EEZ]'.[41] The context and purpose of Article 73 thus suggests that a balancing exercise is indeed warranted in the application of Article 73(1), but it should not be limited to merely comparing the offence and the sanction. Judge Paik in his Separate Opinion argued that ITLOS should have considered both the extent to which the measure contributes to the achievement of the objective sought and the degree to which the measure encroaches upon the protected rights of other States.[42] On that basis, he proposed four general criteria to assess the necessity of Guinea-Bissau's confiscation measure.[43] Judge Paik's approach added the much-needed clarity that the judgment regrettably did not offer.

out a three-fold test. They examined: (i) the 'relative importance' of the interests that the measures are designed to protect, (ii) the contribution of the measure to the ends pursued', that is, whether there were any reasonably available alternatives and (iii) the measures' 'restrictive impact on international commerce'. See *European Communities–Measures Affecting Asbestos and Asbestos-Containing Products*, AB Report (12 March 2001) WT/DS135/AB/R; *Korea–Measures Affecting Imports of Fresh, Chilled and Frozen Beef*, AB Report (11 December 2000) WT/DS161,169/AB/R; *United States–Measures Affecting Cross-Border Supply of Gambling and Betting Services*, AB Report (7 April 2005) WT/DS285/AB/R. The European Court of Human Rights, in examining whether the State's interferences with rights protected by the European Convention on Human Rights was necessary required that the State's measure satisfy a three-prong test: (i) whether the 'interference' complained of corresponded to a 'pressing social need', (ii) whether it was 'proportionate to the legitimate aim pursued', and (iii) whether the reasons given by the national authorities to justify it are 'relevant and sufficient'. See *Sunday Times (I) v UK* 30 Eur. Ct. H.R. (ser. A), [62].

41 Harrison (n 36) 557.

42 *M/V 'Virginia G' (Panama/Guinea-Bissau)* (Judgment, Sep. Op. Paik) ITLOS Reports 2014, 4 [25]. See also: Dissenting Opinion of Judge ad hoc Sérvulo Correia (n 28) [18].

43 These criteria include: the availability of other measures (equally effective and less onerous); the importance to Guinea-Bissau of the objective sought in taking the confiscation measure (i.e., protection of living resources in the EEZ); the impact of that measure on protected rights of Panama and other states; and the circumstances and manner in which the confiscation measure was taken. Separate Opinion of Judge Paik (n 42) [29]).

This is not to suggest that ITLOS erred in considering the gravity of the offence and that of the sanction. Severe sanctions, including severe enforcement measures, are not uncommon. They are in fact encouraged in order to deter illegal fishing, for example in the International Plan of Action (IPOA) Prevent, Deter, and Eliminate Illegal, Unreported and Unregulated Fishing,[44] which despite not being legally binding, is 'the most cited, high-profile and widely diffused global fisheries instrument in the world after the 1982 UN Convention'.[45] The point is simply that ITLOS should have explained why the severity of the sanction, or that of the offence, were the only factors taken into account in the balancing exercise to determine necessity under Article 73(1).

Another issue raised by ITLOS's approach to interpreting the scope of coastal States' enforcement jurisdiction in the EEZ concerned the margin of discretion reserved for coastal States in deciding the necessary enforcement measures in their EEZ. Margin of appreciation is a principle that is widely recognised and applied in other areas of international law, such as human rights or trade law. However, under UNCLOS and particularly before UNCLOS tribunals, it rarely arises. As will be analysed in Section 2.1.1.3, the issue of coastal States' margin of discretion and international courts' standard of review has primarily come up before ITLOS in prompt release proceedings in relation to the assessment reasonable bond. *Virginia* G was the first time it was raised in connection with coastal States' enforcement power. In their Joint Dissenting Opinion, Judges Hoffmann, Marotta Rangel, Rao, Kateka, Gao, Bouguetaia argued that in the context of Article 73(1), 'term "sovereign rights" ought to carry with it a degree of deference to the coastal State in its exercise of those rights'.[46] As a result, according to the six judges, 'the Tribunal does not sit as a court of appeal in assessing whether or not the enforcement measures are necessary in the circumstances of the case'.[47] These judges believed that, while coastal States are not given

[44] Paragraph 21 of the IPOA–IUU provides, in relevant parts: States should ensure that sanctions for IUU fishing by vessels and, to the greatest extent possible, nationals under its jurisdiction are of sufficient severity to effectively prevent, deter and eliminate IUU fishing and to deprive offenders of the benefits accruing from such fishing. See: FAO, International Plan of Action to Prevent, Deter, and Eliminate Illegal, Unreported and Unregulated Fishing www.fao.org/3/a-y1224e.pdf accessed 25 January 2022. (emphasis added).

[45] FAO, Code of Conduct for Responsible Fisheries www.fao.org/iuu-fishing/international-framework/code-of-conduct-for-responsible-fisheries/en/ accessed 25 January 2022.

[46] *M/V 'Virginia G' (Panama/Guinea-Bissau)* (Judgment, Joint Dis. Op. Hoffman, Rangel, Rao, Kateka, Gao and Bouguetaia) ITLOS Reports 2014, 4 [49].

[47] Ibid [47].

unlimited power of appreciation under UNCLOS,[48] they should be given a broad margin of appreciation as the national courts and authorities 'are better placed to appreciate all the relevant considerations of law and fact in the State concerned'.[49]

Finally, and perhaps rather confusingly, ITLOS also found that 'the principle of reasonableness applies generally to enforcement measure under Article 73 of the Convention' and concluded that the enforcement measure against the M/V Virginia G 'was not reasonable' in the light of the circumstances of the case and the gravity of the violation.[50] In so doing, ITLOS incorporated the standard of 'reasonableness' applicable to prompt release proceedings under Article 73(2) into Article 73(1). It did not, however, explain the basis for applying 'reasonableness' – a criterion intended for a payment to be made by the flag State in a prompt release proceeding in paragraph (2) – to an enforcement measure taken by the coastal State in the EEZ in paragraph (1). Moreover, it did not clarify what was meant by 'reasonable' or how to assess it. In any case, the threshold for the fulfilment of the test of reasonableness undoubtedly differs from that of necessity,[51] and thus ITLOS's statement would leave it unclear as to which threshold should be applied to assess the coastal State's enforcement measure.

In sum, with regards to the scope of coastal States' enforcement jurisdiction, ITLOS's decision in the *Virginia* G case made clear that Article 73(1) does not establish an exhaustive list of enforcement measures, and that coastal States can take enforcement measures not listed under this provision, so long as they are 'necessary' to ensure compliance with their legislation concerning fisheries. However, ITLOS failed to provide clear criteria to guide the determination of how a measure would be considered 'necessary'. This lack of guidance, as observed by Judge Jesus, made ITLOS's interpretation of Article 73(1) 'arbitrary and subjective'.[52] As such, it may create serious difficulties for coastal States to grasp the exact extent of the enforcement power granted to them to conserve and manage their

[48] Ibid [53].
[49] Ibid [50].
[50] *M/V 'Virginia G'* (n 14) [270].
[51] Judge ad hoc Sérvulo Correia held that 'necessary' cannot be regarded as synonymous with 'reasonable'. See Dissenting Opinion of Judge ad hoc Sérvulo Correia (n 28) [18].
[52] *M/V 'Virginia G'* (Panama/Guinea-Bissau) (Judgment, Dis. Op. Jesus) ITLOS Reports 2014, 4 [20].

fisheries resources, especially in the context of growing global concern for the conservation and sustainability of fishing resources.[53]

ENFORCEMENT JURISDICTION OVER NON-LIVING RESOURCES. Article 73(1) deals only with enforcement jurisdiction in relation to living resources. With respect to non-living resources, Article 56(3) specifies that sovereign rights in respect of the seabed and subsoil are to be exercised in accordance with Part VI governing the continental shelf. Unlike Part V, Part VI however does not contain a provision on coastal States' enforcement jurisdiction for non-living resources. As remarked by ITLOS Judges Wolfrum and Kelly in the *Arctic Sunrise* provisional measure phase, '[a]s far as enforcement actions in the exclusive zone in general are concerned the enforcement jurisdiction of the coastal State is limited if it is not legitimized by one of the exceptions [under the Convention].'[54] The question that arises is then, in the absence of a clear legal basis to that effect under both Part V and Part VI, are coastal States allowed to take enforcement measures with respect to the exploration and exploitation of non-living resources in the EEZ – or in continental shelf for that matter?

The arbitral tribunal in *Arctic Sunrise* had the opportunity to deal with this question. The tribunal first recalled that during UNCLOS III, proposals to extend coastal States' enforcement powers to non-living resources were not accepted.[55] However, as non-living resources in the seabed and subsoil are regulated under Part VI, the tribunal then turned its attention to Article 77 dealing with non-living resources in the continental shelf. It found that the International Law Commission (ILC) Commentary to the relevant draft provision of the 1958 Convention on the Continental Shelf, which Article 77 UNCLOS reproduces, confirmed that coastal States' rights connected to the exploration and exploitation of resources in the continental shelf include 'jurisdiction in

[53] By way of illustration, questions regarding the permissibility of coastal States' enforcement measures such as burning or sinking of foreign vessels allegedly engaged illegal fishing in the EEZ have attracted much attention in have in the past years. See, for example, Dita Liliansa, 'The Necessity of Indonesia's Measures to Sink Vessels for IUU Fishing in the Exclusive Economic Zone' (2020) 10 Asian J. Int. Law 1; Lan Ngoc Nguyen and Yen Hoang Tran, 'Coastal States' Enforcement Power over Fishing Activities in the South China Sea: Where Is the Line under International Law?' (2019) 37 Chinese (Taiwan) Yearbook of International Law and Affairs 110–145.

[54] *'Arctic Sunrise' (Kingdom of the Netherlands v Russian Federation)* (Provisional Measures, Order of 22 November 2013, Joint Sep. Op. Wolfrum and Kelly) ITLOS Reports 2013, 256 [13].

[55] Ibid [281].

connexion with the prevention and punishment of violations of the law'.[56] Based on this commentary, the tribunal concluded that coastal States' right to enforce laws in relation to non-living resources in the EEZ exists, but that it was not necessary for the tribunal to reach a view on the extent of this right.[57]

The *Arctic Sunrise* tribunal thus clarified that the absence of a provision conferring enforcement jurisdiction over non-living resources to coastal States in the EEZ does not mean that such jurisdiction does not exist. The reasoning provided, however, raises some interesting points. The tribunal did not explain how to reconcile its finding based on the ILC Commentary to the 1958 Convention on the Continental Shelf with the negotiating history of UNCLOS. As the tribunal acknowledged, the latter showed that the drafters of UNCLOS did not wish to extend coastal States' enforcement powers to non-living resources in the EEZ. By using an article belonging to Part VI to answer a question relating to Part V, the tribunal seems to have treated the continental shelf and EEZ regimes as one integral regime. It should be recalled that in *Barbados v Trinidad and Tobago*, the respondent made a similar argument, stating that the phrase 'in accordance with' under Article 56(3) signified that the drafters intended the terms of Part V to be subject to those of Part VI.[58] The applicant, on the other hand, argued that 'in accordance to' is distinct from 'subject to' and that 'the legal concepts of the EEZ and the CS exist side by side, with neither taking precedence over the other'.[59] The arbitral tribunal, in response, stated that the EEZ and continental shelf regimes '[coexist] with significant elements in common'[60] and that there was a 'trend towards harmonization of legal regimes'.[61] The negotiating history of UNCLOS also indicated that the rejection of the proposal to include enforcement jurisdiction within the ambit of Article 73 was based on the understanding that enforcement powers in relation to non-living sources in the EEZ were to be governed by Part VI.[62] The tribunal's

56 Ibid [283].
57 Ibid [284].
58 *Arbitration between Barbados and the Republic of Trinidad and Tobago, Relating to the Delimitation of the Exclusive Economic Zone and the Continental Shelf Between Them (Barbados v Trinidad and Tobago)* (2006) RIAA XXVII 147 [175].
59 Ibid [181].
60 Ibid [226].
61 Ibid [227].
62 Myron H Nordquist, Shabtai Rosenne and Satya N Nandan (eds), *United Nations Convention on the Law of the Sea 1982: A Commentary*, Vol II (Martinus Nijhoff 1985) 794. [Virginia Commentary, vol II]

reasoning would have been more nuanced if it had addressed this point in a more explicit manner.

Finally, it is interesting to note that in *Arctic Sunrise*, the arbitral tribunal showed particular willingness to engage with the question of enforcement jurisdiction over non-living resources despite the fact that, as the tribunal acknowledged, Russia has neither charged the Arctic 30 with any offences related to Russia's non-living resources in the EEZ nor did Russia consider that the vessel had committed such an offence.[63] Such willingness could perhaps be explained by Russia's nonappearance in this case, thus prompting the tribunal to make extra efforts to discuss all possible legal arguments that could be raised so as to ensure that, in case of default of appearance, 'the claim is well-founded in fact and in law' as required under Article 9 of Annex VII. Nevertheless, it is also open to question whether the tribunal's keenness to address an issue for which there is a gap in UNCLOS is indicative of how it views its own role in clarifying and developing the law of the sea.[64]

2.1.1.3 Coastal States' Obligation to Promptly Release Fishing Vessels

Coastal States have the right to arrest vessels allegedly violating their laws and regulations on the exploitation and conservation of living resources in the EEZ under Article 73(1). However, they also have the obligation to release the vessel and the crew upon the posting of a reasonable bond or other security under Article 73(2). Should the coastal State fail to do so, the flag State of the detained vessel may bring the question of release from detention pursuant to the prompt release proceedings under Article 292. Prompt release proceedings were introduced into UNCLOS with a view to balancing the rights of coastal States to take measures to ensure compliance with their fisheries laws and regulations on the one hand, and the interests of flag States to prevent their vessel and crew from prolonged detention, on the other.[65] Coastal States have the discretion to set the bond at a level they deem fit in accordance with their respective domestic laws, but Article 73(2) requires that the bond must be 'reasonable'.

[63] *Award in the Arbitration regarding the Arctic Sunrise (Kingdom of the Netherlands v Russian Federation)*, Award on Merits (2015) RIAA XXXII 183 [279].

[64] See further discussion in Section 7.2.3.2.

[65] Myron H Nordquist (ed), *United Nations Convention on the Law of the Sea 1982: A Commentary*, Vol V (Martinus Nijhoff 1985) 67.

The term 'reasonable' is neither defined under the Convention, nor is there any guidance in the Convention as to how this requirement should be applied in practice.[66] In fact, this term was intentionally left open as a compromise for the diverging opinions expressed during the negotiation of UNCLOS regarding whether the coastal State or the flag State should have jurisdiction to prosecute violations of the coastal State's sovereign rights in the EEZ.[67] The founders of UNCLOS thus expected the competent courts and tribunals to give concrete content to the reasonableness criterion.[68] As all prompt release procedures have hitherto been initiated only before ITLOS and prompt release cases make up nearly a third of its case law,[69] the Tribunal has managed to develop over the years a list of criteria to provide guidance for the determination of 'reasonable bond'.

In *M/V Saiga* – the first case in which ITLOS assessed the reasonableness of a bond – ITLOS simply explained that 'the criterion of reasonableness encompasses the amount, the nature and the form of the bond or financial security. The overall balance of the amount, form and nature of bond or financial security must be reasonable'.[70] However, it was not until *Camouco* that ITLOS for the first time provided a list of factors relevant to an assessment of the reasonableness of bonds or other financial security.[71] These factors included the gravity of the alleged offences, the penalties imposed or imposable under the laws of the detaining State, the value of the detained vessel and of the cargo seized, the amount of the bond imposed by the detaining State and its form.[72] However, when applying these factors to the case, ITLOS only focused on two factors, namely: the maximum penalty that could be imposed on the Master of the Camouco; and the value of Camouco and of the catch on board.

[66] Erik Franckx, 'Reasonable Bond in the Practice of the International Tribunal for the Law of the Sea' (2002) 32(2) California Western International Law Journal 303.

[67] Virginia Commentary, vol II (n 62) 784–795.

[68] Vincent P Cogliati-Bantz, 'International Tribunal for the Law of the Sea, Hoshinmaru (*Japan v Russian Federation*) and Tomimaru (*Japan v Russian Federation*), Prompt Release Judgments of 6 August 2007' (2009) 58(1) ICLQ 241.

[69] Prompt release cases account for 9 out of 29 cases ITLOS has received to date. See ITLOS List of Cases www.itlos.org/cases/list-of-cases/ accessed 25 January 2022.

[70] *M/V 'SAIGA'* (Prompt Release, Judgment) (n 11) [82].

[71] The Camouco, a fishing vessel flying the flag of Panama, was arrested by the French authorities and the Master was charged for breaching French fisheries law in the EEZ of the Crozet Islands near the Antarctic. *'Camouco' (Panama v France)* (Prompt Release, Judgment) ITLOS Reports 2000, 10.

[72] ibid [67].

The list of factors relevant for the determination of reasonable bond in *Camouco* was later adopted in the *Monte Confurco*[73] and *Juno Trader*.[74] In *Monte Confurco*, ITLOS emphasised, however, that 'it did not intend to lay down rigid rules' as to the exact weight to be attached to each one of the factors.[75] ITLOS instead placed special emphasis on the balance of interests emerging from Articles 73 and 292 of the Convention, and stated that this balance provided the guiding criterion in the assessment of the reasonableness of the bond.[76] It was the maintenance of this balance that led ITLOS in the subsequent *Volga* case to find that coastal States could not impose additional nonfinancial conditions, including a 'good behaviour bond' such as the carriage of a fully operational Vessel Monitoring System on board as a condition, among others, for the release of the Volga and the crew.[77] In its view, the inclusion of such conditions would defeat the purpose of Article 73(2) read in conjunction with Article 292 of the Convention, which was to provide a mechanism through which vessel and crew could be released promptly by posting a security of a financial nature.[78] On a more general point, ITLOS held that the reasonableness of the bond or other security should take into account 'the terms of the bond or security set by the detaining State, having regard to all the circumstances of the particular case',[79] but this did not include the circumstances of the seizure.[80]

The approach of ITLOS to determining what constituted a reasonable bond, focusing particularly on quantifiable factors, was repeatedly met with criticism from individual judges. In *Camouco*, for example, Judge Anderson

73 The Monte Confurco, a fishing vessel flying the flag of Seychelles, was boarded by the crew of a French surveillance frigate in the EEZ of the Kerguelen Islands in the French Southern and Antarctic Territories. Monte Confurco was charged with violating French fisheries law for having entered the EEZ without prior authorisation and for not declaring the toothfish caught on board. *'Monte Confurco' (Seychelles v France)* (Prompt Release, Judgment) ITLOS Reports 2000, 86.

74 The Juno Trader was a refrigerated cargo vessel flying the flag of Saint Vincent and the Grenadines. The vessel was boarded and charged with illegal fishing and subsequently detained and confiscated by the authorities of Guinea-Bissau. *'Juno Trader' (Saint Vincent and the Grenadines v Guinea-Bissau)* (Prompt Release, Judgment) ITLOS Reports 2004, 17.

75 *Monte Confurco* (n 73) [76].

76 Ibid [72].

77 *'Volga' (Russian Federation v Australia)* (Prompt Release, Judgment) ITLOS Reports 2002, 10 [53].

78 Ibid [80].

79 Ibid [65].

80 Ibid [83].

was of the opinion that the determination of the bond could not depend solely on the monetary value of the vessel, its gear, catch or the monetary value of the penalties.[81] The gravity of the alleged offence, which was illegal fishing, and the discretion of the coastal State in laying down law to deal with this,[82] should have been given more weight given the widespread problems of illegal fishing, flags of convenience as well as the problems faced by coastal States in ensuring the effective conservation of fish stocks in extensive and remote EEZs.[83] In the same vein, in *Volga*, several judges expressed disappointment with ITLOS's repeated disregard for the problem of widespread IUU fishing, in assessing the reasonableness of the bond. Judge ad hoc Shearer believed that the imposition of nonfinancial bond should have been considered reasonable in order for coastal States to fulfil their duties to ensure the conservation of fisheries resources in the EEZ.[84]

ITLOS was not oblivious to the concerns relating to IUU fishing. In *Monte Confurco*, for example, it stated that it took note of the general context of unlawful fishing in the region, the threat posed by illegal fishing to the future resources and the measures taken under the Convention on the Conservation of Antarctic Marine Living Resources (CCAMLR) for the conservation of toothfish.[85] However, in the final judgment, it is difficult to see how the concerns about illegal fishing were taken note of; it was also not clear the extent to which these concerns informed the final amount of the bond. Not until *Hoshinmaru* could one see a shift in ITLOS's examination of the reasonableness of the bond.[86] While still holding that '[t]he amount of a bond should be proportionate to the gravity of the alleged offence',[87] ITLOS no longer assessed the gravity of offence in isolation from the wider context in which the offence was committed. The Hoshinmaru held a valid fishing licence and was authorised to be present and to fish in the Russian EEZ.

[81] *'Camouco' (Panama v France)* (Prompt Release, Dis. Op. Anderson) ITLOS Reports 2000 [5].

[82] *'Camouco' (Panama v France)* (Prompt Release, Dis. Op. Wolfrum) ITLOS Reports 2000 [11].

[83] Ibid [6].

[84] *'Volga' (Russian Federation v Australia)* (Prompt Release, Dis. Op. Shearer) ITLOS Reports 2002, 10 [16]. Contra: *'Volga' (Russian Federation v Australia)* (Prompt Release, Sep. Op. Volga) ITLOS Reports 2002, 10 [26]. Judge Cot, while acknowledging Australia's right to take conservation measures in order to protect a common heritage, agreed with ITLOS that, in the context of a prompt release case, the bond or financial security provided for in Articles 73(2) and 292 was in fact of a purely financial nature.

[85] *Monte Confurco* (n 73) [79].

[86] The Hoshinmaru was a fishing vessel flying the flag of Japan and was arrested by Russia for falsely declaring 20 tons of raw sockeye salmon as the cheaper chum salmon. *'Hoshinmaru' (Japan v Russian Federation)* (Prompt Release, Judgment) ITLOS Reports 2005–2007, 18.

[87] Ibid [89].

However, ITLOS noted that between Russia and Japan, there existed a high level of cooperation in respect of fishing activities in the area in question, including the establishment of an institutional framework for consultations concerning the management and conservation of fish stocks.[88] Pointing to the need for proper conservation and management measures to ensure that living resources in the EEZ are not endangered by overexploitation as stipulated under Article 61(1) UNCLOS,[89] ITLOS was of the view that the offence committed by the Master of the Hoshinmaru could not be considered a minor offence or an offence of a purely technical nature.

The *Hoshinmaru* case presented a commendable development in ITLOS's approach to determining a reasonable bond. In previous cases, ITLOS assessed the gravity of the offence based mainly on the penalty prescribed in the relevant domestic legislation and only paid lip service to IUU fishing concerns. By contrast, in this case, ITLOS placed what might at first glance be a minor offence in the wider context of IUU fishing, taking into account the rights of coastal States under UNCLOS and the cooperation framework between Russia and Japan to conserve and manage living resources in assessing the gravity of the offence. This is an extremely important step forward in recognising and reinforcing States' obligations to combat IUU fishing.

The preceding discussion shows that the clarification of the term 'reasonable bond' under Article 73(2) presents one of the most significant contributions of ITLOS to the clarification of ambiguous terms under the UNCLOS. As mentioned above, the UNCLOS drafters deliberately left the term 'reasonable bond', which holds the key to the operation of both Articles 73(2) and 292, unspecified. The consolidated factors emerging from prompt release judgments have filled the void left by the drafters and provided some guidance as to how reasonableness is to be determined. ITLOS progressed from setting out general criteria in the first case to elaborating on more specific criteria for determining the reasonableness of the bond. By drawing up a list of factors relevant for the determination of reasonableness while still maintaining that this list is not exhaustive, ITLOS has clearly endeavoured to allow both predictability and flexibility in its assessment of reasonableness.[90]

On the other hand, while the list may be clear, there still exists some ambiguity when it comes to the application of the above-mentioned factors to

88 Ibid [98].

89 Ibid [99].

90 Helmut Türk, 'The Work of the International Tribunal for the Law of the Sea' (2012) 26 Ocean Yearbook Online 181.

specific cases. As one scholar commented, 'when all relevant factors have been discussed and applied in a case, the setting of the bond itself still resembles as much a *deus ex machina* as it did during the first case'.[91] Even though ITLOS made clear in the *Monte Confurco* case that it did not wish to attach any weight to the factors, ITLOS had the tendency to only look at factors that could be quantified,[92] paying particular attention to the gravity of the offence. ITLOS's assessment of the gravity of offence has itself been an evolving exercise. In earlier cases, the gravity of the offence was determined with reference, almost exclusively, to the penalty imposed under domestic law; whereas in subsequent cases, the broader context of the offence, including States' international commitments relating to the conservation of living resources and the community interests, started to creep into the examination. Since all prompt release cases brought before ITLOS have stemmed from allegations of illegal fishing, the attention to conservation obligations is arguably more in line consistent with the focus on conservation and management of the marine environment under UNCLOS.[93] More importantly, continued consideration of the problems posed by illegal fishing activities and coastal States' rights to tackle this problem will also allow ITLOS to better ensure the balance between coastal States and flag State's rights and obligations in the EEZ. Until *Hoshinmaru*, the balance seems to have tilted in favour of the flag State.

That said, several scholars have argued that prompt release is not exactly the appropriate procedure to strengthen the legal framework for combating IUU fishing. One contended that prompt release proceedings are geared towards securing speedy release of the vessel and the crew, that is, ensuring humanitarian considerations within the UNCLOS regime. Consequently, 'ITLOS and, more specifically, the prompt release mechanism are ineffective at properly addressing the issue of regulating IUU fishing'.[94] Other commentators, pointing to the narrow approach that ITLOS has adopted in interpreting a reasonable bond and the inherent jurisdictional

91 Franckx (n 66) 335.

92 Edward Arthur Laing, 'ITLOS Procedures and Practices: Bond' in John Moore and Myron H Nordquist (eds), *Current Marine Environmental Issues and the International Tribunal for the Law of the Sea* (Martinus Nijhoff 2001).

93 Andrew Serdy and Michael Bliss, 'Prompt Release of Fishing Vessels: State Practice in the Light of the Cases before the International Tribunal for the Law of the Sea' in Alex G Oude Elferink and Donald Rothwell, *Oceans Management in the 21st Century: Institutional Frameworks and Responses* (Martinus Nijhoff 2002) 293; Seline Trevisanut, 'Twenty Years of Prompt Release of Vessels: Admissibility, Jurisdiction, and Recent Trends' (2017) 48(3–4) ODIL 300.

94 Taisaku Ikeshima, 'The "Reasonableness" of Unreasonable Arguments in Prompt Release Cases in the ITLOS' (2010) 6 Waseda Global Forum 107, 123.

limit under Article 292, which prevents ITLOS from prejudicing to the merits of the case before domestic courts,[95] concluded that 'it is wishful thinking to expect Herculean efforts by the Tribunal to address the general problem of IUU fishing'.[96] However, it appears that such contentions have adopted a rather pessimistic view of ITLOS's power in prompt release cases. Although its jurisdiction is indeed only limited to examining the question of release, ITLOS made clear in the *Monte Confurco*, echoed in *Hoshinmaru*, that it 'is not prevented from examining the facts and circumstances of the case to the extent necessary for a proper appreciation of the reasonableness of the bond as set by the Respondent'.[97] Considerations of responsible fishing practices can, therefore, enter into prompt release procedures through the reasonableness test, without necessarily constituting any misuse of the procedure or abuse of the legal process.

Finally, it is interesting to note that since 2007, ITLOS has not received any requests for prompt release. This stands in great contrast to the first ten years of its existence when the bulk of docket was made up of prompt release cases. It is not exactly certain why this is the case, but one can speculate two reasons. First, the consolidated criteria for determining the bond as established in ITLOS case law have provided useful guidance for both coastal States and flag States to deal with prompt release cases out of court. Second, prompt release proceedings are initiated by flag States or owners of the vessel on behalf of flag States with a view to not only securing a rapid release of the vessel but also a lower bond than that set by the detaining State. In earlier cases, this was certainly true, but ITLOS is gradually paying more attention to coastal States' rights and obligations to conserve fish stocks in the determination of the bond, and thus showing more deference to the bond set by the coastal State. A reasonable argument could be made, thus, that the amount of bond and the manner in which ITLOS decides on the bond no longer make prompt release proceedings an attractive option for flag States.

In conclusion, ITLOS's decisions on coastal States' rights and obligations concerning fisheries in the EEZ have clarified several provisions under UNCLOS. First, it shed light on the scope of coastal States' regulatory power in the EEZ under Articles 56 and 62(4). Coastal States now have the competence to regulate under their fisheries law any activity which has a direct connection with fishing. In such a framework, the bunkering of fishing vessels is now firmly placed under coastal States' regulation, ending decades of

95 Article 292(3).
96 Rothwell and Stephens (n 1) 187.
97 *Monte Confurco* (n 73) [74].

uncertainty surrounding this particular activity. Second, with regards to the scope of their enforcement power under Article 73(1), coastal States are permitted to take enforcement measures which are not listed under this article, including confiscation of vessels, provided that such measures are necessary to ensure compliance with their fisheries laws and regulations. This allows coastal States to adopt more stringent measures than those explicitly contained in Article 73(1). Third, ITLOS's prompt release judgments have given important guidance to the interpretation and determination of what constitutes a 'reasonable bond' under Article 73(2) for the release of foreign vessels arrested for illegal fishing activities.

2.1.2 *Coastal States' Jurisdiction over Artificial Islands, Installations and Structures*

Article 56(1)(b)(i) gives coastal States jurisdiction with regard to the establishment and use of artificial islands, installations and structures. Elaborating on Article 56(1)(b)(i), Article 60 specifies that coastal States' rights and jurisdiction over the construction, operation and use of artificial islands, installations and structures are exclusive. In *South China Sea*, the arbitral tribunal reaffirmed the exclusive nature of the coastal State's jurisdiction with regards to installations and structures with regards to Mischief Reef which was located within the Philippines' EEZ. It held that 'only the Philippines' had 'decision-making and regulatory power artificial islands, and of installations and structures covered by Article 60(1), on Mischief Reef'.[98]

UNCLOS itself does not provide a definition for any of the features mentioned in Article 60(1) or any other guidance to distinguish these three categories of features. The tribunal in *South China Sea* found that the initial structures that China had built on Mischief Reef 'constituted installations or structures for the purposes of Article 60(1)'[99], which subsequently 'evolved into ... an artificial island'.[100] The tribunal briefly explained that 'China has elevated what was originally a reef platform that submerged at high tide into an island that is permanently exposed' and thus '[s]uch an island is undoubtedly "artificial" for the purposes of Article 60'.[101] This statement suggests that in order to qualify an artificial island, a feature has to be above water at high

98 *South China Sea Arbitration* (n 7) [1035].
99 Ibid [1036].
100 Ibid [1037].
101 Ibid.

tide – which seems to follow the definition of islands in Article 121(1)[102] – but that the elevation had to be man-made. By emphasising this characteristic, the tribunal seemed to distinguish between installations and structures on the one hand and artificial islands on the other upon the former two being submerged at high tide.[103] Moreover, the tribunal also held that the installations and structures built on Mischief Reef were for economic purposes.[104] This is an explicit requirement under Article 60(1)(b). Many States have, however, claimed jurisdiction over all types of installations and structures including those without economic purposes.[105] It is not entirely clear, therefore, whether the tribunal's finding can be construed to exclude installations and structures without an economic purpose from the ambit of Article 60(1) or merely to confirm one particular category of installations and features.

Paragraphs (4) and (5) of Article 60 further allow coastal states to establish safety zones around artificial islands, installations and structures, which should not exceed a distance of 500 metres, and to take appropriate measures to ensure the safety of navigation as well as artificial islands, installations and structures. The arbitral tribunal in *Arctic Sunrise* had the opportunity to engage with these two paragraphs. In particular, it dealt with two questions: (i) what constitutes a safety zone, and (ii) what are the appropriate measures that can be taken with regards to the safety zone?

UNCLOS does not define what constitutes a safety zone for the purposes of Article 60. In *Arctic Sunrise*, the issue of safety zone around installations and structures arose when the Netherlands argued that Russia had breached UNCLOS by establishing a 3 nautical miles safety zone around the Prirazlomnaya. This submission would seem to require the tribunal consider two issues, namely whether a safety zone was created and whether the Convention allowed Russia to extend it to 3 nautical miles. The arbitral tribunal answered the first question in the negative. Even though Russia had declared an area with a radius of 3 nautical miles, the tribunal was of the opinion that the relevant Russian instruments only labelled the 3 nautical miles zone around the Prirazlomnaya as 'dangerous to navigation' not a safety zone.[106] Further, Russia did not enact safety laws and regulations or impose

[102] For a more detailed discussion regarding the status of insular features, see Section 4.1.2.

[103] This view has received support from scholars, see, for example, Alexander Proelss, 'Article 60' in Proelss (n 36) 471; Alex G. Oude Elferink, 'Artificial Islands, Installations and Structures', *Max Planck Encyclopedia of Public International Law* (OUP 2013) [5].

[104] *South China Sea Arbitration* (n 7) [1036].

[105] Proelss (n 103) 471–472.

[106] Ibid [210].

mandatory rules on foreign ships,[107] nor did it prohibit navigation within 3 nautical miles of the Prirazlomnaya.[108] Based on these reasons, the tribunal did not agree with the Netherlands that Russia had created a safety zone within the meaning of Article 60 (4).

It follows from the tribunal's reasoning that a safety zone is only established when the coastal State has not only clearly designated it as such but has also enacted and enforced mandatory law and rules within this safety zone. In other words, whether a safety zone has been established would depend on 'the structure and content' of the coastal State's laws and regulations.[109] The tribunal's requirement for the application of prescriptive and mandatory measures has been criticised for being too strict and formalistic for the purposes of Article 60(4).[110] As the tribunal concluded that Russia had not established a safety zone of 3 nautical miles,[111] it avoided having to answer the more general question as to whether the breadth of a safety zone could exceed 500 metres as stipulated under Article 60(5). It is to be noted that while this same paragraph allows safety zones to exceed 500 metres if authorised 'by generally accepted international standards or as recommended by the competent international organization', the International Maritime Organization (IMO) has 'resisted a general expansion of the 500 m limit for safety zones'.[112]

In terms of what measures would be considered 'appropriate' in the safety zone, the arbitral tribunal stated that Article 60(4) 'allows the coastal State to take, in the safety zone, appropriate measures in the nature of the enactment of laws or regulations, and of the enforcement of such laws and regulations, provided that such measures are aimed at ensuring the safety of both navigation and artificial islands, installations, or structures'.[113] This statement sheds light on the nature of the measures that coastal states may take in relation to safety zones in the EEZ in two respects.

First, coastal States are entitled to exercise not only prescriptive but also enforcement jurisdiction over activities in the safety zone. This finding is reminiscent of the views expressed by Judges Kelly and Wolfrum in their Joint

[107] Ibid [212–213].
[108] Ibid [214].
[109] Ibid [216].
[110] Robin Churchill, 'Revealing a Mosaic: International Jurisprudence Concerning the Non-Fisheries Elements of the Exclusive Economic Zone Regime' in Øystein Jensen (ed), *The Development of the Law of the Sea Convention* (Edward Elgar 2020) 55.
[111] *Arctic Sunrise Arbitration* (n 63) [216].
[112] Richard Caddell, 'Platforms, Protestors and Provisional Measures: The Arctic Sunrise Dispute and Environmental Activism at Sea' in Mónika Ambrus and Ramses A Wessel (eds), *Netherlands Yearbook of International Law* (T.M.C. Asser Press 2014) 14.
[113] *Arctic Sunrise Arbitration* (n 63) [211].

Separate Opinion, as well as Judge Golitsyn in his Dissenting Opinion in the provisional measures phase of the same case before ITLOS.[114] The legislative and enforcement measures, however, cannot be of a general nature; they have to be aimed at ensuring the safety of navigation and the installations themselves. Prior to the case, commentators had raised questions as to whether coastal States may adopt laws and regulations that go beyond these purposes in safety zones established around their installations and structures.[115] While this question was not at issue before the tribunal, its statement above seems to hint at a restrictive understanding of the scope of legislation that could apply to safety zones.

Second, the statement suggests a spatial limit for the measures that can be taken, including enforcement measures under Article 60(4), namely that they must be taken *within* the safety zone. As a result, even when law enforcement measures were taken outside of the safety but on the basis of the actions taken within the safety zone,[116] the *Arctic Sunrise* tribunal still found that coastal States did not have the rights to board a foreign vessel without the consent of the flag State outside of the safety zone.[117] Churchill has contended that the tribunal's view of the scope of enforcement competence 'seems to be too narrow' based on the argument that breaches of a coastal State's legislation in a safety zone constitute part of an interference with the coastal state's sovereign rights over non-living resources.[118] It follows, in his view, that 'a coastal state should be able to seize a foreign vessel for such a breach (as well as for any other interference with its seabed rights) anywhere within the waters overlying its continental shelf that constitute its EEZ'.[119] The tribunal indeed alluded to the fact that an attack on an installation or structure of the coastal State 'would involve a direct interference with the exercise by the coastal State of its sovereign rights to exploit the non-living resources of its seabed'.[120] However, this could not be taken to mean that coastal States' jurisdiction regarding installations and structures, including their safety zones, is subsumed under jurisdiction relating to the exploitation of non-living resources and consequently, enforcement measures against violations of law relating to

[114] Joint Separate Opinion of Judges Wolfrum and Kelly (n 54) [120]; *'Arctic Sunrise' (Kingdom of the Netherlands v Russian Federation)* (Provisional Measures, Order of 22 November 2013, Dis. Op. Golitsyn) ITLOS Reports 2013, 278 [25].

[115] Alexander Proelss, 'The Law on the Exclusive Economic Zone in Perspective: Legal Status and Resolution of User Conflicts Revisited' (2012), Ocean Yearbook Online 26, 107.

[116] *Arctic Sunrise Arbitration* (n 63) [242].

[117] Ibid [244].

[118] Churchill (n 110) 52–53.

[119] Ibid 53.

[120] *Arctic Sunrise Arbitration* (n 63) [314].

installations and structures could be taken anywhere in the EEZ. As is clear from Article 60(1), the rights and jurisdiction conferred upon the coastal states under Article 60 are attached to 'the construction, operation and use' of the installations and structures themselves, not to the *purpose* of their constructions, operation and use. As mentioned above, many States have claimed jurisdiction over all types of installations and structures,[121] indicating that in practice their existence is not to be tied to economic activities alone. It follows that coastal States' rights and jurisdiction over installations and structures could not be equated as merely a subset of their sovereign rights and jurisdiction over resources, living or non-living, in the EEZ and as such would allow coastal States to extend their enforcement jurisdiction beyond the safety zones. This restrictive interpretation of coastal States' enforcement jurisdiction, as argued by Oude Elferink, is further confirmed by Article 111 on hot pursuit, which explicitly refers to coastal States' right of hot pursuit from safety zones around continental shelf installations.[122]

In sum, the leading cases on the scope of coastal States' jurisdiction over artificial islands, installations and structures in the EEZ have been *South China Sea* and *Arctic Sunrise*. The *South China Sea* tribunal confirmed the exclusive nature of coastal States' jurisdiction in this regard, and made a vague attempt to distinguish between artificial islands on the one hand and installations and structures on the other based on their relative height to high-water tide. The *Arctic Sunrise* tribunal, for its part, shed light on issues involving the safety zone around the installations and structure. In particular, the tribunal identified the conditions for an area to be considered a safety zone within the meaning of Article 60(4). It also confirmed that coastal States are entitled to exercise both prescriptive and enforcement jurisdiction over activities in the safety zone, but that enforcement measures relating to the safety zone need to be limited only within the safety zone itself. In arriving at these findings, however, tribunals were rather modest with providing both explanation and reasoning.

2.1.3 *Obligation of Due Regard in the EEZ*

The obligation of due regard exists under general international law, albeit under different names,[123] and can be found in various provisions under

[121] Proelss (n 103) 471.

[122] Alex G. Oude Elferink, 'The Arctic Sunrise Incident: A Multi-faceted Law of the Sea Case with a Human Rights Dimension' (2014) 29 IJMCL 2, 258.

[123] For a discussion of the general nature and content of 'due regard', see Mathias Forteau, 'The Legal Nature and Content of "Due Regard" Obligations in Recent International Case Law' (2019) 34 IJMCL 1, 27.

UNCLOS.[124] In the EEZ, the obligation of due regard is found in both Article 56(2) and Article 58(3) dealing with the rights and duties of the coastal State and those of other States, respectively. As mentioned above, the EEZ is a *sui generis* maritime zone that hinges on the mutuality in the relationship of the coastal State and other States.[125] Exemplifying this mutual relationship, the obligation of due regard is of a reciprocal nature, whereby both the coastal State and the other States are required to have due regard to the rights and duties of one another in the EEZ. UNCLOS provides little guidance on what this obligation entails, leaving it 'so indeterminate that its application by different decision makers will necessarily be unpredictable'.[126] UNCLOS tribunals have had the opportunity to examine the obligation of due regard in several cases. This section examines how UNCLOS tribunals have dealt with the obligation of due regard and the extent to which the scope and content of this obligation has been clarified in the relevant case law.

To start with, case law has not been consistent regarding when the obligation of due regard can be invoked. In *M/V Norstar*, ITLOS held that Article 58 could not be invoked when a State has not declared an EEZ.[127] Arguably, this finding could be extended to Article 56 and the obligation of due regard found in both articles. It follows that in the absence of an EEZ, the obligation of due regard within the meaning of Articles 56 and 58 does not apply. By contrast, in *Chagos Marine Protected Area*, the tribunal found that the UK had violated Article 56(2) in declaring the establishment of an marine protected area even when it had not declared an EEZ around the Chagos Archipelago but only an Environmental Protection and Preservation Zone/Fisheries Conservation and Management Zone.[128]

Different interpretations of the term 'due regard' have emerged from UNCLOS tribunals' decisions – largely dependent on the context in which due regard was examined, but not all of which provided clear guidance. In *Virginia G*, ITLOS found that the obligation of due regard found in Article 56(2) also applied to the coastal States' enforcement powers under

[124] For a general overview of the mention of 'due regard' under UNCLOS, see Hasjim Djalal, '"Due Regards" and "Abuse of Rights" in UNCLOS' in Shicun Wu, Mark Valencia and Nong Hong (eds), *UN Convention on the Law of the Sea and the South China Sea* (Routledge 2015).

[125] Alexander Proelss, 'Article 56' in Proelss (n 36) 432.

[126] Louis B. Sohn and others, *Cases and Materials on the Law of the Sea* (2nd ed, Martinus Nijhoff 2014) 79; Julia Gaunce, 'On the Interpretation of the General Duty of "Due Regard"' (2018) 32 Ocean Yearbook Online 1, 28.

[127] *The M/V 'Norstar' Case (Panama v Italy)* (Preliminary Objections) ITLOS Reports 2016, 44 [116]. Contra

[128] *Chagos Marine Protected Area Arbitration (Mauritius v United Kingdom)* (2015) RIAA XXI 359 [536].

Article 73(1). This entailed that, in ITLOS's view, 'the competent authorities of the coastal State shall proceed with all possible consideration'.[129] ITLOS then proceeded to examine this issue in connection with whether Guinea-Bissau used excessive force in boarding and arresting the Virginia G. However, it is unclear in the discussion on the use of force what the 'possible consideration' should be or whether Guinea-Bissau had proceeded with 'all possible consideration'. Not much guidance can thus be glimpsed from ITLOS's conclusion in this case.

A clearer answer was subsequently provided in *Chagos MPA*, in which the tribunal conducted the most extensive analysis of this obligation to date. In this case, in examining whether the UK had violated, inter alias, Article 56(2) by declaring an MPA around the Chagos Archipelago, the tribunal provided an interpretation of due regard which shed light on several aspects of this obligation. It found that first, coastal States must have due regard for the rights other States 'as is called for by the circumstances and by the nature of those rights'.[130] This means that due regard has to be determined on a case-by-case basis, and as such, there is no 'universal rule of conduct'.[131] In each case, as held by the tribunal, the extent of regard will depend upon 'the nature of the rights held by [other States], their importance, the extent of the anticipated impairment, the nature and importance of the activities contemplated by the [coastal State], and the availability of alternative approaches'.[132] Second, in order to discharge of the obligation of due regard, coastal States would at least be required to engage in 'both consultation and a balancing exercise' between other States' rights and interests and those of its own.[133] It follows that the obligation of due regard, in the tribunal's view, comprises of both the procedural aspect of consultation and the substantive aspect of balancing two sets of rights and interests.

With respect to consultations, the tribunal did not explicitly set out a threshold for this obligation to be met. Instead, it concluded that the UK had failed to '[fulfil] the basic purpose of consulting' based on evidence indicating the lack of information provided to Mauritius, the absence of a

[129] *M/V 'Virginia G'* (n 14) [347].

[130] *Chagos Marine Protected Area* (n 128) [519].

[131] Ibid. Note, however, that the tribunal did not conclude that the UK was the coastal State in relation to the Chagos Archipelago. The examination of the UK's declaration of the MPA in Submission 4 proceeded on the assumption that the UK was exercising coastal states' rights under UNCLOS without prejudice to the question of sovereignty. For an examination of the jurisdictional scope of UNCLOS tribunals, see Chapter 6.

[132] Ibid [519].

[133] Ibid [534].

reasoned exchange between the Parties and the frustration of the expectation that there would be further opportunities for Mauritius to respond and exchange views by the sudden declaration of the MPA.[134] Using the UK's approach to consultations with the US, which the tribunal considered 'provides a practical example of due regard and a yardstick against which the communications with Mauritius can be measured',[135] the tribunal found that consultation should be conducted in a timely manner and with the provision of information.[136]

The balancing exercise, for its part, confirms the nature of EEZ in which coastal States' sovereign rights and jurisdiction are exclusive but not absolute.[137] As argued by one commentator, 'any specific application of the duty of due regard, a coastal State would not benefit from a presumption of priority simply on the basis of the sovereign character of its entitlements in the EEZ'. Likewise, a flag State could not claim benefits in the EEZ simply on the basis that its entitlements in the EEZ are extensions of freedoms of the high seas.[138] In order to conduct this balancing exercise, two questions needed to be addressed, namely: (i) what rights can enter into the balancing exercise? and (ii) how is the balance to be achieved?

In response to the first question, the tribunal in *Chagos MPA* held that Mauritius' rights for the purposes of Article 56(2) were those arising from the Lancaster House Undertaking made by the UK to Mauritius in 1965 in connection with the detachment of the Chagos Archipelago.[139] It is clear, as acknowledged by the tribunal itself, that the rights that are taken into account for the purposes of due regard include not only the rights arising under the Convention, but also 'legal rights as they otherwise arise as a matter of international law'.[140] While such an interpretation has received support from some scholars,[141] one wonders whether it is in line with the wording of

[134] Ibid.
[135] Ibid [528].
[136] Ibid.
[137] Gemma Andreone, 'The Exclusive Economic Zone' in Donald R. Rothwell et al. (eds), *The Oxford Handbook of the Law of the Sea* (2015), 159, 165.
[138] Gaunce (n 126) 55.
[139] *Chagos Marine Protected Area* (n 128) [294], [536].
[140] Ibid [293].
[141] See, for example, Shotaro Hamamoto, 'The Genesis of the "Due Regard" Obligations in the United Nations Convention on the Law of the Sea' (2019) IJMCL 34, 24, (arguing that the negotiating history of Articles 56(2) and 58(3) confirms that 'where the coastal state is obliged to "have due regard to the rights and duties of other States", these "rights and duties" are not limited to those explicitly listed in the Convention'. However, it is not clear from the exposition of the history of these articles how he came to this conclusion).

Article 58(3). To recall, Article 58(3) stipulates that other States must have due regard to the rights and duties of the coastal State 'in exercising their rights and performing their duties *under this Convention* in the EEZ'. As observed by one author, 'Article 58(3) obligates all States to have due regard to the rights and duties of the coastal State when exercising their freedoms in terms of Article 58(1).'[142] Under Article 58(1), apart from the freedoms as specified under UNCLOS including freedom of navigation and overflight, laying of submarine cables and pipelines, States are entitled to enjoy 'other internationally lawful uses of the sea' but only insofar as they are 'related to' the aforementioned freedoms. The *Arctic Sunrise* arbitration provided a good illustration of a right that is not explicitly mentioned under Article 58(1) but is nonetheless an international lawful use of the sea related to a freedom contained therein, namely the right to protest at sea. The tribunal held that while '[p]rotest at sea is an internationally lawful use of the sea related to the freedom of navigation',[143] it is subjected to limitations defined, inter alias, by the law of the sea including the obligation to have due regard under Article 58(3) when it occurs at sea.[144] Similarly, for the coastal State, the tribunal found that even though it has the right to take measures to prevent interferences with its sovereign rights over non-living resources, including interferences caused by protest actions, '[d]ue regard must be given to rights of other States, including the right to allow vessels flying their flag to protest'.[145] The tribunal concluded that as the conduct of the Arctic Sunrise did not interfere with Russia's exercise of its sovereign rights over non-living resources, Russia violated, inter alias, the obligation of due regard under Article 56(2).[146] The balancing exercise in this case involved on the one hand, the right of the coastal State to prevent interferences with its exercise of sovereign rights in the EEZ and, on the other hand, the right of the flag State to allow its vessel exercise a right associated with the freedom of navigation, namely right to protest at sea.

A combined reading of paragraphs (1) and (3) of Article 58 suggests that the internationally lawful uses of the sea available to other States in the coastal State's EEZ are not as unlimited as the *Chagos MPA* tribunal made out to be.[147] In fact, the arbitral tribunal in *South China Sea*, when considering whether China can claim to have historic rights in the EEZ,[148] adopted a

[142] Alexander Proelss, 'Article 58' in Proelss (n 36) 455.
[143] *Arctic Sunrise Arbitration* (n 63) [227].
[144] Ibid [228].
[145] Ibid [328].
[146] Ibid [330], [333].
[147] Ibid, 452.
[148] For a more detailed analysis of historic rights, see Section 2.2.

narrow understanding of the scope of non-coastal State's rights in the EEZ under Article 58(1), stating that UNCLOS does not intend for other States to have rights in the exclusive economic zone 'in excess of those specified'.[149] In light of the contrasting interpretations provided by these two tribunals, it remains open to question whether non-coastal States' rights in the EEZ include only those expressly provided for under UNCLOS or also those existing in other sources of law. It should be noted, however, that while the tribunal in *South China Sea* situated its conclusion within an extensive analysis of coastal States' sovereign rights in the EEZ, the tribunal in *Chagos MPA* did not support its conclusion with much reasoning. The latter tribunal simply equated the obligation of due regard in the EEZ to the obligation to exercise sovereignty in the territorial sea 'subject to other rules of international law' under Article 2(3).[150] Such an interpretation does not seem tenable in light of both the different wording of Articles 2(3) and 56(2) and the different nature of the coastal States' rights in these two maritime zones.[151]

Turning to the second question, namely how the balance to is be achieved, the tribunal in *Chagos MPA* stated that degree of regard to be had by the coastal State corresponds to the significance of the rights of other states.[152] This means, as commented by one author, '[t]he more important the right, the wider the possibility for states to make that right prevail over other rights.'[153] In this case, Mauritius' rights included fishing rights in the territorial sea and the eventual return of the Chagos Archipelago to Mauritius, which were either extinguished or significantly affected by the declaration of the MPA.[154] The tribunal did not comment on the significance of these rights vis-à-vis the UK's purported environmental purpose for declaring the MPA. In any case, it would seem that the balancing exercise was not at all conducted due to the UK's total disregard for Mauritius' rights, leading to a breach of the due regard obligation.

The need to consider the importance of the rights at stake also applies to non-coastal States' obligation to have due regard under Article 58(3) as confirmed by the *South China Sea* tribunal. In examining China's obligation of due regard in the Philippines' EEZ, the tribunal highlighted 'the importance of fisheries to the entire concept of the exclusive economic zone, the

[149] *South China Sea Arbitration* (n 7) [243].
[150] *Chagos Marine Protected Area* (n 128) [293].
[151] Churchill (n 110); Forteau (n 123).
[152] *Chagos Marine Protected Area* (n 128) [521].
[153] Forteau (n 123) 42.
[154] *Chagos Marine Protected Area* (n 128) [521].

degree to which the Convention subordinates fishing within the exclusive economic zone to the control of the coastal State, and the obligations expressly placed on the nationals of other States by Article 62(4) of the Convention'.[155] On that basis, the tribunal required China to exercise due diligence to prevent its nationals from unlawfully fishing in the Philippines' EEZ,[156] the failure of which resulted in China's breach of its obligation of due regard under Article 58(3).

It follows from the two above-mentioned cases that balancing does not mean giving equal weight to the two sets of rights. When balancing the Philippines' sovereign rights over living resources in its EEZ against Chinese-flagged vessels rights to fish in the Philippines's EEZ, it is not difficult to conclude that the former should prevail in light of coastal States' exclusive sovereign rights in the EEZ, making the latter inconsistent with the Convention. When the two sets of rights are both provided for under the Convention and are of equal importance, such as in the case of *Arctic Sunrise*, the balancing exercise seems then to turn on the level of interference that one set of rights may cause to the other.

In sum, the due regard obligation found under Articles 56(2) and 58(3) has been given some shape through the decisions of the tribunals in *Chagos MPA*, *South China Sea* and *Arctic Sunrise*. What has become clear is that the obligation of due regard has both procedural and substantive components. In essence, it requires consultation between coastal States and other States, and a balancing exercise between the rights and the interests of those involved. The balancing exercise, however, does not require that the two sets of rights at stake ought to be given equal weight. The significance of the rights plays the key role in determining which one prevails. Due to the seemingly contrasting positions taken by the *Chagos MPA* and *South China Sea* tribunals, however, what remains uncertain is whether the rights that may be taken into account for the purposes of balancing include only those arising under UNCLOS or also those stemming from other sources of international law.

2.2 COASTAL STATES AND HISTORIC CLAIMS

UNCLOS refers to 'historic bay' and 'historic title' under Articles 10, 15 and 298(1). In addition to historic bays and historic title, there also exist under international law other categories of historic claims, namely 'historic waters' and 'historic rights'. However, UNCLOS does not provide for 'historic

[155] *South China Sea Arbitration*, (n 7) [744].
[156] Ibid [744].

fishing', only 'habitual fishing'[157] or 'traditional fishing'.[158] The fact that these different terms exist under and beyond UNCLOS has given rise to three questions: (i) Do these different terms have the same normative content or scope? (ii) What is the relationship between rights existing UNCLOS, particularly sovereign rights over resources, and historical or traditional rights, and (iii) What are the requirements for the existence of historical title or historical rights? This section assesses the extent to which the relevant decisions rendered by UNCLOS tribunals have shed satisfactory light upon these questions. The analysis will focus particularly on the decisions of *Barbados v Trinidad and Tobago*, *Chagos MPA* and *South China Sea*.[159] As disputes concerning historic title and historic fishing rights have also been brought before other international courts and tribunals, references are also made to these disputes for comparative purposes.

2.2.1 *Distinguishing 'Historic' Claims*

The term 'historic bays' is found under Article 10(6) as an exception to the application of the technical rules for defining a bay under UNCLOS. The term 'historic title' is found under Article 15 as one of the reasons to depart from the application of the equidistance line to delimit overlapping territorial seas. Under Article 298(1)(a)(i), disputes concerning historic bays or historic titles are excluded from the compulsory jurisdiction of UNCLOS tribunals. In all these provisions, the characterisation of a bay or title as 'historic' creates an exception to the relevant rule prescribed by UNCLOS.[160] 'Historic fishing rights' and 'historic waters' are not mentioned as such under UNCLOS. In some of the cases before the ICJ and ad hoc tribunals in which they appear, the terms 'historic rights' and 'historic title' or historic rights' and 'historic waters' were used interchangeably, creating further confusion regarding whether they carry the same meaning under international law.[161] Most of these cases, however,

[157] Article 62 UNCLOS.

[158] Article 51 UNCLOS.

[159] 'Historic title' under Article 15 was raised in *Bangladesh/Myanmar* before ITLOS. However, ITLOS did not engage with this issue because 'The Tribunal finds no evidence of an historic title in the area to be delimited and notes that neither Party has invoked the existence of such title.' *Dispute concerning delimitation of the maritime boundary between Bangladesh and Myanmar in the Bay of Bengal (Bangladesh/Myanmar)* (Judgment) ITLOS Reports 2012, 4 [130].

[160] *Continental Shelf (Tunisia/Libyan Arab Jamahiriya)* (Merits) [1982] ICJ Rep 18 [100].

[161] See, for example, *Tunisia/Libya* (n 160) [100]; *Territorial Sovereignty and Scope of the Dispute (Eritrea and Yemen)* (1998) RIAA XXII 209 [23]–[26]. See also: Florian Dupuy and Pierre-Marie Dupuy, 'A Legal Analysis of China's Historic Claims in the South China Sea' (2013) 107 American Journal of International Law 124.

were concerned with the effect of historic fishing rights or historic title on maritime delimitation and not with their existence per se.[162] As such, they provided little guidance on the distinction between these different terms. *South China Sea* is the only case to date which directly engaged with this issue.

In *South China Sea*, the question of distinction arose in the context of the interpretation and application of Article 298(1)(a)(i). China had made a declaration under Article 298 excluding all the three categories contained therein from the compulsory jurisdiction of UNCLOS tribunals.[163] In determing whether Article 298(1)(a)(i) applied to hear the Philippines' submissions against China, the tribunal therefore had to consider whether China had claimed historic title in the South China Sea.[164] After stating that 'the meaning of the Convention's reference to "historic titles" should be understood in the particular context of the evolution of the international law of the sea',[165] the tribunal proceeded to survey the development of the law of the sea starting from the League of Nations Conference in 1930 to identify the meaning of different 'historic' terms.[166] On that basis, the tribunal acknowledged that 'there exists, within the context of the law of the sea, a cognizable usage among the various terms for rights deriving from historical processes'.[167] The tribunal then made a distinction between these different terms, which deserves to be quoted in full:

> The term 'historic rights' is general in nature and can describe any rights that a State may possess that would not normally arise under the general rules of international law, absent particular historical circumstances. Historic rights may include sovereignty, but may equally include more limited rights, such as fishing rights or rights of access, that fall well short of a claim of sovereignty. 'Historic title', in contrast, is used specifically to refer to historic sovereignty to land or maritime areas. 'Historic waters' is simply a term for historic title over maritime areas, typically exercised either as a claim to internal waters or as a claim to the territorial sea .... Finally, a 'historic bay' is simply a bay in which a State claims historic waters.[168]

[162] In some of these cases, they are called traditional fishing rights. See, for example. *Fisheries (United Kingdom v Norway)* (1951); *Fisheries jurisdiction (Federal Republic of Germany v Iceland)* (1974); *Continental shelf (Tunisia/Libyan Arab Jamahiriya)* (1982); *Delimitation of the maritime boundary in the Gulf of Maine Area (Canada/United States)* (1984); *Maritime delimitation in the Area between Greenland and Jan Mayen (Denmark v Norway)* (1993); *Eritrea/Yemen* (1996).

[163] For an analysis of the scope of Article 298, see Chapter 6.

[164] *South China Sea Arbitration* (n 7) [205].

[165] Ibid [217].

[166] Ibid [218]–[224].

[167] Ibid [225].

[168] Ibid.

This was the first time an international tribunal explicitly spelled out the differences between different historical claims. It seems clear from the passage above that 'historic bay' is a subset of 'historic water', which in turn is a subset of 'historic title', which is then a subset of 'historic rights'. In other words, 'historic rights' has the broadest scope and encompasses the other three terms implying a claim of sovereignty. 'Historic rights', however, may also include nonexclusive rights falling short of sovereignty such as fishing rights. Essentially, different historic claims can now be classified into two groups: historic rights based on sovereignty and historic rights short of sovereignty. As an illustration of the former, the tribunal found that China's claim within the nine-dash line could not be one to historic title because China had unequivocally accepted the freedom of navigation and overflight, signifying that it did not consider the areas within the nine-dash line to be equivalent to its territorial sea or internal waters.[169] Put differently, because China did not claim rights on the basis of sovereignty, its claim did not qualify as a 'historic title' claim.

As regards historic rights short of sovereignty, the tribunal has been criticised for failing to further distinguish between two different forms of historic rights short of sovereignty, namely historic rights short of sovereignty that has a quasi-territorial or zonal impact beyond the territorial sea, and nonexclusive historic rights (mainly related to fishing rights).[170] The category of historic rights short of sovereignty that has a quasi-territorial or zonal impact seems to have been taken from *Qatar/Bahrain* before the ICJ, in which the Court held that 'even if it had been found that this activity was exclusively performed by Bahrain, this activity seems in any event never to have led to the recognition of an exclusive quasi-territorial right to the fishing grounds themselves or to the superjacent waters'.[171] This statement, however, does not show that the ICJ was recognising a category of rights known as 'quasi-territorial rights'. Rather they Court was merely acknowledging such claims, even if held by one of the parties, had never been accepted.[172]

[169] Ibid [213].

[170] Sophia Kopela, 'Historic Titles and Historic Rights in the Law of the Sea in the Light of the South China Sea Arbitration' (2017) 48 ODIL 2, 188.

[171] *Maritime Delimitation and Territorial Questions between Qatar and Bahrain (Qatar v Bahrain)* (Merits) [2001] ICJ Rep 2001, 40 [236]. Kopela interpreted this statement to mean that 'the ICJ did not preclude the possibility of the existence of "exclusive quasi-territorial rights" over certain maritime areas'. See: Kopela (n 170) 189.

[172] See also: Leonardo Bernard, 'Historic Rights and the Exclusive Economic Zone' (2022) 18 Indonesian J Int'L 161, 164. (who read the ICJ's statement to mean 'even if the historic pearling rights of Bahrain were recognized, it would not have amounted to sovereignty or any form of 'quasi-sovereignty' over the pearling banks or to the superjacent waters').

Furthermore, the *South China Sea* tribunal also shed light on the relationship between 'historic' terms used in different UNCLOS articles. Two issues were clarified. First, prior to the arbitration, opinions differed regarding whether 'historic title' under Articles 15 and 298(1)(a) had the same scope. One author, for instance, has argued that historic title in the latter article 'must have a broader meaning' than that in the former,[173] although no explanation was provided to substantiate this argument. Others, however, have argued that 'both references in UNCLOS to "title" – in Art. 15 and Art. 298 – have the same meaning'.[174] The tribunal clarified that 'the reference to "historic titles" in Article 298(1)(a)(i) of the Convention is a reference to claims of sovereignty over maritime areas derived from historical circumstances. This accords with the only other direct usage of the term, in Article 15 of the Convention, where historical sovereignty would understandably bear on the delimitation of the territorial sea.'[175] The tribunal's statement clearly showed that the latter approach was preferable.

Second, when examining the Philippines' claim to fishing rights in the territorial sea of Scarborough Shoal, the tribunal did not use the term 'historic fishing rights'. Instead, the tribunal used the terms 'traditional fishing rights'[176] – found under Article 51(1) UNCLOS – and 'artisanal fishing' which it recalled from the *Eritrea/Yemen* arbitration.[177] The question again arises as to whether these terms carry the same meaning. The manner in which the tribunal described artisanal fishing rights and the authorities invoked to support its discussion of traditional fishing rights[178] suggest that the tribunal did not intend for traditional fishing rights to be different category to that of historic fishing rights, at least in terms of the requirements for their establishment.[179] However, in using the term 'traditional fishing rights' or 'artisanal fishing rights', the tribunal seemed to have wanted to highlight their private nature of belonging to 'the individuals and communities that have traditionally fished in an area'.[180] Thus a distinction is drawn not between traditional

173 Ted L McDorman, 'Rights and Jurisdiction over Resources in the South China Sea: UNCLOS and the "nine-dash line"' in S. Jayakumar, Tommy Koh and Robert Beckmna (eds), *The South China Sea Disputes and Law of the Sea* (Edward Elgar 2014) 152.

174 Clive R Symmons, 'Article 15' in Proelss (n 36) 163.

175 *South China Sea Arbitration* (n 7) [226].

176 Ibid [758]

177 Ibid [795].

178 Ibid [795]–[797].

179 See also: Sophia Kopela, 'Historic Fishing Rights in the Law of the Sea and Brexit' (2019) LJIL 32, 700.

180 *South China Sea Arbitration* (n 7) [798]. See also: Clive Symmons, *Historic Waters and Historic Rights in the Law of the Sea: A Modern Reappraisal* (2nd ed, Martinus Nijhoff 2019) 27.

fishing rights and historic fishing rights, but between traditional fishing rights based on the activities of individual or communities of a State and historic rights belonging to States, based on the activities performed by a state in the exercise of its sovereignty, such as historic title.

Finally, it is interesting to note that the *South China Sea* tribunal also mentioned 'historic *maritime* rights to the living and non-living resources within the 'nine-dash line',[181] which were labelled as 'exclusive historic rights'.[182] At first glance, this suggests that there exists a separate category of historic rights called 'exclusive historic rights to living and non-living resources'. This type of historic rights would appear to fall within the category of historic rights short of sovereignty as defined by the tribunal earlier, since it only purports to establish rights to resources. Vested with exclusivity, however, exclusive fishing rights then become a hybrid between sovereignty-based historic rights and nonexclusive historic rights. Upon closer inspection, the tribunal's inquiry could not be construed to support the existence of such a category of historic rights. Due to China's nonappearance in the case, the tribunal seemed to have taken upon itself the task of predicting and addressing the possible arguments that China might have come up with, had it decided to participate in the proceedings 'for the sake of completeness'.[183] In other words, the tribunal was simply conducting an inquiry into China's claims of historic rights to living and non-living resources which it understood to be of an exclusive nature, not endorsing them.[184] In any case, the tribunal found that China was merely exercising the freedoms of the high seas beyond the territorial sea and there was no evidence to show that China had 'historically regulated or controlled fishing in the South China Sea'.[185] Consequently, the tribunal concluded that China had not established exclusive historic right to resources within the nine-dash line. In short, exclusive historic rights to natural resources, particularly in the high seas, do not exist.

In short, the *South China Sea* tribunal provided the much-needed clarification of the meaning of the different terms relating to historic claims and 'is a welcome development in a formerly arcane and obscure area of international law'.[186] The tribunal paid careful attention to situating 'historic title' within

[181] *South China Sea Arbitration* (n 7) [267]. (emphasis added)
[182] Ibid [270].
[183] Ibid [263].
[184] Ibid [214].
[185] Ibid [270].
[186] Clive R Symmons, 'Historic Rights in the Light of the Award in the South China Sea Arbitration: What Remains of the Doctrine Now?' in S. Jayakumar et al. (eds), *The South China Sea Arbitration: The Legal Dimension* (Edward Elgar 2018) 125.

the development of the law of the sea and existing case law. This provided continuity in the development of these concepts and lent credence to conclusion reached.[187]

2.2.2 *Requirements for the Establishment of Historic Fishing Rights*

The requirements for the formation of historic title are well-established under general international law.[188] Those for historic rights, including historic fishing rights, by contrast are not. The question of historic fishing rights was brought before the Annex VII arbitral tribunals in two cases, namely: *Barbados v Trinidad and Tobago* and *South China Sea*. However, in *Barbados v Trinidad and Tobago*, historic or traditional fishing rights were raised as a special circumstance in a maritime delimitation dispute,[189] thus the tribunal did not deal with the issue in too much detail. It was only in *South China Sea* that the tribunal was asked to specifically examine the existence of historic fishing rights. Consequently, this section mainly focuses on the findings of *South China Sea* on the requirements for the establishment of historic fishing rights, with references to *Barbados v Trinidad and Tobago* where relevant. As will be shown below, the requirements for the establishment of historic fishing rights have also been discussed by other international courts and tribunals beyond Part XV. Comparison is thus made where appropriate to identify convergences and divergences in the approach of the different tribunals.

In *South China Sea*, the tribunal examined historic fishing rights when dealing with two separate claims, namely: whether China had historic fishing rights within the nine-dash line in Submissions 1 and 2; and whether China had prevented the traditional fishing by Filipinos at Scarborough Shoal in Submission 10. In examining the first two submissions, the tribunal held that 'historic waters are merely one form of historic right and the process is the same for claims to rights short of sovereignty'.[190] This statement thus confirmed that the requirements for existence of nonexclusive historic fishing rights are the same as for sovereignty-based historic rights. These include: the continuous exercise of the claimed rights and acquiescence on the part of

[187] Yoshifumi Tanaka, 'Reflections on Historic Rights in the South China Sea Arbitration (Merits)' (2017) 32 IJMCL 3, 466; Seokwoo Lee and Lowell Bautista, 'Historic Rights' in Øystein Jensen (ed), *The Development of the Law of the Sea Convention* (Edward Elgar Publishing 2020), 260.

[188] See: *United Nations, Juridical Regime of Historic Waters, Including Historic Bays*, U.N. Doc A/CN.4/143 (9 March 1962).

[189] *Barbados v Trinidad and Tobago* (n 58) [247].

[190] *South China Sea Arbitration* (n 7) [265].

other affected States.[191] That the requirements for these two categories of historic rights are similar has been noted by various scholars,[192] but this was the first time the similarities were acknowledged by an international tribunal. However, when the tribunal elaborated on the elements for the establishment of historic rights, the tribunal seemed to have focused only on the latter requirement, namely acquiescence. It summarised the elements of historic rights as follows:

> the assertion by a State of a right at variance with the Convention, acquiescence therein by the other States Parties, and the passage of sufficient time to establish beyond doubt the existence of both the right and a general acquiescence.[193]

As remarked by one commentator, '[u]nder the Tribunal's approach, the role of the historical element is to be reduced almost to a vanishing point.'[194]

The importance of a right being at variance with the Convention and the role of acquiescence are highlighted in the tribunal's examination of whether China had historic rights within the nine-dash line. It stated that historic rights are exception rights which 'accord a right that a State would not otherwise hold, were it not for the operation of the historical process giving rise to the right and the acquiescence of other States in the process'.[195] It follows from this exceptional nature that, as the tribunal further observed, 'the exercise of freedoms permitted under international law cannot give rise to a historic right; it involves nothing that would call for the acquiescence of other States and can only represent the use of what international law already freely permits'.[196] The tribunal concluded that 'historical navigation and fishing, beyond the territorial sea, cannot therefore form the basis for the emergence of a historic right'.[197].

In Submission 10 concerning the Philippines' claim of traditional fishing rights in the territorial sea of Scarborough Shoal, the tribunal elaborated on the requirements for the establishment of such rights. As analysed above, the tribunal did not seem to distinguish between historic fishing rights and traditional fishing rights, thus the requirements identified below would

[191] Ibid.
[192] See, for example, Bernard (n 171), 164; McDorman (n 173) 157.
[193] *South China Sea Arbitration* (n 7) [275].
[194] Tanaka (n 187) 475.
[195] *South China Sea Arbitration* (n 7) [268].
[196] Ibid [268].
[197] Ibid [270].

equally apply to historic fishing rights. As the name suggests, fishing has to be of a traditional character. Traditional fishing in this context was, as the tribunal found, synonymous to artisanal fishing[198] and 'the distinguishing characteristic will always be that, in contrast with industrial fishing, artisanal fishing will be simple and carried out on a small scale, using fishing methods that largely approximate those that have historically been used in the region'.[199] Elaborating on the methods of fishing that would be considered traditional, the tribunal further observed that they would be 'those that broadly follow the manner of fishing carried out for generations: in other words, artisanal fishing in keeping with the traditions and customs of the region'[200] and 'largely in keeping with the longstanding practice of the community'.[201] While the tribunal was 'not prepared to specify any precise threshold for the fishing methods that would qualify as artisanal fishing',[202] it seems clear that traditional fishing not only has to be of a small scale, but has also to be more importantly rooted in traditional practices and closely connected with a local community. As is apparent from its reference to existing case law, particularly *Eritrea/Yemen*, the *South China Sea* tribunal was not the first to note the link between traditional fishing rights and the traditions of the local community.[203] The tribunal's statement built upon the existing case law on this issue.

The requirement of long usage – a natural correlation of the traditional character of fishing – had already been confirmed in several cases dealing with traditional fishing.[204] In *Barbados v Trinidad and Tobago*, Barbados recognised the significance of the temporal element and argued that 'there is a centuries-old history of Barbadian artisanal fishing in the waters off Tobago'[205]. However, the tribunal found that Barbadian fisherfolk had only

[198] *South China Sea Arbitration* (n 7) [795].
[199] Ibid [797].
[200] Ibid [806].
[201] Ibid [798].
[202] Ibid [806].
[203] *Award of the Arbitral Tribunal in the Second Stage – Maritime Delimitation (Eritrea/Yemen)* (1999) RIAA XXII 335 [67], [92]. The importance of the traditional character of fishing and of the relationship with the local community was also noted in other cases. See, for example, *Maritime Delimitation in the Area between Greenland and Jan Mayen (Denmark v.Norway)* (Judgment) [1993] ICJ Rep 1993, 38.
[204] See: *Fisheries (United Kingdom v Norway)* (Judgment) [1951] ICJ Rep 1951, 116, 30; *Fisheries Jurisdiction (Federal Republic of Germany v Iceland)* (Merits) ICJ Rep 1974, 175 [55]; *Jan Mayen* (n 203) [74]; *Tunisia/Libyan* (n 160) [98].
[205] *Barbados v Trinidad and Tobago* (n 58) [250].

been fishing for flying fish in the period 1978–1980 and concluded that '[t]hose short years are not sufficient to give rise to a tradition.'[206] In the context of historic title, it has been remarked that 'no precise length of time can be indicated as necessary to build the usage on which the historic title must be based'.[207] It would seem that in the view of the tribunal, the duration of thirty years was not sufficient not because it was short per se but more importantly because such a short passage of time could not enable the formation of a tradition. The temporal element is thus closely connected with the traditional character of fishing underlying historic fishing. In *South China Sea*, the tribunal also acknowledged the need for the existence of a long-standing tradition in several places by noting that 'traditional fishing rights are customary rights, acquired through long usage',[208] which 'extend to artisanal fishing that is carried out largely in keeping with the longstanding practice of the community'[209] and by requiring that 'generations of fishermen' need to have pursued a livelihood through artisanal fishing 'over an extended period'.[210] The acquisition of rights through long usage is manifested not only by the length of time but also, as the tribunal recalled from *Eritrea/Yemen*,[211] through the continuous exercise of the entitlements through the ages. The frequency and intensity of the exercise of rights are thus of the essence.

In conclusion, Annex VII arbitral tribunals, particularly the *South China Sea* tribunal, have brought some clarity to the requirements for the establishment of historic fishing rights. By confirming that the requirements for the establishment of historic title or historic waters also apply to historic fishing rights, it would seem that the contribution made by the tribunals is limited. After all, these conditions are well-established under general international law. The transfer of these requirements to historic rights is thus largely uncontroversial. What was noticeable was the weight that the tribunal attached to the different conditions when applying these requirements to different claims to historic fishing rights. While for some claims, the tribunal paid more attention to the requirements of acquiescence, for other long usage was the main point of analysis. The different approaches could perhaps be explained by the fact that the tribunal was dealing with historic claims in different maritime zones. In any case, the tribunal should be commended for providing clear

[206] Ibid [266].
[207] Juridical Regime of Historic Waters including Historic Bays (n 188) [104].
[208] *South China Sea Arbitration* (n 7) [806].
[209] Ibid [798].
[210] Ibid.
[211] Ibid.

reasoning and situating its findings within existing law, showing consistency and continuity in the clarification of this issue.

2.2.3 *Relationship between Historic Rights and UNCLOS*

In *Tunisia/Libya*, the ICJ stated that while there are references to historic bays, or historic titles in the then-draft UNCLOS, 'it seems clear that the matter continues to be governed by general international law'.[212] This does not necessarily mean that historic rights exist independently from UNCLOS, yet the question as to what their interaction looks like is not always clear. In respect of historic rights in the narrow sense, that is nonexclusive historic rights to living and non-living resources, the question becomes even more pertinent due to the existence of exclusive sovereign rights over natural resources that UNCLOS confers upon coastal States in the EEZ and continental shelf. The relationship between historic rights and UNCLOS, particularly the question as to whether they continue to exist in the maritime zones specified in UNCLOS, has been brought before Annex VII arbitral tribunals in *Chagos MPA* and *South China Sea*. This section analyses the decisions of the tribunals in these two cases and assess whether they have managed to provide some clarity on this question.

Starting with historic rights in the territorial sea, in *Chagos MPA*, Mauritius argued that it enjoyed fishing rights based on a bilateral agreement between Mauritius and the UK – the Lancaster House Undertaking – in waters around the Chagos Archipelago and that in any case, it enjoyed traditional fishing rights in the territorial sea of the Archipelago.[213] The issue of traditional fishing rights in the territorial sea seemed to have been raised only as an alternative argument. Having found that Mauritius was indeed entitled to fishing rights in the territorial sea pursuant the bilateral agreement, the tribunal did not address the question of traditional fishing rights.[214] However, when examining Mauritius' claim that the UK had violated its obligations under Article 2(3), the tribunal interpreted this article to contain 'an obligation on States to exercise their sovereignty subject to "other rules of international law"',[215] and that the reference to 'other rules of international law' included only general rules of international law and not bilateral commitment that a State might

[212] *Tunisia/Libya* (n 160) [100].
[213] *Chagos Marine Protected Area* (n 128) [414]–[415].
[214] Ibid [456].
[215] Ibid [514].

undertake in the territorial sea.[216] Such an interpretation leaves open the possibility that historic fishing rights may indeed be recognised in the territorial sea by virtue of their existence under general international law. Such a possibility was explicitly confirmed by the tribunal in *South China Sea*. After endorsing the *Chagos MPA* tribunal's interpretation of Article 2(3), the tribunal stated that '[t]raditional fishing rights constitute a vested right, and the Tribunal considers the rules of international law on the treatment of the vested rights of foreign nationals to fall squarely within the "other rules of international law" applicable in the territorial sea.'[217] Of note here is the fact the 'other rule of international law' within the meaning of Article 2(3) was not 'traditional fishing rights' per se but 'the protection due in customary international law to the acquired rights of individuals and communities engaged in traditional fishing'.[218] The tribunal concluded that UNCLOS did not alter acquired rights in the territorial sea and thus established that traditional fishing rights remain protected in this maritime zone.

Beyond the territorial sea, the tribunal in *Eritrea/Yemen* had found that, '[b]y its very nature [the traditional fishing regime] is not qualified by the maritime zones specified under the United Nations Convention on the Law of the Sea . . .. The traditional fishing regime operates throughout those waters beyond the territorial waters of each of the Parties'.[219] It follows from *Eritrea/Yemen* that historic fishing rights, once established, continue to exist in the EEZ, continental shelf, high seas and Area; that traditional fishing rights exist possibly extended to the EEZ, continental shelf and the high seas. The tribunal in *South China Sea*, however, took the opposite view and explicitly stated that it 'disagrees with the conclusions of the tribunal in *Eritrea/Yemen*'.[220] In examining the Philippines' contention that any claim to historic rights within the nine-dash line in excess of that provided for in the Convention is prohibited,[221] tribunal was faced with the question of whether 'the Convention, and in particular its rules for the exclusive economic zone and continental shelf, allow for the preservation of rights to living and non-living resources that are at variance with the provisions of the Convention?'[222] The answer to this question, in the tribunal's view, rest upon the relationship between UNCLOS and other possible sources of rights under international

[216] Ibid [516].
[217] *South China Sea Arbitration* (n 7) [259], [808].
[218] Ibid [812].
[219] *Eritrea/Yemen* (n 203) [109]
[220] Ibid [803].
[221] Ibid [233].
[222] Ibid [234].

law',[223] which is set out in Articles 311 and 293(3). These provisions in turn 'mirror the general rules of international law concerning the interaction of different bodies of law, which provide that the intent of the parties to a convention will control its relationship with other instruments'.[224]

Applying these provisions to the relationship between UNCLOS and historic rights, the tribunal found that historic claims that are expressly permitted or reserved by the Convention, such as historic bays and historic titles under Articles 10 and 15 'shall remain unaffected'.[225] This would presumably also apply to traditional fishing rights in archipelagic waters, which are expressly protected under Article 51(1). By contrast, historic rights that are not expressly permitted or preserved by the Convention can only continue to exist 'where their operation does not conflict with any provision of the Convention or to the extent that interpretation indicates that the Convention intended the prior agreements, rules, or rights to continue in operation'.[226] Having found that UNCLOS does not expressly permit or provide for the continued existence of historic rights to living and non-living resources in the EEZ, continental shelf, the high seas or the Area, the tribunal then embarked on an inquiry as to whether UNCLOS intended the continued operation of such historic rights.[227]

In conducting this inquiry, the tribunal resorted to the text and context of Articles 56 and 77 relating to coastal States' sovereign rights in the EEZ and continental shelf, respectively,[228] to the negotiating history of the Convention and the creation of the EEZ, as well as existing decisions in which claims involving rights in the EEZ of another State. Based on the text and context of Articles 56 and 77, the tribunal found that the Convention was 'clear in superseding any historic rights that a State may once have had in the areas that now form part of the exclusive economic zone and continental shelf of another State'.[229] As for the negotiating history of the Convention, based on the fact that UNCLOS was negotiated by consensus and that the final text represented a package deal, the tribunal observed that '[i]t is simply inconceivable that the drafters of the Convention could have gone to such lengths to forge a consensus text and to prohibit any but a few express reservations while, at the same time, anticipating that the resulting Convention would be

[223] Ibid [235].
[224] Ibid [237].
[225] Ibid [238(a)].
[226] Ibid [238(b)].
[227] Ibid [239].
[228] Ibid [243]–[246].
[229] Ibid [247].

subordinate to broad claims of historic rights'.[230] In its survey of relevant case law, the tribunal paid particular attention to distinguishing its findings with those in previous cases that were contradictory, such as the *Fisheries Jurisdiction Cases* before the ICJ,[231] or *Eritrea/Yemen* as noted above. All these considerations then led the tribunal to conclude that 'any historic rights that China may have had to the living and non-living resources within the "nine-dash line" were superseded, as a matter of law and as between the Philippines and China, by the limits of the maritime zones provided for by the Convention'.[232]

It follows that according to the *South China Sea* tribunal, historic rights continue to exist in the territorial sea, but not in the EEZ and continental shelf as they have been superseded by the coastal State's sovereign rights in these maritime zones. The tribunal was conscious that this could be seen as a contradiction, but stated that 'the law reflects the particular circumstances of the creation of the [EEZ]'.[233] While the tribunal saw 'nothing that would suggest that the adoption of the Convention was intended to alter acquired rights in the territorial sea',[234] it concluded that 'the degree of control over fisheries that was ultimately given to the coastal State'[235] and more specifically the inclusion of Article 62(3) 'which would be entirely unnecessary if traditional fishing rights were preserved in the exclusive economic zone – confirms that the drafters of the Convention did not intend to preserve such rights'.[236]

Even though the tribunal did not directly discuss historic rights in the high seas, its exposition of China's purported exclusive historic rights to living and non-living resources as discussed above shed some light on this matter.[237] The tribunal's approach suggests that claims to historic rights based on fishing activities in the high seas would unlikely succeed as such rights are by nature not at variance with the Convention.[238] In other words, historic fishing rights simply cannot exist in the high seas in the first place. This is different to historic fishing rights in the EEZ, which might have existed but have now been 'superseded' by the Convention.

230 Ibid [254].
231 *Fisheries jurisdiction (Federal Republic of Germany v Iceland)* (Merits) [1974] ICJ Rep 1974, 175 [258].
232 Ibid [262].
233 Ibid [801].
234 Ibid [804(c)].
235 Ibid [803].
236 Ibid [804(b)].
237 See Section 2.2.2
238 See also: Tanaka (n 187) 475; Symmons (n 180) 31.

In clarifying the relationship between historic rights and UNCLOS, the *South China Sea* tribunal should be commended for providing clear justification and an abundance of reasoning to support its conclusion. The tribunal resorted to the rules of treaty interpretation found under Article 31 of the Vienna Convention on the Law of Treaties (VCLT) even though the tribunal did not explicitly invoke this article, conducted an extensive survey of the negotiating history of the relevant provisions of the Convention and situated its findings within existing case law. Despite the detailed justification, some issues with the tribunal's reasoning remain and merit further consideration.

First, the tribunal's understanding of the relationship between UNCLOS and historic rights through Articles 311 and 293 is not without problems. In particular, the invocation of Article 293 was certainly out of place as this article does not regulate the relationship between different sources of law, but merely to specify the law that an UNCLOS tribunal may apply in the course of dispute settlement. As for Article 311, the tribunal did not provide any explanation as to how this article, which governs the relationship between the Convention and *other international agreements*, could 'appl[y] equally to the interaction of the Convention with other norms of international law, such as historic rights, that do not take the form of an agreement'.[239] In other words, Article 311 deals specifically with the relationship between treaties,[240] as does Article 30 VCLT that the tribunal invoked as an example of the general rules concerning the interaction of different bodies of law. As the tribunal seemed to have accepted that historic rights exist under customary international law, the relationship between UNCLOS and historic rights then becomes one between treaty law and an existing rule of customary law. As historic rights are those asserted at variance with the Convention, the treaty rule and the customary rule are in conflict. The rules of international law applicable to resolve conflict between treaty law and customary law are not straight forward. One suggestion for dealing with this conflict has been to apply 'the traditional legal presumptions that later law trumps prior law (*lex posterior derogat priori*) and that specialized law trumps general law (*lex specialis derogat generali*)'.[241] Since the tribunal was dealing with the relationship between UNCLOS and a rule that had arisen prior to the entry into force of the Convention, the application of the principle of lex posterior would seem to be apposite to

[239] *South China Sea Arbitration* (n 7) [235].

[240] Nele Matz-Lück, 'Final Provisions' in Alexander Proelss (n 36) 2010.

[241] Brian D Lepard, *Customary International Law: A New Theory with Practical Applications* (CUP 2010) 272.

resolve the conflict between the two.[242] Besides this principle, other authorities have also suggested that states may agree in treaties to derogate from existing customary rules,[243] in which case, treaties prevail over custom as between the parties to the treaty'.[244] If the tribunal in *South China Sea* had approached the relationship between UNCLOS and historical fishing rights in this manner, its reasoning would arguably have been more nuanced.

Second, the fact that historic rights were deemed to continue to exist in the territorial sea – in which coastal States have full sovereignty – but not in the EEZ in which coastal States only have sovereign rights has not gone unnoticed.[245] The tribunal did acknowledge this seeming contradiction by referring to the drafters' different intention behind the establishment of the territorial sea regime and that of the EEZ in UNCLOS.[246] Some questions, however, remain in relation to its reasoning. Neither in the territorial sea nor the EEZ does the Convention explicitly preserve historic fishing rights. However, with regards to the territorial sea, the tribunal accepted that historic or traditional fishing rights are protected by virtue of the reference to 'other rules of international law' contained in Article 2(3). Such a reference to 'other rules of international law' is also found under Article 58(2) regarding non-coastal States' rights and duties the EEZ. This notwithstanding, the tribunal still found that other States are not entitled to have rights in the EEZ in excess of those specified.[247] As analysed above,[248] the approach of the *Chagos MPA* tribunal to expand non-coastal States' scope of rights under Article 58 beyond the Convention implies that historic fishing rights may still be protected in the EEZ through Article 58(2).

Third, the *South China Sea* tribunal particularly highlighted the importance of Article 62(3) which requires the coastal State in giving access to other States in its EEZ to take into account 'the need to minimize economic dislocation in States whose nationals have habitually fished in the zone' to underscore the extinguishment of historic rights in the EEZ. The tribunal's reliance on a provision that explicitly mentions habitual fishing in order to

[242] Contra: Kopela (n 170) 184 (arguing that the principle of *lex specialis* should apply as historic rights are 'established on the basis of a particularized regime'.

[243] *North Sea Continental Shelf Cases (Federal Republic of Germany/Denmark; Federal Republic of Germany/Netherlands)* (Judgment) [1969] ICJ Rep 3, 42 [72].

[244] Christopher Greenwood, 'Sources of International Law: An Introduction' (2008).

[245] Symmons (n 186) 124; Kopela (n 170) 188; Ryan North, 'Traditional Fishing Rights in International Law: The South China Sea Arbitration' (2017) 36 UTLR 101, 106.

[246] South China Sea Arbitration (n 7) [804].

[247] Ibid [243].

[248] See Section C on due regard

extinguish historic rights in the EEZ at first glance sends a confusing message, given that the tribunal equated the term habitual fishing with 'historic fishing'[249] and that, as the tribunal had earlier found, where the Convention explicitly permits or preserves historic rights, they remain unaffected.[250] Following this logic, because habitual or historic fishing is explicitly protected in the EEZ by virtue of Article 62(3), they should continue to exist.[251] However, it is argued that the tribunal was correct in holding that Article 62 (3) supports the interpretation that the Convention intended to extinguish historic rights in the EEZ. The reference to habitual fishing in Article 62(3) cannot be understood to mean a preservation of historic fishing to the extent that it should remain unaffected by the Convention. Article 62(3) provides an illustrative list of factors that a coastal States may take into account when giving access to other States to its EEZ.[252] As has been noted by one commentator, the mere existence of such an illustrative list with no hierarchy shows that the coastal State has 'the broadest discretion to decide to whom and under what conditions access will be granted'.[253] In other words, habitual fishing constitutes one of the considerations that coastal States may take into account, it does not imply a right held by other States on the same footing as the exclusive sovereign rights of the coastal State. Under Article 62(3), the factor that need to be taken into account is not even habitual fishing itself, but rather 'the need to minimize economic dislocation in States whose nationals have habitually fished in the zone'.

Finally, as mentioned, the approach taken by the South China Sea tribunal drastically differed from that taken by the tribunal in *Eritrea/Yemen*. The tribunal was again cognisant of the divergence and explained that '[t]he arbitral tribunal in *Eritrea/Yemen* was empowered to – and in the Tribunal's view did – go beyond the law on traditional fishing as it would exist under the Convention',[254] and thus 'that tribunal was able to reach the conclusions it did only because it was permitted to apply factors other than the Convention itself under the applicable law provisions of the parties' arbitration agreement'.[255] It is not clear, however, how this explanation supported its contention that the

[249] *South China Sea Arbitration* (n 7) [242].
[250] Ibid [238].
[251] See also Kopela (n 170) 195.
[252] James Harrison and Elisa Morgera, 'Article 62' in Proelss (n 36) 500.
[253] Francisco Orrego Vicuna, 'The Exclusive Economic Zone: Regime and Legal Nature under International Law' (1989), 40 ICLQ 232, 54.
[254] *South China Sea Arbitration* (n 7) [259].
[255] Ibid [803].

drafters of UNCLOS did not intend for traditional fishing to survive the introduction of the EEZ. Instead, what it seems to acknowledge is that historic fishing rights continue to exist beyond the Convention, because only then could the tribunal in *Eritrea/Yemen* have considered such rights and their relationship with the Convention. Article 2 of the Arbitration Agreement between the parties in *Eritrea/Yemen* for phase II requested the tribunal to take into account both UNCLOS and any other pertinent factor.[256] By stating that the arbitral tribunal in *Eritrea/Yemen* 'was not bound by Article 293 to apply only the Convention and rules of law not incompatible therewith',[257] the *South China Sea* tribunal seemed to have suggested that the former either did not realise or did not need to consider the relationship between historic rights and UNCLOS since they could apply both. However, it would seem inconceivable that the *Eritrea/Yemen* tribunal, having been empowered to apply both UNCLOS and other pertinent factors, would blindly apply one source of law that is incompatible with another without any explanation. The finding of the *Eritrea/Yemen* tribunal could perhaps be better explained by the fact the Eritrean fishermen's traditional fishing rights had been recognised and approved by Yemen.[258] As has been pointed out by some scholars, '[i]n practice … some States still recognize historic rights that existed prior to the Convention'.[259] This means that historic fishing rights may continue to exist subject to the recognition of the coastal State. The *South China Sea* tribunal itself acknowledged this possibility when discussing Article 62(3), stating that '[t]he Convention does not, of course, preclude that States may continue to recognise traditional fishing rights in the exclusive economic zone in their legislation, in bilateral fisheries access agreements, or through regional fisheries management organisations.'[260]

In sum, the tribunals in *Chagos MPA* and *South China Sea* have provided important clarification on the relationship between historic rights and rights existing under UNCLOS. The approach taken by the tribunals shows both continuity and departure from existing case law. While the *South China Sea* tribunal's findings were support by detailed reasoning,

[256] *Eritrea/Yemen* (n 203) [7].
[257] *South China Sea Arbitration* (n 7) [259].
[258] *Eritrea/Yemen* (n 203) [107], [109].
[259] Leonardo Bernard, 'The Effect of Historic Fishing Rights in Maritime Boundaries Delimitation' in Harry N. Scheiber and Moon Sang Kwon (eds), *Securing the Ocean for the Next Generation* (Berkeley Law School 2013) 9 (listing examples India and Sri Lanka, Japan accepting fishing rights of fishermen from Korea and China, Australia and Papua New Guinea).
[260] *South China Sea Arbitration* (n 7) [804(b)].

they have not been without controversy due to the gaps in the justification provided by the tribunal.

2.3 CONCLUDING REMARKS

UNCLOS tribunals' decisions relating to coastal States' rights and obligations have mainly revolved around those in the EEZ. UNCLOS tribunals' decisions have therefore not only contributed to clarifying the scope of coastal States' rights and obligation with respect to particular issues but also more broadly to elucidating on the nature of the EEZ regime.

The case law concerning the interpretation of Articles 56, 62 and 73 has strengthened coastal States' exclusive sovereign rights over resources as well as their exclusive jurisdiction over artificial islands, installations and structures. ITLOS's decisions relating to activities which are not explicitly regulated under UNCLOS but which are prevalent in State practice such as bunkering activities or confiscation of vessels provide clarity and much-needed guidance for States in conducting activities at sea. The *South China Sea* tribunal's interpretation of the requirements of the establishment of historic rights and the interaction between UNCLOS and historic rights has further cemented the primacy and exclusivity of coastal States' sovereign rights in the EEZ. By contrast, while ITLOS was comfortable with expanding coastal States' regulatory and enforcement powers over fisheries activities in the EEZ, it essentially tilted the balance towards flag States' right in prompt release proceedings by giving little weight to coastal States' rights and obligations to conserve the fish stocks in the EEZ under both UNCLOS and other international agreements.

With respect to the nature of EEZ, the reconciliation achieved during UNCLOS III resulted in ambiguity in the legal status of the EEZ.[261] On the one hand, due to the a *sui generis* functional nature of the EEZ, the general legal relationship between all States in the EEZ is believed to be 'based on legal equality, as it is in the high seas'.[262] On the other hand, scholars have questioned this assumption, arguing that the history and rationale of the EEZ,[263] as well as the measures and control that coastal States are entitled to exercise in the EEZ,[264] ultimately shift the balance in favour of coastal States. In light of a new focus on the conservation of the marine resources, it

[261] Barbara Kwiatkowska, *The 200 Mile Exclusive Economic Zone in the New Law of the Sea* (Martinus Nijhoff 1989), 230.
[262] Gaunce (n 126) 36.
[263] Proelss (n 125) 432–433.
[264] Leanza and Caracciolo (n 3) 186.

has further been argued that the balance between the interests of the flag States and the sovereign rights of the coastal States 'needs a new equilibrium' altogether.[265] The decisions of UNCLOS tribunals seem to suggest that this equilibrium has been tilted in favour of coastal States. UNCLOS tribunal's decisions relating to bunkering of fishing vessels, the obligation of due regard, as well as to the relationship between historic rights and UNCLOS, reiterate the shift to coastal States by giving supremacy to coastal States' sovereign rights and jurisdiction in the EEZ. It should be noted, however, that some of ITLOS's conclusion was based, to a large extent, on State practice as recorded in subsequent international agreements or in States' national legislations. This indicates that the tribunals did not invent the new balance, it was merely affirming a balance that has been set by States themselves.

UNCLOS tribunals have not, however, been consistent in the extent to which they justify their decision with clear reasoning. For some issues, such as the relationship between historic rights and UNCLOS, the tribunal in question meticulously applied the tools of interpretation found under the VCLT, in addition to carefully situating its decision within existing case law and differentiating the differences. In other issues, such as coastal States' enforcement power in the EEZ, ITLOS provided only sparse reasoning to justify its findings.

[265] Seline Trevisanut, 'The Exercise of Administrative Functions by ITLOS: A Comment on Prompt Release Case-Law' in Nerina Boschiero et al. (eds), *International Courts and the Development of International Law: Essays in Honour of Tullio Treves* (Springer 2013) 322.

3

Flag States' Rights and Obligations under the Law of the Sea

The rights and duties of flag States go hand in hand under the United Nations Convention on the Law of the Sea (UNCLOS) legal framework. A State bears the right to grant a ship its nationality and is entitled to exercise exclusive jurisdiction over the ship.[1] At the same time, the flag State has the obligation to effectively exercise its jurisdiction and control over the ship sailing under its flag.[2] While the provisions relating to flag States' rights and obligations are found in Part VII UNCLOS entitled 'High seas', as scholars have argued, 'their application is much broader since they reflect the general international law on the topic and effectively apply wherever the ship may be'.[3] Given the omnipresence of ships at seas, clarity and certainty regarding flag States' rights and obligations are crucial for the effective implementation of UNCLOS, as well as for ensuring delicate balance between the rights and obligations of coastal States and of flag States upon which UNCLOS hinges. This chapter examines the decisions of UNCLOS tribunals which touched upon flag States' rights and obligations, in order to examine whether and to what extent UNCLOS tribunals have contributed to the clarification and development of the relevant rules pertaining to flag States. Section 3.1 focuses on the concept of flag States, followed by Section 3.2 examining the principle of flag States' exclusive jurisdiction and the freedom of navigation and Section 3.3 on flag States' obligations. Section 3.4 concludes with an assessment regarding the contribution of UNCLOS tribunals to the development of flag States' rights and obligations under UNCLOS.

1 Article 92 UNCLOS. In other maritime zones, flag States' jurisdiction is exercised concurrent with that of coastal States.

2 Article 94 UNCLOS.

3 Donald R Rothwell and Tim Stephens, *The International Law of the Sea* (2nd ed, Hart Publishing 2016) 167. See also, Henrik Ringbom, 'Introduction' in Henrik Ringbom (ed), *Jurisdiction over Ships* (Brill 2014) 3.

3.1 CONCEPT OF 'FLAG STATE'

UNCLOS does not provide for a clear definition of 'flag State'. Based on Article 91(1), a flag State is understood as a State whose flag ships are entitled to fly. This understanding, as well as several definitions existing elsewhere,[4] points to the inextricable link between the flag State and the ship. While UNCLOS also does not provide for a definition of the term 'ship', it should be noted that the International Tribunal for the Law of the Sea (ITLOS) in *Saiga (No 2)* held that a 'ship' is understood broadly to encompass 'the ship, everything on it, and every person involved or interested in its operations'.[5] The link between the State and the ship is, in turn, established by the concept of 'nationality of the ship' regulated under Article 91(1). Article 91(1) provides that '[e]very State shall fix the conditions for the grant of its nationality to ships, for the registration of ships in its territory, and for the right to fly its flag. . . . There must exist a genuine link between the State and the ship'. This article, on the one hand, allows States to determine the conditions by which to grant nationality to ships; and on the other hand, requires that a genuine link exists between the State and the ship. ITLOS has had the opportunity to engage with both these aspects of Article 91(1) in several of its decisions. The remainder of this section examines ITLOS's interpretation of (a) the conditions for granting nationality to ships and (b) the genuine link requirement.

3.1.1 *Conditions for Granting Nationality to Ships*

M/V Saiga (No. 2) was the first case – and to date remains the most authoritative decision – to examine the issue of nationality of vessel. In this case, Guinea as the respondent challenged the legal standing of Saint Vincent

4 For example, Article 2 of the 1986 Convention on Conditions for the Registration of Ships defines a flag State as 'a State whose flag a ship flies and is entitled to fly'. Other definitions include: 'the State which has granted to a ship the right to sail under its flag' (Robin Churchill and Vaughan Lowe, *The Law of the Sea* (3rd ed, Manchester University Press 1999) 208); 'the State whose nationality the ship possesses' (Michael B Akehurst, A *Modern Introduction to International Law* (Unwin Hyman 1988) 182.

5 *M/V 'Saiga' (No. 2) (Saint Vincent and the Grenadines v Guinea)* (Judgment) ITLOS Reports 1999, 10 [106]. This doctrine of 'ship as a unit' has been endorsed and developed in subsequent cases. See: *M/V 'Virginia G' (Panama/Guinea-Bissau)* (Judgment) ITLOS Reports 2014, 4 [127]–[128]; *The M/V 'Norstar' Case (Panama v Italy)* (Judgment) ITLOS Reports 2019 [230]–[231]. Note, however, that Article 18 of the International Law Commission Draft Articles on Diplomatic Protection recognises both nationality of the crew members and the flag of the vessel as relevant criteria for the exercise of jurisdiction over seafarers. See: United Nations, Draft articles on Diplomatic Protection (2006) https://legal.un.org/ilc/texts/instruments/english/draft_articles/9_8_2006.pdf accessed 25 January 2022.

and the Grenadines to bring claims regarding the Saiga. One of the grounds invoked by Guinea was that on the day of its arrest, the ship was not validly registered under the flag of Saint Vincent and the Grenadines as the Provisional Certificate of Registration issued by Saint Vincent and the Grenadines had expired and the Permanent Certificate of Registration had not been issued.[6] Saint Vincent and the Grenadines, on the other hand, argued that when a vessel was registered under its flag 'it remains so registered until deleted from the registry'.

In response, ITLOS recalled that Article 91 gives the State the exclusive jurisdiction over the granting of its nationality to ships and thus it was for the flag State to fix the conditions for granting its nationality to ships, for the registration of ships in its territory and for the right to fly its flag in its domestic law.[7] In the case of merchant ships, it held that 'the normal procedure used by States to grant nationality is registration in accordance with domestic legislation adopted for that purpose'.[8] As a result, it considered that 'the nationality of a ship is a question of fact to be determined ... on the basis of evidence adduced by the parties'.[9] On this basis, it found that Saint Vincent and the Grenadines had produced sufficient evidence to show that Saiga still had its nationality, which includes references to the relevant provisions of the Merchant Act confirming the validity of the Provisional Certificate of Registration and indications of Vincentian nationality on the ship and on board.[10] Moreover, ITLOS also relied on the conduct of both parties – that of Saint Vincent and the Grenadines to act as the flag State during all the phases of the proceedings,[11] and the failure of Guinea to raise any challenge reading the national of the ship – to strengthen its argument that Saiga still had the nationality of Saint Vincent and the Grenadines.[12]

The question of whether a State qualified as the flag State and thus the nationality of a ship also took centre stage in several prompt release proceedings. This was due to the fact that, according to Article 292(2), 'the application for release may be made only by or on behalf of the flag State of the vessel'.

6 *M/V 'Saiga' (No. 2)* (n 5) [55], [58].
7 Ibid [63].
8 Ibid [64].
9 Ibid [66].
10 Ibid [67].
11 Ibid [68].
12 Note, however, that in his Dissenting Opinion, Judge Warioba criticised ITLOS's reliance on the conduct of Saint Vincent the Grenadines for the purposes of determining nationality as 'trying to amend the Convention by introducing new conditions outside article 91'. See *M/V 'SAIGA' (No. 2) (Saint Vincent and the Grenadines v Guinea)* (Judgment, Dis Op Warioba) ITLOS Reports 1999, 10 [46], [47].

In *Grand Prince*, ITLOS attached particular importance to the act of registration in determining whether a fishing vessel had the right to fly the Belizean flag, stating that '[i]t is necessary that there is sufficient evidence to establish that a vessel is registered and, therefore, has the right to fly the flag of Belize at the relevant time.'[13] In this case, the only document issued to the Grand Prince by Belize was the provisional patent of navigation which had already expired before the institution of prompt release proceedings and had not been extended or replaced by another statutory certificate.[14] Even though there was a letter and a certification from the International Merchant Marine Registry of Belize which asserted that 'despite the expiration of the Patent of navigation and Ship station license, the vessel is still considered as registered in Belize',[15] ITLOS was not satisfied that these communications could be treated as 'documents' within the meaning of Article 91(2) of the Convention.[16] Moreover, Belize also sent an official communication to France, which declared that it had deregistered the vessel as a punitive measure.[17] In the light of the expiration of the provisional patent of navigation, and of the deregistration of the Grand Prince, ITLOS concluded that Belize was not the flag State of the vessel.[18]

ITLOS's approaches in these two cases at first glance seemed to be inconsistent. In both cases, the parties presented expired domestic provisional documents showing the nationality of the ship. ITLOS, however, accepted the document for the purposes of determining nationality in one case but rejected the relevance of the document in the other. Scovazzi interpreted ITLOS's approach in *Grand Prince* as a deliberate departure from Saiga because '[t]he position taken in the M/V "Saiga No. 2" judgment was so weak that the ITLOS itself preferred a completely different solution in a subsequent and similar situation'.[19] However, it is worth asking whether ITLOS had actually intended to send such a message. On closer inspection, the circumstances of the two cases do not appear to be entirely similar. The document produced in *Saiga (No 2)* proved that the ship had been registered in accordance with domestic law. Even though the Provisional Certificate of Registration had expired, it was followed by a permanent one shortly after. More importantly, Saint Vincent and the Grenadines were able to show that

[13] *'Grand Prince' (Belize v France)* (Prompt Release, Judgment) ITLOS Reports 2001, 17 [83].
[14] Ibid [84].
[15] Ibid [85].
[16] Ibid.
[17] Ibid [87].
[18] Ibid [93].
[19] Tullio Scovazzi, 'ITLOS and Jurisdiction over Ships' in Ringbom (n 3) 392.

its domestic legislation confirmed the validity of a provisional certificate and the consequences flowing from an expired one. In contrast, in *Grand Prince*, the document presented was not a certificate of registration, moreover it had expired and had not been replaced by any other official document in accordance with domestic law to confirm the nationality of the ship.[20] It follows that ITLOS's approach remained the same in both cases, namely that the nationality of a ship depends entirely on States' registration procedures as provided in their domestic laws. In other words, compliance with domestic procedures for registration was the only criterion that mattered. Therefore, the difference in the outcome of the two cases simply reiterates the importance of compliance with domestic law for the purposes of determining nationality. ITLOS's approach to determining nationality in *Saiga (No 2)* also suggests strong deference to the flag State in determining the nationality of ships. Neither an international tribunal nor any other State would be in the position to determine the sufficiency or otherwise of the State's domestic law providing for the nationality of ships. The State has exclusive power on this matter.

While the above-mentioned cases demonstrated the importance of registration as evidence for the nationality of ships, Article 94(2) provides a registration exemption for small vessels. The Annex VII arbitral tribunal in *Enrica Lexie* dealt specifically with this provision when it had to consider whether St Antony – a small fishing vessel which was exempted from registering under the Indian Merchant Shipping Act – had Indian nationality. The tribunal answered this question in the affirmative as it found that St Antony had met the relevant conditions under Indian law to be granted Indian nationality.[21] This conclusion did not change even when St Antony did not acquire the right to fly the Indian flag, because in the tribunal's view '[a] flag may thus be regarded as "visual evidence" or "a symbol" of nationality, but is not determinative for that vessel's nationality'.[22] While reiterating the desirability of registration, the tribunal also accepted that in light of Article 94(2), 'States may, exceptionally, exercise their freedoms under Article 87 of the Convention also through small non-registered vessels'.[23] *Enrica Lexie* thus

[20] Guilfoyle argues that the difference between the two cases 'may simply be one of burden of proof' as Saint Vincent and the Grenadines were able to show evidence to rebut the inference arising from the expired document while Belize did not. See: Douglas Guilfoyle, 'Article 91' in Alexander Proelss (ed), *United Nations Convention on the Law of the Sea: A Commentary* (CH Beck, Hart, Nomos 2017) 698.

[21] *The 'Enrica Lexie' Incident (Italy v India)*, Arbitral Award of 21 May 2021, [1025] https://pcacases.com/web/sendAttach/16500 accessed 25 January 2022 [Enrica Lexie]

[22] Ibid [1029].

[23] Ibid [1034].

confirmed the importance of compliance with domestic law and procedures concerning the granting of nationality, in which registration usually plays the key role but is not the only condition.

3.1.2 *The (In)significance of 'Genuine Link' for Granting Nationality*

The second part of Article 91(1) provides that '[t]here must exist a genuine link between the State and the ship'. The term 'genuine link' is believed to originate from the *Nottebohm* case before the International Court of Justice (ICJ).[24] In this case, the Court when examining the relationship between a State and its nationals, held that 'nationality is a legal bond having as its basis a social fact of attachment, *a genuine connection* of existence, interests and sentiments, together with the existence of reciprocal rights and duties'.[25] A ship is, however, not the same as an individual and neither is its relationship with the State. The mention of 'genuine link' in an article that deals with nationality of ships raises questions regarding what role it plays in the granting of nationality of ships, and whether the lack of a genuine link between the State and the ship would mean that the former cannot grant nationality to the latter. It should be remembered that the term 'genuine link' was already included in Article 5(1) of the 1958 Convention on the High Seas. Thus debates surrounding the meaning of this evasive term and related questions as to whether it should be considered a precondition for registration of a ship and whether nonrecognition of nationality is permissible in the absence of genuine link have had a long history.[26] Despite the decades-old discussion, Churchill has remarked that 'there is no consensus among writers as to what is meant by a genuine link or the consequences that follow from its absence'.[27] 'Genuine link' has thus always remained 'nebulous and controversial'.[28] ITLOS had the opportunity to provide clarity to the issue; and its decisions in *Saiga*

[24] Robin R Churchill and Christopher Hedley, 'The Meaning of the "Genuine Link" Requirement in Relation to the Nationality of Ships' (A *Study prepared for the International Transport Workers' Federation*, October 2000) 22 https://orca.cardiff.ac.uk/45062/1/ITF-Oct2000.pdf accessed 25 January 2022; Richard A Barnes 'Flag States' in Rothwell and others (eds), *Oxford Handbook on Law of the Sea* (OUP 2015); Doris König, 'Flag of Ships', Max Planck Encyclopedias of International Law (2009).

[25] *Nottebohm (Liechtenstein v Guatemala)* (Judgment, Second Phase) [1955] ICJ Rep 1955, 4, 23. (emphasis added)

[26] For a summary of the debate, see Churchill and Hedley (n 24) 33–37.

[27] Churchill and Hedley (n 24) 37. See also Guilfoyle (n 20) 699.

[28] G C Kasoulides, *Port State Control and Jurisdiction: Evolution of the Port State Regime* (Springer 1993) 75, cited in Rosemary Gail Rayfuse, *Non-Flag State Enforcement in High Seas Fisheries* (Martinus Nijhoff Publishers 2004) 28.

(*No* 2) and *Virginia* G together provided an authoritative interpretation of Article 91(1) UNCLOS.

The requirement of 'genuine link' was put before ITLOS in *Saiga* (*No.* 2) when Guinea contended that it was not bound to recognise the Vincentian nationality of the M/V Saiga because 'there was no genuine link between the Saiga and Saint Vincent and the Grenadines'.[29] In response, Saint Vincent and the Grenadines argued that there was nothing under UNCLOS to support the contention that the existence of a genuine link between a ship and a State was a necessary precondition for the grant of nationality to the ship.[30] ITLOS, for its part, first considered whether the absence of a genuine link between a flag State and a ship would entitle another State to refuse to recognise the nationality of the ship. It found that none of the UNCLOS articles, including Articles 91(1), 92 or 94, provided an explicit answer to this question. It then turned to the negotiating history of the 1958 Convention on the High Seas on the question of nationality – whose approach UNCLOS follows – and found that a proposal to include 'genuine link' as a criterion not only for the attribution of nationality to a ship but also for the recognition by other States of such nationality was not adopted.[31] More importantly, ITLOS pointed out that Article 94 set out the procedures to be followed when 'a State has clear grounds to believe that proper jurisdiction and control with respect to a ship have not been exercised'; it did not permit a State which discovered 'evidence indicating the absence of proper jurisdiction and control by a flag State over a ship to refuse to recognize the right of the ship to fly the flag of the flag State'.[32] ITLOS, therefore, concluded that:

> [T]he purpose of the provisions of the Convention on the need for a genuine link between a ship and its flag State is to secure more effective implementation of the duties of the flag State, and not to establish criteria by reference to which the validity of the registration of ships in a flag State may be challenged by other States.[33]

ITLOS recalled this approach in *Virginia* G when it was faced with a challenge on admissibility raised by Guinea-Bissau against Panama's claims on the basis that there was no genuine link between the M/V Virginia G and Panama.[34] ITLOS concluded that the requirement of genuine link in Article

[29] *M/V Saiga (No. 2)* (n 5) [75].
[30] Ibid [77].
[31] Ibid [80].
[32] Ibid [82].
[33] Ibid [83].
[34] *Virginia* G (n 5) [102]–[103].

91(1) 'should not be read as establishing prerequisites or conditions to be satisfied for the exercise of the right of the flag State to grant its nationality to ships.[35] ITLOS's examination of the requirement of 'genuine link' in *M/V Saiga*, affirmed and applied in *Virginia G*, made clear that this requirement does not play a role in determining the nationality of a vessel.

In both of the cases, ITLOS clarified the function that 'genuine link' should play but they did not shed much light on what constituted genuine link. In *M/V Saiga*, ITLOS simply concluded that 'the evidence adduced by Guinea is not sufficient to justify its contention that there was no genuine link between the ship and Saint Vincent and the Grenadines'.[36] This statement suggests that the genuine link between the State and the ship is presumed to exist and the burden of proof is on the party contesting such an existence to show otherwise. In *Virginia G*, ITLOS held that:

> [O]nce a ship is registered, the flag State is required, under article 94 of the Convention, to exercise effective jurisdiction and control over that ship in order to ensure that it operates in accordance with generally accepted international regulations, procedures and practices. This is the meaning of 'genuine link'.[37]

By virtue of the phrase 'once a ship is registered', it seems clear that genuine link is detached from the issue of granting nationality to a ship. It is again linked to the duties of a flag State under Article 94.

ITLOS's interpretation has provided some clarity regarding the role of genuine link in the granting of nationality for ships.[38] However, the reasoning used by the Tribunal has been criticised as 'far from being impeccable from the logical and legal point of view'.[39] This point merits further scrutiny. ITLOS's reasoning in *Saiga (No 2)* was based on both the negotiating history of Article 91(1) UNCLOS and its predecessor Article 5(1) of the 1958 Convention on the High Seas, as well as subsequent international agreements dealing with the issue of nationality of ships. In relation to the question of whether the absence of genuine link could constitute a ground for one State to not recognise the nationality of a ship of another State, it seemed reasonable for ITLOS to take account of the fact that an explicit mention of the need for recognition was removed from the final version of Article 5(1) of

35 Ibid [110].

36 *M/V Saiga (No. 2)* (n 5) [87].

37 *M/V 'Virginia G'* (n 5) [113].

38 Vincent P Cogliati-Bantz, 'Introductory Note to the M/V "Virginia G" Case (Panama/Guinea-Bissau) (ITLOS)' (2014) 53(6) ILM 1161, 402.

39 Ibid.

the 1958 Convention on the High Seas. However, with regards to the question of whether genuine link should be considered as a requirement for the granting of nationality, it would seem the negotiating history would be of little help. The rejection of recognition was primarily due to the fear that it would give States 'an uncontrollable unilateral discretion to question and deny other states' ascription of nationality to their ships'.[40] The emphasis was therefore not on the rejection of the genuine link as a requirement in the granting of nationality but rather on preventing other States from exerting control on the right of flags State to grant nationality to ships. The fact that ITLOS in *Virginia* G recalled its conclusion in *Saiga* (*No* 2) to support its conclusion that genuine link could not serve as a precondition for the granting of nationality was thus not entirely convincing. ITLOS in *Virginia* G conflated the two questions without much explanation.

Instead of placing too much emphasis on the negotiating history, ITLOS could have paid more attention to States practice on this matter. In *Saiga* (*No* 2), the fact that the Tribunal referred to the 1986 United Nations Convention on Conditions for Registration of Ships (the Registration Convention) and other international agreements suggested that ITLOS was mindful of the need to interpret Article 91(1) UNCLOS in line with subsequent State practice. Indeed, the Registration Convention only contains vague wording concerning the requirement of genuine link, which suggests a compromise between States wishing to strengthen the requirement of genuine and those that do not. More importantly, it has not to date entered into force, which has been interpreted to mean that, 'the attempt to establish, as a legally binding concept, an economic genuine link as a prerequisite for registration of ships has failed'.[41] Attempts to have a clearer definition of 'genuine link' at the International Maritime Organization (IMO) and the Food and Agriculture Organization (FAO) also did not make much progress. Developments since 1982 demonstrate that States have not been in favour of harmonising or controlling the conditions for the granting of nationality, but rather on increasing and strengthening flag States' obligations.[42] While a more stringent interpretation of 'genuine link' might have been more conducive to tackling the issue of flags of

40 Myres S McDougal, William T Burke and Ivan A Vlasic, 'The Maintenance of Public Order at Sea and the Nationality of Ships' (1960) 54(1) The American Journal of International Law 25, 41.

41 König (n 24) [11]. See also: Barnes (n 24) 307 (who contends that, 'the Registration Convention stands as a salutary lesson about States' resistance to limits on the exercise of sovereign powers').

42 Cogliati-Bantz (n 38) 40; König (n 24) 54–55.

convenience, this would not have been in line with the practice of States.[43]

In conclusion, the concept of 'flag States' in UNCLOS tribunals' case law has been defined through the notion of 'nationality of ships'. In dealing with the question of nationality, ITLOS has consistently adopted the approach taken in *Saiga* (*No. 2*) by which the most important factor is whether the ship has complied with domestic law and procedures concerning nationality of ships. Registration plays an important role particularly in this regard as it 'constitutes both a formal link and proof of connection between the ship and the flag State'.[44] Even though the requirement of a genuine link between the flag State and the ship is found in Article 91(1) regulating the nationality of ships, ITLOS has consistently found that it does not establish a prerequisite or condition to be satisfied for the exercise of the right of the flag State to grant its nationality to ships.[45] Instead, 'genuine link' constitutes part of the duties of flag States. ITLOS's interpretation of genuine link seems to be in line with State practice. By emphasising compliance with domestic rules relating to the granting of nationality, as well as by rejecting the connection between 'genuine link' and the establishment of nationality and by rejecting the possibility of nonrecognition of nationality based on genuine link, ITLOS has reinforced the flag State' sole discretion in granting ships the right to acquire its nationality. As ITLOS succinctly put in *Tomimaru*, 'it is for each State to establish the conditions for the granting of its nationality to ships and for the registration of ships'.[46]

3.2 FREEDOM OF NAVIGATION AND THE PRINCIPLE OF FLAG STATES' EXCLUSIVE JURISDICTION

Freedom of the high seas is without doubt one of the oldest principles of the law of the sea.[47] In the modern law of the sea, freedom of the high seas is encapsulated in Article 87 of UNCLOS, whose paragraph (1) confirms that

43 Scovazzi's argument that ITLOS provided 'an implicit support to flags of convenience' does not therefore seem tenable. See: Scovazzi (n 19) 388.

44 Moira L McConnell, 'ITLOS and the Tale of the Tenacious "Genuine Link"' in Øystein Jensen (ed), *The Development of the Law of the Sea Convention* (Edward Elgar Publishing 2020) 214.

45 *M/V Saiga (No. 2)* (n 5) [110].

46 *'Tomimaru' (Japan v Russian Federation)* (Prompt Release, Judgment) ITLOS Reports 2005–2007, 74 [70]. ITLOS in this case held that when a ship was confiscated by a coastal State, confiscation only resulted in a change of ownership, it did not automatically lead to the change or loss of the ship's flag. The unilateral act of another State such as confiscation cannot replace the flag States' right to grant nationality.

47 This principle is usually credited to Hugo Grotius and his famous Mare Liberum doctrine, but traces its history back to even earlier in Roman and Greek law. See: Rayfuse (n 28) 18.

'the high seas are open to all States'. The principle of freedom of the high seas is, in turn, closely linked to the principle of flag States' exclusive jurisdiction codified under Article 92(1) UNCLOS. This article reads, in relevant parts, 'ships . . . shall be subject to [the flag State's] exclusive jurisdiction on the high seas'. UNCLOS tribunals have often dealt with flag States' exclusive jurisdiction and freedom of the high seas together in their decisions even when the parties invoked only one of the two principles. This section examines the decisions of UNCLOS tribunals relating to the principle of flag States' exclusive jurisdiction and the one freedom of the high seas that has come before UNCLOS tribunals, namely the freedom of navigation. It analyses the extent to which UNCLOS tribunals have clarified two main issues that have arisen including: the scope of freedom of navigation under Article 87(1) and the scope of flag States' exclusive jurisdiction under Article 92.

3.2.1 *Scope and Applicability of the Freedom of Navigation*

Article 87(1)(a) provides for the freedom of navigation in the high seas. While the plain wording of this freedom suggests unimpeded passage in the high seas,[48] UNCLOS tribunals have clarified the scope of freedom of navigation, including the activities that are encompassed within this freedom and the spatial scope of the exercise of this freedom. More importantly – and controversially – UNCLOS tribunals have also provided answers to the questions as to when the freedom of navigation is applicable and relatedly when it is breached. Each of these issues is examined in turn.

3.2.1.1 Scope of the Freedom of Navigation

With respect to the activities included within the freedom of navigation, the Annex VII arbitral tribunal confirmed in *Arctic Sunrise* that protest at sea is part of freedom of navigation. However, the tribunal was careful to add that there were limitations to such right, emphasising, particularly, that it must be peaceful and when in the exclusive economic zone (EEZ) must be exercised with due regard to the rights and duties of the coastal State.[49] As mentioned by the tribunal itself, the emphasis on peaceful protest certainly paid heed to both

[48] Douglas Guilfoyle, 'Article 87' in Proelss (n 20) 681.

[49] *Award in the Arbitration Regarding the Arctic Sunrise (Kingdom of the Netherlands v Russian Federation)*, Award on Merits (2015) RIAA XXXII 183 [227]–[228].

developments in the law of the sea[50] and those in the field of human rights.[51] It also narrowed down the kind of protest at sea that is considered lawful as part of freedom of navigation, thereby potentially preempting the Award from being used as a legal basis to justify violent protests at sea.[52] The tribunal also made clear that the coastal State may take measures to to prevent protest actions that interfere with the exercise of its sovereign rights,[53] but otherwise it should 'tolerate some level of nuisance through civilian protest'.[54] Another activity that has been included within the scope of freedom of navigation is bunkering activities in the high seas as confirmed by ITLOS in *M/V Norstar*.[55] It should be recalled that ITLOS in *Virginia G*, while confirming that the bunkering of fishing vessels fell within the coastal State's regulatory power, did not directly address the classification of bunkering activities in general. By explicitly stating that bunkering activities in the high seas are encompassed within the freedom of navigation, ITLOS in *M/V Norstar* has settled this question.

Turning to the spatial limits of the freedom of navigation, the fact that the freedom of navigation is one of the freedoms of the high seas suggests a spatial application of the exercise of this freedom to high seas and, by virtue of Article 58(1), to the EEZ. However, a question that has been raised in several cases before UNCLOS tribunals is whether freedom of navigation refers to the right to navigate in the EEZ and on the high seas or the right to navigate to and from these maritime zones. In *ARA Libertad* provisional measures proceedings, which concerned Ghana's detention of the Argentinian-flagged warship ARA Libertad in its port, Argentina made the argument that Ghana's detention prevented the warship from enjoying its freedom of navigation under Article 87(1).[56] As ITLOS had to deal only with *prima facie* jurisdiction in provisional measures proceedings, it did not engage with this argument in detail but only stated that Article 87(1) did not relate to the immunity of warships in internal waters.[57] As the Tribunal seemed to have framed the main contention of the dispute as one relating to immunity of warships, it is difficult

50 Ibid [227].
51 Ibid [197].
52 See, for example, Gerry Nagtzaam and Douglas Guilfoyle, 'Ramming Speed': The Sea Shepherd Conservation Society and the Law of Protest' (2018) 44 Monash University Law Review 360.
53 *Arctic Sunrise* (n 49) [327].
54 Ibid [328].
55 *M/V 'Norstar' Case (Panama v Italy) (Preliminary Objections)* ITLOS Reports 2016, 44 [219].
56 *The 'ARA Libertad' Case (Argentina v Ghana)* (Provisional Measures, Order of 20 November 2012) ITLOS Reports 2012, 326 [43].
57 Ibid [61].

to conclude whether ITLOS, by making this statement, accepted or rejected Argentina's argument – although one may be tempted to lean towards the latter. An explicit answer was only provided in a subsequent case *M/V Louisa*, in which ITLOS rejected a similar argument, thereby confirming the spatial limit of the freedom of navigation. In this case, the vessel M/Louisa was detained in a Spanish port. Saint Vincent and the Grenadine, the flag state of M/V Louisa argued that 'because of the detention of the M/V "Louisa" the vessel was denied access to the high seas and that this detention violates the freedom of vessels under the flag of Saint Vincent and the Grenadines to navigate on the high seas'.[58] This argument thus turned the freedom of navigation into one that allowed not only free sailing within the high seas but also the freedom to traverse into the high seas. ITLOS rejected this expansive reading of Article 87 stating that this article 'cannot be interpreted in such a way as to grant the M/V "Louisa" a right to leave the port and gain access to the high seas notwithstanding its detention in the context of legal proceedings against it'.[59] As interpreted by one commentator, '*M/V Louisa* seems to suggest that under UNCLOS navigational rights extinguish at the limits of their respective maritime zones.'[60] ITLOS's findings thus clarified that the freedom of navigation is conferred upon vessels operating on the high seas and in the EEZ, it does not extend to vessels that find themselves in other maritime zones.

3.2.1.2 Applicability and Breach of the Freedom of Navigation

The questions as to when the freedom of navigation is applicable and when this freedom may be breached were examined in detail for the first time by ITLOS in *M/V Norstar*. In this case, a Panamanian-flagged oil tanker that gave the dispute its name had engaged in supplying gasoil to mega yachts off the coasts of France, Italy and Spain.[61] Investigations carried out by the Italian policed showed that the M/V Norstar had involved in a tax fraud scheme by purchasing tax-exempted fuel in Italy and reselling it to Italian and other EU leisure boats in international waters.[62] After instituting criminal proceedings

58 *The M/V 'Louisa' Case (Saint Vincent and the Grenadines v Kingdom of Spain)* ITLOS Reports 2013, 4 [106].
59 Ibid [109].
60 Arron N Honniball, 'Extraterritorial Port State Measures: The Basis and Limits of Unilateral Port State Jurisdiction to Combat Illegal, Unreported and Unregulated Fishing' (PhD thesis, Utrecht University 2019) 167.
61 *M/V 'Norstar' Case* (n 55)[69].
62 Ibid [70].

against eight individuals on board of M/V Norstar, Italy issued a Decree of Seizure to seize the vessel. A request for judicial assistance to execute the Decree was then sent to a Spanish court, which was subsequently granted, resulting in the seizure of the M/V Norstar by the Spanish authorities while it was anchored in a Spanish bay. This summary of the facts of the case illustrates that the maritime zones relevant for the purposes of this case not only included the high seas but also the territory of Italy and the internal waters of Spain. However, after finding that 'the detention carried out by Spain was part of the criminal investigation and proceedings conducted by Italy against the M/V "Norstar" '[63] and that 'the Decree of Seizure and the request for its enforcement by Italy were central to the eventual arrest of the vessel',[64] ITLOS limited the question that it had to address to whether the Decree of Seizure concerned Norstar's bunkering activities in the high seas or crimes that Norstar was alleged to have committed in the Italian territory.

ITLOS took into account references to the activities of M/V Norstar on the high seas in the Decree of Seizure, including description of the *modus operandi* of the bunkering activity in the high seas,[65] and came to the conclusion that '[t]he Decree of Seizure and its execution … concern both alleged crimes committed in the territory of Italy and bunkering activities conducted by the M/V "Norstar" on the high seas'.[66] The Tribunal went even further to say that 'the bunkering activities of the *M/V "Norstar"* on the high seas in fact constitute not only an integral part, but also a central element, of the activities targeted by the Decree of Seizure and its execution'.[67] While characterising the case as one that centred upon bunkering activities in the high seas, ITLOS still held that it would have to examine how the freedom of navigation was to be interpreted and applied to the case in order to determine whether Article 87 was indeed applicable and breached.[68] The fact that ITLOS stated that it would assess these issues separately indicated a distinction between the applicability and a violation of Article 87.[69]

In its assessment, however, it is not clear which analysis pertained to applicability and which to breach. After classifying bunkering on the high seas as an exercise of freedom of navigation as analysed above, ITLOS swiftly moved to the question of what constituted a breach of Article 87. ITLOS

63 Ibid [167].
64 Ibid [165].
65 Ibid [176], [177].
66 Ibid.
67 Ibid [186].
68 Ibid [187].
69 Ibid [188].

found that 'any act of interference with navigation of foreign ships or any exercise of jurisdiction over such ships on the high seas constitutes a breach of the freedom of navigation, unless justified by the Convention or other international treaties'.[70] ITLOS adopted a broad understanding of the term 'any act' and held that 'even acts which do not involve physical interference or enforcement on the high seas may constitute a breach of the freedom of navigation'[71] if it 'subjects activities of a foreign ship on the high seas to the jurisdiction of States other than the flag State ... save in exceptional cases expressly provided for in the Convention and other international treaties'.[72] This broad understanding was further confirmed when ITLOS reached the conclusion that:

> [I]f a State applies its criminal and customs laws to the high seas and criminalizes activities carried out by foreign ships thereon, it would constitute a breach of article 87 of the Convention, unless justified by the Convention or other international treaties. This would be so, even if the State refrained from enforcing those laws on the high seas.[73]

While rejecting Panama's contention that the freedom of navigation encompassed the right to leave port and gain access to the high seas,[74] ITLOS also disagreed with Italy's argument that since the Decree of Seizure was enforced in internal waters, Article 87 was neither applicable nor breached. More specifically, ITLOS found that 'article 87 may still be applicable and be breached if a State extends its criminal and customs laws extraterritorially to activities of foreign ships on the high seas and criminalizes them'.[75]

ITLOS in *M/V Norstar* thus adopted the view that Article 87 is applicable and breached by both non-flag State physical interference and enforcement on the high seas and by any non-flag State's application of its laws to activities carried out by a vessel on the high seas. This is a very broad interpretation of a breach of the freedom of navigation which substantially favours and bolsters the right flag State vis-à-vis other States. Moreover, in reaching this conclusion, ITLOS muddled the distinction between when Article 87 is applicable and when it would be breached.[76] While ITLOS at first suggested that these

70 Ibid [222].
71 Ibid [223].
72 Ibid [224].
73 Ibid [225].
74 Ibid [221].
75 Ibid [226].
76 Arron N Honniball, 'Freedom of Navigation Following the M/V "Norstar" Case' (*NCLOS Blog*, 4 June 2019) https://site.uit.no/nclos/2019/06/04/freedom-of-navigation-following-the-m-v-norstar-case/ accessed 25 January 2022.

were the two distinctive tests, it seems clear that the Tribunal in the end viewed these two steps as one and the same. It used the same fact, namely the extension of Italian law to the high seas, to find that Article 87 was both applicable and breached. The Tribunal's finding would seem to suggest that any extension of non-flag State domestic law to activities of a foreign vessel in the high seas would simultaneously trigger and violate Article 87.

This conclusion was met with strong criticism from the seven judges of the case – almost one third of the judges sitting on bench – in their Joint Dissenting Opinion.[77] In the view of the minority, just because the Decree of Seizure and other relevant domestic documents mentioned and described the bunkering activity, did not mean that they 'targeted' the activity. Instead, 'the activity must be criminally prosecutable under the law of that State.[78]' The Decree concerned the act of tax evasion and smuggling of fuel, both of which took place in Italian territory and both were criminal offences under Italian domestic law. By pointing out that the Decree of Seizure did not target bunkering activities, thereby separating applicability from relevance for the purposes of establishing jurisdiction, the Joint Dissenting Opinion thus 'set a higher threshold and standard for invoking and applying Article 87 than the judgment did'.[79]

The *Enrica Lexie* was the next case that required interpretation and application of Article 87 and 92 before an Annex VII arbitral tribunal, albeit in the EEZ. By virtue of Article 58(1), the freedom of navigation also applies to the EEZ; as a result the flag State's exclusive jurisdiction with regard to navigation is also extended to the EEZ. The freedom of navigation was raised before the tribunal in relation to two separate claims.

The first was raised by Italy that India interfered with the freedom of navigation of the Italian-flagged ship in the latter's EEZ by directing interdicting, escorting and perpetrating a ruse in order to bring the Enrica Lexie into India's territorial waters. The question before the tribunal then essentially revolved around which acts constituted an interference with the freedom of navigation in breach of Article 87(1). In response the arbitral tribunal stated that:

> [A] breach of freedom of navigation may result from acts including physical or material interference with navigation of a foreign vessel, the threat or use

77 *The M/V 'Norstar' Case (Panama v Italy)* (Judgment, Joint Dis Op Cot, Pawlak, Yanai, Hoffmann, Kolodkin and Lijnzaad and Judge *ad hoc* Treves) ITLOS Reports 2019).

78 Ibid [18].

79 Haomei Li, 'Coastal State Jurisdiction in the "Norstar" Case at the ITLOS' (2020) 19 CJIL 177, 180.

> of force against a foreign vessel, or non-physical forms of interference whose effect is that of instilling fear in, or causing hindrance to, the exercise of the freedom of navigation.[80]

It is interesting to see here that the tribunal included within the scope of interference with freedom of navigation the element of 'instilling fear to the exercise of freedom of navigation'. While this element was not applied to the facts of this case and thus did not receive further attention from the tribunal, one is reminded of the argument made by Italy in *M/V Norstar* that an act falling short of enforcement action could breach Article 87 if such acts produce some 'chilling effect'.[81] While ITLOS in that case dismissed the importance of 'chilling effect',[82] the statement by the arbitral tribunal in *Enrica Lexie* seems to lend support to such an effect in the context of enforcement actions in violation of the freedom of navigation.[83]

The second claim was raised as part of India's counterclaim alleging that Italy had breached Article 87(1)(a) and Article 90 UNCLOS when the Marines fired shots at the 'St. Antony' and caused it to change course and veer away in order to avoid further gunfire. Applying the same reasoning as mentioned above, the tribunal found that by shooting at the St Antony and changing its direction, Italy as the flag State interfered with the freedom of navigation of the St Antony.

The Enrica Lexie arbitral tribunal's findings relating to a breach of the freedom of navigation did not raise so much controversy as those of *M/V Norstar*. This was primarily due to the fact that the case only concerned the potential infringement of the freedom of navigation in the context of an enforcement operation. Even then, the tribunal seemed to have adopted a broad understanding of the types of actions that could constitute a breach of the freedom of navigation.

80 *Enrica Lexie* (n 21) [472]. *M/V Saga* could have tied the claim on the use of force to freedom of navigation.
81 *The M/V 'Norstar' Case* (n 55) [223].
82 Ibid [224].
83 In *M/V Saiga (No. 2)*, ITLOS found that the use of firearms by Guinean officers before and after boarding the M/V Saiga constituted an excessive use of force in violation of general international law. *M/V Saiga (No. 2)* (n 6) [157]–[159]. As will be argued in Chapter 6, ITLOS's exercise of jurisdiction to find a violation of international law beyond the scope of UNCLOS raised some criticism. If ITLOS in that case had also adopted the reasoning that the threat to use force against a foreign vessel constituted a violation of the freedom of navigation under UNCLOS, perhaps it could have avoided having to expand its jurisdictional scope so broadly.

3.2.2 Flag State Exclusive Jurisdiction

The principle of exclusive flag State jurisdiction is well-established under the law of the sea, constituting 'an essential element in the public order of the oceans'.[84] However, what is encompassed within the scope of flag State exclusive jurisdiction has not been entirely clear. While scholarly opinions seem to lean towards a restrictive understanding of Article 92 as including only enforcement jurisdiction,[85] recent decisions have adopted a different understanding of the scope of this article.

Article 92 was examined in two cases before UNCLOS tribunals, namely *M/V Norstar* before ITLOS and *Enrica Lexie* before an Annex VII arbitral tribunal. In *M/V Norstar*, even though Article 92 was not invoked by either party, ITLOS still found it necessary to consider this article in determining whether Article 87 was breached.[86] The Tribunal established a close link between the principle of freedom of navigation and principle of flag State exclusive jurisdiction by stating that 'freedom of navigation would be illusory if a ship – a principal means for the exercise of the freedom of navigation – could be subject to the jurisdiction of other States on the high seas'.[87] The close link between the two principles, coupled with the ITLOS's expansive understanding of the scope of freedom of navigation under Article 87(1), not surprisingly also resulted in a broad understanding of the scope of flag State exclusive jurisdiction under Article 92. In fact, ITLOS explicitly held that:

> this principle prohibits not only the exercise of enforcement jurisdiction on the high seas by States other than the flag State but also the extension of their prescriptive jurisdiction to lawful activities conducted by foreign ships on the high seas.[88]

This bold statement was perhaps the most controversial point of *M/V Norstar* and has thus attracted much criticism. In their Joint Dissenting Opinion, the seven judges strongly rejected such an expansive understanding of the scope of flag State exclusive jurisdiction on the basis that 'nothing in the text of the Convention, in its *travaux préparatoires*, in other international treaties, in customary international law, or in the practice of States suggests that article

[84] Vasco Becker-Weinberg, 'The Interpretation and Application of the Freedom of Navigation and Flag State Jurisdiction in the M/V "Norstar" and the M/T "San Padre Pio" Cases' (2021) 9 Korean Journal of International and Comparative Law 108, 115.

[85] Douglas Guilfoyle, 'Article 92' in Proelss (n 20), Rayfuse (n 28).

[86] *The M/V 'Norstar' Case* (n 55) [218].

[87] Ibid [216].

[88] Ibid [225].

87 and its corollary article 92 altogether excludes the right of non-flag States to exercise their prescriptive criminal jurisdiction with respect to activities on the high seas'.[89] The judges were instead of the view that exclusive flag state jurisdiction within the meaning of Article 92 referred only to exclusive enforcement jurisdiction. As a result, 'a State may extend its prescriptive criminal jurisdiction to conduct beyond its territory when a constituent element of an alleged crime has occurred in its territory or where there is a sufficient connection to it'.[90]

What is perhaps most striking about the *M/V Norstar* judgment is the absence of any reasoning to explain how the conclusions were reached. The failure to provide some sort of justification is even more remarkable given the controversial nature of the Tribunal's findings, something the Tribunal must have foreseen given the number of dissenting judges. ITLOS neither engaged with the interpretation of the wording of Article 92, nor did it pay attention to the context in which this article finds itself within UNCLOS. As argued by Ringbom, while UNCLOS *does* provide for non-flag State exceptional enforcement in specific cases, '[n]o corresponding express exceptions exist with respect to prescription. Every express exception from exclusive flag State jurisdiction in [UNCLOS], in other words, relates only to enforcement.'[91] The extension of flag State exclusive jurisdiction to include prescriptive jurisdiction hardly finds support in this context. Similarly, ITLOS in this case made no reference to the negotiating history of the relevant provisions nor did it acknowledge and engage with state practice which allows for the exercise of non-flag State exclusive jurisdiction, including States' extraterritorial jurisdiction over their nationals on board a foreign ship on the high seas,[92] or extraterritorial port state measures in regards of fishing or shipping.[93]

The only basis provided by ITLOS for extending flag State exclusive jurisdiction to including prescriptive jurisdiction was reference to the Permanent Court of International Justice (PCIJ) S.S. *Lotus* case. However, the reliance on S.S. *Lotus* was misplaced for several reasons. First, S.S. *Lotus*

[89] Joint Dissenting Opinion of Judges Cot, Pawlak, Yanai, Hoffmann, Kolodkin and Lijnzaad and Judge ad hoc Treves (n 77) [19].

[90] Ibid [31].

[91] Henrik Ringbom, 'Ships in ABNJ – Broadening Jurisdictional Opportunities for Non-flag States' in Vito De Lucia, Alex Oude Elferink, and Lan Ngoc Nguyen (eds), *International Law and Marine Areas beyond National Jurisdiction* (Brill 2022) 322.

[92] Becker-Weinberg (n 84) 115.

[93] Judith Swan, 'Port State Measures – from Residual Port State Jurisdiction to Global Standards' (2016) 31 IJMCL 395; Sophia Kopela, 'Port-state Jurisdiction, Extraterritoriality and the Protection of Global Commons' (2016) 47 Ocean Development and International Law 89.

revolved around enforcement jurisdiction as the PCIJ was asked to examine the prosecution of a French national by Turkey, the prescriptive jurisdiction was not an issue.[94] It is also worth mentioning in this connection that in *M/V Norstar*, the Decree of Seizure should be considered an enforcement act,[95] not an prescriptive act as its main content was to order the vessel as well as the oil produce transported therein to be seized as corpus delicti in an ongoing criminal investigation. It would seem, therefore, that ITLOS did not even have to go so far as to pronounce on prescriptive jurisdiction in this case. Second, ITLOS only cited the parts of the S.S. *Lotus* judgment that supported its position, namely its statement that '[i]n virtue of the principle of the freedom of the sea, that is to say, the absence of any territorial sovereignty upon the high seas, no State may exercise any kind of jurisdiction over foreign vessels upon them'.[96] It did not mention that the PCIJ in S.S *Lotus* also held that 'it by no means follows that a State can never in its own territory exercise jurisdiction over acts which have occurred on board a foreign ship on the high seas'.[97] Since this statement contradicts the conclusion reached by the majority, the fact that the judgment failed account for and engage with it was highly unfortunate. Third, as has been pointed out by the Joint Dissenting Opinion, the PCIJ in S.S. *Lotus* in fact allows States to exercise prescriptive jurisdiction on the high seas unless there is a prohibitive rule against such exercise, which in this case did not exist.[98]

In *Enrica Lexie*, Italy specifically alleged a violation of Article 92 and the parties had disagreements regarding the application this article. Italy claimed that Article 92 concerned both the vessel and its crew,[99] an argument which seemed to have been based on the 'ship as a unit' doctrine mentioned above. India, by contrast, argued that Article 92 concerned only the vessel, not the crew, and India did not exercise any jurisdiction over the vessel in the EEZ,[100] as the target of its action was the marines on board. In any case, it did not exercise any jurisdiction over the Enrica Lexie either through physical interference or indirect means. The arbitral tribunal eventually sided with

94 Cameron Miles, 'The M/V "Norstar" Case (*Panama v Italy*)' (2020) 114 American Journal of International Law 116, 121.

95 See: *The M/V 'Norstar' Case (Panama v Italy)* (Judgment, Joint Sep Op Wolfrum and Attard) ITLOS Reports 2019 [31].

96 *The M/V 'Norstar' Case* (n 55) [216].

97 *S.S. 'Lotus' (France v Turkey)* (Judgment) PCIJ Series A, No. 10 [25].

98 Joint Dissenting Opinion of Judges Cot, Pawlak, Yanai, Hoffmann, Kolodkin and Lijnzaad and Judge ad hoc Treves (n 77) [36]. See also: Li (n 79) 181.

99 *Enrica Lexie* (n 21) [509].

100 Ibid [512].

India due to the lack of convincing evidence to support Italy's claims. The tribunal thus did not address the arguments put forward by the parties as mentioned-above.

Notwithstanding the fact that the tribunal in *Enrica Lexie* only had to deal with enforcement jurisdiction and that it had disposed of the dispute regarding Article 92 based on evidentiary grounds, the arbitral tribunal still felt the need to recall and reiterate the *M/V Norstar* finding that the principle of exclusive flag State jurisdiction extends to prescriptive jurisdiction.[101] Such an endorsement of exclusive prescriptive jurisdiction is striking in at least two respects.

First, strictly speaking, such a statement was not necessary for the purposes of deciding the case. One wonders whether this *obiter dictum* could be seen as a show of support for ITLOS amidst the criticism that it had received in the aftermath of *M/V Norstar*.[102] In any case, the tribunal did not provide any reasoning or explanation to support the extension of flag State exclusive jurisdiction to include prescriptive jurisdiction.

Second, by reaffirming flag State exclusive prescriptive jurisdiction, the tribunal seems to have contradicted itself. Earlier in the award, the tribunal had found that the subjective territoriality principle and objective territoriality principle were both applicable in the context of vessels, meaning that 'where an offence was commenced on board one vessel and completed on board another vessel, the flag States of both vessels may have concurrent jurisdiction over the offence'.[103] This meant that as the alleged offence was commenced on board the Italian vessel, the Enrica Lexie, and completed on board the Indian vessel, the St. Antony, both Italy and India were entitled to exercise jurisdiction over the incident.[104] These statements suggested that the tribunal recognised that jurisdiction over a vessel may be concurrent and not exclusive. In light of its conflicting statements, the *Enrica Lexie* tribunal's interpretation of Article 92 might have caused more confusion rather than adding clarity to the interpretation of the principle of exclusive flag State jurisdiction.[105]

[101] Ibid [527].

[102] In its submission, India also dismissed Italy's reliance on *M/V Norstar*, pointing out that its finding on prescriptive jurisdiction 'has been highly controversial as evident from the dissents of seven ITLOS judges'. Ibid [336].

[103] Ibid [366].

[104] Ibid [357].

[105] Arron N Honniball, 'The "Enrica Lexie" Incident Award and Exclusive Flag State Jurisdiction' (*CIL*, 2020) https://cil.nus.edu.sg/the-enrica-lexie-incident-award-and-exclusive-flag-state-jurisdiction-by-arron-n-honniball/ accessed 25 January 2022; James G Devaney and Christian J Tams, 'In Re Arbitration between the Italian Republic and the Republic of India Concerning the "Enrica Lexie" Incident' (2021) 115 AJIL 513.

In short, UNCLOS tribunals have clarified activities that fall within the scope of freedom of navigation under Article 87(1) and, to a certain extent, the spatial limits of the freedom. However, the tribunals' decisions regarding a breach of the freedom of navigation and scope of flag State exclusive jurisdiction under Article 92 have been much less convincing and thus have not managed to provide the needed clarity.

3.3 FLAG STATES' DUTIES UNDER UNCLOS

The duties of flag States are set out in Article 94 UNCLOS. The gist of the article is spelled out in paragraph (1) which requires flag States to 'effectively exercise its jurisdiction and control in administrative, technical and social matters over ships flying its flag'. The list of duties and measures that flag States are required to take contained in paragraphs (3) and (4) of Article 94 extends to a variety of different issues. These measures must, in accordance with paragraph (5), 'conform to generally accepted international regulations, procedures and practices'. UNCLOS tribunals have had the opportunity to examine Article 94 and other related articles when dealing with two aspects of flag States' obligations. They include: flag States' duties to ensure safety at sea in *South China Sea* and flag States' obligation with regard to the conservation of marine living resources in the EEZ in the *Advisory Opinion on IUU Fishing*. Each of these obligations is examined below in order to assess the contribution of UNCLOS tribunals to the development of flag States' obligations under UNCLOS.

3.3.1 *Duty to Ensure Safety at Sea and the Role of the Rule of Reference*

Article 94(3) imposes on flag States an obligation to 'ensure safety at sea' and, to that end, to take measures as specified in paragraphs (3) and (4). Paragraph (5) in turn requires that these measures conform to 'generally accepted international regulations, procedures and practices'. Paragraph (5) thus introduces what is commonly referred to as the 'rule of reference' in relation to safety at sea. UNCLOS does not use the term 'rule of reference'. It is but an umbrella term referring to instances in which UNCLOS provisions incorporates rules, standards and practices which exist in other sources of law into the Convention.[106] By using the term 'conform to', the rule of reference employed

[106] Judge Paik in his Separate Opinion to the *Advisory Opinion on IUU Fishing* explained the rule of reference as follows: UNCLOS 'first formulates a general duty, and then refers to and incorporates those rules or standards developed in other legal instruments into its ambit' and these rules and standards will 'give specific content to the general duty enunciated by the

in Article 94(5) creates an obligation for flag States that are parties to UNCLOS to implement external regulations, procedures and practices, which may otherwise not be binding on the flag State in the first place. As such, the rule of reference has a powerful impact on the scope of flag States' obligations under Article 94. The external regulations may, however, only become binding on flag States if they meet the threshold of being 'generally accepted', for which no definition or interpretative guidance can be found under UNCLOS. According to the International Law Association, the term 'generally accepted' was 'intentionally kept vague in order not to upset the delicate balance which the notion incorporates'.[107]

South China Sea remains the only case to date in which an international tribunal examined the threshold for 'generally accepted international regulations, procedures and practices' as contained in Article 94(5). In this case, the Philippines argued that by operating its law enforcement vessels in a dangerous manner, causing risk of collision to Philippine vessels, China had violated its obligations relating to safe navigation under Article 94 UNCLOS as well as the Convention on the International Regulations for Preventing Collisions at Sea (COLREGS). The Philippines pointed out that the International Maritime Organization (IMO) had recognised COLREGS as fulfilling the requirement of Article 94(5) 'on account of their worldwide acceptance'.[108] The tribunal agreed with the Philippines and held that 'with 156 contracting parties representing more than 98 percent of world tonnage, the COLREGS comprise one of the most widely adopted multilateral conventions in force'.[109] On that basis, the tribunal concluded that although the Philippines was not bound by COLREGS at the time of the incident in question 'the COLREGS to bind both Parties relating to the conduct of their respective vessels by virtue of Article 94 of the Convention'.[110] It also spelled out the consequences of a rule of reference, stating that 'a violation of the COLREGS, as "generally accepted international regulations" concerning measures necessary to ensure maritime safety, constitutes a violation of the Convention itself'.[111]

Convention'. *Request for Advisory Opinion submitted by the Sub-Regional Fisheries Commission* (Advisory Opinion, Sep Op Paik) ITLOS Reports 2015, 4 [23]. [Advisory Opinion on IUU Fishing]

107 International Law Association, Committee on Coastal State Jurisdiction relating to Marine Pollution, 2000 Final Report, 38.

108 *The South China Sea Arbitration between the Republic of the Philippines and the People's Republic of China (Philippines v China)* (2016) RIAA XXXIII 153 [1063].

109 Ibid [1081].

110 Ibid [1082].

111 Ibid [1083].

The tribunal's examination of Article 94(5) sheds light on several aspects of the rule of reference and its application to flag States' duties. First, it provides some guidance as to what constitutes 'generally accepted internationally regulations'. Two considerations would need to be taken into account: the number of States that are parties to the instrument containing the regulation and whether this number includes States taking part in implementing the rules and standards in question. The arbitral tribunal thus confirmed the quantitative and functional majority approach in determining the threshold for 'generally accepted international rules and regulations', which was in line with that adopted earlier by the International Law Commission.[112]

Second, the tribunal also confirmed two important effects of the rule of reference. By stating that the Philippines was bound by COLREGS even at the time when it had not become a party to this convention, the tribunal confirmed that the legal effect of the rule of reference on UNCLOS parties. In particular, it renders external rules binding on State parties regardless of whether they have agreed to these rules independently of UNCLOS. Further, by proceeding to interpret and apply COLREGS in order to make a decision on the Philippines' submission under UNCLOS, the tribunal made clear that the rule of reference has the effect of bringing other international treaties or nonbinding instruments within the scope of an UNCLOS tribunal's jurisdiction.

In sum, the tribunal in *South China Sea* contributed to confirming that, by virtue of the rule of reference, the measures to be taken by flag States to ensure safety of navigation under Article 94 safety may include those which are found international instruments other than UNCLOS itself. As the first international decision to discuss the rule of reference, the case also lent an authoritative voice to clarifying the threshold of 'generally accepted rules and standards', which holds the key to the application of the rule of reference. As such, the tribunal provided important guidance for the operationalisation of this rule in other contexts beyond safety of navigation.[113]

[112] See: Lan Ngoc Nguyen, 'Expanding the Regulatory Scope of LOSC for Environmental Issues through the Rule of Reference: Potentials and Limits' (2021) 52(4) Ocean Development & International Law 419–444

[113] The rule of reference can be found in provisions relating to shipping, navigation and most abundantly in protection of the marine environment under Part XII UNCLOS relating to the protection and preservation of the marine environment.

3.3.2 *Flag States' Duty to Conserve Marine Living Resources in the EEZ of Another State*

Illegal, unregulated and unreported (IUU) fishing is one of the greatest threats to the sustainable management of living resources worldwide. As IUU fishing is facilitated by the exploitation of flags of convenience as well as flag States' unwillingness to exercise control over their vessels engaged in fishing activities,[114] strengthening the duties of flag States in monitoring and controlling their fishing vessels is of paramount importance in combatting IUU fishing. However, even though the bulk of global IUU fishing takes place in the EEZ of coastal States,[115] UNCLOS itself is silent on flag State obligations with regards to fishing vessels operating in the EEZ of another State. Article 94 lists the 'duties of the flag State', which, by virtue of Article 58(2), are also applicable to the EEZ. However, Article 94 only provides for flag States' jurisdiction over a limited number of matters, namely 'administrative, technical and social matters'. The question that arises is then, in absence of an explicit provision to that effect, do flag States have an obligation over fishing activities conducted by their vessels in the EEZ of another State under UNCLOS?[116] This question was addressed for the first time and in detail by ITLOS in the *Advisory Opinion on IUU Fishing*,[117] and its approach was subsequently followed by the arbitral tribunal in *South China Sea*. This section discusses the two tribunals' examination of flag States' obligations over their fishing vessels in the EEZ of another State, focusing in particular on the

[114] There is no one single definition of 'flag of convenience'. But 'flag of convenience' has been used to refer to flag of States with 'open registries' which place minimal or no restrictions on the kind of ship that may fly their flag. It is estimated that large-scale, industrialised flag of convenience fishing fleet makes up half of the world's fishing capacity. See Judith Swan, 'Fishing Vessels Operating under Open Registers and the Exercise of Flag State Responsibilities: Information and Options 2', FAO, Fisheries Circular No. 980, 2002; Jessica K Ferrell, 'Controlling Flags of Convenience: One Measure to Stop Overfishing of Collapsing Fish Stocks' (2005) 35 Envtl L 323; DF Matland, 'Re-evaluating the Status of Flags of Convenience Under International Law' (1990–1991) 23 Vanderbilt Journal of Transnational Law 1017.

[115] Valentin J. Schatz, 'Combating Illegal Fishing in the Exclusive Economic Zone – Flag State Obligations in the Context of the Primary Responsibility of the Coastal State' (2016) 7(2) Goettingen Journal of International Law 383, 386.

[116] D'Andrea, for example, contends that under UNCLOS flag States' obligations in the EEZ do not extend to fisheries activities. See Ariella D'Andrea, 'The "Genuine Link" Concept in Responsible Fisheries: Legal Aspects and Recent Developments' (2006) FAO Legal Papers Online No. 6 www.fao.org/3/a-bb094e.pdf accessed 25 January 2022.

[117] *Request for Advisory Opinion submitted by the Sub-Regional Fisheries Commission* (Advisory Opinion, 2 April 2015) ITLOS Reports 2015, 4. [Advisory Opinion on IUU Fishing]

Advisory Opinion on IUU Fishing in order to determine to what extent they have contributed to clarifying this issue.

3.3.2.1 Flag State's Obligations Regarding IUU Fishing Activities in UNCLOS Tribunals' Decisions

The request for the *Advisory Opinion on IUU Fishing* was brought by the Sub-Regional Fisheries Commission (SRFC) on the basis of the Convention on the Determination of the Minimal Conditions for Access and Exploitation of Marine Resources within the Maritime Areas under Jurisdiction of the Member States of the SRFC (MCA Convention). The reason behind the request was the difficulties that SRFC Member States had encountered in securing the cooperation of flag States when the latter's vessels, which were involved in IUU fishing, escaped the former's control. The SFRC thus sought a clarification on the nature and content of flag States' obligation under Article 94, and on whether a flag State could be held responsible for illegal fishing activities committed by a vessel flying its flag.[118] At the outset, ITLOS acknowledged that the issue of flag State responsibility for IUU fishing activities was not directly addressed in UNCLOS. Yet, it stated that the framework within which this question was to be examined was provided by the Convention. This framework consisted of two layers of obligations: first, general obligations concerning the conservation and management of marine living resources in Articles 91, 92, 94 as well as Articles 192 and 193; and second, specific obligations of the flag State in the EEZ of the coastal State.[119]

With regard to the general obligations, Article 91 provides for the nationality of ships, Article 92 confirms the exclusive jurisdiction of flag State and Article 94(2) specifies the matters over which the flag State effectively exercises its jurisdiction. Even though none of these articles mention fishing activities, ITLOS interpreted the words 'in particular' contained in Article 94(2) to mean that 'the list of measures that are to be taken by the flag State to ensure effective exercise of its jurisdiction and control over ships flying its flag in is only indicative, not exhaustive'.[120] As a result, ITLOS held that the flag State, in fulfilment of its responsibility to exercise effective jurisdiction and control in administrative matters:

[118] Written Statement of SFRC, 12 www.itlos.org/fileadmin/itlos/documents/cases/case_no.21/written_statements_round1/C21_19_CSRP_orig_Eng_rev.pdf accessed 25 January 2022.

[119] *Advisory Opinion on IUU Fishing* (n 117) [109].

[120] Ibid [117].

> must adopt the necessary administrative measures to ensure that fishing vessels flying its flag are not involved in activities which will undermine the flag State's responsibilities under the Convention in respect of the conservation and management of marine living resources.[121]

ITLOS thus used the term 'administrative measures' as an anchor to read flag States' obligations relating to conservation of marine living resources into Article 94(2)(b). ITLOS further supported its findings on flag State jurisdiction by invoking Article 192 that provides for an obligation on all States to protect and preserve the marine environment.[122] Recalling the statement made in the *Southern Bluefin Tuna* Order that 'the conservation of living resources of the sea was an element in the protection and preservation of the marine environment',[123] ITLOS held that flag States were under an obligation to ensure compliance by vessels flying their flags with the relevant conservation measures concerning living resources enacted by the coastal State for its EEZ.[124] Finally, turning to specific obligations of flag States in the EEZ, ITLOS held that Article 58(3) together with Article 62(4) suggested that flag States were obliged to take necessary measures to ensure that their nationals and vessels flying their flags do not engage in IUU fishing activities.[125]

Based on an examination of flag States' general and specific obligations under UNCLOS, ITLOS concluded that flag States had an 'obligation to ensure' that vessels flying their flag do not conduct IUU fishing activities within the EEZ of the SRFC Member States.[126] This was not the first time the 'obligation to ensure' appeared in ITLOS's case law. The Seabed Disputes Chamber (SDC) had already expounded on the meaning and nature of this obligation in the *Advisory Opinion on Activities in the Area.*[127] It held that this 'obligation to ensure' was an obligation of due diligence and an obligation of conduct.[128] Recalling *Pulp Mills*, the SDC held that the connection between the obligation of due diligence and obligation of conduct meant that the

[121] Ibid [119].

[122] Ibid [120].

[123] *Southern Bluefin Tuna (New Zealand v Japan; Australia v Japan)* (Provisional Measures, Order of 27 August 1999) ITLOS Reports 1999, 280 [70] [Southern Bluefin Tuna Order].

[124] *Advisory Opinion on IUU Fishing* (n 117) [120].

[125] Ibid [124]. Article 58(3) requires other States operating in the EEZ of the coastal State to have due regard to the latter's rights and duties, and Article 62(4) stipulates that 'Nationals of other States fishing in the [EEZ] shall comply with the conservation measures and with the other terms and conditions established in the law and regulations of the coastal State'.

[126] *Advisory Opinion on IUU Fishing* (n 117) [120].

[127] *Responsibilities and obligations of States with respect to Activities in the Area* (Advisory Opinion, 1 February 2011) ITLOS Reports 2011, 10 [110].

[128] Ibid [110].

sponsoring State was not obliged to achieve, in each and every case, the result that the sponsored contractor complies with the obligations. Rather, it was an obligation to deploy adequate means, to exercise best possible efforts, to do the utmost, to obtain this result.[129] In terms of what the 'obligation to ensure' entailed, the SDC, again echoing *Pulp Mills*, stated that it was not possible to describe the content of 'due diligence' in precise terms, as the standard of due diligence varied over time and depended on the level of risk and on the activities involved.[130] At the minimum, ITLOS stated that sponsoring States were under the obligation to take measures within their legal system, which must consist of laws and regulations and administrative measures. The applicable standard was that the measures must be 'reasonably appropriate'.[131] Adopting the approach of that Advisory Opinion, ITLOS also interpreted the flag State's 'obligation to ensure' as an obligation of due diligence and an obligation of conduct. This meant that, '[t]he flag State is under the "due diligence obligation" to take all necessary measures to ensure compliance and to prevent IUU fishing by fishing vessels flying its flag.[132]

With regards to the measures to be taken by the flag States to ensure compliance with the due diligence, ITLOS noted that, 'the Convention is the key instrument which provides guidance regarding the content of the measures that need to be taken by the flag State'.[133] On that basis, ITLOS specified that flag States had wide-ranging obligations, including the obligation to take necessary measures to ensure compliance by vessels flying their flags with the laws and regulations adopted by the SRFC Member States;[134] to adopt the necessary measures prohibiting their vessels from fishing in the EEZs of the SRFC Member States, unless so authorised by the SRFC Member States;[135] to take the necessary measures to ensure that vessels flying their flag comply with the protection and preservation measures adopted by the SRFC Member States;[136] to exercise effectively their jurisdiction and control in administrative matters over fishing vessels flying its flag, by ensuring, in particular, that such vessels are properly

[129] Ibid.
[130] Ibid [117].
[131] Ibid [242].
[132] *Advisory Opinion on IUU Fishing* (n 117) [129].
[133] Ibid [133].
[134] Ibid [134].
[135] Ibid [135].
[136] Ibid [136].

marked;[137] and to include enforcement mechanisms to monitor and secure compliance with these laws and regulations.

Subsequent to the *Advisory Opinion on IUU Fishing*, the arbitral tribunal in *South China Sea* was the first to apply the flag State's due diligence obligation as elaborated by ITLOS in a contentious proceeding. It held that the flag State – in this case China – had failed to exercise due diligence to prevent fishing by Chinese flagged vessels at Mischief Reef and Second Thomas Shoal. While acknowledging the difficulties that flag States face to effectively exercise due diligence over their vessels, since 'unlawful fishing will be carried out covertly, far from any official presence',[138] the tribunal found that China had in fact escorted, organised and coordinated the fishing activities.[139] Based primarily on China's failure to take steps to enforce its rules and to take measures against fishermen engaged in unlawful activities, the tribunal found that China violated the flag State's due diligence under Articles 192 and 194(5).[140]

3.3.2.2 Appraisal of the Advisory Opinion on IUU Fishing

UNCLOS establishes a framework to regulate flag State jurisdiction that does not sufficiently address all issues, including flag State obligation with regards to the conservation of marine living resources in the EEZ of another State. ITLOS itself admitted as much.[141] As the first international tribunal to address this issue, ITLOS in the *Advisory Opinion on IUU Fishing* made some important contributions to clarifying the legal basis for as well as the contours of flag States' obligations concerning illegal fishing activities.

First, ITLOS made clear that although the primary obligation to prevent IUU fishing rested with coastal States, this did not relieve flag States from the obligation to exercise due diligence over their fishing vessels. Coastal States and flag States have concurrent obligations to prevent illegal fishing in the EEZ.

Second, even though ITLOS has been criticised for not going far enough in clarifying the measures that must be taken to satisfy the due diligence obligation,[142] a closer look at the Advisory Opinion shows that ITLOS *did* in fact

[137] Ibid [137].
[138] *South China Sea Arbitration* (n 108) [754].
[139] Ibid [755].
[140] See Chapter 5, section 5.1.2.
[141] *Advisory Opinion on IUU Fishing* (n 117) [110].
[142] *Request for Advisory Opinion submitted by the Sub-Regional Fisheries Commission* (Advisory Opinion, Sep Op Paik) ITLOS Reports 2015, 4 [25]. See also Victor Alencar Mayer Feitosa

specify specified the content of this obligation and identified concrete measures to be taken in order to satisfy the due diligence obligation.[143] The measures identified provide a minimum standard and a yardstick to assess whether the due diligence obligation has been met. This is especially important given the fact that, in contrast to other areas such as marine pollution and sea safety, there are no globally agreed minimum standards of flag State responsibilities in the fishing sector.[144] What is clear is that flag States now bear the burden of proof to show that they have taken the measures specified in the Advisory Opinion in order to discharge of their obligation to ensure over their fishing vessels. Whether or not a flag State can be considered to have satisfactorily implemented the measures specified would have to be assessed on a case-by-case basis taking into account the particular circumstances of the case. In the context of an advisory proceeding, it would have been impossible for ITLOS to go into much more detail.

Third, even though ITLOS attempted to limit its answer to a specific group of flag States, that is, States whose vessels were fishing in the EEZ of the SRFC Member States, there was no such spatial limit in the eventual answer that it provided. ITLOS based its interpretation of the 'obligations to ensure' entirely on UNCLOS provisions, thus there is nothing in the Advisory Opinion that restricts the 'obligation to ensure' to flag States operating the waters of SRFC State Members. This means that the Advisory Opinion could have a much more general application than ITLOS made out to be; indeed it could be applicable to any other flag State whose vessels are engaged in fishing activities in any other States' EEZ.[145] What is more, as Articles 94 and 192 are applicable to all maritime zones, flag States would also have to exercise due diligence with regard to fisheries in the high seas. The extension of flag States obligations to areas beyond the EEZ based on the Advisory Opinion may raise

Ventura, 'Tackling Illegal, Unregulated and Unreported Fishing: The ITLOS Advisory Opinion on Flag State Responsibility for IUU Fishing and the Principle of Due Diligence' (2015) 12 Brazilian Journal of International Law 50, 62.

143 *Advisory Opinion on IUU Fishing* (n 117) [134]–[140].

144 Tamo Zwinge, 'Duties of Flag States to Implement and Enforce International Standards and Regulations – And Measures to Counter Their Failure to Do So' (2011) 10(2) Journal of International Business Law 297, 306.

145 Michael A Becker, 'Request for an Advisory Opinion Submitted by the Sub-Regional Fisheries Commission (SRFC)' (2015) 109(4) AJIL 851, 856; Tom Ruys and Anemoon Soete, 'Creeping' Advisory Jurisdiction of International Courts and Tribunals? The Case of the International Tribunal for the Law of the Sea' (2016) 29(1) LJIL 155, 174; Solène Guggisberg, *The Use of CITES for Commercially-exploited Fish Species: A Solution to Overexploitation and Illegal, Unreported and Unregulated Fishing?* (Springer 2015) 173.

problems from a jurisdictional point of view.[146] However, it cannot be denied that the Advisory Opinion may have a spillover effect and contributes to strengthening flag States' obligations relating to conservation of livings resources in the high seas.[147]

Finally, it is worth recalling that in earlier prompt release cases, ITLOS only paid scant attention to both coastal States' and flag States' obligations to conserve marine living resources in the EEZ in determining a reasonable bond. More specifically, ITLOS hardly recognised the deterrent purposes of a high bond as a sanction for illegal fishing.[148] In this Advisory Opinion, however, ITLOS held that 'sanctions applicable to involvement in IUU fishing activities must be sufficient to deter violations and to deprive offenders of the benefits accruing from their IUU fishing activities'.[149] The Advisory Opinion shows a welcome development in ITLOS case law and it is arguably much more in line with the broader emphasis that UNCLOS places on all States to protect the marine environment, including conserving marine living resources. The conclusion in the Advisory Opinion may well have a significant impact on the balancing exercise as well as the consideration of reasonableness in future prompt release cases.

Notwithstanding the importance of ITLOS's findings in strengthening the UNCLOS legal framework for combatting IUU fishing, a close examination of the Advisory Opinion reveals significant shortcomings in the Tribunal's reasoning process and interpretative method adopted.

First, throughout the Advisory Opinion, ITLOS provided little explanation or reasoning to support its interpretation of relevant UNCLOS provisions. For example, while the list of measures to be taken by flag States in Article 94(1) may not be exhaustive, the Tribunal did not explain how the term 'administrative measures' could be expanded to include flag States' responsibilities in respect of conservation and management of marine living resources. The wording of this paragraph specifically stipulates jurisdiction 'in respect of administrative, technical and social matters concerning the ship'. As this provision only refers to administrative matters concerning *the ship* itself, it is

[146] See Section 6.1.2.

[147] See Budislav Vukas and Davor Vidas, 'Flags of Convenience and High Seas Fishing: The Emergence of a Legal Framework' in Olav Schram Stokke (ed), *Governing High Seas Fisheries: The Interplay of Global and Regional Regimes* (OUP 2001) 56; Ellen Hey, 'The Fisheries Provisions of the LOS Convention' in Ellen Hey (ed), *Developments in International Fisheries Law* (Kluwer Law International 1999) 35.

[148] See Section 2.1.1.3.

[149] *Advisory Opinion on IUU Fishing* (n 117) [138].

not entirely clear on what basis it could be extended to fishing activities.[150] Similarly, ITLOS merely recited the wording of Articles 58(3) and 62(4) UNCLOS without providing any actual analysis. The Tribunal's interpretation of these two articles as providing the basis for flag States' obligations concerning fishing activities has in fact been subjected to scholarly criticism.[151]

Second, in clarifying the scope of flag State obligation over its vessels, ITLOS relied solely on the wording of UNCLOS provisions. It did not resort to any other means of treaty interpretation as stipulated under Article 31 VCLT.[152] More importantly, even though ITLOS insisted that the provisions of UNCLOS provided the basis for different flag State obligations as enumerated in the Advisory Opinion, it is difficult to see how this was the case for all these obligations. For instance, ITLOS held that flag States had the obligation to include enforcement mechanisms to monitor and secure compliance with the coastal State's laws and regulations, including the imposition of sanctions. However, nowhere in Articles 58(3), 62(4), 192 or 193 of UNCLOS can one find any reference to or indication of enforcement mechanisms or sanctions. The requirement to put in place such mechanisms is instead found under Article 19(2) of the 1995 Agreement for the Implementation of the Provisions of the Convention relating to the Conservation and Management of Straddling Fish Stocks and Highly Migratory Fish Stocks (UN Fish Stocks Agreement or 'UNFSA').[153] Similarly, the obligation to ensure that vessels are properly marked finds no basis under UNCLOS, but rather under Article 18(3)(d) UNFSA. Therefore, ITLOS's statement that UNCLOS provided the framework for flag State obligations did not hold true.

The law on fisheries and specifically the rules on coastal States and flag States obligations with regards to fishing vessels in both the EEZ and the high seas have been developed to a large extent by post-UNCLOS instruments. In order to tackle the issue of ineffective flag State control over fishing vessels,

[150] Note that the Virginia Commentary seems to have adopted a broad understanding of Article 94(2)(b) to include 'not so much matters concerning "the ship" as concerning the activities of the ship, or more accurately, the person on board'. Myron H Nordquist (ed), *United Nations Convention on the Law of the Sea 1982: A Commentary*, Vol III (Martinus Nijhoff 1985) 146. [Virginia Commentary, vol III].

[151] For criticism regarding ITLOS's reliance on Articles 58(3) and 62(4), see, for example, Schatz (n 115) 399.

[152] Vienna Convention on the Law of Treaties, 1155 UNTS 331 (23 May 1969).

[153] The United Nations Agreement for the Implementation of the Provisions of the United Nations Convention on the Law of the Sea of 10 December 1982 relating to the Conservation and Management of Straddling Fish Stocks and Highly Migratory Fish Stocks, 2167 UNTS 3 (4 August 1995).

several fisheries instruments have been put in place, including the Agreement to Promote Compliance with International Conservation and Management Measures by Fishing Vessels on the High Seas (the Compliance Agreement),[154] the UNFSA, and a series of soft law instruments developed under the auspices of the FAO, most importantly the FAO International Plan of Action to Prevent, Deter and Eliminate Illegal, Unreported and Unregulated Fishing.[155] Instead of feigning that it was relying solely on UNCLOS to answer the advisory request, ITLOS should have acknowledged the existence and relevance of fisheries agreements, and provided some explanation as to whether and how these agreements could be relevant to the interpretation of the 'obligation to ensure' under UNCLOS.

Judge Paik, in his Separate Opinion, proposed the use of 'the rule of reference' in order to take into account the UNFSA as well as other bilateral fisheries agreements in the interpretation of flag States' obligations under UNCLOS. As this rule was already employed in the Convention, particularly in Part XII of UNCLOS and in Article 94(5) in regard to the exercise of flag State duties to ensure safety at sea,[156] Judge Paik was of the view that the rule of reference can be employed to 'give effective content to the general yet rather vague obligations of the flag State in respect of IUU fishing',[157] and 'to impose legal obligations on a State to apply certain rules and standards which it would otherwise not have been legally bound to apply'.[158] Judge Paik's proposal has merits to the extent that, unlike the Advisory Opinion which failed to take note of other fisheries agreements, it provided the basis for the incorporation of the rules contained in non-UNCLOS instruments to clarify the content of the obligations imposed on flag States under UNCLOS. Having said that, extending the 'rule of the reference' to fisheries issues is not without problem. UNCLOS provides for the rule of reference in only specific cases. Although the rules, standards and procedures to which the relevant UNCLOS provisions make reference may not always be explicitly specified in the Convention, States parties to UNCLOS have given their consent to incorporate these rules into the Convention and thus implicitly

[154] Agreement to Promote Compliance with International Conservation and Management Measures by Fishing Vessels on the High Seas (24 November 1993) 2221 UNTS 91.

[155] FAO, Code of Conduct for Responsible Fisheries (31 October 1995); FAO, International Plan of Action to Prevent, Deter and Eliminate Illegal, Unreported and Unregulated Fishing (23 June 2001). [FAO IPOA-IUU]; FAO, Agreement on Port State Measures to Prevent, Deter and Eliminate Illegal, Unreported and Unregulated Fishing (22 November 2009).

[156] *Advisory Opinion on IUU Fishing*, Separate Opinion of Judge Paik (n 106) [24].

[157] Ibid.

[158] Ibid.

agreed to be bound by them. Thus the fact that the Convention does not include the rule of reference in the field of fisheries means that the use of analogy to extend the rule of reference to flag State obligations over IUU fishing may go against the drafters' intention. Such an extension also potentially upsets the carefully negotiated balance between coastal States' and flag States' rights and obligations in the EEZ.

Instead, ITLOS could have considered the use of Article 293(1) on Applicable Law or had recourse to post-UNCLOS fisheries instruments on the basis of Article 31(3) of the Vienna Convention on the Law of Treaties (VCLT) to shed light on flag States' obligations under UNCLOS.[159] The question then becomes whether the UNFSA, the Compliance Agreement and other nonbinding soft law fisheries instruments as mentioned above qualify as subsequent agreements for the purposes of interpreting UNCLOS? Article III, the core of the Compliance Agreement, specifies that flag States are responsible for vessels flying their flags, and no authorisation shall be given unless the flag State is able to exercise effective responsibilities.[160] The UNFSA, as an implementing agreement of UNCLOS, elaborates on the fundamental obligations specified under UNCLOS to conserve and manage straddling stocks and highly migratory species by providing at great length the duties of the flag State and by making more stringent the obligation of flag States to exercise control over their fishing vessels in the high seas. Admittedly, the obligations imposed on flag States whose vessels are fishing in the high seas cannot be automatically transferred and imposed on flag States whose vessels are fishing in the EEZ, due to the concurrent coastal States' sovereign rights and jurisdiction in the EEZ. However, ITLOS had already recognised that, by virtue of Article 58(2), flag State duties in the high seas are applicable to the EEZ insofar as they are not incompatible with coastal State obligations. The flag States' obligations contained under the Compliance Agreement and the UNFSA, therefore, can provide guidance for the interpretation of flag States' obligations over fishing vessels in the EEZ.

[159] Article 31(3) VCLT provides that: There shall be taken into account, together with the context:
(a) any subsequent agreement between the parties regarding the interpretation of the treaty or the application of its provisions;
(b) any subsequent practice in the application of the treaty which establishes the agreement of the parties regarding its interpretation;
(c) any relevant rules of international law applicable in the relations between the parties.

[160] Erik J Molenaar, 'Current Legal and Institutional Issues Relating to the Conservation and Management of High-Seas Deep-Sea Fisheries' (FAO Report for the FAO Expert Consultation on Deep Sea Fisheries in the High Seas, 2007) www.fao.org/tempref/docrep/fao/010/a1341e/a1341e02c.pdf accessed 25 January 2022.

Alternatively, ITLOS could have examined whether Article 31(3)(c) could be used to read flag States obligations found under other fisheries agreement. into UNCLOS Article 31(3)(c) essentially provides the principle of systemic integration in treaty interpretation, in order to avoid treaties from being interpreted and applied in a vacuum, detached from the rest of the corpus of international law.[161] Indeed, the ICJ has acknowledged in several cases that treaties are to be 'interpreted and applied within the framework of the entire legal system prevailing at the time of the interpretation'.[162] Thus Article 31(3)(c) has been used by various courts and tribunals as a tool to resort to external rules in order to interpret certain terms or provisions in a particular convention.[163] Following the same logic, it can be argued that flag States obligations over fishing vessels under UNCLOS cannot and should not be interpreted in isolation, without regard to relevant rules on the matter.

In the *Advisory Opinion on IUU Fishing*, the reference to subsequent fisheries agreements would not necessarily mean that ITLOS was seeking to impose additional obligations on the SRFC Member or UNCLOS Member States in general. Instead, the resort to other fisheries agreements would shed light on the contours of the obligation to ensure. Thus resort to those instruments should be viewed as the interpretation of UNCLOS in light of the development of the rules on flag States' obligations which has taken place since the adoption of the Convention.[164]

In sum, as ITLOS was the first international tribunal to deal with the question of flag State obligation over fishing vessels in the EEZ of another State under UNCLOS, there was high hope for the Tribunal to provide authoritative guidance on this question.[165] ITLOS confirmed that despite the absence of explicit provision to this effect, flag States bear the obligation to ensure that their vessels do not engage in IUU fishing in the EEZ of

[161] See, for example, Panos Merkouris, *Article 31(3)(c) VCLT and the Principle of Systemic Integration: Normative Shadows in Plato's Cave* (Brill 2015).

[162] *Legal Consequences for States of the Continued Presence of South Africa in Namibia (South West Africa) Notwithstanding Security Council Resolution 276 (1970)* (Advisory Opinion) [1971] ICJ Rep 1971, 16 [53];
Aegean Sea Continental Shelf (Greece v Turkey) [1978] ICJ Rep 1978, 3 [32]–[33].

[163] See, for example, *Proceedings Pursuant to the OSPAR Convention (Ireland/United Kingdom)* (2003) RIAA XXIII 59 [93]–[105], [137-38]; *United States – Import Prohibition of Certain Shrimp and Shrimp Products*, WT/DS58/AB/R (12 October 1998) [158].

[164] Campbell MacLachlan, 'The Principle of Systemic Integration and Article 31(3)(c) of the Vienna Convention' (2005) 54 ICLQ 279, 315 (arguing that by resorting to other instruments, 'the tribunal is using other treaties not so much as sources of binding law, but as a rather elaborate dictionary').

[165] Nele Matz-Luck and Johannes Fuchs, 'Marine Living Resources' in Donald R Rothwell and others (n 24) 505.

another State under the Convention. This 'obligation to ensure' is an obligation of due diligence requiring a host of measures on the part of flag States. However, the preceding analysis also shows that ITLOS failed to provide nuanced and convincing reasoning to support its findings. While there are arguably flaws in the method that ITLOS employed to reach the above conclusion, its answer provided an important clarification in the law on fisheries.

3.4 CONCLUDING REMARKS

UNCLOS tribunals have had the opportunity to hear several cases concerning the arrest and detention of ships or concerning activities conducted by ships at sea such as navigation or fishing. Through the decisions rendered on these issues, UNCLOS tribunals' decisions have clarified different aspects of flag States' rights and obligations under UNCLOS. In the course of doing so, they have upheld primacy accorded to flag States under the Convention in several respects.

First, flag States have the sole discretion in granting their nationality to ships. ITLOS has repeatedly emphasised that compliance with a State's domestic regulations, and particularly registration in accordance with domestic law, remains the sole requirement for a ship to acquire the nationality of that State. While ITLOS has not clarified what role genuine link plays under the law of the sea, what has become clear is that genuine link has no role to play with respect to the nationality of Ship. Genuine link does mean require the flag State to show proof of its effective exercise of duties over the ship as a requirement for the granting of nationality. The lack of a genuine link does not constitute a ground for other States to not recognise the nationality of a ship.

The significance of flag States' power under the law of the sea can also be seen in flag State exclusive jurisdiction over the ship flying its flag as stipulated under Article 92(1). Exclusive flag State jurisdiction has raised a myriad of issues, particularly in relation to IUU fishing. UNCLOS tribunals have contributed to both exacerbating and addressing this issue. On the one hand, the tribunals expanded the scope of exclusive flag State jurisdiction to include not only enforcement jurisdiction as has conventionally been understood but also exclusive prescriptive jurisdiction. UNCLOS tribunals have also adopted a low threshold for finding a breach of the freedom of navigation on the high seas. Such an expansion strengthens the power of flag States over their ships to the exclusion of other States. This may potentially aggravate the problems associated with flags of convenience as flag States now enjoy a much broader level of discretion and freedom under international law. On the other hand, ITLOS in the *Advisory Opinion on IUU Fishing* read flag States' obligations over fishing vessels engaging in IUU fishing in the EEZ into UNCLOS, despite the Convention's silence on this matter. The fact that UNCLOS now imposes a due diligence obligation on flag States over vessels engaged in IUU fishing activities provides a balance to the exclusive jurisdiction that flag States retain over their ships. It also turns UNCLOS into an authoritative legal tool in the fight against IUU fishing, and thus strengthened the role that UNCLOS can play in the sustainable development of ocean resources.

UNCLOS tribunals have thus provided answers to some key issues relating to the scope of flag States' rights and obligations. However, UNCLOS tribunals' conclusions on some of these issues were not supported with sound legal reasoning, For certain issues, such as the interpretation of genuine link, although ITLOS did not specify the interpretative technique used, it was clear that the tribunal relied both on the negotiating history of the relevant article as well as State practice evidenced in other relevant treaties. By contrast, for issues such as flag States' due diligence obligation over IUU fishing or exclusive prescriptive jurisdiction, UNCLOS tribunals did not specify the interpretative technique used and only provided sparse reasoning. As a result, the answers provided by the tribunals either appeared overly contrived and predetermined as in the case of the *Advisory Opinion on IUU Fishing*, or were met with strong criticism, from within the tribunal itself as in the case of *M/V Norstar*.

4

Maritime Entitlement and Maritime Delimitation

Maritime entitlement and maritime delimitation are two distinct but related concepts.[1] These two concepts are distinct in that entitlement concerns a coastal State's maritime zones and their limits, and is established unilaterally by the coastal State, while delimitation refers to the establishment maritime boundaries which require agreement by States concerned.[2] They are related, however, in that delimitation is premised upon overlapping entitlements. This chapter examines the United Nations Convention on the Law of the Sea (UNCLOS) tribunals' contribution to the clarification of these two legal issues. In light of the distinct nature, each issue is discussed separately. Where relevant, the interconnectedness of the two issues is highlighted.

4.1 MARITIME ENTITLEMENT

For maritime zones whose entitlement is based on distance, such as the territorial sea, exclusive economic zone (EEZ) or continental shelf within 200 nautical miles (nm), the question of entitlement is rarely problematic, insofar as it is generated from continental coasts. However, for the continental shelf beyond 200 nm (also known as the outer continental shelf), the determination of entitlement becomes more complicated. The International Tribunal for the Law of the Sea (ITLOS) and the Annex VII arbitral tribunal in *Bangladesh/Myanmar* and *Bangladesh/India*, respectively, were the first international tribunals to engage with Article 76 concerning the continental

1 *Continental Shelf (Libyan Arab Jamahiriya/Malta)* (Judgment) [1985] ICJ Rep 13, 29–30 [27].

2 Nuno Marques Antunes and Vasco Becker-Weinberg, 'Entitlement to Maritime Zones and Their Delimitation: In the Doldrums of Uncertainty and Unpredictability' in Alex G Oude Elferink, Tore Henriksen and Signe Veierud Busch (eds), *Maritime Boundary Delimitation: The Case Law: Is It Consistent and Predictable?* (CUP 2018) 72.

shelf to clarify some key issues relating to the entitlement to the outer continental shelf.

Apart from continental territory, insular features can also generate maritime entitlement as stipulated under Article 121. In practice, the presence of insular features and the impact of their entitlements on the maritime boundary have occupied a prominent place in case law concerning maritime delimitation. However, in all these cases, the court or tribunal in question limited their examination to the effect of insular features' entitlement on boundary, thus avoiding the question maritime entitlement from insular features per se. In fact, the only case in which this question has been examined in detail was not one that concerned maritime delimitation, namely the *South China Sea* arbitration.

It seems clear from this brief overview that UNCLOS tribunals were the first international tribunals to examine two important issues concerning maritime entitlement, namely entitlement to a continental shelf beyond 200 nm and entitlement from insular features. The tribunals' contribution to clarifying these two issues is analysed in turn.

4.1.1 *Entitlement to a Continental Shelf beyond 200 Nautical Miles*

The concept of the 'continental shelf' is not new to UNCLOS as it was already included in the 1958 Convention on the Continental Shelf,[3] and prior to that, the Truman Proclamation.[4] UNCLOS however, introduced fundamental changes in the criteria for determining the seaward limits of the continental shelf. According to Article 76(1) UNCLOS, the continental shelf can extend to a distance of 200 nm or to the outer edge of the continental margin. If the outer edge of the continental margin extends beyond 200 nm, the limits of the continental shelf are determined in accordance with the technical requirements in paragraphs (4)–(6) of Article 76. When establishing the limits of the continental shelf that extends beyond 200 nm, coastal States are required, under Article 76(8), to submit information relating to the limits of the continental shelf to a technical body established under UNCLOS called the Commission on the Limits of the Continental Shelf (CLCS or 'the Commission'). The CLCS is comprised of experts in the fields of geology, geophysics or hydrography, and its main function is to consider data and other

[3] Article 1 of the 1958 Convention on the Continental Shelf defines the continental shelf as 'the seabed and subsoil of the submarine areas adjacent to the coast but outside the area of the territorial sea'. See 1958 Convention on the Continental Shelf (29 April 1958) 499 UNTS 311.

[4] Proclamation No. 2667 of September 28, 1945 'Policy of the United States with Respect to the Natural Resources of the Subsoil of the Sea Bed and the Continental Shelf www.gc.noaa.gov/documents/gcil_proc_2667.pdf accessed 25 January 2022.

material submitted by coastal States and to make recommendations regarding where the outer limits are located.

Unlike the EEZ, coastal States do not need to make an express claim to a continental shelf. As the International Court of Justice (ICJ) made clear in the *North Sea Continental Shelf* cases, the rights of coastal States in the continental shelf 'exist ipso facto and ab initio, by virtue of its sovereignty over land'.[5] Article 77(3) confirms this by providing that 'the rights of the coastal State over the continental shelf do not depend on occupation, effective or notional, or on any express proclamation'. Yet ITLOS in *Bangladesh/Myanmar* acknowledged that 'not every coast generates entitlements to a continental shelf extending beyond 200 nm'.[6] The question thus arises as to the basis for a coastal State to claim entitlement to a continental shelf beyond 200 nm and how to prove such an entitlement. This section examines these two issues in turn and considers whether the decisions of UNCLOS tribunals have satisfactorily provided an answer to these questions.

4.1.1.1 Legal Basis of Entitlement to an Outer Continental Shelf

Since it was first introduced by the ICJ in the *North Sea Continental Shelf* cases, 'natural prolongation' has long been accepted as the basis of entitlement to a continental shelf.[7] However, for the establishment of a continental shelf that extends beyond 200 nm within the UNCLOS framework, the concept of 'natural prolongation' is used alongside with that of 'the outer edge of the continental margin' under Article 76(1) UNCLOS – whose location is, in turn, identified using the formulae provided under Article 76(4). The emergence of the concept of the 'outer edge of the continental margin' raises two important questions: (i) what is the relationship between the concepts of 'natural prolongation' and 'continental margin' under Article 76 and (ii) does entitlement depend on 'natural prolongation' or the establishment of the outer edge of the continental margin?

Turning to the first question, the concept of 'natural prolongation' performs multiple functions including 'a basis of title, a means of delimitation, an equitable principle of delimitation, a criterion for delimitation and as a

5 *North Sea Continental Shelf Cases (Federal Republic of Germany/Denmark; Federal Republic of Germany/Netherlands)* (Judgment) [1969] ICJ Rep 3 [19].

6 *Dispute concerning delimitation of the maritime boundary between Bangladesh and Myanmar in the Bay of Bengal (Bangladesh/Myanmar)* (Judgment) ITLOS Reports 2012, 4 [439].

7 *North Sea Continental Shelf Cases* (n 6) [19]. See also: Lindsay Parson, 'Article 76' in Alexander Proelss (ed), *United Nations Convention on the Law of the Sea: A Commentary* (CH Beck, Hart, Nomos 2017) 590.

relevant circumstance'.[8] It has, however, often been considered 'a source of mystery and confusion'[9] in establishing entitlement to a continental shelf. While 'natural prolongation' has been discussed in several cases before international courts and tribunals,[10] it was raised in the context of delimitation, not in relation to entitlement to an outer continental shelf within the UNCLOS framework. The meaning of 'natural prolongation' was a key point of contention in *Bangladesh/Myanmar*. In this case, on the one hand, Bangladesh interpreted the phrase 'natural prolongation of its land territory' found in Article 76(1) providing for the definition of a continental shelf as referring to the need for geological and geomorphological continuity between the land mass of the coastal State and the seabed beyond 200 nm.[11] Myanmar, on the other hand, was of the view that the controlling concept was not natural prolongation but that of the 'outer edge of the continental margin'.[12]

ITLOS eventually agreed with Myanmar on this issue. It held that while Article 76(1) mentions the term 'natural prolongation', it is clear from the wording of this article that 'the notion of "the outer edge of the continental margin" is the essential element in determining the extent of the continental shelf'.[13] Moreover, while the notion of 'the outer edge of the continental margin' is elaborated in paragraphs 3 and 4 of Article 76 UNCLOS,[14] no such definition or elaboration of 'natural prolongation' could be found in any other paragraphs of Article 76.[15] Finding further support in the *North Sea Continental Shelf* cases before the ICJ,[16] the negotiating records of UNCLOS,[17] and the test of appurtenance adopted in the Scientific and Technical Guidelines on the Limits of the Continental Shelf by the CLCS,[18] ITLOS found that the notions of 'natural prolongation' and 'continental margin' under Article 76 paragraphs (1) and (4), respectively, are closely

8 Malcolm D Evans, *Relevant Circumstances and Maritime Delimitation* (Clarendon Press 1989) 100.

9 Clive Schofield, Anatasia Telesetsky and Seokwoo Lee, 'A Tribunal Navigating Complex Waters: Implications of the Bay of Bengal Case' (2013) 44 ODIL 363, 375.

10 *Delimitation of the Anglo-French Continental Shelf Arbitration (UK/France)*, (First) Decision (1977) RIAA XVIII:3, 63; *Continental Shelf (Tunisia/Libyan Arab Jamahiriya)* [1982] ICJ Rep 18; *Delimitation of the Maritime Boundary in the Gulf of Maine Area (Canada/United States)* [1984] ICJ Rep 246; *Continental Shelf (Libyan Arab Jarnahiriya/Malta)* [1985] ICJ Rep 13.

11 *Bangladesh/Myanmar* (n 7) [426].

12 Ibid [427].

13 Ibid [429].

14 Ibid [430].

15 See also: Parson (n 8) 592.

16 *Bangladesh/Myanmar* (n 7) [432].

17 Ibid [433].

18 Ibid [436].

interrelated and they refer to the same area.[19] This means that entitlement to a continental shelf beyond 200 nm should be determined by reference to the outer edge of the continental margin, to be ascertained in accordance with the formulae provided in Article 76(4).[20] ITLOS thus concluded that natural prolongation did not constitute an independent, separate criterion for the establishment of entitlement to an outer continental shelf.[21]

ITLOS's rejection of the requirement of 'natural prolongation' as a separate criterion in the establishment of entitlement to outer continental shelf has been criticised by Judge Gao in his Separate Opinion in *Bangladesh/Myanmar*, as well as by some other scholars.[22] ITLOS was, however, arguably correct in rejecting 'natural prolongation' – interpreted as requiring continuity from the land territory to the seabed area – as a separate and additional criterion for the establishment of an outer continental shelf.[23] Nowhere under Article 76 UNCLOS or the CLCS Technical Guidelines can the requirement of similarities in the geological or geomorphological condition in the seabed of the coastal State from its landmass to the outer continental margin be found. Beyond the Technical Guidelines, the CLCS has in practice 'treated the natural prolongation and continental margin as synonymous with each other and did not assign to natural prolongation an autonomous role in determining the entitlement to the continental shelf beyond 200 nm'.[24] Moreover, the negotiating records of UNCLOS III also show that the concept of 'natural prolongation' was understood with reference to the concept of 'the continental margin'.[25] The negotiating texts of UNCLOS, therefore, do not lend support to the argument that 'natural prolongation' constituted an

19 Ibid [434].

20 Ibid [437]. Note that the close connection between paragraphs (1) and (4) of Article 76 had earlier been rejected by scholars. See: Suzette V Suarez, *The Outer Limits of the Continental Shelf: Legal Aspects of their Establishment* (Springer 2008) 151.

21 Ibid [435].

22 Huang Yao and Liao Xuexia, 'Natural Prolongation and Delimitation of the Continental Shelf Beyond 200 nm: Implications of the Bangladesh/Myanmar Case' (2014) 4 Asian Journal of International Law 281, 287–293; Bing Bing Jia, 'The Notion of Natural Prolongation in the Current Regime of the Continental Shelf: An Afterlife?' (2013) 12(1) CJIL 87.

23 Hyun Jung Kim, 'Natural Prolongation: A Living Myth in the Regime of the Continental Shelf?' (2014) 45 ODIL 374, 379.

24 Xuexia Liao, *The Continental Shelf Delimitation Beyond 200 Nautical Miles: Towards a Common Approach to Maritime Boundary-Making* (CUP 2021) 32.

25 Official Records, 18th Meeting, Statement of Uruguay, para 61–62, Statement of Trinidad and Tobago, para 86; Statement of Burma, para 91; Official Records, 19th Meeting, Statement of Switzerland, para 26; *Official Records of the Third United Nations Conference on the Law of the Sea*, Volume II *(Summary Records of Meetings of the First, Second and Third Committees, Second Session)*, 20th Meeting A/CONF.62/C.2/SR.20, Statement of Jamaica, para 95.

independent requirement upon the fulfilment of which States would be entitled to an outer continental shelf.[26] Finally, as ITLOS acknowledged, the term 'natural prolongation' originated from the *North Sea Continental Shelf* cases. The concept of natural prolongation used by the ICJ in these cases was not meant to impose a condition based on which entitlement for the outer continental shelf could be established, but 'to justify the appurtenance of the continental shelf to the coastal State'.[27]

Apart from the concept of 'outer edge of the continental shelf', Article 76 also employs the term 'outer limits of the continental shelf'. Myanmar in *Bangladesh/Myanmar* argued that ITLOS could not deal with the issue of entitlement to an outer continental shelf due to the 'crucial role' of the CLCS.[28] Given that the tasks of the CLCS involve reviewing and giving recommendations to coastal States regarding the location of the outer limits of the continental shelf, in essence, Myanmar's objection implied that a coastal State's entitlement to an outer continental shelf depended on the establishment of the outer limits of the shelf. ITLOS, however, drew a clear a distinction between the notions of 'entitlement to the continental shelf beyond 200 nm' and 'the outer limits of the continental shelf',[29] stating that the coastal State's entitlement to an outer continental shelf 'does not depend on' the establishment of the outer limits of the continental shelf.[30] It further held that the procedures set out under Article 76(8), whereby States are required to submit information to the CLCS and then to wait for the latter's recommendation regarding the outer limits, did not imply that entitlement to the continental shelf depended on any procedural requirements.[31] In ITLOS's view, Article 77(3) confirms that the existence of entitlement does not depend on the establishment of outer limits but only on 'the sole fact that the basis of entitlement, namely, sovereignty over the land territory, is present'.[32]

There are merits in ITLOS's view regarding the independent relationship between the establishment of 'entitlement' to an outer continental shelf and the identification of the 'outer limits' of the continental shelf. Under UNCLOS,

[26] See Steinar Thor Gudlaugsson, 'Natural Prolongation and the Concept of the Continental Margin for the Purposes of Article 76' in Myron N Nordquist, John Norton Moore and Tomas H Heidar, *Legal and Scientific Aspects of Continental Shelf Limits* (Martinus Nijhoff 2004) 69.

[27] Barbara Kwiatkowska, *The 200 Mile Exclusive Economic Zone in the New Law of the Sea* (Martinus Nijhoff 1989) 11.

[28] *Bangladesh/Myanmar* (n 7) [405].

[29] Ibid [406].

[30] Ibid [409].

[31] Ibid [408].

[32] Ibid [409].

entitlement is determined with reference to the outer edge of the continental margin, which is ascertained in accordance with Article 76(4).[33] On the other hand, the outer limits of the continental shelf, pursuant to Article 76(5), are drawn 'in accordance with paragraph 4(a)(i) and (ii)' *and* subject to the technical requirements under paragraphs (5), (6) and (7) of the same article. In other words, in addition to identifying the outer edge of the continental margin, the coastal State would have to take further steps and consider all of the requirements under paragraphs (5), (6) and (7) in order to establish the outer limits of the continental shelf. It follows that the identification of the line indicating the outer edge of the continental margin is only the starting point of the delineation process to determine the outer limits of the shelf. Further, the 'test of appurtenance' set out by the CLCS requires that a coastal State must first prove that it has a continental shelf entitlement that extends beyond 200 nm before it is permitted to delineate the outer limits of the shelf. Such a test affirms that the establishment of entitlement to an outer continental shelf precedes and predicates the identification of the outer limits of the shelf.[34] Having said that, the close relationship between paragraphs (4) and (5) as well as the practice of the CLCS indicates that 'the task of establishing the outer limits is not confined to defining the precise limits of the continental shelf beyond 200 nm; the ascertainment of the existence of the entitlement is also integral to this procedure'.[35] As a result, while the determination of entitlement does not depend on the establishment of the outer limits, it is important to acknowledge that they may have a bearing on one another.

4.1.1.2 Evidence for Entitlement to an Outer Continental Shelf

As mentioned, ITLOS found in *Bangladesh/Myanmar* that coastal State's entitlement to an outer continental shelf does not depend on the establishment of the outer limits of the continental shelf. The basis of a coastal State's entitlement to an outer continental shelf is the existence of a juridical continental margin that extends beyond 200 nm, the identification of which quires the involvement of a technical body, the CLCS. How can a coastal State then prove that the outer edge of its continental margin lies beyond 200 nm so that it has entitlement to an outer continental shelf?

33 Ibid [437].

34 See also: *Question of the Delimitation of the Continental Shelf between Nicaragua and Colombia Beyond 200 Nautical Miles from the Nicaraguan Coast (Nicaragua v Colombia)*, Joint Dissenting Opinion of Vice-President Yusuf, Judges Cançado Trindade, Xue, Gaja, Bhandari, Robinson and Judge ad hoc Brower [55].

35 Liao (n 25) 47.

In *Bangladesh/Myanmar* and *Bangladesh/India*, all three States had made submissions to the CLCS in respect of their claims beyond 200 nm. In both cases, UNCLOS tribunals acknowledged that the parties had entitlement to an outer continental shelf and thus proceeded to delimitation. This approach suggests that full submissions to the CLCS were considered necessary and sufficient evidence for entitlement. In fact, one commentator argued that 'in order to continue the delimitation beyond 200 nautical miles, it was crucial that the parties had each made their submissions to the Commission'.[36] However, on closer inspection, interpreting the approaches taken by UNCLOS tribunals as establishing an evidentiary threshold for coastal States' entitlement beyond 200 nm is arguably mistaken. In the Bay of Bengal cases, UNCLOS tribunals were, based on available scientific evidence to which neither party objected, certain that the parties had entitlements to an outer continental shelf. ITLOS itself stated that, '[n]otwithstanding the overlapping areas indicated in the submissions of the Parties to the Commission, the Tribunal would have been hesitant to proceed with the delimitation of the area beyond 200 nm had it concluded that there was significant uncertainty as to the existence of a continental margin in the area in question'.[37] Thus it was not the submission *per se* that assured the tribunals that they should exercise jurisdiction, it was the availability of uncontested scientific evidence which removed any doubt as to the existence of the outer continental shelf.

In *Ghana/Côte d'Ivoire*, both parties had lodged their submissions to the CLCS, and Ghana, for its part, had received the recommendation from the CLCS. Neither party contested the entitlement of the other party to a continental shelf beyond 200 nm,[38] thus the question of uncertainty regarding the existence of entitlement did not arise in this case. Ghana nonetheless questioned the scope of Côte d'Ivoire's entitlement,[39] arguing that the latter's Revised Submission to the CLCS in 2016 indicated an overlap between the entitlements of the two States which had not existed previously.[40] The Special Chamber of ITLOS eventually dismissed this objection on procedural grounds.[41] The fact that the Chamber did not itself scrutinise the information

36 Øystein Jensen, 'Maritime Boundary Delimitation Beyond 200 Nautical Miles: The International Judiciary and the Commission on the Limits of the Continental Shelf' (2015) 84 Nordic Journal of International Law 580, 587.

37 *Bangladesh/Myanmar* (n 7) [443].

38 *Delimitation of the Maritime Boundary in the Atlantic Ocean (Ghana/Côte d'Ivoire)* ITLOS Reports 2017, 4 [503], [507].

39 Ibid [498].

40 Ibid [504].

41 Ibid [515].

provided by Côte d'Ivoire in its Revised Submission to the CLCS to determine whether entitlement existed or whether there was an overlap suggests that the Chamber gave substantial weight to the submissions to CLCS as evidence of entitlements. That the parties did not contest one another's entitlement presumably played an important role in this case as well.

ITLOS and the Annex VII tribunal in the abovementioned cases did not explicitly confirm that submissions to the CLCS constituted conclusive evidence of coastal States' entitlement to an outer continental shelf, despite signs pointing to such a direction. By contrast, the ICJ seems to have increasingly been more prepared to accept such evidence. In the 2012 *Nicaragua v Colombia* judgment, rendered after *Bangladesh/Myanmar*, the Court distinguished its decision to not delimit the boundary between Nicaragua and Colombia beyond 200 nm from that of ITLOS on the basis that both Bangladesh and Myanmar had made full submissions to the CLCS,[42] whereas Nicaragua had not established that its continental margin extended far enough to overlap with Colombia's 200-nautical-mile entitlement to the continental shelf.[43] In 2016, when Nicaragua again invited the ICJ to delimit its maritime boundary with Colombia in an area beyond 200 nm from Nicaragua's mainland coast, the ICJ interpreted its 2012 Judgment as requiring Nicaragua to submit its information to the CLCS, stating further that this was 'a *prerequisite* for the delimitation of the continental shelf beyond 200 nautical miles by the Court'.[44] As Nicaragua had, following the 2012 Judgment, furnished complete information and documentation to the CLCS, the ICJ then found that it had jurisdiction to delimit the maritime boundary independently of a recommendation of the CLCS.[45] This confirmation of jurisdiction suggested that the ICJ accepted Nicaragua's full submission to the CLCS per se as evidence of its entitlement beyond 200 nm, it did not inquire any further into the information contained in Nicaragua's submission.[46] In the more recent *Somalia v Kenya*, the ICJ was again satisfied that both parties had entitlement to an outer continental shelf, relying primarily on the fact that the

[42] *Territorial and Maritime Dispute (Nicaragua v Colombia)* (Judgment) [2012] ICJ Rep 2012, 624 [125].

[43] Ibid [129].

[44] *Question of the Delimitation of the Continental Shelf between Nicaragua and Colombia beyond 200 Nautical Miles from the Nicaraguan Coast (Nicaragua v Colombia)* Preliminary Objections, Judgment, [2016] ICJ Rep 100 [105]. (emphasis added)

[45] Ibid [114].

[46] See, however, Joint Dissenting Opinion of Vice-President Yusuf, Judges Cançado Trindade, Xue, Gaja, Bhandari, Robinson and Judge ad hoc Brower (n 35) [56].

parties had made full submissions to the CLCS.[47] The ICJ acknowledged that '[t]he situation in the present case is not the same' as *Bangladesh/Myanmar*,[48] indicating that the Court was aware of 'scientific uncertainty' test put forward by ITLOS as mentioned above. However, on the basis that the parties' claims to an outer continental shelf were based on 'scientific evidence' and that 'neither Party questions the existence of the other Party's entitlement to a continental shelf beyond 200 nautical miles or the extent of that claim',[49] the Court seemed to have simply relied on the parties' submissions to the CLCS to obtain scientific certainty.

In summary, ITLOS in *Bangladesh/Myanmar* clarified four important issues relating to the entitlement to a continental shelf beyond 200 nm. First, the basis of a coastal State's entitlement to an outer continental shelf is the existence of a juridical continental margin as defined under Article 76(3) that extends beyond 200 nm, ascertained pursuant to Article 76(4). Second, natural prolongation is still relevant to the establishment of an outer continental shelf, but not in the sense that there has to be geological or geomorphological continuity between the land territory and the seabed area beyond 200 nm. 'Natural prolongation' is defined with reference to Article 76(4), which means that the natural prolongation of a coastal State's territory is the seabed area that extends to the outer edge of the continental margin as determined by Article 76(4). Third, the establishment of the outer limits of the continental shelf does not constitute the basis for entitlement. A coastal State does not need to identify the exact scope of the continental shelf – or the limits of its entitlement – in order to establish that it has entitlement beyond 200 nm. Finally, while entitlement to an outer continental shelf does not depend on the establishment of outer limits, courts and tribunals have to date tended to rely on the parties' submissions to the CLCS – the starting point of the process to establish the outer limits of the continental shelf – as evidence of the entitlement. This approach was pioneered by ITLOS in *Bangladesh/Myanmar* and subsequently followed by other courts and tribunals. However, it should be pointed out that ITLOS in that case was careful to note the importance of significant scientific certainty for the purposes of determining the existence of entitlement. The fact that the parties had both made submissions to the CLCS in itself therefore might not be sufficient evidence in case significant scientific uncertainty exists.

[47] *Maritime Delimitation in the Indian Ocean (Somalia v Kenya)* (Judgment) 2021 [188]. www.icj-cij.org/public/files/case-related/161/161-20211012-JUD-01-00-EN.pdf accessed 25 January 2022

[48] Ibid [193].

[49] Ibid [194].

4.1.2 *Maritime Entitlement from Insular Features*

While the law of the sea generally does not regulate issues relating to land – only the maritime zones and activities taking place therein – UNCLOS dedicates an entire Part VIII to the regime of islands. Part VIII only contains one article, namely Article 121 which provides for the definition of 'island' in paragraph (1), their maritime entitlements in paragraph (2), and the entitlements of a category of insular features called 'rocks' in paragraph (3). Apart from islands, other insular features are also mentioned elsewhere under UNCLOS, for example, in Article 13 on low-tide elevations or in Article 60 concerning artificial islands. Disputes concerning insular features and their entitlement have been brought before international courts and tribunals in different contexts. However, as will be shown below, courts and tribunals generally avoided the classification of islands, rocks or low-tide elevations. *South China Sea* was the first instance in which an international tribunal engaged in a detailed interpretation of the legal terms contained in Article 121. This section seeks to examine the arbitral tribunal's interpretation and application of Article 121 and assess the extent to which the arbitral tribunal contributed to clarifying: (i) the distinction between high-tide and low-tide elevations and (ii) the distinction between islands and rocks.

4.1.2.1 Distinction between High-Tide Features and Low-Tide Elevations

The term 'high-tide features' was used by the tribunal in *South China Sea* to refer to 'islands' or 'rocks' under Article 121 to distinguish them from low-tide elevations which are regulated under Article 13. The common feature between these two categories is that they both need to be 'naturally formed area of land' – which distinguishes them with artificial islands regulated under Article 60. The difference between the two categories of features lies in their height relative to high tide. In order to qualify as an island or a rock, the feature must be 'above water at high tide', whereas low-tide elevations are those 'above water at low tide but submerged at high tide'. While these conditions seem rather straightforward, their application to specific cases requires an interpretation of key terms such as 'naturally formed' as well as the consideration of technical data to determine what is 'high tide', what is 'above' or 'below' water.

'NATURALLY FORMED'. The *South China Sea* tribunal first clarified that the term 'naturally formed' 'indicates that the status of a feature is to be evaluated on the basis of its natural condition',[50] and that 'human modification cannot change the seabed into a low-tide elevation or a low-tide elevation into an island'.[51] In case the features have been subject to extensive human modification, the tribunal remarked that the status of a feature must be 'ascertain on the basis of its earlier, natural condition, prior to the onset of significant human modification'.[52] It is clear from these statements that the tribunal placed considerable emphasis on the natural state of the feature. Such focus seems to have been prompted by the factual situation in the South China Sea, in which, as the tribunal observed, many features had been subjected to substantial human modification.[53] However, on a more general basis, the question remains as to the extent to which human modification is allowed for a feature to still be considered 'naturally formed'? The tribunal itself seems to have provided a brief answer to this question with the use of the term 'significant', which seems to suggest that the tribunal did not completely rule out the possibility of human intervention in the natural state of a feature. The threshold for 'significant' was, however, not clarified. The tribunal stated that it would rely on 'the best available evidence of the previous status of what are now heavily modified coral reefs'.[54] The use of the term 'previous' in turn suggests a point in time – a critical date – at which human modification reaches the threshold of significant so that anything that follows thereafter will be disregarded for the purposes of determining the status of the feature.[55] On this particular point, the tribunal has been criticised for assuming that 'natural formation is a "one-off" event, whereas it is likely to be a process over time'.[56] However, while the tribunal did not explicitly identify the critical date when examining the status of the features in the South China Sea, it considered evidence ranging from the nineteenth century to as recent as 2005.[57] The selection of evidence suggests that the tribunal did not consider natural formation a 'one-off' event.

50 *The South China Sea Arbitration between the Republic of the Philippines and the People's Republic of China (Philippines v China)* (2016) RIAA XXXIII 153 [305].

51 Ibid.

52 Ibid [306].

53 Ibid.

54 Ibid.

55 Warwick Gullett, 'The South China Sea Arbitration's Contribution to the Concept of Juridical Islands' (2018) 47 CIL 5, 34.

56 Malcolm D Evans and Reece Lewis, 'The Regime of Islands' in Øystein Jensen (ed), *The Development of the Law of the Sea Convention: The Role of International Courts and Tribunals* (Edward Elgar Publishing 2020) 30.

57 *South China Sea Arbitration* (n 51) 159.

'HIGH TIDE'. As mentioned, whether a feature is considered an island or a low-tide elevation depends on its height relative to high tide. While there exist different datums for measuring high tide water, the tribunal in *South China Sea* stated that there is 'nothing in the Convention, and no rule of customary international law, that would mandate that the status of low-tide elevations and high-tide features/islands be determined against any particular high-water datum'.[58] As a result, the tribunal granted States discretion in choosing high-water datum as long as it 'reasonably corresponds to the ordinary meaning of the term "high tide" in Articles 13 and 121'.[59] Despite discrepancies between Chinese and Filipino charts with regards to height datum,[60] the tribunal found that the divergences in the parties' views did not prevent the tribunal from conducting its own examination based on available evidence. This approach seems to be less stringent than that of the ICJ, whereby the Court would only consider a feature as above water at high tide if the models used by the parties, regardless of which model chosen, showed the same result of being above high tide.[61] The arbitral tribunal and the ICJ's different approaches could perhaps be explained by the non-appearance on the part of China, depriving the tribunal of the opportunity to have a clear view of the parties' position on the matter.

The tribunal in *South China Sea* decided to rely primarily on hydrographic surveys produced by the United Kingdom, Japan, China, which, as it noted, contained 'direct observations' and therefore 'can be assumed to have been based on an accurate understanding of the tidal conditions at the time the observations were made'.[62] The tribunal also remarked that the historical observations of tidal ranges in the Spratly Islands were consistent with each other, and also consistent with recent tidal observations from the modern Chinese charts.[63] The tribunal's reliance on historical observations has been criticised for being overly static in time, in that if at one point in time an above-water feature was considered to be above high tide based on sailors' observation, such a feature would remain qualified as a high-tide feature.[64]

[58] Ibid [311].
[59] Ibid.
[60] Ibid [133].
[61] Stefan Talmon, 'Article 121' in Proelss (n 8) 866.
[62] *South China Sea Arbitration* (n 51) [318].
[63] Ibid [317].
[64] Youna Lyons, Luu Quang Hung and Pavel Tkalich, 'Determining High-tide Features (or islands) in the South China Sea under Article 121(1): A Legal and Oceanography Perspective' in S Jayakumar and others (eds), *The South China Sea Arbitration: The Legal Dimension* (Edward Elgar Publishing 2018) 134.

Some of the surveys relied upon by the tribunal were actually more than a century old,[65] and as such, did not reflect natural changes that had occurred since, such as sea level rise due to global warming since the beginning of the twentieth century. Moreover, as pointed out by scholars, 'the sea level used as reference in charts and sailing directions does not follow a single clear convention globally and has evolved over time'.[66] As a result of both natural changes and developments in referencing techniques, historical observations may not accurately reflect the current status of the features and thus the heavy reliance on historical evidence may lead to incorrect results. The particular weight given to historical observations was, as the tribunal explained, due to the fact that 'the majority of charts of the South China Sea issued by different States . . . are to a greater or lesser extent copies of one another'.[67] Thus, the tribunal believed that recourse to original survey data would be most beneficial.

The tribunal acknowledged that its approach differed to that of the ICJ in *Nicaragua v Colombia* in 2012, in which the ICJ attached little importance to historical surveys when examining whether Quitasueño had any naturally formed areas of land which were above water at high tide.[68] The arbitral tribunal, however, strived to distinguish the case before it. The tribunal remarked that *Nicaragua v Colombia* involved States 'presenting information concerning its own coastlines in areas that can be expected to be well surveyed and well charted by that State', which was distinguishable from that of the South China Sea which involved 'the status of remote features, subject to the demands of competing States, that have been carefully surveyed only infrequently'.[69] The arbitral tribunal also acknowledged the shortcomings of direct, inperson observations, and took into account other more modern forms of evidence, such as satellite imagery, sailing directions, while being similarly wary of the limitations of these forms of evidence.[70] It is also noteworthy that while the tribunal reached the same conclusion as the Philippines' submission regarding the status of the features, it did not agree with all of the Philippines' arguments and interpretation of the evidence.[71] Due to absence of one of the parties, the tribunal took extra care in examining the evidence presented to it

65 For example, survey charts by the British Royal navy are dated between 1862 and 1868, and whiles those of the Japanese Navy between 1920s and 1930s.

66 Lyons, Hung and Tkalich (n 65) 142.

67 Ibid [330].

68 *Nicaragua v Colombia* (2012) (n 43) [35].

69 *South China Sea Arbitration* (n 51) [331].

70 *South China Sea Arbitration* (n 51) [321].

71 Ibid [371].

by the appearing party and sought the help of independent experts to assist its work, considered a rare case for international dispute settlement bodies.[72]

The foregoing discussion shows that the determination of whether a feature is a high-tide feature or low-tide elevations requires not only the interpretation of legal terms in Articles 13 and 121(1) such as 'naturally formed' but also the application of evidence to specific cases. The *South China Sea* tribunal's contribution in this regard pertains to both aspects, to varying degrees. The tribunal clarified the that the assessment of 'naturally formed' has to be based on the natural condition of the feature, before significant human modification takes place. Such an examination rests upon the determination of the critical date and the level at which modification is considered 'significant'. The tribunal, however, did not set out specific criteria for these two tests. In terms of evidence, the tribunal made clear that States are free to choose high-water datum in order to determine whether the feature is above water at high tide. The tribunal itself favoured historical observations, even though its approach showed that the types of evidence used needs to be determined on a case-by-case basis depending on the location of the features, the accessibility as well as the frequency of survey that has been conducted.

4.1.2.2 Distinction between Islands and Rocks

Within the category of high-tide features, Article 121 distinguishes between 'islands' and 'rocks'. Paragraph (3) introduces the term 'rocks' but does not define it. Rather, this paragraph provides that 'rocks which cannot sustain human habitation or economic life of their own shall have no exclusive economic zone or continental shelf'. As such, it focuses on specifying the maritime entitlement of rocks, or to be more precise, of a certain subset of rocks, that is, those 'which cannot sustain human habitation or economic life of their own'. While the definition of islands in paragraph (1) of Article 121 finds its origin in the 1958 Convention on the Territorial Sea and the Contiguous Zone,[73] paragraph (3) is a new addition to UNCLOS. This paragraph has been a source of confusion and debate since the Convention was adopted, for it contains terms that are 'intolerably imprecise'[74] as a result of the

72 Nulifer Oral, 'The South China Sea Arbitral Award: Casting Light on Article 121 of UNCLOS, Law and Practice of International Courts and Tribunals' (2017) 16(2) The Law and Practice of International Courts and Tribunals 354, 360.

73 Article 10, Convention on the Territorial Sea and the Contiguous Zone (29 April 1958) 516 UNTS 205

74 ED Brown, 'Rockall and the Limits of National Jurisdiction of the UK' (1978) 2 Marine Policy 181, 206.

disagreements during UNCLOS III. As one commentator noted, the vague wording of the paragraph 'is a reflection of the (meagre) outcome of 10 years of negotiations'.[75] Even though international courts and tribunals have, to different extents, made observations regarding the maritime entitlements of insular features under Article 121, to date, the *South China Sea* arbitration remains the only jurisprudence in which each key term of paragraph (3) was interpreted and applied to concrete features. Consequently, this section focuses on discussing the *South China Sea* key findings and its reasoning in order to assess the contribution of the tribunal to the development of Article 121(3).

THE INTERPRETATION OF ARTICLE 121(3). The tribunal approached its task of interpreting Article 121(3) in a systematic manner. At the outset, the tribunal explicitly stated that it would apply the interpretative canons found in the VCLT, on the basis of which it 'will separately review the text, its context, the object and purpose of the Convention, and the *travaux préparatoires*, before setting out the conclusions'.[76]

Starting with the text of Article 121(3), the tribunal interpreted the term 'rocks' in a non-restrictive manner to include features that may 'not necessarily be composed of rock',[77] as well as those which have a different geological or geomorphological composition.[78] This conclusion was not based only on the ordinary meaning of the word 'rocks' but more importantly, on the intent behind this paragraph, which, according to the tribunal, was to limit the entitlement of features that are not capable of sustaining human habitation or an economic life their own, rather than focusing on the composition of the feature itself.[79] This understanding of the term 'rock' has received support from commentators and seems to be in line with the negotiating history of Article 121(3).[80]

75 Erik Franckx, 'The Regime of Islands and Rocks' in David J Attard, Malgosia Fitzmaurice and Norman A Martínez Gutiérrez (eds), *The IMLI Manual on International Maritime Law, Volume I: The Law of the Sea* (OUP 2014) 102.

76 *South China Sea Arbitration* (n 51) [477].

77 Ibid [482].

78 Ibid [480], [481].

79 Ibid [481].

80 Talmon (n 62) 871; Victor Prescott and Clive Schofield, *The Maritime Political Boundaries of the World* (2nd ed, Martinus Nijhoff 2005) 76; Clive R Symmons, 'Maritime Zones from Islands and Rocks' in S Jayakumar, Tommy Koh and Robert Beckman (eds), *The South China Sea Disputes and Law of the Sea* (Edward Elgar Publishing 2014) 100. Contra: Judge Gilbert Guillaume, 'Rocks in the Law of the Sea: Some comments on the South China Sea Arbitration Award' (*EJIL: Talk!*, 25 February 2021) www.ejiltalk.org/ricks-in-the-law-of-the-sea-some-comments-on-the-south-china-sea-arbitration-award/ accessed 25 January 2022.

Next, the tribunal interpreted the term 'cannot' to signify the objective capacity of the feature rather than 'whether the feature actually does sustain human habitation or an economic life'.[81] The term 'sustain', for its part, was interpreted to contain three components, which taken together, led the to the understanding of 'sustain' as 'provid[ing] that which is necessary to keep humans alive and healthy over a continuous period of time, according to a proper standard'.[82] As noted by one commentator, this new qualification of 'proper' level introduces a requirement of 'something more than enabling humans to survive on a feature'.[83] However, the tribunal did not explain further what would be considered as 'proper'. In setting out this requirement of 'proper', the tribunal essentially interpreted an unqualified term, that is, 'sustain' by reference to a subjective standard that is as equally vague.

As for 'human habitation', the tribunal stated that paragraph (3) requires 'settled human habitation', as opposed to the mere presence of humans. This means that a feature needs to be able to 'support, maintain, and provide food, drink, and shelter to some humans to enable them to reside there permanently or habitually over an extended period of time'.[84] While no precise number of persons was set, the tribunal held that the presence of a single individual would not suffice; rather a group or community of persons is required.[85] Based on historical evidence, the tribunal found that the features in the Spratly Islands were only temporarily inhabited by fishermen or labourers only for short periods of time mostly to engage in economic activities before returning to the mainland. The tribunal considered that the presence of these people could not constitute a settled community within the meaning of 'human habitation'.[86] The tribunal emphasised that it saw 'no evidence that would suggest that the historical absence of human habitation on the Spratly Islands is the product of intervening forces'[87] However, it is not clear what the tribunal meant by 'intervening forces'. An argument could be made that the lack of permanent habitation could be attributed to other factors such as the feature's remoteness as well as vulnerability to annual natural disasters such as typhoons or hurricanes, and the entailing difficulties of raising a family, making a stable income to support a decent standard of life all year round. In other words, the absence of a stable community does not necessarily speak to the capacity of

[81] *South China Sea Arbitration* (n 51) [483].
[82] Ibid [487].
[83] Gullett (n 56) 13.
[84] *South China Sea Arbitration* (n 51) [490].
[85] Ibid [491].
[86] Ibid [619].
[87] Ibid [622].

the feature itself to sustain human habitation but may relate to the need for a 'settled' stable social life of human beings.

The tribunal then turned its attention to the word 'or' and found that, as a result of the negative overall structure of the sentence, a feature needs to only have the capacity to sustain either human habitation or an economic life of its own.[88] However, the tribunal still noted that the two concepts are linked in practical terms[89] and that 'the two will in most instances go hand in hand'.[90] With regards to the remainder of the sentence 'shall have not exclusive economic or continental', while the word 'or' is again used, the tribunal found that it should mean 'and' in this context. As a result, the tribunal concluded that paragraph (3) should be understood to mean that 'an island that is able to sustain either human habitation or an economic life of its own is entitled to both an exclusive economic zone and a continental shelf'.[91] This conclusion is based not only on formal logic but again on the intent of the drafters.[92] The tribunal practically used the intention behind paragraph (3) in order to explain away any linguistic inconsistences found in this paragraph.[93]

Finally, the last criterion of 'economic life of their own' was construed to require more than the mere presence of resources. Instead, 'some level of local human activity to exploit, develop, and distribute those resources would be required' over a period of time.[94] The phrase 'of their own', for its part, was interpreted to mean that the feature must have the ability to support an independent economic life.[95] The tribunal adopted a rather high threshold for this requirement, stating that economic activities dependent on external resources, purely extractive activities which do not accrue benefit for the feature or its population, or economic activity derived from the EEZ or continental shelf all do not meet the requirement of 'of their own'.[96] By establishing a close connection between economic activities and the population, as remarked by one scholar, 'the Tribunal sought to laden the description of a 'fully entitled' island with strong connections to human life and human activity'.[97] As such, the tribunal opted for a conjunctive interpretation of

88 Ibid [494].
89 Ibid [497].
90 Ibid [543].
91 Ibid [496].
92 Ibid [495], [496].
93 Ibid [496], [497].
94 Ibid [499].
95 Ibid [500].
96 Ibid [500]–[502].
97 Natalie Klein, 'Islands and Rocks after the South China Sea Arbitration' (2016) 34 Australian Yearbook of International Law 21, 24.

paragraph (3) even though, as mentioned above, it stated that a disjunctive approach is required by virtue of the word 'or'.

After examining the ordinary meaning of the relevant terms, the tribunal proceeded to consider the context of Article 121(3) and the object and purpose of the Convention, as required under Article 31 VCLT. The tribunal found that two aspects of the context of Article 121(3) were of relevance, namely the system of classifying features and the purpose behind the introduction of the EEZ. The former led the tribunal to confirm the interpretation that it adopted based on the ordinary meaning of the word, specifically that the status of a feature must be based on its earlier, natural condition, before intensive human modification. This reading, according to the tribunal, was consistent with the purpose of Article 121(3) as 'a provision of limitation' in order to 'prevent States from claiming for themselves potentially immense maritime space'.[98] As regards the purpose of the EEZ, the tribunal was of the view that the genesis of Article 121(3) 'is inextricably linked with the expansion of coastal State jurisdiction through the exclusive economic zone',[99] and thus the meaning of the Article 121(3) is shaped by this connection. Having found that the purpose of the EEZ was to 'to extend the jurisdiction of States over the waters adjacent to their coasts and to preserve the resources of those waters for the benefit of the population of the coastal State',[100] the tribunal understood that Article 121(3) 'serves to disable tiny features from unfairly and inequitably generating enormous entitlements to maritime space that would serve not to benefit the local population, but to award a windfall to the (potentially distant) State to have maintained a claim to such a feature'.[101] Using the purpose of Article 121(3) to give more concrete guidance to the meaning of the words 'human habitation', the tribunal concluded that human habitation 'should be understood to refer to the habitation of a feature by a settled group or community for whom the feature is a home'.[102]

In order to shed further light on the purpose of Article 121(3), the tribunal then resorted to the *travaux préparatoires* of this paragraph. After a lengthy survey of its negotiating history from 1923 until the conclusion of UNCLOS III, the tribunal found that while the *travaux préparatoires* were 'an imperfect guide', they still helped to confirm the purpose of paragraph (3) as a limiting provision and that the general language of Article 121(3) was a deliberate

98 *South China Sea Arbitration* (n 51) [509].
99 Ibid [512].
100 Ibid [513].
101 Ibid [516].
102 Ibid [520].

choice by the drafters as a result of 'the difficulty in setting, in the abstract, bright-line rules for all cases'.[103] As a result, the assessment of a feature's status has to be made on a case-by-case basis.

Finally, the tribunal examined the relevance of state practice in implementing Article 121(3) as provided under Article 31(3) VCLT. On this point, the tribunal was noticeably brief. It simply stated that the threshold for state practice to constitute an agreement concerning the interpretation of the provision in question 'is quite high'.[104] The tribunal found that 'there is no evidence for an agreement based upon State practice on the interpretation of Article 121(3) which differs from the interpretation of the Tribunal'.[105]

THE TRIBUNAL'S INTERPRETATIVE METHOD. What emerged from the *South China Sea* tribunal's interpretative exercise is the imposition of high thresholds for and strict application of the elements of Article 121(3). In reaching this outcome, three issues relating to the tribunal's interpretative method merit further observations.

First, it seems clear that while the tribunal applied all the elements of treaty interpretation to Article 121(3), the element that carried the most weight in the tribunal's interpretative exercise was the intended purpose of the article. In other words, the tribunal was guided by the goal to give effect to the intended purpose of Article 121(3), which as the tribunal interpreted, was a 'provision of limitation' to 'prevent States from claiming for themselves potentially immense maritime space'.[106] In order to fulfil this purpose, the tribunal's general approach was to impose on Article 121(3) requirements that more or less resembled those required for human life on normal land territory, evidenced particularly in the tribunal's interpretation of the 'human habitation' and 'economic life'. This resulted in a strict interpretation of the conditions of Article 121(3), with a strong focus on the natural state of the feature, excluding any human interference or reliance on extraneous factors. This at first glance suggests that the tribunal was guided by a teleological approach to interpreting Article 121(3). However, what is noteworthy is that the tribunal's understanding of the purpose of Article 121(3) primarily derived from its examination of the negotiating history of this article. Not only did the tribunal conduct a lengthy perusal of the negotiating history of the article itself, but it also frequently referred to the 'intent' of the drafters when it was determining the ordinary

[103] Ibid [537].
[104] Ibid [552].
[105] Ibid [553].
[106] Ibid [621].

meaning of the terms or examining the context of the article. As a result, it could be argued that ultimately what guided the tribunal in its interpretation of Article 121(3) was the intention of the drafters.

The reliance on the intention of the drafters for interpretative purposes, particularly in the case of Article 121(3), raises some problems. First, as the tribunal admitted, the *travaux préparatoires* 'are an imperfect guide'.[107] Due to the nature of the negotiations during UNCLOS III, the reliability or usefulness of the drafting history of the article for interpretative purposes has been cast in doubt.[108] Assuming that the negotiating history of Article 121(3) could shed light on its purpose, it has been observed by several commentators, including those present at the negotiation, that paragraph (3) was the subject of debate between States that wished to expand their maritime entitlements and those which wanted to limit these entitlements and to prevent encroachment on the common heritage of (hu)mankind.[109] The wording of paragraph (3) was initially a synthesis of different alternatives and as such, 'was not a mere amalgamation or choice between conflicting alternatives, but rather was one in which a 'middle course was adopted'.[110] In that sense, it seems difficult to conclude that either side of the debate was successful with regards to the final outcome of paragraph (3). The tribunal's interpretation of the *travaux préparatoires*, however, seems to paint a different picture and suggests that those wishing to limit entitlements had prevailed. Its brief summary of the positions advanced during UNCLOS III provided little support for such a conclusion, rather the tribunal merely discussed proposals for different criteria to include in the wording of Article 121(3).

That said, the tribunal's emphasis on the need to prevent an abuse of Article 121(3) to generate vast EEZ and continental was not unreasonable. As will be discussed below, coastal States' claim to insular features based on Article 121(3) are primarily aimed at maximising their entitlement. At the same time, the approach of international courts and tribunals in delimitation cases involving small, remote insular features has been to limit the entitlement of these features where they have a disproportionate effect compared to the

107 Ibid [534].

108 See, for example, Clive Schofield and Dustin Kuan-Hsiung Wang, 'The Regime of Islands under UNCLOS: Implications for the South China Sea' in Clive Schofield (ed), *Maritime Energy Resources in Asia: Legal Regimes and Cooperation* (National Bureau of Asian Research, Special Report No. 37, February 2012); David Anderson, 'Islands and Rocks in the Modern Law of the Sea' in Myron H Nordquist (ed), *The Law of the Sea: US Accession and Globalisation* (Martinus Nijhoff 2012).

109 Franckx (n 76) 159

110 Ibid.

landmass.[111] The practice of states and international courts suggests that a narrow interpretation is warranted in order to ensure the balance between the rights and the obligations of different States under UNCLOS. In light of China's extensive claims in the South China Sea, the need to ensure the balance was perhaps even more justified.[112] However, it is argued that relying on the *travaux préparatoires* was not the right approach to support this balancing exercise.

Second, questions also arise as to the extent to which the purpose of an article could be relied upon to interpret its wording beyond the ordinary meaning of the terms contained therein. For example, when examining the status of the Spratly Islands, the tribunal found that 'the principal high-tide features in the Spratly islands are capable of enabling the survival of small groups of people'[113] but that this capacity is 'limited'.[114] However, whether or not the capacity to sustain human habitation and economic life is limited arguably does not rule out the capacity of the feature to do so, which is all the wording of Article 121(3) requires. As alluded to above, the tribunal placed particular emphasis on the natural state of feature, reading this requirement into not only the physical characteristics of the feature,[115] but also into the interpretation of terms such as 'sustain', 'economic life of their own'. The tribunal thus adopted a high threshold for the fulfilment of these conditions, ruling out any 'artificial addition',[116] injection of external sources or purely extractive activities not bringing benefits for the local population. In this sense, 'natural' in the tribunal's view seems to be synonymous with 'self-sustained'. Such an interpretation has attracted criticism,[117] for it would exclude the use of technological developments to enhance the capacity of a feature to sustain human habitation or economic life or to enhance the quality of the human habitation up to the minimal 'proper standard' requested by the tribunal itself.[118] As one commentator has argued, 'th[e] text as discussed in its legislative history does not read that all future developments are to rely solely upon

[111] For a general discussion on the effects of islands on maritime delimitation, see, for example: Massimo Lando, *Maritime Delimitation as a Judicial Process* (CUP 2019), 181–193.

[112] Yoshifumi Tanaka, *The South China Sea Arbitration: Toward an International Legal Order in the Oceans* (Hart Publishing 2019) 378 ('the Tribunal's view can be thought to be the antithesis of unilateralism demonstrated by China's claim in the South China Sea').

[113] *South China Sea Arbitration* (n 51) [615].

[114] Ibid [616].

[115] Ibid [508], [511].

[116] Ibid [510].

[117] See, for example, Joanna Mossop, 'The South China Sea Arbitration and New Zealand's Maritime Claims' (2017) 15 New Zealand Journal of Public and International Law 265, 284.

[118] Sondra Faccio, '"Human Habitation or Economic Life of their Own": The Definition of Features between History, Technology and the Law' (2021) 42 Liverpool Law Review 15, 17.

nature, but to take into account ordinary improvements to facilitate sustainability by humans'.[119] However, this commentator's contention that the determination of the status of a feature should be made based on the conditions of the feature at the time of the proceedings, regardless of the conditions of the feature in the past, is not unproblematic. It incentivises States to modify features for the purposes of claiming extensive maritime areas. A loose approach based solely on current and future developments would favour States with advanced technological capacity to claim vast maritime areas based on modified features. The more appropriate view should instead be that so long as the application of technology improves the feature's capacity, and not intensively modified or change the original status of the feature, the role of technology should not be disregarded.

Third, the tribunal's brief examination of the relevance of state practice within the meaning of Article 31(3) VCLT was perhaps the most controversial aspect of its interpretative exercise. To start with, the tribunal searched for 'an agreement based on state practice on the interpretation of Article 121(3) which differs from the interpretation that the tribunal adopted'.[120] This statement places the interpretation adopted by an international tribunal at a higher level of authority than that by States. The test under Article 31(3) VCLT should rather be to determine whether state practice has established an agreement with the interpretation of Article 121(3) then to assess whether the tribunal's interpretation is in line with such an agreement.[121]

In any case, the tribunal did not at all conduct a survey of state practice, and merely reached a conclusion in one sentence. It is questionable whether there even exists 'an agreement based upon State practice' concerning the interpretation of Article 121(3). In practice, a number of States have claimed vast maritime zones from insular features that would arguably not meet the high threshold set by the tribunal under Article 121(3), prompting the critique that 'there is an abyss between the tribunal's approach and the practice of many States'.[122] However, only a handful of States have asserted maximum maritime claims from insular features that are small, uninhabited, remote and

[119] Myron H Nordquist and William G Phalen, 'Interpretation of UNCLOS Article 121 and Itu Aba (Taiping) in the South China Sea Arbitration Award' in Myron H. Nordquist, John Norton Moore, Ronán Long (eds) *International Marine Economy* (Brill Nijhoff Publishers 2017) 196.

[120] *South China Sea Arbitration* (n 51) [553].

[121] See also: Tanaka (n 113) 373.

[122] Alex G Oude Elferink, 'The South China Sea Arbitration's Interpretation of Article 121(3) of the LOSC: A Disquieting First' (*JCLOS Blog*, 7 September 2016) https://site.uit.no/nclos/2016/09/07/the-south-china-sea-arbitrations-interpretation-of-article-1213-of-the-losc-a-disquieting-first/ accessed 25 January 2022.

desolate.[123] Some of these claims have been met with protests from other States,[124] others have not.[125] For example, Australia has claimed an EEZ and continental shelf from Heard and McDonald Islands, both of which would likely not meet the standards set out by the *South China Sea* tribunal. No other States have protested against these claims, even when a submission to an outer continental shelf around these features was lodged with the CLCS. It should be noted that protests lodged at the CLCS are aimed primarily at barring the CLCS from considering or qualifying a submission pertaining to a land or maritime dispute.[126] Heard and McDonald islands are neither currently under dispute between Australia and any other State, nor do the entitlements that the features generate overlap with those of any other States. The lack of protest may be prompted by the lack of political interests on the part of other States, rather than their acquiescence to Australia's application of Article 121(3).[127] As observed by one commentator, '[i]t seems likely that any dispute over the classification of a feature has more to do with its location, rather than the characteristics of the rock itself . . . Where the feature is remote, it is less likely to be challenged'.[128]

In light of the limited State practice that contradicts the tribunal's findings, as well as the existence of protests to some extensive claims and the reasons for the lack of protests to others, it is neither possible to conclude that state practice to the contrary is 'significant' as has been suggested[129] nor that there exists no agreement which differs from the interpretation of the tribunal. Simply put, 'State practice has yet to coalesce around a particular understanding of Article 121'.[130] A closer examination of state practice would have added more nuance to the conclusion reached.

[123] For example: France (Clipperton), Australia (Heard and McDonald), Japan (Okinotorishima), New Zealand (the Kermadec Islands group), Portugal (Savage Islands), Venezuela (Aves Island), Brazil (St Peter and Paul rocks), the US (Johnson Atoll, Jarvis Island, Palmyra Atoll and Kingman Reef). Note UK decided to relinquish the claim to a 200 nm maritime zone surrounding Rockall when acceding to UNCLOS in 1997.

[124] Such as those of Japan, Portugal and Venezuela.

[125] Such as Australia, the United States, New Zealand and Brazil.

[126] Rule 46 of the Rules of Procedure of the (CLCS/40/Rev.1); Paragraph 5(a) of Annex I to the Rules of Procedure of the CLCS.

[127] Symmons (n 81) 112. Note also Judge Vukas, in his Declaration in *Volga* remarked that the establishment of a 200 nm EEZ around Head Island and the McDonald Islands was 'contrary to international law'. *'Volga' (Russian Federation v Australia)* (Declaration of Vice-President Vukas) ITLOS Reports 2002, 10, 47.

[128] Mossop (n 118) 283.

[129] Faccio (n 119) 20.

[130] Ted L McDorman, 'An International Law Perspective on Insular Features (Islands) and Low-tide Elevations in the South China Sea' (2017) 32 The International Journal of Marine and Coastal Law 298, 312.

In summary, due to ambiguous wording of Article 121(3) and the limited available State practice, guidance from the decisions of courts and tribunals for the interpretation of this particular paragraph is much needed.[131] Although this paragraph had been brought before international courts and tribunals in prior instances, the *South China Sea* arbitration was the first time an international tribunal provided a detailed interpretation of Article 121(3). The tribunal should be commended for approaching the task in a systematic manner, clearly explaining the method of interpretation that it employed to conduct its task. Guided primarily by the purpose of paragraph (3), the tribunal adopted a narrow interpretation of and imposed high thresholds for the conditions contained therein. While certain aspects of the tribunal's methodology could be more nuanced, it cannot be denied that the tribunal has provided some important guidance for the factors that should be taken into account in interpreting this article, and as such, provided a useful benchmark for future cases to build upon. As the first tribunal to directly engage with Article 121(3), it remains to be seen whether the tribunal's interpretation will be adopted by other stakeholders, including States whose interpretation differs from that of the tribunal. The *South China Sea* arbitration's interpretation of Article 121(3), therefore, provides an excellent example of the 'interstitial' role of international courts and tribunals. For now, as correctly observed by one commentator, 'the Award is welcomed as part of the steady, slow, incremental progressive development of the Law of the Sea'.[132]

4.2 MARITIME DELIMITATION

Much ink has been spilled on the role that international courts and tribunals play in shaping the law on maritime delimitation, specifically the delimitation of the EEZ and continental shelf. The ICJ in particular has been key in this process, and the three-stage approach that it introduced in *Black Sea* in 2009 has been regarded as *the* established method for continental shelf and EEZ delimitation.[133] By contrast, UNCLOS tribunals have been latecomers in the judicial delimitation process. The first decision concerning maritime delimitation within the framework of Part XV was rendered by the Annex VII arbitral tribunal in *Barbados v Trinidad* and *Tobago* in 2006, while ITLOS did not hear its first maritime delimitation case until 2012 – more than 15 years

[131] Franckx (n 76) 120.
[132] Gullett (n 84) 38.
[133] Lando (n 112) 22.

after it came into existence. Not surprisingly, therefore, UNCLOS tribunals cannot be said to be the pioneers in developing the law with respect to the delimitation of the EEZ and the continental shelf. This statement, however, is only correct insofar as the delimitation of maritime zones within 200 nm is concerned. While the ICJ had engaged with delimitation for nearly half a century, UNCLOS tribunals in the Bay of Bengal cases were the first international tribunals to delimit the continental shelf beyond 200 nm.

To date, Annex VII arbitral tribunals have heard three delimitation cases and ITLOS has rendered two decisions with one pending at the time of writing. In order to provide a complete picture of the development of maritime delimitation as a whole by UNCLOS tribunals, this section is devoted to analysing UNCLOS tribunals' decisions relating to maritime delimitation within and beyond 200 nm. In light of the different roles that UNCLOS tribunals play with respect to the delimitation of maritime zones within and beyond 200 nm as mentioned above, Section 4.2.1 focuses on examining the convergences and divergences in the decisions of UNCLOS tribunals in the application of the established delimitation approaches, and on assessing the implications of the divergences on the law on maritime delimitation within 200 nm. Section 4.2.2 analyses the contribution of UNCLOS tribunals to clarifying the legal ambiguities concerning the delimitation of the continental shelf beyond 200 nm.

4.2.1 *Delimitation of Maritime Zones within 200 Nautical Miles*

Articles 15, 74 and 83 of UNCLOS govern the delimitation of the territorial sea, EEZ and continental shelf, respectively. While the latter two are identical, a major difference exists in the approach of Article 15 and Articles 74/83. Article 15 clearly stipulates the delimitation method, namely equidistance/special circumstances, whereas Articles 74/83 merely states the objective to be achieved by delimitation, namely an equitable solution. As a result, when it comes to the delimitation of the territorial sea, international courts and tribunals are merely called upon to apply the detailed rule contained in Article 15. Their contribution, therefore, does not lie in developing a delimitation method, but rather in clarifying how the two elements of the method are to be applied and how they relate to one another. By contrast, as Articles 74 and 83 are silent as to the method of delimitation, there is much more room available for international courts and tribunals to determine and refine the applicable method. The contribution of UNCLOS tribunals is thus examined in this light. As mentioned above, this section does not rehearse the development of the law on maritime delimitation by international courts

The focus of analysis is limited to situating UNCLOS tribunals' application of the established delimitation method within existing case law in order to identify the extent to which UNCLOS tribunals contributed to clarifying Articles 15, 74 and 83.

4.2.1.1 Delimitation of the Territorial Sea

The delimitation of the territorial sea was brought before the Annex VII arbitral tribunals in two cases, namely *Guyana v Suriname* and *Bangladesh/India*, and before ITLOS in two cases, namely *Bangladesh/Myanmar* and *Ghana/Côte d'Ivoire*. In all of these cases, the parties as well as the relevant UNCLOS tribunal reaffirmed the application of the equidistance/special circumstances as stipulated in Article 15.[134] While the two elements of the delimitation process are clear, questions still remain as to the interaction between the equidistance line and special circumstances. As explained by the ICJ in *Qatar/Bahrain*, '[t]he most logical and widely practised approach is first to draw provisionally an equidistance line and then to consider whether that line must be adjusted in the light of the existence of special circumstances.'[135] However, in all three cases *Guyana v Suriname*, *Bangladesh/Myanmar* and *Bangladesh/India*, the relevant tribunals started the delimitation process not with a provisional equidistance line, but instead by inquiring into the existence or otherwise of special circumstances.

In *Guyana v Suriname*, despite the observation from the outset that 'Article 15 of the Convention places primacy on the median line as the delimitation line between the territorial seas of opposite or adjacent States',[136] the arbitral tribunal began the delimitation process by considering 'whether there are any special circumstances which might justify a departure from the median line approach'.[137] As the tribunal found that 'the 10° Line is established between the Parties from the starting point to the 3 nm limit',[138] it only drew the delimitation line for the territorial sea from 3 to 12 nm, which was 'a line

[134] *The Bay of Bengal Maritime Boundary Arbitration between the People's Republic of Bangladesh and the Republic of India, (Bangladesh/India)* (2014) RIAA XXXII 1 [246]–[247]. In *Ghana/Côte d'Ivoire*, as requested by the parties, the Special Chamber of ITLOS did not delimit the territorial sea separately from the EEZ and the continental shelf. Therefore, the Special Chamber did not apply Article 15.

[135] *Maritime Delimitation and Territorial Questions between Qatar and Bahrain (Qatar v Bahrain)* (Merits) [2001] ICJ Rep 2001, 40 [176].

[136] *Arbitration between Guyana and Suriname (Guyana v Suriname)* (2007) RIAA XXX 1 [296].

[137] Ibid [298].

[138] Ibid [307].

continuing from the seaward terminus of the N10°E line at 3 nm, and drawn diagonally by the shortest distance to meet the line ... to delimit the Parties' continental shelf and [EEZ]'.[139] In constructing this line, however, the tribunal returned to special circumstances and found that 'special circumstance is constituted by the very need to determine such a line from a point at sea fixed by historical arrangements of an unusual nature'.[140] The approach of the tribunal in this case has been interpreted in different ways. One commentator understood the tribunal's approach as merely adjusting the median line over the first three-mile leg of the boundary on account of special circumstances.[141] Another scholar, by contrast, has argued that 'the tribunal had got rid of the equidistance almost from the outset of the delimitation' and as such only paid lip service to this method.[142] Yet another commentator took the view that the tribunal still upheld the two-stage approach consistent with Article 15 in that it adhered to a prior boundary agreement between the parties up to 3 nm, and implicitly considered a provisional equidistance line between 3 and 12 nm.[143] Whatever the debate, what is clear is that the construction of an equidistance line was not the departure point of the delimitation process.

This order of conduct was explicitly confirmed by ITLOS in *Bangladesh/Myanmar*, in which it stated that '[i]t follows from article 15 of the Convention that before the equidistance principle is applied, consideration should be given to the possible existence of historic title or other special circumstances relevant to the area to be delimited.[144] Following this approach, ITLOS proceeded with examining whether St Martin's Island constituted a special circumstance for the purposes of delimiting the territorial sea.[145] Only after it was satisfied that this was not the case did the tribunal engage in the step of constructing the equidistance line. In *Bangladesh/India*, the tribunal similarly first addressed Bangladesh's arguments regarding special circumstances, and only proceeded to constructing the equidistance line after finding that none of the considerations invoked by Bangladesh justified a deviation from the application of the equidistance method.[146] After having established the

[139] *Guyana v Suriname* (n 137) [323]

[140] Ibid.

[141] Stephen Fietta, 'Arbitral Tribunal Decision Guyana v. Suriname' (2008) 46 International Legal Materials 164, 164.

[142] Jianjun Gao, 'Comments on Guyana v Suriname' (2009) 8 CJIL191, 195–196.

[143] Massimo Lando, 'Judicial Uncertainties Concerning Territorial Sea Delimitation Under Article 15 of the United Nations Convention on the Law of the Sea' (2017) 70 ICLQ 589, 595.

[144] *Bangladesh/Myanmar* (n 7) [129].

[145] Ibid [146–152].

[146] *Bangladesh/India* (n 135) [248].

equidistance line, however, the tribunal again looked into special circumstances but this time to see whether 'special circumstances exist which call for an adjustment of the median line in the delimitation of the territorial sea'.[147] It found that indeed 'the need to connect the land boundary terminus to the median line constructed by the Tribunal for the delimitation of the territorial sea constitutes a special circumstance in the present context'.[148] As a result, special circumstances were examined twice,[149] but seemingly for different purposes, namely to consider whether the equidistance line should be used and to see whether the equidistance line should be adjusted. What is even more interesting is that in constructing the equidistance line, the tribunal conducted a separate step for identifying the base points, in which it chose 'the base points it considers appropriate'.[150] It is arguable that by taking upon itself the task of choosing the 'appropriate' base points, particularly by discounting low-tide elevations as base points for the purpose of delimiting the territorial sea, the tribunal in fact considered special circumstance three times, before, during and after drawing the provisional equidistance line. One commentator has termed base points 'pseudo-special circumstances' which find no basis in Article 15.[151]

It follows from the above discussion that the contribution of UNCLOS tribunals to the law on territorial sea lies mainly in clarifying the relationship between the two elements of the delimitation method stipulated in Article 15, namely equidistance and special circumstances. While confirming the applicability of the equidistance line, neither ITLOS nor the Annex VII arbitral tribunals drew provisional equidistance line as the first step in the delimitation process, opting instead to inquire into the existence of special circumstances. This approach of the tribunals stands in contrast with the order set out by the ICJ in *Qatar/Bahrain* as mentioned above. However, it should be noted UNCLOS tribunals were not the first to 'reverse' the order of the steps to be taken pursuant to Article 15. The ICJ in *Nicaragua v Honduras* in 2007, having decided to consider special circumstances as the first step, found that coastal instability constituted a special circumstance which excepted the applicability of any equidistance line and instead opted for the angle-bisector method. The decisions of UNCLOS tribunals would thus seem to follow the approach of

147 Ibid [272].

148 Ibid [274].

149 Lando, 'Judicial Uncertainties Concerning Territorial Sea Delimitation' (n 144) 598.

150 *Bangladesh/India* (n 135) [253].

151 Davor Vidas, 'The Delimitation of the Territorial Sea, the Continental Shelf, and the EEZ' in Oude Elferink, Henriksen and Busch (n 2) 57.

the ICJ in *Nicaragua v Honduras*, suggesting that UNCLOS tribunals have strengthened a new development of the application of the two-stage approach to territorial sea delimitation. More recent decisions involving the delimitation of the territorial sea by the ICJ and other ad hoc tribunals have, however, not endorsed such a development but rather reverted to the order set out in *Qatar/Bahrain*.[152] What is perhaps noteworthy is that the ICJ in *Kenya v Somalia* seems to have followed the approach of the tribunal in *Bangladesh/India* in selecting base points in the construction of the equidistance line. It remains to be seen whether such a trend will be adopted in future cases. In the light of the inconsistency in case law, it cannot be concluded that UNCLOS tribunals have in fact helped to clarify the delimitation rule under Article 15.

4.2.1.2 Delimitation of the EEZ and Continental Shelf

Most maritime delimitation cases brought before international courts and tribunals are concerned with the delimitation of the EEZ and continental shelf. This, coupled with the vagueness of Articles 74 and 83 regarding the applicable delimitation method, means that the law on the delimitation of the EEZ and continental shelf has primarily been judge-made.[153] As mentioned, the ICJ has played an instrumental role in this process. The Court's most significant contribution in this respect can be found in the 2009 *Black Sea* case, in which it laid down a three-stage approach to delimiting the EEZ and the continental shelf.[154] The first stage of this approach is for a court or tribunal to draw an equidistance line as the provisional boundary, followed by the second stage in which the court has to consider whether the equidistance line needs adjustment in light of any relevant circumstances and finally, the third stage consists of the disproportionality test to verify

[152] *Maritime Delimitation in the Caribbean Sea and the Pacific Ocean (Costa Rica v Nicaragua)* (Judgment) [2018] ICJ Rep 2018 and *Land Boundary in the Northern Part of Isla Portillos (Costa Rica v Nicaragua)* (Merits) [2018] ICJ Rep 2018 [98]; *Somalia v Kenya* (n 48) [111]–[112] (the ICJ drew a equidistance line and did not even consider special circumstances); *Arbitration Between the Republic of Croatia and the Republic of Slovenia (Croatia/Slovenia)*, Final Award [1002] https://pcacases.com/web/sendAttach/2172 accessed 25 January 2022.

[153] Yoshifumi Tanaka, *The International Law of the Sea* (3rd ed, CUP) 268.

[154] Note, however, that certain authors have considered that the starting point of the consistent application of the three-stage approach was *Qatar v Bahrain*, even though the ICJ had yet to explicitly spell out this delimitation method. Alex G Oude Elferink, Tore Henriksen and Signe Veierud Busch, 'The Judiciary and the Law of Maritime Delimitation' in Oude Elferink, Henriksen and Busch (n 2) 7.

that the equidistance line, whether adjusted or not, leads to an equitable result.[155] Since *Black Sea*, all international courts and tribunals have applied this method to the delimitation of the EEZ and the continental shelf. This section is neither an attempt to trace the development of the three-stage approach nor does it examine in detail how each of the steps has been applied in case law. It instead focuses on two issues: (i) examining whether and to what extent UNCLOS tribunals have upheld the three-stage approach and (ii) identifying peculiarities, if any, in the operationalisation of the three-stage approach by UNCLOS tribunals that may have repercussions beyond the particular cases. The aim of the section is therefore to again situate the contributions of UNCLOS tribunals to clarifying the delimitation method for the EEZ and continental shelf within existing jurisprudence.

With regards to the first question, it should be noted at the outset that the decisions concerning the delimitation of the EEZ and continental shelf in *Barbados v Trinidad and Tobago* and *Guyana v Suriname* were rendered prior to *Black Sea*. As a result, the three-stage approach as spelled out in *Black Sea* as such was not applied in these cases. In both cases, however, the tribunals adopted what the so-called two-stage approach which, in their view, had until then been applied by different courts and tribunals as well as in state practice.[156] The two-stage approach bore much resemblance to the three-stage approach, save for the third stage of verification by reference to the disproportionality test. However, this difference may just be in name. In these cases, the tribunals still implicitly conducted the third stage, albeit merging it with the second stage by viewing proportionality as a relevant circumstance to consider whether the provisional line produced an equitable result. As a result, while strictly not applying the three-stage approach, the decisions of these two cases will still be taken into consideration for the analysis.

The other three delimitation cases before UNCLOS tribunals, namely *Bangladesh/Myanmar*, *Bangladesh/India* and *Ghana/Côte d'Ivoire*, all explicitly recalled the three-stage approach. However, what is noteworthy is that in all these cases, UNCLOS tribunals did not apply this approach a priori without inquiring into the appropriateness of this approach. In *Bangladesh/Myanmar*, ITLOS stated that:

[155] *Maritime Delimitation in the Black Sea (Romania v Ukraine)* (Judgement) [2009] ICJ Rep 2009, 61 [118]–[122].

[156] *Arbitration between Barbados and the Republic of Trinidad and Tobago, Relating to the Delimitation of the Exclusive Economic Zone and the Continental Shelf Between Them* (2006) RIAA XXVII 147 [242]; *Guyana v Suriname* (n 137) [342].

> the issue of which method should be followed in drawing the maritime delimitation line should be considered in light of the circumstances of each case . . . the method to be followed should be one that, under the prevailing geographic realities and the particular circumstances of each case, can lead to an equitable result.[157]

The arbitral tribunal in *Bangladesh/India* similarly considered that the appropriate delimitation method needs to be determined based on the paramount objective of achieving an equitable result, adding further that 'transparency and the predictability of the delimitation process as a whole are additional objectives to be achieved in the process'.[158] The Special Chamber in *Ghana/Côte d'Ivoire* simply recalled the above statements.[159]

Despite their initial hesitation, UNCLOS tribunals in all three cases eventually adopted the equidistance/relevant circumstances approach. The reason for such a decision in *Bangladesh/Myanmar* was based on the finding that the bisector constructed by Bangladesh 'fails to give adequate effect to the southward projection of the coast of Bangladesh',[160] and that 'jurisprudence has developed in favour of the equidistance/relevant circumstances method'.[161] In *Bangladesh/India*, the arbitral tribunal assessed the appropriateness of the two equidistance/relevant circumstances and the angle-bisector methods at a more abstract level. It found that 'the advantage of the equidistance/relevant circumstances method lies in the fact that it clearly separates the steps to be taken and is thus more transparent'.[162] On that basis, it concluded that equidistance/relevant circumstances 'is preferrable'[163] though still noting that there may be cases which make the application of this method inappropriate. Using similar language, the Special Chamber in *Ghana/Côte d'Ivoire* acknowledged that 'the international jurisprudence concerning the delimitation of maritime spaces in principle favours the equidistance/relevant circumstances methodology' and that 'in the absence of any compelling reasons that make it impossible or inappropriate to draw a provisional equidistance line, the equidistance/relevant circumstances methodology should be chosen'.[164] After conducting a lengthy examination of the arguments put forward by Côte d'Ivoire for the use of the angle-bisector methodology, the Special

157 *Bangladesh/Myanmar* (n 7) [235].
158 *Bangladesh/India* (n 135) [339].
159 *Ghana/Côte d'Ivoire* (n 39) [289].
160 *Bangladesh/Myanmar* (n 7) [237].
161 Ibid [238].
162 *Bangladesh/India* (n 135) [343].
163 Ibid [345].
164 *Ghana/Côte d'Ivoire* (n 39) [289].

Chamber concluded that it saw 'no convincing reason to deviate in this case from the equidistance/relevant circumstances methodology'[165]

Although UNCLOS tribunals eventually decided to draw the equidistance line in these three cases, their examination suggests that this was only so because it was the most appropriate in the specific circumstances of the case in question. The fact that the tribunals conducted an inquiry into the appropriateness of the delimitation method, and particularly the emphasis placed on achieving an equitable result, further indicated that they did not view the equidistance/relevant circumstances as the compulsory starting point for the delimitation process in every case.[166] In other words, while preferrable, equidistance/relevant circumstances method is not required as a matter of law.[167] UNCLOS tribunals' inquiry into the appropriateness of this method before applying it can be contrasted with the ICJ's willingness to embrace this method with little hesitation in cases post-Black Sea.[168] In *Somalia v Kenya*, however, the Court, similar to UNCLOS tribunals, began the delimitation process with the observation that the three-stage approach 'is not mandatory' and thus should not be applied if there are factors that make the application of this method inappropriate.[169] UNCLOS tribunals' approach highlights that the result-oriented approach to delimitation advanced in earlier case law has not completely disappeared. What guided the tribunals' determination of the appropriate delimitation method was the goal that it was to fulfil, which consisted of not only achieving an equitable solution as required by Articles 74/83 but also providing certainty and transparency in the process. The equidistance/relevant circumstances method was thus favoured, not because it is mandatory as such, but because it met these criteria.

With regards to the application of the three-stage approach, UNCLOS tribunals in all relevant cases systematically engaged with each stage of the process. However, while the method is described as having three separate consecutive stages, UNCLOS tribunals have applied these stages in a rather fluid manner. This is most prominently demonstrated in the merging of the first and second stages. In conducting constructing what supposed to be an

165 Ibid [324].

166 See: Donald McRae, 'The Applicable Law' in Oude Elferink, Henriksen and Busch (n 2) 114 (arguing that equidistance has been elevated into an almost mandatory provision – a result that seems at odds with the objectives behind Article 74/83).

167 Malcom D Evans, 'Relevant Circumstances' in *Maritime Boundary Delimitation: The Case Law* (n 167) 239.

168 See, for example, *Nicaragua v Colombia* (2012) (n 43) [190]; *Maritime Dispute (Peru v Chile)* (Judgment) [2014] ICJ Rep 2014 [180]; *Costa Rica v Nicaragua* (n 153) [135].

169 *Somalia v Kenya* (n 48) [128], [129].

objective equidistance line on the basis of the relevant baselines pursuant to the rules contained in UNCLOS,[170] the tribunals in fact considered relevant circumstances. These considerations were motivated by the need to ensure an equitable result, which belongs to the latter stages. In *Bangladesh/Myanmar*, for example, ITLOS when constructing the provisional equidistance line, disregarded St. Martin's Island as a base point for the purposes of constructing an equidistance line for the EEZ and continental shelf. ITLOS explained that 'the selection of a base point on St. Martin's Island would result in a line that blocks the seaward projection from Myanmar's coast'.[171] As argued by one commentator, 'cut-off seaward projections and considerations of small insular features that unduly distort the direction of a delimitation line are quintessential relevant circumstances'.[172] While the *Bangladesh/India* tribunal's and the *Ghana/Côte d'Ivoire* Special Chamber's selection of base points did not raise serious problems per se, on a more general level, by assuming the task of selecting 'appropriate' baselines for constructing the provisional equidistance line, UNCLOS tribunals have allowed the weighing and balancing of more subjective factors to enter into the first stage. As remarked by one commentator, whilst '[t]he airtight distinction between stages of the delimitation process appears to be artificial . . . it is feasible practically to apply [the] process without pre-empting at an earlier stage a decision belonging in a later stage.'[173] Yet this seems to be exactly what ITLOS did in *Bangladesh/Myanmar*. If the equidistance line constructed in the first phase has already been adjusted with a view to ensuring an equitable result, what remains for the second stage, particularly in light of the fact the relevant circumstances have increasingly been found to only consist of geographical-based factors?[174]

That said, UNCLOS tribunals' application of the three-stage approach as analysed above is not peculiar. The discretion to select 'appropriate' base points and the exclusion of islands in the construction of the provisional equidistance line were already present in *Black Sea* in which the ICJ spelled out the three-stage approach as well as in subsequent cases.[175] In that light, for better or worse, it may be concluded that UNCLOS tribunals' application of

[170] Alex G Oude Elferink, Tore Henriksen and Signe Veierud Busch, 'Conclusions' in Oude Elferink, Henriksen and Busch (n 2) 379.

[171] *Bangladesh/Myanmar* (n 7) [265].

[172] Coalter G Lathrop, 'The Provisional Equidistance Line' in Oude Elferink, Henriksen and Busch (n 2) 218.

[173] Lando, *Maritime Delimitation as a Judicial Process* (n 112) 24.

[174] McRae (n 167) 111.

[175] See: Malcolm D Evans, 'Maritime Boundary Delimitation' in Donald R Rothwell and others (eds), *The Oxford Handbook of the Law of the Sea* (OUP 2015) 274.

the three-stage approach has been consistent with existing case law – at least at the theoretical level.

In the end, *Ghana/Côte d'Ivoire* was the only case in which the final delimitation line was the provisional equidistance line. By contrast, in both Bay of Bengal cases, ITLOS and the Annex VII arbitral tribunal, on account of the cut-off effect resulting from the concavity of Bangladesh's coast as a relevant circumstance, adjusted the provisional line by drawing an azimuth of a particular angle, resulting in the final delimitation line that is anything but equidistance. Both tribunals have been criticised for not providing satisfactory explanation for neither the adjustment of the equidistance nor the angle chosen for the azimuth.[176] The tribunals' similar approaches in these cases raise the question of whether they were actually applying the three-stage approach or merely paying lip service to it.[177]

In sum, UNCLOS tribunals have embraced the two-stage method as specified in Article 15 for the delimitation of the territorial sea and the three-stage method as established by the ICJ for the delimitation of the EEZ and the continental shelf. While there may be issues in the way UNCLOS tribunals have applied these methods in the relevant cases, these issues are by no means unique to UNCLOS tribunals. In other words, UNCLOS tribunals have more or less followed the approach of the ICJ in applying the different stages of the delimitation methods. As a result, it may be concluded that UNCLOS tribunals have contributed to a collective endeavour to maintain continuity and certainty in the development of the law on maritime delimitation.

4.2.2 *Delimitation of the Continental Shelf Beyond 200 Nautical Miles*

Even though Article 83 UNCLOS relating to the delimitation of the continental does not distinguish between the continental shelf within and beyond 200 nm, the delimitation of the outer continental shelf undoubtedly raises complicated issues due to the unique nature of the outer continental shelf regime. ITLOS and the Annex VII arbitral tribunal have rendered decisions relating to the delimitation of the continental shelf beyond 200 nm in three

[176] See, for example, *Robin Churchill*, 'The *Bangladesh/Myanmar* Case: Continuity and Novelty in the Law of Maritime Boundary Delimitation' (2012) 1(1) Cambridge Journal of International and Comparative Law 137, 144.

[177] Malcolm D Evans, 'Maritime Boundary Delimitation: Whatever Next?' in Jill Barrett and Richard Barnes (eds) *Law of the Sea: UNCLOS as a Living Treaty* (British Institute of International and Comparative Law, 2017).

cases,[178] namely *Bangladesh/Myanmar*, *Bangladesh/India*, and *Ghana/Côte d'Ivoire*. This section critically examines the significance of UNCLOS tribunals' decisions, with references to the decisions of other courts where appropriate, in clarifying the following issues: (i) the relationship between delimitation and delineation in the case of the outer continental shelf, (ii) the delimitation method for the outer continental shelf and (iii) the grey area.

4.2.2.1 Relationship between Delimitation and Delineation

In the context of the outer continental shelf, 'delimitation' refers to the establishment of a boundary that divides overlapping entitlements lying beyond 200 nm from the baselines of one or more States, whereas delineation refers to the establishment of the limits of the continental shelf, in the process of which the CLCS is involved. While there has been some confusion relating to the two terms 'delimitation' and 'delineation',[179] ITLOS made clear in *Bangladesh/Myanmar* that delineation and delimitation are two distinct concepts.[180] Delimitation does not depend on delineation, meaning that delimitation can be carried out regardless of whether the outer limits of the continental shelf have been identified. Delimitation only requires that the parties' entitlements to an outer continental shelf exist and that those entitlements overlap.[181]

On the basis of this distinction, UNCLOS tribunals in the two *Bangladesh/Myanmar* and *Bangladesh/India* cases also clarified the much debated relationship between the UNCLOS tribunals and the CLCS.[182] In particular,

[178] The Annex VII arbitral tribunal confirmed jurisdiction to delimit the outer continental shelf in *Barbados v Trinidad and Tobago* in 2007, but it did not proceed to delimit the outer continental shelf after finding that 'the single maritime boundary which the Tribunal has determined is such that, as between Barbados and Trinidad, there is no single maritime boundary beyond 200 nm'. See *Barbados v Trinidad and Tobago* (n 157) [368].

[179] Several scholars have used the terms 'delimitation' and 'delimitation' interchangeably; in particular, 'delimitation' has been used in place of 'delineation' when referring to the procedures under Article 76 UNCLOS. See, for example, Ron Macnab, 'The Case for Transparency in the Delimitation of the Outer Continental Shelf in Accordance with UNCLOS Article 76' (2004) 35 ODIL, 1; Vincente Marotta Rangel, 'Settlement of Disputes Relating to the Delimitation of the Outer Continental Shelf: The Role of International Courts and Arbitral Tribunals' (2006) 21(3) IJMCL 347.

[180] *Bangladesh/Myanmar* (n 7) [376].

[181] Ibid [397]–[399].

[182] See Bjorn Kunoy, 'The Terms of Reference of the Commission on the Limits of the Continental Shelf: A Creeping Legal Mandate' (2012) 25(1) LJIL 109; Alex G Oude Elferink, 'The Continental Shelf beyond 200 Nautical Miles: The Relationship between the CLCS and Third Party Dispute Settlement' in Alex G Oude Elferink and Donald Rothwell, *Oceans Management in the 21st Century: Institutional Frameworks and Responses* (Brill 2004) 118.

ITLOS stated that, as a dispute settlement body, it has the legal expertise to interpret and apply the provisions of the Convention; while the CLCS deals with scientific and technical issues.[183] As 'the question of the Parties' entitlement to a continental shelf beyond 200 nm raises issues that are predominantly legal in nature', ITLOS was in a position to examine this issue under Article 76.[184] With regard to the interaction between the tasks of the two bodies, that is, between delimitation and delineation, ITLOS noted that there was nothing in the Convention, the Rules of Procedure of the Commission or in its practice to indicate that delimitation of the continental shelf constituted an impediment to the performance by the Commission of its functions.[185] ITLOS thus adopted the view, which was subsequently followed by the Annex VII arbitral tribunal in *Bangladesh/India*, that the absence of a CLCS recommendation relating to the limits of the continental shelf beyond 200 nm could not prevent it from determining the existence of entitlement to the continental shelf and delimiting the continental shelf between the parties concerned.[186]

It should be noted, however, that even though ITLOS took pains to show that 'delimitation by an international tribunal would not prejudice the work of the CLCS',[187] such a blanket statement might not be true for all cases. ITLOS' pronouncement must be properly situated in the context of the Bay of Bengal, which is unique in terms of the thickness of the layer of sediment on its the sea floor as acknowledged by the tribunal,[188] and indicated in Bangladesh, Myanmar and India's submissions to the CLCS.[189] It was beyond any doubt that the parties had entitlement even when the CLCS had not issued its recommendations. In cases which do not share the same characteristics as the Bay of Bengal, that is, where significant uncertainty exists regarding entitlement, the delimitation effected by a dispute settlement body before

[183] *Bangladesh/Myanmar* (n 7) [411].
[184] Ibid [413].
[185] Ibid [377].
[186] *Bangladesh/India* (n 135) [410].
[187] *Bangladesh/Myanmar* (n 7) [379].
[188] Ibid [444].
[189] Continental Shelf Submission of the Union of Myanmar, 3 /www.un.org/Depts/los/clcs_new/submissions_files/mmr08/mmr_es.pdf accessed 25 January 2022; Submission by the People's Republic of Bangladesh to the Commission on the Limits of the Continental Shelf, para 6.5 / www.un.org/Depts/los/clcs_new/submissions_files/bgd55_11/Executive%20summary%20final.pdf accessed 25 January 2022; The Indian Continental Shelf, Partial Submission to the Commission on the Limits of the Continental Shelf, Pursuant to Article 76, paragraph 8 of the United Nations Convention on the Law of the Sea, Appendix 1 www.un.org/Depts/los/clcs_new/submissions_files/ind48_09/ind2009executive_summary.pdf accessed 25 January 2022.

the outer limits have been identified may in fact encroach on the work of the CLCS and thus caution should be exercised.[190]

The clarification of the interrelated but independent relationship between the two institutions has a significant bearing on the temporal order in which delimitation and delineation are to be carried out. Before the Bay of Bengal decisions, some scholars had argued that delimitation should not and could not be conducted prior to delineation.[191] The UNCLOS tribunals decisions, however, rejected this absolute view. Consequently, as has been noted, 'States are now free to choose whichever course of action to first undertake, be it the CLCS path or the delimitation of the continental shelf with their neighbouring States'.[192] The decisions of ITLOS and the Annex VII arbitral tribunal in the Bay of Bengal cases regarding the relationship between a dispute settlement body and the CLCS stood in contrast with earlier decisions by other international courts and tribunals.[193] However, in subsequent cases such as *Nicaragua v Colombia* (2016) and *Somalia v Kenya* the ICJ essentially adopted the view of UNCLOS tribunals in the Bay of Bengal cases[194] As a result, despite some initial inconsistencies, the approach of international courts and tribunals regarding the relationship between a dispute settlement body and the CLCS, along with its implications on the former's jurisdiction to delimit the outer continental shelf, seems to have converged.

In short, UNCLOS tribunals have provided an answer to the long-debated relationship between the two newly established institutions of UNCLOS, the dispute settlement bodies and the CLCS, thereby clarifying to a certain extent the application of Article 76(10) UNCLOS. However, while the approach adopted by UNCLOS tribunals was enlightening, the decisions reached were limited to the factual circumstances of the cases. Consequently, caution

[190] See: Lan Ngoc Nguyen, 'UNCLOS Tribunals and the Development of the Outer Continental Shelf Regime' (2018) 67(2) International and Comparative Law Quarterly 425, 442–447.

[191] Bjorn Kunoy, 'The Admissibility of a Plea to an International Adjudicative Forum to Delimit the Outer Continental Shelf Prior to the Adoption of Final Recommendations by the Commission on the Limits of the Continental Shelf' (2010) 25 IJMCL 237.

[192] Bjarni Már Magnússon, 'Is there a Temporal Relationship between the Delineation and the Delimitation of the Continental Shelf beyond 200 Nautical Miles?' (2013) 28 IJMCL 465, 483.

[193] See, for example, *Delimitation of Maritime Areas between Canada and France* (1992) RIAA XXI 265 [81]; *Territorial and Maritime Dispute between Nicaragua and Honduras in the Caribbean Sea (Nicaragua v Honduras)* [2007] ICJ Rep 659 [319] (although only implicitly); *Nicaragua v Colombia* (2012; *Territorial and Maritime Dispute (Nicaragua v Colombia)*, Separate Opinion of Judge Donoghue [25].

[194] *Nicaragua v Colombia* (2016) (n 45) [106].

should be exercised when attempting to generalise the tribunal's conclusions in the Bay of Bengal cases to all other situations.

4.2.2.2 Delimitation Method Applicable to the Outer Continental Shelf

UNCLOS tribunals in the three cases *Bangladesh/Myanmar*,[195] *Bangladesh/India*[196] *and Ghana/Côte d'Ivoire*[197] all stated that the delimitation method to be employed for the continental shelf beyond 200 nm should not differ from that applicable to the continental shelf within 200 nm. In other words, the delimitation method applicable to the outer continental shelf continued to be the equidistance/relevant circumstances method. As one commentator noted, '[t]he approach of the ITLOS, including the references to LOSC Article 83, gives strong support to the equidistance/relevant circumstances methodology *prima facie* applying to overlapping shelf claims beyond 200 nm'.[198]

While the equidistance/relevant circumstances method was purportedly used in all the three cases, the way it was applied differed drastically in each case. In *Bangladesh/Myanmar*, ITLOS completed the delimitation of the EEZ and continental shelf within 200 nm before moving on to delimiting the continental shelf beyond 200 nm. For this task, based on the argument that 'Article 83 applies equally to the delimitation of the continental shelf within and beyond 200 nm', meaning that 'the delimitation method for the continental shelf beyond 200 nm should not differ from that within 200 nm',[199] ITLOS simply concluded that the maritime boundary within 200 nm 'continues in the same direction beyond the 200 nm limit of Bangladesh until it reaches the area where the rights of third States may be affected'.[200] In *Bangladesh/India*, the arbitral tribunal did not conduct the delimitation of the areas within and beyond 200 nm in two distinct phases like ITLOS. The tribunal first drew a provisional equidistance line for the delimitation of the areas within 200 nm but did not adjust it at this stage, deciding rather to adjust the equidistance line within and beyond 200 nm together. For the delimitation of the continental shelf beyond 200 nm, the tribunal again applied this method from scratch by constructing a provisional equidistance line and then

195 *Bangladesh/Myanmar* (n 7) [455].
196 *Bangladesh/India* (n 135) [465].
197 *Ghana/Côte d'Ivoire* (n 39) [526].
198 Ted L McDorman, 'The Continental Shelf Regime in the Law of the Sea Convention: A Reflection on the First Thirty Years' in David Freestone (ed), *The 1982 Law of the Sea Convention at 30: Successes, Challenges and New Agendas* (Brill 2013) 76.
199 *Bangladesh/Myanmar* (n 7) [456].
200 Ibid [462].

considering the relevant circumstances. In *Ghana/Côte d'Ivoire*, the Special Chamber, having constructed a single equidistance line for the delimitation of the territorial sea, EEZ and continental shelf within 200 nm and having found that were not relevant circumstances that would justify an adjustment of the provisional line,[201] simply stated that the delimitation line for the areas within 200 nm 'continues in the same direction until it reaches the outer limits of the continental shelf'.[202] It would seem that the Special Chamber's approach in *Ghana/Côte d'Ivoire* bore greater resemblance to that of ITLOS in *Bangladesh/Myanmar*.

Judge Treves commended ITLOS in *Bangladesh/Myanmar* – being the first international tribunal to have proceeded with delimitation of the outer continental shelf – for having '[kept] in mind the need to ensure consistency and coherence' by following the methodology developed by the ICJ and recent arbitral awards on delimitation, but still contributing 'its own grain of wisdom and particular outlook'[203] in applying the notion of relevant circumstances and in its decision to delimit the continental shelf beyond 200 nm. Judge Treves commented that ITLOS, in so doing, had 'become an active participant in a collective interpretative endeavour of international courts and tribunals'.[204] However, the differences among the three cases show that there is hitherto little consistency in the application of the equidistance/relevant circumstances in the delimitation of the outer continental shelf.

More generally at the conceptual level, there is the question of whether the equidistance/relevant circumstances method should be the appropriate method for the delimitation of the outer continental shelf. Article 83 only specifies that the result for delimitation of the continental shelf, be it within or beyond 200 nm, should be equitable; it does not say that the method has to be the same.[205] Both the ITLOS and the Annex VII tribunal relied on the 'one continental shelf' argument to determine that the equidistance/relevant circumstances method, which had only been developed through case law for the delimitation of areas *within* 200 nm, was also applicable to the delimitation of

[201] *Ghana/Côte d'Ivoire* (n 39) [480].
[202] Ibid [527].
[203] *Delimitation of the Maritime Boundary in the Bay of Bengal (Bangladesh/Myanmar)* (Judgment, Decl. Treves) ITLOS Reports 2012 [2].
[204] Ibid.
[205] Alex G Oude Elferink, 'ITLOS' Approach to the Delimitation of the Continental Shelf Beyond 200 Nautical Miles in the Bangladesh/Myanmar Case: Theoretical and Practical Difficulties' in Rüdiger Wolfrum, Maja Seršić and Trpimir M Šošić (eds), *Contemporary Developments in International Law: Essays in Honour of Budislav Vukas* (Brill 2016) 240.

areas *beyond* 200 nm without undertaking a serious examination of its ability to produce an equitable outcome beyond this distance. ITLOS explained in *Bangladesh/Myanmar* that the equidistance/relevant circumstances method was 'rooted in the recognition that sovereignty over the land territory is the basis for the sovereign rights and jurisdiction of the coastal State with respect to both the exclusive economic zone and the continental shelf'.[206] However, it is difficult to see how sovereignty over land territory accounts for extending the equidistance/relevant circumstances method beyond 200 nm. Due to the differences between the inner and the outer continental shelf in terms of the basis for entitlement, the criteria for establishing the limits as well as the role that the Convention assigns to the CLCS, the automatic application of the equidistance/relevant circumstances method by UNCLOS tribunals to delimiting the outer continental shelf may raise certain questions. In particular, it is questionable whether (i) equidistance should be used as the starting point; (ii) whether circumstances deemed relevant within 200 nm continue to be appropriate beyond 200 nm, and (iii) whether the proportionality test provides an accurate outcome in the absence of the outer limits.

First, as has been argued by several scholars, the use of the equidistance line as the starting point of the three-stage approach is grounded on the basis for entitlement.[207] The International Law Association Committee on Legal Issues of the Outer Limits of the Continental Shelf was of the opinion that 'the fact that the basis for entitlement to continental shelf and its delimitation are linked suggests that the process of delimitation may be different within and beyond 200 nm'.[208] On the one hand, the basis for entitlement for the continental shelf within 200 nm – similar to that of the EEZ – is the distance from the coast. On the other hand, entitlement to the continental shelf beyond 200 nm, as analysed above,[209] is the location of the outer edge of the continental margin determined by geomorphological and geological criteria. Given the importance the geomorphology and geology conditions of the seabed for the outer continental shelf, it is not clear whether equidistance line should still retain its primacy as the first step in delimitation, or whether a method that is more consistent with the basis of entitlement needs

[206] *Bangladesh/Myanmar* (n 7) [91].
[207] Yoshifumi Tanaka, *Predictability and Flexibility in the Law of Maritime Delimitation* (2nd ed, Hart 2006) 147–148.
[208] Committee on 'Legal Issues of the Outer Limits of the Continental Shelf' (the ILA Committee) (Preliminary Report) in International Law Association Report of the Seventy Conference (New Delhi, 2002) (International Law Association 2002) 741, 751.
[209] See Section 4.1.1.1.

to be used.[210] The simple argument of 'one single continental shelf' does not provide an adequate answer to this question.

This is not to say that the use of equidistance is categorically inappropriate for delimitation beyond 200 nm. The point is simply that UNCLOS tribunals should have provided clearer explanation for this issue, on which opinions remain divided. Lando has argued that 'Article 76 suggests that distance is not unrelated to the basis of title over the continental shelf beyond 200 nm.'[211] Based on the references to distance contained in paragraphs (4)–(6) of Article 76, the author concludes that 'using equidistance as a delimitation method beyond 200 nm could be legally grounded in UNCLOS'.[212] By contrast, Liao took the view that the use of equidistance is not inherently connected with distance, it was chosen merely because it is likely to result in an equitable result.[213] Accordingly, Liao contends that there does not exist a normative link between entitlement and delimitation methods.[214] Given the attention devoted to clarifying the basis of entitlement to the continental shelf beyond 200 nm in the Bay of Bengal cases, it would have been desirable if a more detailed examination had been conducted on the relationship between the basis of entitlement and the delimitation method chosen for the continental shelf beyond 200 nm.

Second, regarding relevant circumstances calling for the adjustment of the provisional boundary, both ITLOS and Annex VII arbitral tribunal only took into account those that had already been considered relevant for the areas of water within 200 nm, such as concavity of the coast producing cutoff effects. No mention was made to those that are peculiar to the areas beyond 200 nm, namely geological or geomorphological circumstances. ITLOS in *Bangladesh/Myanmar* rejected Bangladesh' argument relating to 'the most natural prolongation' as a relevant circumstance in the delimitation of the outer continental shelf.[215] However, this decision cannot be taken to mean,

210 David Anderson, 'Developments in Maritime Boundary Law and Practice' in David A Colson and Robert W Smith (eds), *International Maritime Boundaries*, Volume V (Brill Nijhoff Publishers 2005), 3214; Liao (n 25) 228.

211 Lando, *Maritime Delimitation as a Judicial Process* (n 112) 132.

212 Ibid.

213 Liao (n 25) 235. See also: Prosper Weil, *The Law of Maritime Delimitation – Reflections* (Maureen MacGlashan tr, Cambridge Grotius Publications Limited 1989) 282.

214 Liao (n 25) 245.

215 This decision received support from Judges ad hoc Mensah and Oxman in their Joint Declaration in *Bangladesh/Myanmar*. See: *Delimitation of the Maritime Boundary in the Bay of Bengal (Bangladesh/Myanmar)* (Judgment, Joint Decl. Mensah and Oxman) ITLOS Reports 2012, 4 [11].

as one author has contended, that ITLOS 'rejects geology as a relevant circumstance for the delimitation of the outer continental shelf; in other words, geology is completely immaterial beyond 200 nm'.[216] ITLOS's rejection of 'the most natural prolongation' argument flowed from a conclusion it adopted earlier that 'natural prolongation' could not constitute an independent criterion to prove entitlement to the outer continental shelf. In ITLOS's view, therefore, Bangladesh could not claim that because it had more 'natural prolongation', it should be entitled to a bigger shelf. There is no basis to suggest that ITLOS's rejection of the 'most natural prolongation' argument amounted to a complete rejection of the relevance of geological and/or geomorphological criteria in the delimitation process. In fact, in the Bay of Bengal cases, neither the ITLOS nor the Annex VII arbitral tribunal explicitly said anything to endorse or reject the relevance of geological factors in the delimitation of the outer continental shelf. Interestingly, however, in *Bangladesh/Myanmar*, ITLOS declined to accept that the Bengal depositional system was relevant to the delimitation of the EEZ and the continental shelf *within* 200 nm as:

> The location and direction of the single maritime boundary applicable both to the seabed and subsoil and to the superjacent waters within the 200 nm limit are to be determined on the basis of geography of the coasts of the Parties in relation to each other and not on the geology or geomorphology of the seabed of the delimitation area.[217]

This statement is reminiscent of the statement made by the ICJ in *Libya/Malta* that there was no 'reason why a factor which has no part to play in the establishment of title should be taken into account as a relevant circumstance for the purposes of delimitation'.[218] In fact, in no cases in which the delimitation of the continental shelf within 200 nm was at issue before the ICJ did the Court find geophysical factors put forward by the parties relevant.[219] This would seem to suggest that, *a contrario*, if a factor has a part to play in the establishment of the shelf, it should be taken into account. It follows that the decisions of international courts and tribunals to date, including those of UNCLOS tribunals, leave open the possibility that geological and geomorphological factors may be deemed relevant to delimitation on the outer

[216] Bjarni Már Magnússon, *The Continental Shelf Beyond 200 nm: Delineation, Delimitation and Dispute Settlement* (Brill 2016) 170.
[217] *Bangladesh/Myanmar* (n 7) [322].
[218] *Libya v Malta* (n 1) [40].
[219] *Tunisia v Libyan* (n 11) [67]; *Gulf of Maine* (n 11) [45]; *Libya v Malta* (n 1) [34].

continental shelf since they do in fact have a role to play in forming the basis of entitlement to such an area.[220]

Moreover, if, as UNCLOS tribunals reiterated, there is only 'one continental shelf', Article 76 including those paragraphs that pertain to the outer continental shelf and Article 83 should have a close connection. This strengthens the contention that geological and geomorphological factors should have a role to play in the delimitation of the outer continental shelf. Of course, this does not suggest that geomorphological or geological factors 'operate to the exclusion of other relevant facts in the delimitation of the outer continental shelf'.[221] The decision as to which factor could be deemed relevant can only be made on a case-by-case basis, so long as the solution is equitable as required by Article 83.

Finally, the last step in the equidistance/relevant circumstances method is a (dis)proportionality test in order to ensure that the boundary line drawn by the tribunal produces an equitable result for the parties concerned. The proportionality test requires the tribunal to check if the boundary line, whether adjusted or not, 'results in any significant disproportion between the ratio of the respective coastal lengths and the ratio of the relevant maritime areas allocated to each Party'.[222] However, in both the Bay of Bengal cases, the outer limits of the continental shelf had not been identified, giving rise to the question as to whether it was even possible for the tribunals to have definitively known the total area overlapping the outer continental shelf of the two parties? ITLOS determined that the relevant maritime area for the purpose of the delimitation of the EEZ and the continental shelf between Bangladesh and Myanmar was that resulting from the projections of the relevant coasts of the Parties.[223] No attention was paid to the outer limits of the shelf, or the lack thereof. In *Bangladesh/India*, the arbitral tribunal took cognisance of the outer limits of the continental shelf by referring to Bangladesh's submission to CLCS in order to determine the south and southwest limits of the relevant area.[224] However, this also meant that an Annex VII arbitral tribunal took upon itself to validate Bangladesh's submission regarding its outer continental shelf limits, which could prejudice the work of the CLCS.[225] In *Ghana/Côte*

[220] See also: Øystein Jensen, 'The Delimitation of the Continental Shelf beyond 200 nm' in Oude Elferink, Henriksen and Busch (n 2) 371.

[221] David A Colson, 'The Delimitation of the Outer Continental Shelf between Neighboring States' (2003) 97 AJIL 91, 100–103.

[222] *Bangladesh/Myanmar* (n 7) [240].

[223] Ibid [489].

[224] *Bangladesh/India* (n 135) [309], [310].

[225] Kunoy, 'The Admissibility of a Plea' (n 192) 258.

d'Ivoire, ITLOS conceded that the size of the relevant area 'can only be an approximation' as 'the outer limits of the continental shelf beyond 200 nm have not yet been finally established'.[226] If the relevant maritime area could not be conclusively determined due to the lack of the outer limits of the continental, it is questionable whether the proportionality test could be performed or whether the final boundary line would ensure an equitable result.

In short, the delimitation method applicable to the continental shelf beyond 200 nm has been clarified, but many questions regarding its appropriateness and its ability to produce an equitable result as required by Article 83 remain unresolved.

4.2.2.3 Grey Area

The delimitation of the continental shelf beyond 200 nm in both the Bay of Bengal cases gave rise to an area known as the 'grey area', in which sovereign rights over the seabed and the superjacent water belong to two different States. The grey area results from a situation in which the delimitation line which is not an equidistance line reaches the outer limit of one State's EEZ and continued beyond it in the same direction, until it reaches the outer limit of the other State's EEZ.[227] The tribunals' limited explanation for the creation of the grey area has raised doctrinal questions regarding the relationship between the EEZ and the continental shelf, as well as practical questions regarding the implementation of rights and obligations in the EEZ and continental shelf within the grey area. These two issues are examined in turn.

To start with, in creating the grey area, UNCLOS tribunals practically severed Myanmar's and India's subsoil and seabed in the EEZ from their respective superjacent water, and allowed Bangladesh' 'outer' continental shelf to extend into what would have been the other two parties' 'inner' continental shelf. The implication of the tribunals' decisions is two-fold: (i) the regimes of the EEZ and continental shelf are separable within 200 nm; and (ii) a State's entitlement to an area beyond 200 nm can encroach on another state's entitlement to continental shelf within 200 nm of its coastal baselines. These implications are highly significant for the long-standing debate on the relationship between the EEZ and the continental shelf, as well as that between the 'inner' and 'outer' continental shelf. However, as will

226 *Ghana/Côte d'Ivoire* (n 39) [534].
227 *Bangladesh/Myanmar* (n 7) [464].

be shown below, the tribunals' scarce and unsatisfactory reasoning in support of the grey area seems to have raised more questions than answers.

Both the ITLOS and the Annex VII tribunal invoked Articles 56(3) and 68 to explain the legal basis for the 'grey area'.[228] By relying on these articles, the tribunals seemed to suggest that the Convention already envisioned the separation of the water column and the seabed within 200 nm. It is true that the regimes regulating the waters, and seabed and subsoil within 200 nm are provided for in different parts of UNCLOS. Article 56(3) suggests that notwithstanding the introduction of the EEZ, which significantly impacted the way the limits of the continental shelf are determined under UNCLOS as well as the delimitation method adopted by international tribunals within 200 nm, the EEZ and continental shelf are still two distinct maritime zones. The EEZ regime neither causes the continental shelf regime to cease to exist, nor does the EEZ regime to subsume the continental shelf regime.[229]

However, paragraph (3) of Article 56 cannot be read in isolation. It should instead be interpreted within the context of Article 56 as a whole, including paragraph (1) and taking into account international jurisprudence which emphasises the similarities, even homogeneity, of regimes within the 200 nm zone.[230] Article 56(1) states that the EEZ includes the exploration and exploitation of resources both 'of the waters superjacent and *the seabed and its subsoil*'. If follows that when a coastal State has claimed an EEZ, the seabed and subsoil form an integral part of the EEZ. Since Article 56(3) provides that the rights in seabed and subsoil of the EEZ 'shall be exercised in accordance with Part VI' (on the continental shelf), the EEZ and continental shelf regimes overlap within 200 nm.[231] Thus, within 200 nm, as the ICJ in *Libya/Malta* acknowledged, the two institutions are 'linked together in modern law'.[232] In his partial Dissenting Opinion in *Bangladesh/India*, Judge Rao also opined that, 'the sovereign rights of a coastal State over the

[228] Ibid [473]; *Bangladesh/India* (n 135) [504].

[229] The Exclusive Economic Zone, Working Sessions, ILA 61st Conference, 26 August to 1 September 1984; Allot (n 37) 14; DP O'Connell, *The International Law of the Sea*, Vol II (Claredon Press 1984) 580; Umberto Leanza and Maria Cristina Caracciolo, 'The Exclusive Economic Zone' in David Attard, Malgosia Fitzmaurice and Norman A Martinez Gutierrez (eds), *The IMLI Manual on International Maritime Law*, Volume I: The Law of the Sea (OUP 2014) 208. Contra Lando, *Maritime Delimitations as a Judicial Process* (n 112) 111; Anthony Lucky, 'The Issues Concerning the Continental Shelf: Reflections' (2015) 17 ICLR 95, 108–111.

[230] Surya P Sharma, 'The Single Maritime Boundary Regime and the Relationship between the Continental Shelf and the Exclusive Economic Zone' (1987) 2 International Journal of Estuarine and Coastal Law 203.

[231] Alexander Proelss, 'Article 56' in Proelss (n 8) 421.

[232] *Libya/Malta* (n 1) [34].

water column and the seabed and its subsoil are considered as two indispensable and inseparable parts of the coastal State's rights in the EEZ'.[233] Moreover, the rules governing the rights of the coastal States in the adjacent waters and the seabed are to a large extent uniform. For example, the coastal State's sovereign rights over living and non-living resources, its rights and jurisdiction with regard to artificial islands, marine scientific research, as well as its obligations regarding environmental matters in the EEZ and continental shelf are almost identical.[234]

All the above points to the argument that, while neither the EEZ nor the continental shelf has subsumed one another, the EEZ and continental shelf regimes constitute an integral system of rights and obligation within 200 nm. As discussed in Chapter 2,[235] Article 56(3) is a manifestation of harmonisation of the two legal regimes insofar as coastal States' sovereign rights concerning the exploration and exploitation of resources are concerned in case a coastal State has claimed both the EEZ and the continental shelf. As such, it cannot serve as the legal basis for the separation and distribution of the waters to one State and the seabed and subsoil within 200 nm to another. In the only Dissenting Opinion rendered in *Bangladesh/Myanmar*, Judge Lucky also argued that 'a strict interpretation of the law set out in Parts V and VI of the Convention prohibits the allocation of waters superjacent to the seabed and its subsoil, ie the continental shelf, to two different States'.[236]

Furthermore, by allowing Bangladesh's continental shelf to extend into the seabed within 200 nm of the other two parties, UNCLOS tribunals seem to have rejected a hierarchy between the 'inner' and 'outer' continental shelf.[237] UNCLOS tribunals repeatedly used the argument that 'there is only one continental shelf' as the basis for their decisions. However, this 'one

[233] *Bay of Bengal Maritime Boundary Arbitration (Bangladesh/India)* (Award, Concurring and Dissenting Opinion of Dr. P.S. Rao) [31].

[234] For example, Article 246 regulates coastal State's competence over marine scientific research in both the EEZ and continental shelf, Articles 60 and 80 relating to artificial islands, installations and structures are exactly the same, Part XII on the protection and preservation of the marine environment applies to all maritime zones.

[235] See Section 2.1.1.2.

[236] *Delimitation of the Maritime Boundary in the Bay of Bengal (Bangladesh/Myanmar)* (Judgment, Dis. Op. Lucky) ITLOS Reports 2012, 4, 56.

[237] See: Malcolm D Evans, 'Maritime Boundary Delimitation' (n 176) 265; Antunes and Becker-Weinberg (n 2) 88. In *Barbados v Trinidad and Tobago*, Trinidad argued that its right to a continental shelf could not be 'trumped' by Barbados' claim to an EEZ. *Barbados v Trinidad and Tobago* (n 157) [367]. Similarly, in *Nicaragua v Colombia* (2012), Nicaragua also argued that 'an entitlement to continental shelf based on the distance criterion does not take precedence over an entitlement based on the criterion of natural prolongation'. The arbitral tribunal and ICJ did not address these questions. *Nicaragua v Colombia* (n 43) [121].

continental shelf' argument does not seem tenable from a legal point of view. While it is true that physically speaking, a continental shelf does not stop when it reaches the 200 nm limit, the continental shelf that is regulated under UNCLOS is one of a juridical nature. As a result, there are in fact differences in the legal regime that governs the 'inner' and 'outer' parts of the shelf. Judge Rao in *Bangladesh/India* contended that the non-distinction was true only 'insofar as the resources the shelf encompasses and any regulation that goes with them'.[238] To his comment, one may further add that as far as the regulation over resources is concerned, there are still differences in UNCLOS provisions regarding the coastal State's rights over resources located on the seabed within and beyond 200 nm. For example, Article 82 UNCLOS requires the coastal State to 'make payments or contributions in kind with respect to the exploitation of non-living resources of the continental shelf beyond 200 nm' while no such requirement is in place for activities conducted within 200 nm. Another difference is found in the coastal State's discretion to regulate marine scientific research conducted on the continental shelf within and beyond 200 nm.[239] Consequently, UNCLOS tribunals' use of the continental shelf unity argument failed to account for these differences, which may lead to difficulties in the exercise of rights in practice.

Turning to the practical difficulties for the parties in exercising their rights and jurisdiction within the grey area, it should be recalled that Barbados, in objecting to the arbitral tribunal's jurisdiction to hear Trinidad's claim to an outer continental shelf in *Barbados v Trinidad and Tobago* argued that a grey area would create 'an unprecedented and unworkable situation of overlap between seabed and water column rights'.[240] Although Barbados did not elaborate on what 'unworkable situation' it had in mind, it is not difficult to contemplate such a situation in the grey area. For example, supposing Bangladesh placed a mobile oil rig in the waters of Myanmar's EEZ for the purposes of exploring and exploiting its oil resources in the seabed and the latter alleged that this oil rig in conducting its activities on the seabed was causing pollution to its waters, would Article 208 relating to pollution from seabed activities or Article 211 relating to pollution from vessels apply? Article 208 meant that Bangladesh would have the jurisdiction over the vessel, while Article 211 would confer jurisdiction on Myanmar in accordance with Article 220. Likewise, India, under Article 60, has the exclusive right and jurisdiction over artificial islands, installations and structure in its EEZ. But supposing that

238 Concurring and Dissenting Opinion of Dr RP Rao (n 234) [32].

239 Article 246 UNCLOS.

240 *Barbados v Trinidad and Tobago* (n 157) [180].

the construction of those structures involved the dredging of the seabed, which damaged the living resources on the continental shelf of Bangladesh, which State would have enforcement power in this case? It follows that within 200 nm, the effective exercise of many of the sovereign rights under UNCLOS to a certain extent depends on the fact that only one coastal State is exercising those rights, which is not the case with grey areas.

The problems raised above may not be so significant if the States have in fact agreed to the separation of their rights in the grey area. Some States have in practice agreed, in their maritime boundary delimitation treaties, to an area in which the EEZ belongs to one State and the continental shelf to another. These treaties, however, always include arrangements regarding the exercise of the States' rights and jurisdiction in such areas,[241] which are normally 'heavily dependent upon the goodwill and active cooperation of the State parties'.[242] As the grey area was not envisioned by the parties when submitting the cases, it would have been more desirable if the tribunal had provided some guidance for the States concerned to deal with them. Both Judge Lucky and Judge Rao regarded the decisions to leave the issues involving the grey areas unresolved and to refrain from offering any comment or suggestions to the parties to resolve the matter 'a failure on the part of the UNCLOS tribunals to definitively resolve the disputes brought before them'.[243] The practical difficulties associated with the operationalisation of the grey areas and the lack of guidance provided by the tribunals arguably undermine the purposes of maritime delimitation which, as held by the tribunal in *Barbados v Trinidad and Tobago*, is 'both equitable and as practically satisfactory as possible, while at the same time in keeping with the requirement of achieving a stable legal outcome'.[244]

4.3 CONCLUDING REMARKS

UNCLOS tribunals have been the pioneers in clarifying important legal issues concerning maritime entitlement under the Convention – issues that had

[241] For example, the Torres Strait Treaty between Australia and Papua New Guinea requires that residual jurisdiction, that is, jurisdiction over the seabed or fisheries not related to the exploration and exploitation of these areas, is shared by the parties in the area of overlap and neither party can exercise this jurisdiction without the concurrence of the other. The Australian–Indonesia Maritime Boundary Treaty also recognises areas in which the Australian continental shelf overlapping with the Indonesian EEZ, and Article 7 provides for the regulation of this area. See Stuart Kaye, 'The Use of Multiple Boundaries in Maritime Boundary Delimitation: Law and Practice' (1998) 19 Australian Yearbook of International Law 49.

[242] Kaye (n 242) 71.

[243] Concurring and Dissenting Opinion of Dr RP Rao (n 234) [35]–[36]

[244] *Barbados v Trinidad and Tobago* (n 157) [244].

been avoided, or only superficially examined, by other international courts or tribunals. More specifically, ITLOS was the first tribunal to provide a detailed examination of the entitlement to outer continental shelf. In this process, it clarified the meaning of 'natural prolongation', the relationship between the different concepts that can be found under Article 76 UNCLOS, such as natural prolongation and the edge of the continental margin, entitlement and outer limits of the continental shelf, or delineation and delimitation. In doing so, ITLOS also confirmed the independent relationship between UNCLOS dispute settlement bodies and the CLCS. The *South China Sea* arbitral tribunal, for its part, was the first tribunal engage in depth with Article 121(3) concerning maritime entitlement from insular features. The tribunal managed to set out clear thresholds for the fulfilment of the notoriously vague requirements under this paragraph for a feature to be considered a rock.

The contribution of UNCLOS tribunals to the development of the law on maritime delimitation differs in relation to maritime zones within and beyond 200 nm. For the delimitation of the territorial sea, EEZ and continental shelf within 200 nm, UNCLOS tribunals have embraced and applied the delimitation methods that have been developed by other courts and tribunals over the past decades. As a result, the contribution of UNCLOS tribunals mainly lies in adding another voice to refining the application of the steps of the well-established delimitation methods. With regards to the delimitation of the continental shelf beyond 200 nm, UNCLOS tribunals were the first tribunals to have proceeded with the delimitation of the outer continental shelf. The contribution of UNCLOS tribunals in this regard lies in the clarification of the method of delimitation applicable to the delimitation of the outer continental shelf, which continues to be the equidistance/relevant circumstances method. At the same time, the creation of the grey areas as a result of the application of the adjusted equidistance has caused much uncertainty both with regards to the legal basis of these areas and in the practical exercise of rights and obligations in these areas.

Not all of the tribunals' answers or their accompanying reasoning were provided in a cogently manner, and some of the tribunals' findings were further confined to the particular circumstances of the cases. The significance of these contributions, therefore, lies more in the fact that they laid the first building block to understanding these articles and lent authority to certain interpretations of the legal concepts under these articles amidst various competing ways to understanding them. In consequence, the relevant pronouncements of UNCLOS tribunals have the potential normative power to influence the future development of the outer continental shelf regime. In other words, even with the limitations, they have set out a course for the law regulating the outer continental shelf to develop and take shape. It now remains to be seen whether that course will be followed by other international actors. The first signs from the ICJ seem to be in the positive.

5

Protection of the Marine Environment

The protection of the marine environment assumes a special place under the United Nations Convention on the Law of the Sea (UNCLOS). As the 'first comprehensive codification of international law on the protection and preservation of the marine environment',[1] the Convention not only prescribes States' rights and obligations regarding the conservation of marine resources in the maritime zones falling under their jurisdiction,[2] but also devotes an entire Part XII to the 'Protection and Preservation of the Marine Environment'. Part XII provides for general obligations to protect and preserve the environment as well as more specific provisions concerning the prevention, reduction and control of different sources of marine pollution. Various provisions in Part XII also codify the existing principles of international environmental law. With this structure, Part XII is considered to have set up a 'global legal architecture for the protection and preservation of the marine environment'.[3] At the same time, it is important to remember that Part XII is intended to provide a general framework for the protection of the marine environment. This framework nature is demonstrated not only by the existence of many generally worded provisions and open-ended obligations which need to be further elaborated but also in the existence of numerous reference to external rules and standards, international organisations and regional arrangements.

To date, the International Tribunal for the Law of the Sea (ITLOS) has only dealt with issues relating to the protection of the marine environment in

1 Detlef Czybulka, 'Article 192' in Alexander Proelss (ed), *United Nations Convention on the Law of the Sea: A Commentary* (CH Beck, Hart, Nomos 2017) 1281.

2 See also: Yoshifumi Tanaka, *The International Law of the Sea* (3rd ed, CUP 2019) 284.

3 Donald R. Rothwell and Tim Stephens, *The International Law of the Sea* (2nd ed, Bloomsbury Publishing Plc 2017) 365.

provisional measures and advisory opinion proceedings. Concerning the former, it is pertinent to highlight that under Article 290(1) ITLOS may prescribe provisional measures to not only preserve the rights of the parties as normally seen in other courts, but also to 'prevent serious harm to the marine environment'. This second basis offers ITLOS the unique opportunity to contribute to the protection of the environment even before deciding on the merits of the case. Annex VII arbitral tribunals, for their part, did not have the opportunity to hear disputes concerning marine environment protection until *Chagos MPA* in 2015 and *South China Sea* in 2017.[4] This chapter first examines the contribution of UNCLOS tribunals to clarifying the scope and content of the general obligation to protect and preserve the marine environment (Section 5.1), before moving to discussing the extent to which UNCLOS tribunals have shed light on the normative content of three key environmental obligations and principles in the context of the marine environment. These include: the duty to cooperate (Section 5.2), the duty to conduct environmental impact assessment (Section 5.3) and the precautionary principle (Section 5.4).

5.1 SCOPE OF THE OBLIGATION TO PROTECT AND PRESERVE THE MARINE ENVIRONMENT

5.1.1 *Scope of Marine Environmental Protection*

The majority of provisions in Part XII is concerned with prevention of marine pollution. This suggests at first sight that marine environmental protection under UNCLOS only has the narrow focus of preventing and controlling marine pollution, even when Article 1(4) UNCLOS adopts a rather broad definition of 'pollution'. However, ITLOS in *Southern Bluefin Tuna* took a broader understanding and stated that 'the conservation of living resources of the sea is an element in the protection and preservation of the marine environment'.[5] This approach was followed by both arbitral tribunals in

4 When the cases concerning the marine environment, such as *Southern Bluefin Tuna*, *MOX Plant*, *Land Reclamation*, eventually proceeded to arbitration, they were either terminated and or rejected by the respective arbitral tribunals due to the lack of jurisdiction or to consideration of comity to other courts.

5 *Southern Bluefin Tuna (New Zealand v Japan; Australia v Japan)* (Provisional Measures, Order of 27 August 1999) ITLOS Reports 1999, 280 [70]. [Southern Bluefin Tuna Order] ITLOS subsequently recalled this statement in its *Advisory Opinion on IUU Fishing*. See: *Request for Advisory Opinion submitted by the Sub-Regional Fisheries Commission* (Advisory Opinion, 2 April 2015) ITLOS Reports 2015, 4 [120]. [Advisory Opinion on IUU Fishing]

Chagos MPA and *South China Sea*. In the former, the tribunal made clear that despite being entitled 'measures to prevent, reduce and control pollution to the marine environment', Article 194 is 'not limited to measures aimed strictly at controlling pollution and extends to measures focussed primarily on conservation and the preservation of ecosystems'.[6] In the latter, the tribunal found that Article 192 'may be broadly enough worded to include the obligation to protect and preserve marine biodiversity' and that 'obligations under Article 194 of the Convention may include the protection and preservation of the biological diversity represented by coral reefs'.[7] It would seem that the tribunals in these cases have taken a step further than the ITLOS in *Southern Bluefin Tuna*. These cases moved the focus of marine environmental protection beyond the mere conservation of marine resources as such to the preservation of biodiversity and protection of the ecosystem.

The obligations concerning the conservation of marine resources and prevention of marine pollution are scattered in different parts of UNCLOS, primarily due to the zonal approach that the Convention adopts. By bringing them together, UNCLOS tribunals confirmed that they are integral components of marine environmental protection. As will be shown below, such an approach has enabled UNCLOS tribunals to extend obligations found under Part XII to activities relating to marine resources. While no explanation was provided by the tribunals, such an approach seemed inspired by the United Nations Fish Stocks Agreement (UNFSA) which, compared to UNCLOS, demonstrates a clearer focus of conservation measures to protecting biodiversity and maintaining ecosystem integrity.[8] As argued by one commentator, UNCLOS tribunals' holistic approach to understanding the scope of the protection and preservation of the marine environment under UNCLOS 'could be a typical case of evolutionary interpretation, solidly based on Articles 31(1) and 31(3)(c) of the Vienna Convention on the Law of Treaties (VCLT), where the term is construed in light of changing conditions but with the original intention of the drafters strictly respected'.[9]

[6] *Chagos Marine Protected Area Arbitration (Mauritius v United Kingdom)* (2015) RIAA XXI 359 [538] [Chagos MPA].

[7] *South China Sea Arbitration (Philippines v China)*, Award on Jurisdiction and Admissibility (2015) RIAA XXXIII 1 [284].

[8] See Lan Ngoc Nguyen, 'Principled Challenges: Between Collective Interest and Individual Freedom' in Vito De Lucia, Alex Oude Elferink, Lan Ngoc Nguyen (eds), *International Law and Marine Areas beyond National Jurisdiction: Reflections on Justice, Space, Knowledge and Power* (Brill 2022) 119.

[9] Maria Gavouneli, 'Protection Standards for the Marine Environment: Updating Part XII of the Law of the Sea Convention?' in Stephen Minas and Jordan Diamond (eds), *Stress Testing the Law of the Sea* (Brill 2018) 258.

Not only is the conservation of living resources now part of marine environmental protection, ITLOS in the *Advisory Opinion on IUU Fishing* also confirmed that the conservation and development of living resources, at least with regards to transboundary fishing stocks under Article 63, should also pursue the goal of 'sustainable management'.[10] While the Tribunal's interpretation, strictly speaking, related only to transboundary stocks, the use of Article 61 to shed light on Article 63 shows that there its finding would likely have a broader application. Such an interpretation seems to be in line with the expectation placed upon UNCLOS to provide 'the international legal basis for pursuing the protection and sustainable development of marine and coastal environment and its resources'.[11]

Notwithstanding the desirable interpretation, it is noteworthy that ITLOS relied only on Article 61 to reach this conclusion without explaining which elements of Article 61 'provided guidance' on the meaning of the term 'sustainable development'. As argued by one commentator, the principles to guide conservation and management of the exclusive economic zone (EEZ) in Article 61 are 'at best, vague and ambiguous and, at worst, are based on precepts that are unworkable to maintain the sustainability of the living resources in the [EEZ] in the current environment'.[12] It seems therefore difficult to conclude that Article 61 by itself contains the idea of sustainable development of living resources under UNCLOS. It is suggested that ITLOS could instead have taken into account post-UNCLOS instruments, in which States agreed to use the Convention as the legal foundation for sustainable use of the ocean, to help interpret the terms contained in Articles 61 and 63. For example, Agenda 21 entitled 'Programme of Action for Sustainable Development' adopted by the United Nations Conference on Environment and Development in 1992 clearly acknowledged in its chapter 17 on the 'Protection, Rational Use, and the Development of the Living Resources in Marine and Coastal Areas' that the measures for the sustainable use and conservation of marine living resources are in accordance with the relevant

[10] *Advisory Opinion on IUU Fishing* (n 5) [191].

[11] United Nations General Assembly, Law of the Sea: Report of the United Nations Secretary General, UN Doc A/47/623 (24 November 1992) [62]. See also: Alexander Yankov, 'The Law of the Sea Convention and Agenda 21: Marine Environmental Implications' in Alan Boyle and David Freestone (eds), *International Law and Sustainable Development: Past Achievements and Future Challenges* (OUP 1999) 271.

[12] Donna R Christie, 'The Conservation and Management of Stocks Located Solely within the Exclusive Economic Zone' in Ellen Hey (ed), *Developments in International Fisheries Law* (Kluwer Law International 1999) 406.

provisions of UNCLOS.[13] The Rio+ 20 United Nations Conference on Sustainable Development in 2012 reaffirmed that UNCLOS 'is an important tool for sustainable development'.[14] The concept of sustainability also features prominently in the UNFSA. Article 2 UNFSA defines the objective of the Agreement as 'ensur[ing] long-term conservation and sustainable use of straddling fish stocks and highly migratory fish stocks through the effective implementation of the [UNCLOS]'. It follows, therefore, that ITLOS could have referred to the concept of sustainability in the UNFSA in the interpretation of coastal States' obligations with regard to transboundary fish stocks.

5.1.2 *Scope of General Obligation under Article 192*

Part XII opens with Article 192 which simply provides, 'States have the obligation to protect and preserve the marine environment'. The general wording of Article 192 has raised questions regarding whether it is merely of a hortatory nature,[15] or whether it imposes substantive obligations on State parties, and if so, what is the scope of these obligations. UNCLOS tribunals have adopted the latter approach and significantly contributed to infusing the general obligation to protect and preserve the marine environment found in Article 192 with more specificity than its wording suggests. In particular, UNCLOS tribunals have clarified both the spatial application and the nature and content of Article 192.

In relation to the spatial application of Article 192, ITLOS in its *Advisory Opinion on IUU Fishing* made clear that 'Article 192 applies to all maritime areas'.[16] In the context of this advisory opinion, such a statement was used as the basis for ITLOS to establish the flag State's obligation to ensure that vessels flying its flag comply with the coastal State's conservation of measures in the latter's EEZ.[17] In other words, the term 'all maritime areas' seems to refer specifically to areas within another State's national jurisdiction in which concurrent jurisdiction may exist. The tribunal in *South China Sea*, while echoing ITLOS's above statement that 'the environmental obligations in Part XII apply to States irrespective of where the alleged harmful activities took

[13] Rio Declaration on Environment and Development, 13 June 1992, UN Doc A/CONF.151/26. Rev.1.

[14] *The Future We Want*, UNGA Res A/RES/66/288.

[15] Robin Churchill, 'Dispute Settlement in the Law of the Sea: Survey for 2015 – Part I' (2016) 31(4) IJMCL 555, 565.

[16] *Advisory Opinion on IUU Fishing* (n 5) [120].

[17] See Section 3.3.2.

place'[18] took a step further and specified that 'the obligations in Part XII apply to all States with respect to the marine environment in all maritime areas, both inside the national jurisdiction of States and beyond it'.[19] The term 'beyond' national jurisdiction might give the impression that the tribunal was referring to the high seas and the Area. However, placed in the context of this case, it seemed to refer to areas which may or may not fall under the jurisdiction of another State, in other words, maritime areas whose status is disputed. It follows that, even in disputed maritime zones, the obligation to protect and preserve still applies. That said, UNCLOS contains various provisions relating to the conservation of marine living resources in the high seas and protection of the marine environment in the Area. In light of the tribunals' emphasis on an expansive reading of the spatial scope of the obligation, coupled with the tribunals' holistic approach to understanding the scope of protection of marine environment as discussed above, there is no reason to exclude areas beyond national jurisdiction from the spatial application of Article 192.

As regards the content of the obligation to protect and preserve the marine environment under Article 192, the *South China Sea* tribunal has clarified the obligation in two respects. The tribunal found that this article 'entails the positive obligation to take active measures to protect and preserve the marine environment, and by logical implication, entails the negative obligation not to degrade the marine environment'.[20] Thus the tribunal read into the simple formulation of Article 192 a two-fold obligation comprising of both a positive and a negative aspect.[21] By reading into Article 192 a positive obligation to take preventative measures to protect the marine environment, the tribunal 'incorporated an intertemporal element' into this article. As remarked by one commentator, such an intertemporal understanding of this article is significant as it allows the interpretation of environmental norms to be flexible to adopt to new situations.[22]

More importantly, the *South China Sea* tribunal specified that the content of Article 192 is 'detailed in the subsequent provisions of Part XII, including Article 194, as well as by reference to specific obligations set out in other

[18] *The South China Sea Arbitration between the Republic of the Philippines and the People's Republic of China (Philippines v China)* (2016) RIAA XXXIII 153 [927].

[19] Ibid [940].

[20] Ibid [941].

[21] James Harrison, *Saving the Oceans Through Law: The International Legal Framework for the Protection of the Marine Environment* (OUP 2017) 24; Gavouneli (n 9) 260.

[22] Yoshifumi Tanaka, *The South China Sea Arbitration: Toward an International Legal Order in the Oceans* (Hart 2019) 135.

international agreements, as envisaged in Article 237 of the Convention'.[23] This statement confirms that Article 192 cannot be applied in isolation, but that its content is furnished with reference to other rules found within and beyond UNCLOS.

Within UNCLOS, Article 192, read together with Article 194(5) concerning the protection of fragile ecosystems, includes a due diligence obligation both 'to prevent the harvesting of species that are recognised internationally as being at risk of extinction and requiring international protection'[24] and to '[prevent] harms that would affect depleted, threatened, or endangered species indirectly through the destruction of their habitat'.[25] The tribunal's interpretation has been suggested to mean that 'Article 192 is perhaps better characterized as a statement of principle, whose primary function is to determine the scope of Part XII as a whole'.[26] It would seem, however, that the tribunal in *South China Sea* did not view the general obligation under Article 192 as merely 'a statement of principle'; instead, it interpreted the general obligation contained in this article as one of due diligence. As analysed in Chapter 3, the obligation of due diligence was the subject of detailed scrutiny in the *Advisory Opinion on Activities in the Area* and the *Advisory Opinion on IUU Fishing*.[27] Similar to the two Advisory Opinions, the *South China Sea* tribunal was willing to read the principle of due diligence into UNCLOS provisions which do not expressly provide for such principle – in this case Article 192. The tribunal clarified the content of the obligation, requiring not only legislative measures, but also enforcement measures to be taken on the part of States. In this case, the tribunal placed particular emphasis on the latter component. Despite acknowledging that China had put in place legislation which prohibited the catching and killing of state-protected wildlife,[28] the tribunal emphasised that 'adopting appropriate rules and measures to prohibit a harmful practice is only one component of the due diligence required by States'.[29] As there was no evidence indicating that China had 'taken any steps to enforce those rules and measures against fishermen engaged in poaching of endangered species', the tribunal found that China had violated its obligation under Articles 192 and 194(5) UNCLOS.[30]

[23] *South China Sea Arbitration* (n 18) [942].
[24] Ibid [956].
[25] Ibid [959].
[26] Harrison (n 21) 23.
[27] See Section 3.3.2.
[28] *South China Sea Arbitration* (n 18) [963].
[29] Ibid [964].
[30] Ibid.

Beyond UNCLOS, the tribunal found that Article 192 is to be interpreted 'by reference to specific obligations set out in other international agreements', including '[t]he corpus of international law relating to the environment'.[31] This laid the foundation for the tribunals to then examine two external treaties, namely the Convention on Biological Diversity (CBD)[32] and the Convention on International Trade in Endangered Species of Wild Fauna and Flora (CITES)[33] to interpret Articles 192 and 194(5). In particular, the tribunal relied on Article 2 of the CBD, which contain the definition of 'ecosystem',[34] to find that 'the marine environments where the allegedly harmful activities took place in the present dispute constitute "rare or fragile ecosystems"'.[35] The tribunal also referred to the Appendices of CITES[36] – which it considered to be 'the subject of nearly universal adherence, including by the Philippines and China' and thus 'forms part of the general corpus of international law that informs the content of Article 192 and 194(5)'[37] – to find that the sea turtles and giant clams harvested by Chinese-flagged vessels to be endangered species.

In order to justify recourse to external treaties, the tribunal invoked both Article 293 UNCLOS on Applicable Law and Article 31(3) VLCT in its Award on Jurisdiction and Admissibility, and referred to Article 237 UNCLOS in the Award on the Merits.[38] While all these provisions indeed allowed the tribunal to resort to external sources of law to deal with a dispute arising from UNCLOS, two remarks are warranted.[39] First, the tribunal did not specify under which subparagraph of Article 31(3) the CBD and CITES fell. It would be difficult to maintain that CBD and CITES qualify as 'subsequent

31 Ibid [942].

32 Convention on Biological Diversity 1760 UNTS 79 (05 June 1992).

33 Convention on International Trade in Endangered Species of Wild Fauna and Flora 993 UNTS 243 (03 March 1973).

34 Article 2 of the CBD defines 'ecosystem' as 'a dynamic complex of plant, animal and micro-organism communities and their non-living environment interacting as a functional unit'.

35 *South China Sea Arbitration* (n 18) [945].

36 Appendices I, II and III to the CITES contain lists of species that are afforded different levels or types of protection from overexploitation. Appendix I lists species that are the most endangered among CITES-listed animals and plants. Appendix II lists species that are not necessarily now threatened with extinction but that may become so unless trade is closely controlled. Appendix III is a list of species included at the request of a Party that already regulates trade in the species and that needs the cooperation of other countries to prevent unsustainable or illegal exploitation. See: 'The CITES Appendices', https://cites.org/eng/app/index.php accessed 25 January 2022.

37 *South China Sea Arbitration* (n 18) [956].

38 Ibid [942].

39 For a more detailed analysis of Article 293(1), see Section 6.1.2.

agreements between the parties' regarding the interpretation of the treaty within the meaning of subparagraph (a). It would perhaps be more reasonable to view them as 'relevant rules of international law applicable in the relations between the parties' under sub-paragraph (c). However, as the requirements for the application of sub-paragraph (c) are not free from ambiguity, a more detailed explanation would have both added nuance to the tribunal's reasoning and allowed the tribunal to contribute to clarifying a more general issue of international law. Second, as observed by one scholar, Article 237 'underlines the framework- and "minimum-standard" character of the Convention in its Part XII and consequently the need of advancement or furtherance of the general provisions, especially of Art. 192'.[40] Although Article 237 serves as a conflict-resolving rule between Part XII and other treaties concerning the protection and preservation of the marine environment, the manner in which the tribunal used Article 237 to interpret Article 192 has turned it into a link to connect UNCLOS and external instruments relating to the environment. Taken together, the *South China Sea* tribunal's approach indicates that it did not view the law of the sea as a self-contained regime, and thus it should be 'updated or revised over time by interacting with other treaty regimes'.[41] The tribunal's interpretation of Articles 192 and 194 thus provides a prime example of normative regime interaction.[42] In that sense, while not the first to interpret an obligation under UNCLOS as one of due diligence, *South China Sea* was the first case in which the obligation of due diligence played a key role in enabling resort to external sources to inform the standard of due diligence found under UNCLOS.[43]

The preceding discussion shows that UNCLOS tribunals have greatly expanded the general scope of the marine environment protection. It now encompasses both the prevention of marine pollution as explicitly stated in Part XII and the conservation of living resources whose regulation is scattered elsewhere in the Convention. The tribunals have also given the general obligation contained in Article 192 much greater normative depth. The simple

40 Detlef Czybulka, 'Article 237' in Proelss (n 1) 1597.

41 Chie Kojima, 'South China Sea Arbitration and the Protection of the Marine Environment: Evolution of UNCLOS Part XII Through Interpretation and the Duty to Cooperate' (2015) 21 Asian Yearbook of International Law 166, 172.

42 Seline Trevisanut, Nikolaos Giannopoulos and Rozemarijn Roland Holst, 'Introduction: Regime Interaction in Ocean Governance' in Seline Trevisanut, Nikolaos Giannopoulos and Rozemarijn Roland Holst (eds), *Regime Interaction in Ocean Governance Problems, Theories and Methods* (Brill 2020) 7.

43 Nele Matz-Lück and Erik van Doorn, 'Due Diligence Obligations and the Protection of the Marine Environment' (2017) 42 L'Observateur des Nations Unies 177, 194.

obligation to protect and preserve the environment has significant expanded in its scope of application and the degree of specificity.[44] As Article 192 is not a stand-alone provision, the degree of specificity to be read into this article is determined by reference to not only other provisions of UNCLOS but also external rules existing beyond UNCLOS. The fact that Article 192 has repeatedly been confirmed as including a due diligence obligation, which is 'a variable concept' and 'may change over time',[45] enables UNCLOS to be a living treaty and to be able to deal with new challenges concerning the protection of the marine environment.

It is clear, therefore, that Article 192 has now become a *renvoi* into which rules of international law beyond UNCLOS may be incorporated to determine the content of the due diligence obligation. It should be noted that, true to its framework nature, UNCLOS contains various articles which refer to or incorporate external rules of international law.[46] As with these provisions, the question that arises is to what extent can this renvoi extend and, what would be the limits on judicial bodies in determining the scope of Article 192. As queried by one commentator, 'it is difficult to see how a court or tribunal could give any substantive content to the highly ambiguous terms of Article 192 without overstepping its judicial role and straying into law-making'.[47] While, as discussed in Chapter 1, the concepts of 'judicial role' and 'law-making' may not be as distinct, there are merits in acknowledging the limits of UNCLOS tribunals' jurisdictional scope insofar as resort to rules beyond the Convention is concerned.[48] The *South China Sea* tribunal seems to have been aware of such limits by putting great emphasis on the universal nature of the CBD and CITES, and particularly the fact that both the Philippines and China are parties to this case, setting 'certain standards for future decisions by international courts and tribunals'.[49] Nevertheless, the perception of UNCLOS tribunals crossing these limits may still be used as a ground to cast doubt over the jurisprudential value of its interpretation of Article 192.[50]

44 Gavouneli (n 9) 261.

45 *Responsibilities and Obligations of States with Respect to Activities in the Area* (Advisory Opinion, 1 February 2011) ITLOS Reports 2011, 10 [117] [Advisory Opinion on Activities in the Area].

46 For example, the rule of reference. See discussion in Section 3.3.1.

47 Harrison (n 21) 23.

48 For a more detailed discussion on UNCLOS tribunals' scope of jurisdiction, see Section 6.1.2.

49 Kojima (n 41) [174].

50 See: Zhang Hua, 'The Development of International Law of the Sea by International Courts and Tribunals: A Case Study of Due Diligence Obligation' (2021) 9 Korean Journal of International and Comparative Law 132; Jianping Guo, 'The Developments of Marine Environmental Protection Obligation in Article 192 of UNCLOS and the Operational Impact

5.2 DUTY TO COOPERATE

The duty to cooperate to protect the marine environment is clearly set out in various provisions in the Convention.[51] This duty has come up before UNCLOS tribunals in two contexts, namely in the conservation and management of marine resources and in the prevention of pollution to the marine environment. Each is now analysed in turn.

5.2.1 *Duty to Cooperate in the Conservation and Management of Marine Resources*

In the exercise of its sovereign rights over natural resources in the EEZ, coastal States have the corresponding obligations to conserve and manage living resources that are located in their EEZ as specified under Articles 61 and 62. These articles do not require coastal States to cooperate in taking conservation measures found within their EEZ. It is only with regards to the conservation of transboundary stocks, including straddling stocks and migratory species, that the duty to cooperate arises, even though the wording of Articles 63 and 64 does not specify this duty as such. Article 118 similarly require States to cooperate in the conservation and management of marine living resources in the high seas. While Article 118 has not been brought before UNCLOS tribunals, ITLOS has had the opportunity to shed light on the content of the duty to cooperate in Articles 63 and 64 in the *Southern Bluefin Tuna* provisional measure proceedings and in *Advisory Opinion on IUU Fishing*.[52]

The *Southern Bluefin Tuna* dispute concerning Japan's unilateral experimental fishing of the southern bluefin tuna (SBT) – a highly migratory species under UNCLOS Annex I – was initiated by Australia and New Zealand before an Annex VII arbitration. Australia and New Zealand in this case contended that Japan had breached its obligations under Articles 64 and 116 to 119 UNCLOS in relation to the conservation and management of the SBT.[53] As the Annex VII arbitral tribunal that was eventually constituted decided that it lacked jurisdiction to hear the cases, the content of these

on China's Marine Policy – A South China Sea Fisheries Perspective' (2020) 120 Marine Policy Journal 1.

[51] See, for example, Articles 43, 61(1), 64(1), 65(1), 100, 118, 123.

[52] In *Chagos MPA*, the Annex VII arbitral tribunal touched upon the question of transboundary stocks, but only to the extent that concerned the compulsory jurisdiction over disputes arising from the conservation and management of transboundary stocks, not on the substance of the coastal State's obligations. See: *Chagos MPA* (n 6) [300]–[301].

[53] *Southern Bluefin Tuna Order* (n 5) [28].

articles was not addressed. In the *Southern Bluefin Tuna* provisional measures phase, ITLOS was not allowed to make findings that may prejudice the merits of the case, thus it could only briefly address Articles 64, 116(b) and 119(3) of UNCLOS – the most important provisions underpinning the regime for conservation and management of highly migratory stocks. ITLOS stated that these articles required the parties to cooperate in the conservation and management of the SBT and noted that 'the parties should intensify their efforts to cooperate with the other participants in the fishery for SBT'.[54]

In the *Advisory Opinion on IUU Fishing*, the question that ITLOS was asked neither directly mentioned transboundary fish stocks, nor did it employ the terms used by UNCLOS, that is, 'straddling stocks' and 'migratory stocks'. ITLOS nonetheless determined that, based on the definition of 'shared stocks' in the MCA Convention and of 'stocks of common interest' provided by the Sub-Regional Fisheries Commission (SRFC) in the oral proceedings, these two expressions referred to straddling stocks between two EEZs and between the EEZ and the high seas.[55] This paved the way for ITLOS to examine coastal States' obligations under Articles 63 and 64. ITLOS identified three different regimes under UNCLOS applicable to the three different types of fish stocks.

First, in respect of species that occur within the EEZs of two or more SRFC Member States, ITLOS found that under Article 63(1) these States have the obligation to seek to agree upon the measures necessary to coordinate and ensure the conservation and development of such stocks. Observing that while 'conservation' is provided for under Article 61, UNCLOS remains silent on 'development', ITLOS found that the term 'development of such stocks' used in Article 63(1) of the Convention suggested that 'these stocks should be used as fishery resources within the framework of a sustainable fisheries management regime'.[56] The tribunal, however, did not elaborate on what constituted a 'framework of sustainable fisheries management regime'.

Second, for stocks occurring in coastal States' EEZ and adjacent areas, ITLOS held that coastal States have the obligation to cooperate through competent international organisations to ensure that the shared stocks are not endangered by overexploitation.[57]

Third and finally with regard to migratory stocks – tuna in this case – a highly migratory species under Annex I of UNCLOS, ITLOS held that SRFC

[54] Ibid [70].

[55] *Advisory Opinion on IUU Fishing* (n 5) [186].

[56] Ibid [198].

[57] Ibid [207].

Member States had the obligation under Article 64(1) to seek to agree upon the conservation and management measures in regard to stocks that occur both within the EEZ of the SRFC Member States and in an area beyond and adjacent to these zones.[58] ITLOS particularly emphasised the need for measures taken pursuant to the obligation under Article 64(1) to be consistent and compatible with those taken by the appropriate regional organisations. Although the obligation to cooperate in this case was based on a different convention, ITLOS's statement was reminiscent of the International Court of Justice's (ICJ) Whaling judgment, emphasising the important role of treaty bodies in the conservation of highly migratory species.[59] In ITLOS's view, both the duty to cooperate and the duty to seek to agree were 'due diligence' obligations which required the States concerned to consult with one another in good faith, pursuant to Article 300 of the Convention.[60] These obligations were thus an obligation of conduct, meaning that State parties have to consult each other with a view to reaching an agreement on measures to conserve and develop the fish stocks, but they are not under an obligation to reach such an agreement. ITLOS only required that consultation be meaningful, in the sense that substantial effort should be made by all States concerned.[61] The obligations as interpreted by ITLOS thus have the nature of *pactum de negotiando*, implying a duty to enter into negotiation, not *pactum de contrahendo*, implying a duty to negotiate and to reach an agreement.[62] Such an interpretation sets a rather low threshold for the fulfilment of Articles 63 and 64.

ITLOS also attempted to specify the conservation and management measures that coastal States should take to fulfil the obligation to cooperate. For example, it stated that the measures should ensure that the shared stocks would not be endangered by over-exploitation or that they should be designed to maintain and restore stocks at levels that can produce maximum sustainable yield.[63] These requirements, however, were more focused on the objectives that conservation and management measures should achieve, and not on what the

[58] *Advisory Opinion on IUU Fishing* (n 5) [215].

[59] In its 2014 *Whaling* judgment, the ICJ held that States parties to the International Convention on the Regulation of Whaling had a duty to cooperate with the International Whaling Commission and the Scientific Committee, and thus should give due regard to recommendations of the IWC in implementing the Convention. *Whaling in the Antarctic (Australia v Japan: New Zealand intervening)* [2014] ICJ Rep 226 [83].

[60] Ibid [210].

[61] Ibid.

[62] For a discussion on the distinction between *pactum de negotiando* and *pactum de contrahendo*, see Stuart M Kaye, *International Fisheries Management* (Kluwer Law International 2001) 111.

[63] *Advisory Opinion on IUU Fishing* (n 5) [208].

measures should be. They were, moreover, just repeating what was already provided for more generally under the Articles 61 and 62 on conservation and utilisation of marine sources. It is worth recalling that the purpose of the SRFC's advisory request was to 'bring clarifications on the rights and duties of the coastal State in the sustainable management of shared stocks or stocks of common interest' in light of the 'lack of cooperation among SRFC Member States in managing sustainably the stocks of common interest or shared stocks'.[64] Thus, the request was aimed at asking ITLOS to shed light on the content of the obligation to cooperate in the conservation and management of straddling stocks, not on the objectives of the conservation measures to be taken. It is difficult to see how the fulfilment of the aforementioned objectives would help to address the lack of cooperation among SRFC Member States.

What is interesting is that, apart from obligations, ITLOS held that 'although the Convention approaches the issue of conservation and management of living resources from the perspective of obligations of the coastal State, these obligations entail corresponding rights'.[65] Accordingly, SRFC Member States had the right to seek to agree with other Member States in whose EEZ these stocks occur on the measures necessary to coordinate and ensure the conservation and development of such stocks. These statements imply that the rights which ensue from the obligation to cooperate under UNCLOS are only available to those that have vested interests in the conservation and management of the fish stocks in question, and not to all other State parties to the Convention. In discussing the right to cooperate, Churchill remarked, in the context of the *Southern Bluefin Tuna*, that '[t]here is clearly a duty on Japan under Article 64 but whether this confers a correlative right on Australia and New Zealand is much less certain as is what the scope of such a right might be.'[66] ITLOS's above statements seem to have answered Churchill's first question, but leaves untouched the second one.

In addition to cooperating with other member States of the regional fisheries organisation, ITLOS also held that States also had an obligation to cooperate with non-Member States. This is because, as ITLOS explained, UNCLOS imposes the obligation to cooperate on each and every State Party concerned to conserve and manage shared resources. As a result, it held that 'member States of the SRFC *may* also, directly or through relevant subregional or

[64] Written Statement of SFRC, 17 www.itlos.org/fileadmin/itlos/documents/cases/case_no.21/written_statements_round1/C21_19_CSRP_orig_Eng_rev.pdf accessed 25 January 2022.

[65] *Advisory Opinion on IUU Fishing* (n 5) [205].

[66] Robin Churchill, 'The Jurisprudence of the International Tribunal for the Law of the Sea Relating to Fisheries: Is There Much in the Net?' (2007) 22 IJMCL 383, 413.

regional organizations, seek the cooperation of non-Member States sharing the same stocks along their migrating routes'.[67] The term 'may seek the cooperation' clearly places no binding obligation on coastal States, but merely recognises their discretion to do so. ITLOS's holding is reminiscent of its Order in *Southern Bluefin Tuna*, in which the Tribunal required Australia, New Zealand and Japan not only to make efforts to reach agreement with one another, but also to make efforts to reach agreement with other States and fishing entities engaged in fishing for SBT.[68]

In his Separate Opinion, Judge Ndiyae criticised ITLOS for being 'strikingly mistaken about the extent of the law in force with regard to straddling fish stocks and highly migratory fish stocks'.[69] He believed the question presented to ITLOS was not only governed by UNCLOS but also the UNFSA, as its provisions directly address the main concern of SFRC regarding sustainable management of shared stocks and gives substance to that obligation by establishing mechanism for international cooperation.[70] In other words, ITLOS did not properly situate the obligations found under Article 64 within the wider context of international law dealing with the obligation to conserve migratory stocks. In the same vein, Judge Paik was not overly impressed with the absence of clarification on the meaning and scope of the duty to cooperate in managing the shared resources laid down in the relevant provisions of the Convention.[71] Having considered that 'simply emphasizing the obligation of cooperation or repeating the relevant provisions of the Convention would hardly be sufficient', Judge Paik pointed out that the question that needed to be addressed was 'what specifically is required to discharge that obligation, a question this Opinion does not answer satisfactorily.[72] Similar to Judge Ndiaye, he thus turned to and sought guidance in the UNFSA, Article 7 of which contains several concrete obligations to give effect to the duty to cooperate.[73]

The *Advisory Opinion on IUU Fishing* was the first time in which coastal States' obligations over transboundary stocks under UNCLOS were examined in detail. However, the Advisory Opinion was limited on the substance of the

[67] *Advisory Opinion on IUU Fishing* (n 5) [215] (emphasis added).
[68] *Southern Bluefin Tuna Order* (n 5) [90].
[69] *Request for Advisory Opinion Submitted by the Sub-Regional Fisheries Commission* (Advisory Opinion, Sep Op Ndiyae) ITLOS Reports 2015, 4 [9].
[70] Ibid [10]–[15].
[71] *Request for Advisory Opinion Submitted by the Sub-Regional Fisheries Commission* (Advisory Opinion, Sep Op Paik) ITLOS Reports 2015, 4 [31].
[72] Ibid [34].
[73] Ibid [36].

two important obligations under Articles 63 and 64. Other than elucidating on the nature and objectives of the obligations, it did not provide in any detail on what these obligations entail or what was expected of States to fulfil the obligation to cooperate in conserving and managing transboundary stocks.

5.2.2 *Duty to Cooperate in the Prevention of Marine Pollution*

The duty to cooperate in the prevention of marine pollution took centre stage in the *MOX Plant* and the *Land Reclamation* cases. In *MOX Plant*, Ireland alleged that, inter alia, the UK breached its obligations under Articles 123 and 197.[74] It is interesting to note that while these articles do not specify what would be required of State Parties to fulfil the obligation to cooperate, Ireland's claim incorporated into them other duties also found under UNCLOS, such as the duty to exchange information and to carry out environmental impact assessment (EIA). Although ITLOS did not find that there was urgency requiring the provisional measure requested by Ireland, it still prescribed provisional measures requiring both parties to cooperate and enter into consultations regarding several issues. In one of the most important paragraphs of the Order, ITLOS stated that:

> The duty to cooperate is a fundamental principle in the prevention of pollution of the marine environment under Part XII of the Convention and general international law and that rights arise therefrom which the Tribunal may consider appropriate to preserve under article 290 of the Convention.[75]

With this statement, ITLOS affirmed that the duty to cooperate existed beyond the confines of UNCLOS and had become part of general international law. Interestingly, ITLOS seems to have been saying that the duty to cooperate created a corresponding right on other States to request for cooperation, the latter in need of preservation for the purposes of Article 290.

Furthermore, ITLOS further held that 'prudence and caution require that Ireland and the UK cooperate in exchanging information concerning risks or effects of the operation of the MOX plant and in devising ways to deal with them, as appropriate'.[76] ITLOS used precaution as the basis for the need to cooperate, which in turn, required the exchange of information between the parties. In prescribing provisional measures ITLOS held that 'Ireland and the

74 *MOX Plant (Ireland v United Kingdom)* (Provisional Measures, Order of 3 December 2001) ITLOS Reports 2001, 95 [26]. [MOX Plant Order]

75 Ibid [82].

76 Ibid [84].

UK shall cooperate and shall, for this purpose, enter into consultations'.[77] As argued by one author the insertion of the phrase 'for this purpose' indicated that the duty to enter into consultation was a method of fulfilling the duty to cooperate.[78] The duty to cooperate in this case, thus, included the obligation to exchange information and to enter into consultation. Moreover, the fact that cooperation is required by 'prudence and caution' suggests a close link between the duty to cooperate and the precautionary principle.[79]

The importance of the duty to cooperate is further highlighted in the separate declarations and opinions of the judges. In particular, Judges Caminos, Yamamoto, Park, Akl, Marsit, Eiriksson and Jesus stated that their support for the Order of the Tribunal was a response to 'the almost complete lack of cooperation between the Governments of Ireland and the UK with respect to the environmental impact of the planned operations'.[80] Also supportive of ITLOS's emphasis on the duty to cooperate, Judge Wolfrum added that this duty was the 'Grundnorm' of Part XII of the Convention, as well as of customary international law for the protection of the environment, since it moved the emphasis from States sovereignty and individual interests to the environment and community interests.[81] More interestingly, although he acknowledged the existence of the obligation to cooperate with other States under UNCLOS as a multilateral convention, Judge Wolfrum cautioned against the creation of rights, as a corollary, for every other individual State Party of the Convention.[82] Here again, the relationship between the obligation and the right to cooperate resurfaced. The implication of Judge Wolfrum's statement seems to be that the duty to cooperate did not exist as an *erga omnes* or even *erga omnes partes* obligation, and that a State can only require cooperation from another State in specific cases where its rights may be at stake. Judge Anderson was, however, critical of the majority for finding

77 Ibid., operative paragraph 1.

78 Seokwoo Lee, 'UNCLOS and the Obligation to Cooperate' in Clive Schofield (ed), *Maritime Energy Resources in Asia: Legal Regimes and Cooperation* (National Bureau of Asian Research 2012).

79 Alexander Proelss, 'The Contribution of the ITLOS to Strengthening the Regime for the Protection of the Marine Environment' in Angela Del Vecchio and Roberto Virzo (eds), *Interpretations of the United Nations Convention on the Law of the Sea by International Courts and Tribunals* (Springer 2019) 97.

80 *MOX Plant (Ireland v United Kingdom)* (Provisional Measures, Order of 3 December 2001, Joint Decl. Caminos, Yamamoto, Park, Akl, Marsit, Eiriksson and Jesus) ITLOS Reports 2001, 95, 113.

81 *MOX Plant (Ireland v United Kingdom)* (Provisional Measures, Order of 3 December 2001, Sep Op Wolfrum) ITLOS Reports 2001, 95, 135.

82 Ibid.

that Article 123 provided the basis for the duty to cooperate. In his view, Article 123 'does not require cooperation to be at the bilateral level so long as there is cooperation through an appropriate regional body'.[83] Such an interpretation of Article 123 does, however, not seem tenable. A closer reading of Article 123 suggests that the existence of an appropriate region body does not render bilateral cooperation redundant. The means through which cooperation is taken is not determinative to the fulfilment of Article 123, the key point to consider under Article 123 is whether the States in question have endeavoured to cooperate and coordinate in conducting the activity in question. Judge Anderson's opinion on the irrelevance of Article 123 also touched upon an ongoing debate concerning the normative force of this article due to the weak language that it employs, requiring States merely to 'endeavour' to coordinate. ITLOS could perhaps have paid more attention to this point in its Order.[84]

ITLOS's approach in *MOX Plant* was subsequently adopted in *Land Reclamation*. It should be noted, however, that this case was not entirely similar to *MOX Plant* in two respects. First, Malaysia when requesting provisional measure did not bring up the issue of cooperation, at least by name. In its Request, Malaysia asked the Tribunal to order Singapore to provide Malaysia with full information concerning the current and projected works, to afford Malaysia a full opportunity to comment upon the works and their potential impacts; and to agree to negotiate with Malaysia concerning any remaining unresolved issues.[85] All of these may be part of the duty to cooperate, as has been held in the *MOX Plant* case, but some of them also exist as independent obligations under UNCLOS. Second, in response to several of Malaysia's requests, Singapore gave assurances and undertakings which indicated Singapore's readiness and willingness to enter into negotiations, to give Malaysia a full opportunity to comment on the reclamation works and their potential impacts, and to notify and consult Malaysia before it proceeded to construct any transport links. Singapore also extended an explicit offer to share the information that Malaysia requested, and to re-examine its works in the case that Malaysia was not convinced by the evidence supplied.[86]

83 *MOX Plant (Ireland v United Kingdom)* (Provisional Measures, Order of 3 December 2001, Sep Op Anderson) ITLOS Reports 2001, 95, 129.

84 Erik Franckx and Marco Bernatar, 'The "Duty" to Co-Operate for States Bordering Enclosed or Semi-Enclosed Seas' (2013) 31 Chinese (Taiwan) Yearbook of International Law and Affairs 66.

85 Request for Provisional Measures submitted by Malaysia, [13] www.itlos.org/fileadmin/itlos/documents/cases/case_no_12/C12_Request_Malaysia.pdf accessed 25 January 2022.

86 *Case Concerning Land Reclamation by Singapore in and around the Straits of Johor (Malaysia v Singapore)* (Provisional Measures, Order of 8 October 2003) ITLOS Reports 2003, 4, [76] [Land Reclamation Order].

Despite placing Singapore's commitments on records, ITLOS still found the level of cooperation between the parties insufficient. ITLOS recalled the statement made in the *MOX Plant* case that 'the duty to cooperate is a fundamental principle in the prevention of pollution of the marine environment under Part XII of the Convention and general international law'.[87] In almost identical wording to the *MOX Plant* case, ITLOS then held that 'prudence and caution require that Malaysia and Singapore establish mechanisms for exchanging information and assessing the risks or effects of land reclamation works and devising ways to deal with them in the areas concerned'.[88] The provisional measures eventually prescribed echoed many of Singapore's commitments. The duty to cooperate in this case thus included the duty to exchange information regarding the activities as well as their possible consequences, the duty to consult with other States that may be affected by the planned activities and to devise appropriate measures as deemed necessary for the protection of the marine environment.

Apart from these two cases, in *Chagos MPA*, Mauritius seemed to have interpreted the obligation to 'endeavour to harmonize policies' in preventing pollution to the marine environment under Article 194(1) to be equivalent to the duty to cooperate, or at least to have substantial overlap. Mauritius argued that this obligation required the sharing of information, the exchange of ideas, and some degree of consultation with a view to making pollution-related policies for the Chagos Archipelago consistent or compatible with those of other States in the region.[89] The arbitral tribunal, however, simply held that 'the United Kingdom was under an obligation to 'endeavor to harmonize' its policies with Mauritius'.[90] This endeavour, however, 'is prospective and requires only the United Kingdom's best efforts. It does not require that such attempts precede any action with respect to the marine environment, nor does it impose any particular deadline'.[91] Compared with how the duty to cooperate has been specified by ITLOS in the cases mentioned above, it would seem that the requirements for the fulfilment of the obligation under Article 194(1) is lower, and thus, the obligation to endeavour to harmonise policies cannot be deemed to have the same normative content as the duty to cooperate.

87 Ibid [92].
88 Ibid [99].
89 *Chagos MPA* (n 6) [483].
90 Ibid [539].
91 Ibid.

ITLOS's decisions on the duty to cooperate have made some important contributions to the status and content of this duty. The duty to cooperate is now acknowledged to be part of general international law, as held by ITLOS in *MOX Plant* and confirmed in *Land Reclamation*. While ITLOS has been less successful in defining the contours of the obligation to cooperate with regards to shared stocks, the scope of the duty to cooperate has been clarified in the prevention of marine pollution. It comprises more concrete obligations, namely, the obligations to exchange information, to consult with other States potentially affected by the planned activities, to jointly study the impacts of the activity on the marine environment, monitor risks or the effects of the operation and devise measures to prevent pollution of the marine environment. It should be noted that these obligations already exist as separate obligations under UNCLOS and under general international law. What ITLOS did was to incorporate these independent obligations under the umbrella of the duty to cooperate.

The duty to cooperate the provisional measures phase played a central role in helping the parties in the abovementioned cases to resolve their differences. For example, the establishment of an independent group of experts as required in *Land Reclamation* enabled the parties to reach a Settlement Agreement in their own terms.[92] Similarly, the arbitral tribunal in *MOX Plant* stated that it was 'satisfied that since December 2001, there has been an increased measure of co-operation and consultation, as required by the ITLOS Order'.[93] This acknowledgment notwithstanding, the tribunal also pointed out problems, both before and after the ITLOS Order, concerning 'the absence of secure arrangements, at a suitable intergovernmental level, for coordination of all of the various agencies and bodies involved'.[94] This statement highlights the issue commonly found in the decisions of UNCLOS tribunals concerning the duty to cooperate. With the exception of *Land Reclamation* in which ITLOS prescribed at least one concrete measure to be taken by the parties to discharge of the duty to cooperate, UNCLOS tribunals were generally much more general or, as viewed by Judge ad hoc Shearer in *Southern Bluefin Tuna*, too diplomatic,[95] with regard to the

92 *Case Concerning Land Reclamation by Singapore in and around the Straits of Johor (Malaysia v Singapore)* (2005) RIAA XXVII 133.

93 *MOX Plant (Ireland v United Kingdom)*, Order N° 3 Suspension of Proceedings on Jurisdiction and Merits, and Request for Further Provisional Measures [66] https://pcacases.com/web/sendAttach/867 accessed 25 January 2022.

94 Ibid.

95 *Southern Bluefin Tuna (New Zealand v Japan; Australia v Japan)* (Provisional Measures, Order of 27 August 1999, Sep Op Judge ad hoc Shearer) ITLOS Reports 1999, 280, 324.

measures to be taken so as to fulfil the duty to cooperate. UNCLOS tribunals tend to call on the relevant parties to enter into consultations and exchange information as a means of cooperation. States retain wide discretion as to how to fulfil their duty to cooperate. Consequently, although UNCLOS tribunals have clarified the scope of the duty by reading other independent obligations into the obligation to cooperate, there is still room for further contribution on the part of the tribunals.

5.3 DUTY TO CONDUCT ENVIRONMENTAL IMPACT ASSESSMENT

5.3.1 *UNCLOS Tribunals' Decisions on Environmental Impact Assessment*

The obligation to carry out EIA is provided for in Article 206 UNCLOS.[96] The requirements for conducting EIA found in this article have, however, been considered 'rudimentary' as compared to the standard found elsewhere under international law.[97] This article does not specify what is required of EIA or how it should be conducted. Beyond the Convention, the ICJ in *Pulp Mills* recognised that this obligation also existed under general international law 'where there is a risk that the proposed industrial activity may have a significant adverse impact in a transboundary context, in particular, on a shared resource'.[98] The status of this obligation under international law is, therefore, no longer subject to debate. It is the content of the obligation that is still shrouded in uncertainty. UNCLOS tribunals have had the opportunity to deal with the duty to conduct EIA in several cases, with varying degree of specificity. In earlier cases, the contribution of ITLOS to clarifying the content of this obligation was limited; and it was not until the recent *South China Sea* arbitration that the Annex VII arbitral tribunal managed to engage in a more detailed analysis of this obligation.

In *MOX Plant*, one of Ireland's allegations was that UK had refused to carry out a proper assessment of the impacts on the marine environment of the

96 Article 206 UNCLOS provides that: When States have reasonable grounds for believing that planned activities under their jurisdiction or control may cause substantial pollution or significant and harmful changes to the marine environment, they shall, as far as practicable, assess the potential effects of such activities on the marine environment and shall communicate reports of the results.

97 See: Lingjie Kong, 'Environmental Impact Assessment under the United Nations Convention on the Law of the Sea' (2011) 10 CJIL 651.

98 *Pulp Mills on the River Uruguay (Argentina v Uruguay)* [2010] ICJ Rep 14 [83] [Pulp Mills].

MOX plant and associated activities.[99] Ireland argued that even though the UK in 1993 had carried out EIA on the basis of which the commission of MOX Plant was authorised, the 1993 Impact Assessment Statement was not adequate as it did not address the potential harm of the MOX Plant to the marine environment of the Irish Sea.[100] Meanwhile, the UK contended that it had adduced evidence to establish that the risk of pollution from the operation of the MOX plant would be infinitely small and that the commissioning of the MOX plant would not cause serious harm to the marine environment or irreparable prejudice to the rights of Ireland.[101] ITLOS, for its part, did not address the adequacy or lack thereof of the 1993 Impact Assessment Statement in its Provisional Measure Order. Judge ad hoc Székely took issue with the majority's decision in this regard. Emphasising that 'EIA is a central tool of the international law of prevention', Judge Székely believed that the inadequacy of the UK's EIA, constituting a violation of Ireland's substantive rights under Article 206, should have been sufficient for the prescription of the provisional measures.[102]

In *Land Reclamation*, Malaysia also alleged that Singapore had not, prior to commencing its current land reclamation activities, conducted and published an adequate assessment of their potential effects on the environment and on the affected coastal areas.[103] Agreeing with Malaysia, ITLOS held that in the absence of the EIA, it could not be excluded that the land reclamation works might have adverse effects on the marine environment.[104] Consequently, although ITLOS did not order Singapore to suspend its land reclamation activities as requested by Malaysia, it ordered the establishment of a group of experts whose mandate was to 'study the effects of Singapore's land reclamation and to propose, as appropriate, measures to deal with any adverse effects of such land reclamation'.[105] The task assigned to this group was in effect that of EIA, the results of which would form the basis for any actions as agreed by the two parties. Similar to *MOX Plant*, the lack of EIA did not prompt ITLOS to grant the applicant the provisional measures that Malaysia had requested. However, EIA formed the crux of the provisional measure that ITLOS eventually prescribed.

99 *MOX Plant Order* (n 74) [26].
100 Ibid.
101 Ibid [72]–[73].
102 *MOX Plant (Ireland v United Kingdom)* (Provisional Measures, Order of 3 December 2001, Sep Op Judge ad hoc Székely) ITLOS Reports 2001, 95 [16].
103 *Land Reclamation Order* (n 86) [22].
104 Ibid [96].
105 Ibid [106].

In the *Advisory Opinion on Activities in the Area*, ITLOS – free from the constraints of provisional measures proceedings – managed to shed further light on the obligation to conduct EIA. With regard to activities in the Area, the obligation to carry out an EIA, besides finding basis in Article 206, is also found in the Annex to the 1994 Agreement as well as the Regulations on Prospecting and Exploration for Polymetallic Nodules in the Area (the Nodules Regulations) and the Regulations on Prospecting and Exploration for Polymetallic Sulphides in the Area (the Sulphides Regulations).[106] Notwithstanding this fact, the Seabed Disputes Chamber (SDC) still added that an obligation to conduct an EIA was a general obligation under customary international law.[107] More importantly, while recalling *Pulp Mills*, the SDC effectively expanded the spatial scope of application of EIA by stating that the obligation to conduct EIA 'may also apply to activities with an impact on the environment in an area beyond the limits of national jurisdiction'.[108]

With regard to the content of the obligation to conduct an EIA, the SDC pointed out that the content of the obligation to conduct an EIA in the specific context of activities in the Area was specified in the Nodules Regulations, Sulphides Regulations and the Recommendations for the Guidance of the Contractors for the Assessment of the Possible Environmental Impacts Arising from Exploration for Polymetallic Nodules in the Area.[109] Beyond these instruments, the SDC held that 'EIAs should be included in the system of consultations and prior notifications set out in article 142 of the Convention with respect to resource deposits in the Area which lie across limits of national jurisdiction'.[110] It should be noted that UNCLOS does not contain a specific rule on the relationship between EIA and the duty to consult and notify potentially affected States. Article 142 stipulates the requirement of 'consultation, including a system of prior notification' in cases involving straddling minerals, but it does not specify what should be included in such consultations. Conversely, while Article 206

106 Regulations on Prospecting and Exploration for Polymetallic Nodules in the Area, ISBA/19/C/17 (amended) (22 July 2013); Regulations on Prospecting and Exploration for Polymetallic Sulphides in the Area, ISBA/16/C/L.5 (6 May 2010). The relevant provisions of these Regulations require the sponsoring States not only to individually ensure compliance by the sponsored contractor with this obligation but also to cooperate with the Authority in the establishment and implementation of impact assessments. Advisory Opinion on Activities in the Area (n 45) [141].

107 Ibid [145].

108 Ibid [148].

109 Ibid [149].

110 Ibid [148].

provides for an obligation to communicate the results of EIA, the reference to Article 205 limits this obligation to publishing and communicating the results to competent organisations. At a more general level, the relationship between EIA and the obligation to consult and notify the affected population under general international law is also not entirely clear. Dupuy and Viñuales contend that this 'depends on the source of the obligation' but that 'outside the treaty and administrative framework, the question is less clear';[111] while Okanawa maintains in a more general manner that EIA is implicit in the duty to consult and notify other States of proposed activities that may entail harm.[112] The SDC's abovementioned statement confirmed that EIA was part of the obligation to consult and notify. This statement did not only establish a close connection between Articles 142 and 206 UNCLOS but also gave 'more specific content to these obligations'.[113] While the SDC's finding may be limited to activities in areas beyond national jurisdiction, there is little reason to not extend the close link between EIA and the obligations to consult and notify established to other contexts.[114]

The obligation to communicate the results of EIA is explicitly found under Article 206 UNCLOS, despite not entitled as such. In interpreting this article, the *South China Sea* tribunal again confirmed the customary status of the obligation to conduct EIA and that it was an 'essential part of a comprehensive environmental management system' and a 'particular application of the obligation on states, enunciated in Article 194(2)'.[115] By connecting Article 206 with Article 194(2), the tribunal confirmed that the obligation to conduct EIA is both a standalone procedural obligation and an element of the general obligation to prevent and control pollution. Further, the tribunal distinguished two types of obligations contained in Article 206. These include, first, the obligation to conduct assessment which, according to the tribunal, allows 'an element of discretion for the State concerned' by virtue of the terms

[111] Pierre-Marie Dupuy and Jorge E Viñuales, *International Environmental Law* (CUP 2015) 70.

[112] Phoebe Okanawa, 'Procedural Obligations in International Environmental Agreements' (1997) 67 BYBIL 275; Patricia Birnie, Alan Boyle and Catherine Redgwell, *International Law and the Environment* (3rd ed, OUP 2009) 105.

[113] Laura Pineschi, 'The Duty of Environmental Impact Assessment in the First ITLOS Chamber's Advisory Opinion: Towards the Supremacy of the General Rule to Protect and Preserve the Marine Environment as a Common Value?' in Nerina Boschiero and others (eds), *International Courts and the Development of International Law* (Springer 2013) 434.

[114] The ICJ subsequently confirmed this close relationship between the obligation to conduct EIA and the obligation to notify and consult. See: *Certain Activities Carried out by Nicaragua in the Border Area (Costa Rica v Nicaragua) and Construction of a Road in Costa Rica along the San Juan River (Nicaragua v Costa Rica)* (Merits) [2015] ICJ Rep 665 [110].

[115] *South China Sea Arbitration* (n 18) [948].

'reasonable' and 'as far as practicable'; and second the obligation to communicate reports of the results of the assessment which is 'absolute'. Elaborating on the latter, the tribunal also recalled *Construction of a Road* in which the ICJ stated that the mere assertion of the existence of assessment was not the same as conducting the assessment itself.[116] While the tribunal was not able to conclude whether China had indeed prepared an EIA based on the evidence before it,[117] it nevertheless stated that '[t]o fulfil the obligations of Article 206, a State must not only prepare an EIA but also must communicate it'.[118] On that basis, the tribunal found a violation of Article 206 on the part of China due to the fact that it had never communicated its EIA report to the tribunal or any other international organisations

5.3.2 *Appraisal of UNCLOS Tribunals' Decisions on EIA*

In all the cases brought before UNCLOS tribunals, none of the parties disputed the necessity of EIA or the existence of the obligation to conduct an EIA under international law. Their arguments instead only revolved around whether EIA had been conducted and if so, whether it was adequate and the results were reliable. This clearly shows a high level of consensus among States regarding the existence of such obligation under international law.

With regards to the scope and content of the duty, ITLOS's decisions concerning EIA threw little light on what the duty involves or the criteria based on which an EIA would be considered satisfactory. Both *MOX Plant* and the *Land Reclamation* involved submissions based on Article 206. In neither of the cases, however, was the alleged lack of EIA considered as the basis for the prescription of provisional measures. The only exception was the *Advisory Opinion on Activities in the Area*, in which the SDC was able to clarify the content of the duty to conduct EIA thanks to the specific Rules and Regulations concerning the activities in the Area. Even though these Rules and Regulations contain criteria that are applicable in a very limited context with specific actors, the interpretation provided, particularly the connection between the duty to conduct EIA and the duty to notify and consult, may be of more general guidance beyond the context of deep seabed mining.

The *South China Sea* tribunal was the first to deal with Article 206 in a contentious case and the only case to date in which a violation of the duty to conduct EIA under Article 206 has been found. The tribunal's analysis raises

[116] Ibid [989].
[117] Ibid [991].
[118] Ibid.

interesting points for the broader application of this obligation. First, the tribunal made clear that a State cannot claim to have conducted EIA without showing proof of it. Second, it reaffirmed the connection between the obligation to conduct EIA and the obligation to consult and notify with the potentially affected State, as well as the broader obligation to ensure that pollution is not caused to another State. Third, while the tribunal did not get the chance to elaborate on what should be included in an EIA as there was no EIA report available for scrutiny, it seemed to have placed particular emphasis on the criteria for EIA stipulated in Chinese domestic regulation and the comprehensiveness of EIA reviewed by international courts.

The third point is particularly interesting since despite requiring the conduct of an EIA, Article 206 of UNCLOS does not elaborate on the content of this obligation. In their written submissions to the Annex VII arbitral tribunal in *MOX Plant*, both Ireland and the UK had different views with regards to the specific content of the obligation to conduct EIA. Ireland argued that the arbitral tribunal, in interpreting and applying Article 206, 'should take into account the common standards of EIA in other instruments such as the UNEP EIA Principles or the Espoo Convention'.[119] The UK, for its part, argued that by virtue of the terms 'reasonable grounds' and 'as far as practicable' under Article 206, States retained the discretion as to the manner in which EIA should be carried out.[120] As the arbitration was suspended by the Annex VII arbitral tribunal, it remained open as to which of the two views would have prevailed.

The disagreement between Ireland and the UK also raises the question as to whether and to what extent Article 206 can be informed by existing standards of EIA found in other international instruments.[121] This question is part of a broader discussion concerning whether transboundary EIA is part of international law, or whether it is an outgrowth of domestic EIA regulations.[122] If it is the former, there should be a general standard for EIA imposed on States, whereas if it is the latter, States retain large discretion as to how to carry out their EIA. The ICJ in *Pulp Mills* held that 'general international law does not specify the scope and content of EIA' and that 'it is for each State to determine in its domestic legislation or in the authorization process for the project, the

[119] *MOX Plant Case (Ireland v United Kingdom)* UNCLOS Annex VII Arbitration, Memorial of Ireland [7.16] https://pcacases.com/web/sendAttach/850 accessed 25 January 2022.

[120] Ibid [5.14]–[5.32].

[121] Neil Craik, *The International Law of Environmental Impact Assessment: Process, Substance and Integration* (CUP 2008) 120.

[122] John H Knox, 'The Myth and Reality of Transboundary Environmental Impact Assessment' (2002) 96 AJIL 291.

specific content of the environmental impact assessment required in each case'.[123] However, as observed by one commentator, *Pulp Mills* could not be taken to mean that 'the content of an EIA is for the State to decide in its sole discretion', instead 'international law requires at a minimum that an EIA assess possible effects on people, property and the environment of other States likely to be affected'.[124] The fact that the SDC in the *Advisory Opinion on Activities in the Area* referred to the Mining Code in order to determine the content of EIA seems to support the understanding of a minimum international standard for EIA. In fact, the SDC's approach has been hailed as '[leading] the way to a wider understanding of the content of the EIA; an understanding that looks towards international bodies for the definition of the content of the EIA, thus working towards a global and not a narrow localised approach'.[125] In *South China Sea*, while the tribunal, as discussed above, confirmed the discretion available to States in conducting EIA, its reference to international standards also hints at an inclination to restrict the absolute discretion of States in conducting EIA.

In conclusion, due to the constraints of provisional measure proceedings, ITLOS's earlier cases on EIA have been criticised for '[having] barely scratched the surface'.[126] The approach of ITLOS in *MOX Plant*, however, suggests that the tribunal would be reluctant to assess the adequacy or otherwise of EIA that has been conducted by the State in light of the lack of concrete requirements under general international law and would only find a breach in cases where EIA has not been conducted at all.[127] The SDC in the *Advisory Opinion on Activities in the Area* managed to not only confirm the customary status of EIA but also its normative content and its relationship with other principles of environmental law. While the context in which EIA was discussed, that is, mining activities in the Area, was rather narrow, the SDC's interpretation of EIA is likely to have broader implications on the understanding of the obligation to conduct EIA under general international law. The contribution of *South China Sea* – the only case to date in which an Annex VII arbitral tribunal examined Article 206 – lies primarily in its clarification of the two

[123] *Pulp Mills* (n 98) 205.

[124] Alan Boyle, 'Developments in the International Law of Environmental Impact Assessments and Their Relation to the Espoo Convention' (2011) 20(3) Review of European Community and International Environmental Law 227, 229.

[125] Ilias Plakokefalos, 'Seabed Disputes Chamber of the International Tribunal for the Law of the Sea: Responsibilities and Obligations of States Sponsoring Persons and Entities with Respect to Activities in the Area Advisory Opinion' (2012) 24(1) Journal of Environmental Law 133, 139.

[126] Alan Boyle, 'The Environmental Jurisprudence of the ITLOS' (2007) 22 IJMCL 369, 378.

[127] Eike Blitza, 'Article 206' in Proelss (n 1) 1376.

obligations of a different nature contained in Article 206 and the measures that States would have to undertake to fulfil the obligations of Article 206.

5.4 THE PRECAUTIONARY PRINCIPLE

Even though the precautionary principle can be found in many international instruments,[128] its status under international law as well as its normative content remains unclear due to a number of reasons. First, there is a lack of a single universally accepted definition of the principle. Second, the specific requirements for the elements commonly present in the formulation of the precautionary principle, namely the existence of scientific uncertainty,[129] the threshold of risk,[130] and precautionary action,[131] vary in different agreements. Third, the function of the precautionary principle differs in different versions of the principle, either (i) as a justification to take action, but not as a basis to compel action, in the face of scientific uncertainty, or (ii) as a duty to act, that is, a duty to take preventative measures in cases of scientific uncertainty.[132] Finally, the precautionary principle also generates disagreement regarding its effects on the burden of proof. It is not clear whether the precautionary principle lowers the standard of proof of harm to the environment to trigger response,[133] or

[128] See in general, Arie Trouwborst, *Evolution and Status of the Precautionary Principle in International Law* (Kluwer Law International 2002).

[129] Some instruments require 'lack of full scientific uncertainty'. See, for example, Rio Declaration on Environment and Development, 13 June 1992, UN Doc A/CONF.151/26.Rev.1, Principle 15; Bergen Declaration, Ministerial Declaration on Sustainable Development in the ECE Region, A/CONF/151/PC/10. Others set the level of uncertainty at 'no conclusive evidence'. See, for example, Convention for the Protection of the Marine Environment of the North-East Atlantic (OSPAR Convention), 2354 UNTS 67, Article 2.2; Convention on the Protection of the Marine Environment of the Baltic Sea Area, 1507 UNTS 167, Article 3.2.

[130] A precautionary measure would only be triggered when the threshold of risk is crossed. This threshold comprises two requirements, namely the severity of potential risk and the probability of the risk. The severity of risk varies among 'significant', 'serious' or 'irreversible', while the probability of risk could be 'reasonable grounds to believe' or none at all. See, for example, Rio Declaration (n 129), Principle 15; United Nations Framework Convention on Climate Change, 1771 UNTS 170, Article 3.3; Cartagena Protocol on Biosafety to the Convention on Biological Diversity 39 ILM 1027 (2000), Article 10.6.

[131] Most instruments do not specify the types of measures required in response to the risk. The rare exception is found under Principle 15 of the Rio Declaration which specifies 'cost-effective measures to prevent environmental degradation'. Rio Declaration (n 129) Principle 15.

[132] See Antônio Augusto Cançado Trindade, 'Precaution' in Jorge E Viñuales (ed), *The Rio Declaration on Environment and Development: A Commentary* (OUP 2015) 408.

[133] Boyle (n 126); Arie Trouwborst, 'The Precautionary Principle in General International Law: Combating the Babylonian Confusion' (2007) 16 Review of European Community and International Environmental Law 185.

whether it reverses the burden of proof, by shifting the burden of proof from the party opposing the planned activity to prove that harm will be caused to the party wishing to take certain actions to prove that the actions will not cause harm to the environment.[134]

Due to the above-mentioned disparities, the application of the precautionary principle is specific to the convention or treaty under which it is stipulated. UNCLOS is, however, not among those conventions. While there have been suggestions that the precautionary principle is not completely absent in UNCLOS,[135] the fact remains that UNCLOS does not contain an explicit reference to the precautionary principle. This has, however, not prevented States from invoking the precautionary principle before UNCLOS tribunals, particularly ITLOS, allowing the tribunal to shed some light on this principle.

5.4.1 *UNCLOS Tribunals' Decisions Relating to the Precautionary Principle*

Southern Bluefin Tuna was the first case in which the precautionary principle was invoked before ITLOS. In this case, Australia and New Zealand alleged that Japan, by unilaterally designing and undertaking an experimental fishing programme, failed to comply with, inter alias, 'rules of customary international law'.[136] By 'customary international law', Australia and New Zealand were referring specifically to the precautionary principle.[137] Pending the

[134] Philippe Sands and Jacqueline Peel, *Principles of International Environmental Law* (3rd ed, CUP 2012) 222.

[135] See, for example, Bénédicte Sage-Fuller, *The Precautionary Principle in Marine Environmental Law: With Special Reference to High Risk Vessels* (Routledge 2013) 68 (arguing that the concept of the precautionary principle can be read into UNCLOS by establishing the link between the precautionary principle and the prevention principle); Gerd Winter (ed), *Towards Sustainable Fisheries Law: A Comparative Analysis* (IUCN 2009) 15 (noting that a trace of the precautionary principle can be seen in Articles 61(2) and 119 which create the assumption that if scientific evidence is not available, conservative obligations under the Convention prevail, which is the essence of the precautionary principle); Robin Churchill, 'The LOSC Regime for Protection of the Marine Environment – Fit for The Twenty-First Century?' in Rosemary Gail Rayfuse (ed), *Research Handbook on International Marine Environmental Law* (Edward Elgar 2015) 9 (arguing that there is an 'embryonic use' of the principle in the definition of marine pollution under Article 1(1)(4) UNCLOS which includes the introduction of substances or energy into the marine environment that not only results in deleterious effects but also that 'is likely to result' in such effects).

[136] *Southern Bluefin Tuna* Order (n 5) [45].

[137] Australia and New Zealand asked ITLOS to take into account 'the parties' obligations under general international law, in particular the precautionary principle'. See Request for the Prescription of Provisional Measures Submitted by New Zealand, [1] www.itlos.org/fileadmin/itlos/documents/cases/case_no_3_4/request_new_zealand_eng.pdf accessed 25 January 2022;

constitution of Annex VII arbitral tribunal, the Applicants requested that ITLOS prescribe provisional measures, inter alias, to ensure that 'the parties act consistently with the precautionary principle in fishing for SBT pending a final settlement of the dispute'.[138] ITLOS, for its part, acknowledged that the SBT 'is severely depleted and is at its historically lowest levels and that this is a cause for serious biological concern'.[139] On this basis, it held that 'the parties should in the circumstances act with prudence and caution to ensure that effective conservation measures are taken to prevent serious harm to the stock of SBT'.[140]

Although ITLOS did not explicitly refer to the precautionary principle, there are elements in its reasoning which signalled the application of this principle.[141] In particular, despite highlighting the lack of scientific certainty regarding the effectiveness of the measures to be taken in conserving the stock, ITLOS still decided to prescribe measures to prevent further deterioration to the stock. The decision to take action despite scientific uncertainty clearly paid heed to the precautionary principle as provided for in various instruments mentioned above.[142] Coupled with the reference to 'caution and prudence', it does not seem difficult to conclude that ITLOS intended to apply the precautionary principle. In fact, the precautionary principle served as the main basis for the prescription of provisional measures in this case.[143]

Request for the Prescription of Provisional Measures Submitted by Australia, [1], www.itlos.org/fileadmin/itlos/documents/cases/case_no_3_4/request_australia_eng.pdf accessed 25 January 2022.

138 *Southern Bluefin Tuna* Order (n 5) [34].

139 Ibid [71].

140 Ibid [77].

141 Several judges confirmed in their separate and dissenting opinions that the prescription of the provisional measure was based upon the considerations of the precautionary principle. See *Southern Bluefin Tuna (New Zealand v Japan; Australia v Japan)* (Provisional Measures, Order of 27 August 1999, Sep Op Treves) ITLOS Reports 1999, 280 [8]; *Southern Bluefin Tuna (New Zealand v Japan; Australia v Japan)* (Provisional Measures, Order of 27 August 1999, Sep Op Laing) ITLOS Reports 1999, 280 [19]; *Southern Bluefin Tuna (New Zealand v Japan; Australia v Japan)* (Provisional Measures, Order of 27 August 1999, Sep Op Shearer) ITLOS Reports 1999, 280, 6.

142 Note that Judge Laing argued that ITLOS did not adopt the precautionary principle but merely the precautionary approach. In his view, 'adopting an approach, rather than a principle, appropriately imports a certain degree of flexibility and tends, though not dispositively, to underscore reticence about making premature pronouncements about desirable normative structures'. *Southern Bluefin Tuna*, Separate Opinion of Judge Laing (n 141) [19]. However, it is generally agreed that the use of either of these terms carries little difference in terms of the function that it plays. See also: Cançado Trindade (n 132) 412; Nicolas de Sadeleer, *Environmental Principles: From Political Slogans to Legal Rules* (OUP 2002) 92.

143 Tim Stephens, *International Courts and Environmental Protection* (CUP 2009) 225.

It should be noted, however, that ITLOS did not confirm the customary status of the precautionary principle as contended by the Applicants. Judge Treves in his Separate Opinion attempted to account for this oversight, stating that 'in order to resort to the precautionary approach for assessing the urgency of the measures to be prescribed in the present case, it is not necessary to hold the view that this approach is dictated by a rule of customary international law'.[144] Instead, 'the requirement of urgency is satisfied only in the light of such precautionary approach'[145] and thus, 'a precautionary approach seems to be inherent in the very notion of provisional measures'.[146] Judge Treves' reasoning implied that the basis for the application of the precautionary principle was found in the requirement of 'urgency' under Article 290(5). This view has received support from another scholar, who argues that the inclusion of the 'serious harm to the marine environment' as a basis for the prescription of provisional measure enhances the precautionary aspect of provisional measures.[147]

The precautionary principle also arose in *MOX Plant* concerning Ireland's challenge to the commission and operation of the MOX Plant by the UK.[148] In its Written Request, Ireland contended that the precautionary principle had attained the status of a customary international rule and, as such, it was binding on both parties.[149] On the one hand, in the context of provisional measures proceeding before ITLOS, Ireland adopted a similar line of reasoning as Judge Treves mentioned above and argued that the precautionary principle should inform the Tribunal's assessment of the urgency of the measures that it was required to take in respect of the operation of the MOX plant.[150] The UK, on the other hand, maintained that due to the lack of proof and on the facts of this case, the precautionary principle had no application.[151]

ITLOS in this case adopted a more cautious approach when dealing with the precautionary principle than in *Southern Bluefin Tuna*. Despite both parties' reference to the legal status of the principle and to the insufficiency of scientific data, ITLOS did not address any of these issues in its Order.

144 *Southern Bluefin Tuna*, Separate Opinion of Judge Treves (n 141) [9].
145 Ibid [8].
146 Ibid [9].
147 Caroline Foster, *Science and the Precautionary Principle in International Courts and Tribunals: Expert Evidence, Burden of Proof and Finality* (CUP 2013) 268.
148 *MOX Plant Order* (n 74).
149 Request for Provisional Measures and Statement of Case Submitted on Behalf of Ireland, [97] www.itlos.org/fileadmin/itlos/documents/cases/case_no_10/request_ireland_e.pdf accessed 25 January 2022.
150 Ibid.
151 *MOX Plant Order* (n 74) [75].

ITLOS rejected Ireland's request for provisional measures due to the lack of urgency of the situation required provisional measures under Article 290(5).[152] However, in the Provisional Measures Order, the Tribunal still used the term 'prudence and caution' seen in *Southern Bluefin Tuna* in order to require the parties to cooperate 'in exchanging information concerning risks or effects of the operation of the MOX plant and in devising ways to deal with them'.[153] The use of 'prudence and caution' was not supported by any discussion, particularly on scientific uncertainty or risk of harm, thus it is unclear as to whether ITLOS actually intended to invoke the precautionary principle. In any case, ITLOS's approach could be seen as a retreat from the strong endorsement that ITLOS had shown for the principle in *Southern Bluefin Tuna*. As argued by one commentator, the characteristics of the MOX Plant dispute suggested that it was a 'text book' example of a situation that would require the precautionary principle.[154] Judge Wolfrum, however, supported ITLOS's decision as, in his view, the application of the precautionary principle would have resulted in the fact that '[t]he granting of provisional measures becomes automatic when an applicant argues with some plausibility that its rights may be prejudiced or that there was serious risk to the marine environment.'[155] This statement seems to contrast that of Judge Treves in the *Southern Bluefin Tuna* case mentioned above, in which the latter contended that 'a precautionary approach seems to be inherent in the very notion of provisional measures'.[156]

In *Land Reclamation* concerning Malaysia's allegations that Singapore had violated UNCLOS for conducting land reclamation activities in the Straits of Johor, Malaysia also invoked the precautionary principle when requesting provisional measures. In addition to various provisions under UNCLOS, Malaysia cited, as the legal basis for its claims, 'the precautionary principle, which under international law must direct any party in the application and implementation of those obligations'.[157] Singapore rejected this submission and argued that there was no room to apply the precautionary principle in the case in question.[158] Similar to the approach

[152] Ibid [81].
[153] Ibid [84].
[154] Tim Stephens, *International Courts and Environmental Protection* (n 143) 234; Ted McDorman, 'International Tribunal for the Law of the Sea' (2001) 21 Yearbook of International Environmental Law 531.
[155] *MOX Plant Order*, Separate Opinion of Judge Wolfrum (n 81) 3.
[156] *Southern Bluefin Tuna*, Separate Opinion of Judge Treves (n 141) 8.
[157] *Land Reclamation Order* (n 86) [74].
[158] Ibid [75].

taken in the *MOX Plant* case, ITLOS did not discuss the precautionary principle when considering Malaysia's allegations. However, for activities in the eastern part of Pulau Tekong, it found that EIA had not been conducted,[159] and came to the conclusion that 'the land reclamation works may have adverse effects on the marine environment'.[160] Despite such findings, ITLOS did not find it appropriate to apply the precautionary principle to suspend Singapore's ongoing activities, at least until the results of a more concrete assessment of the environmental impacts of the land reclamation activities would be published. Instead, ITLOS only recalled the familiar phrase 'prudence and caution' to require the parties to 'establish mechanisms for exchanging information and assessing the risks or effects of land reclamation works and devising ways to deal with them in the areas concerned'.[161] The use of the phrase 'prudence and caution' and its connection with the duty to cooperate bore much resemblance to *MOX Plant*.

Finally, the *Advisory Opinion on Activities in the Area* presented the occasion in which ITLOS came the closest to endorsing the customary status of the precautionary principle. In the context of deep seabed mining, the precautionary principle is clearly stipulated in the Nodules Regulations and the Sulphides Regulations which are binding instruments and are applicable to exploration activities in the Area.[162] As a result, unlike previous cases in which the precautionary principle was invoked as a matter of customary international law the precautionary principle was binding on sponsoring States as a matter of treaty law.[163] However, while the precautionary principle is inscribed in a 'standard clause' for exploration contracts in the Sulphides Regulations, it is not included in a parallel standard clause for exploration contracts in the Nodules Regulations.[164] Perhaps it was this absence that prompted the SDC to make the following statement regarding the status of this principle under international law:

[159] Ibid [95].
[160] Ibid [96].
[161] Ibid [99].
[162] Regulation 31, paragraph 2 of the Nodules Regulations and Regulation 33, paragraph 2 of the Sulphides Regulations require sponsoring States as well as the Authority to 'apply a precautionary approach, as reflected in Principle 15 of the Rio Declaration' in order 'to ensure effective protection for the marine environment from harmful effects which may arise from activities in the Area'. See *Advisory Opinion on Activities in the Area* (n 45) [125].
[163] Ibid [127].
[164] Ibid [134].

> [T]he precautionary approach has been incorporated into a growing number of international treaties and other instruments, many of which reflect the formulation of Principle 15 of the Rio Declaration. In the view of the Chamber, this has initiated a trend towards making this approach part of customary international law.[165]

Even though the SDC did not explicitly state that the principle was a customary rule, this in *obiter dictum* came closer to accepting the customary nature of the principle than any other tribunals had, and have, to date.

The SDC also took the opportunity to shed some light on the meaning and application of this principle, albeit only in relation to the activities provided for in the Regulations. The Chamber explained that the second sentence of Principle 15 of the Rio Declaration set the scale of harm to 'serious or irreversible damage' and limited the measures to be taken to only 'cost-effective measures'.[166] Moreover, the Chamber also noted that the Rio Declaration also allowed for certain flexibility in the application of the principle, in light of the phrase 'applied by States according to their capabilities'.[167] The SDC interpreted this to mean that, in the context of the exploration activities, 'the requirements for complying with the obligation to apply the precautionary approach may be stricter for the developed than for the developing sponsoring States'.[168] This statement created a link between the precautionary principle and the principle of 'common but differentiated responsibility' widely recognised under international environmental law.[169] In addition, the SDC also stated that 'the precautionary approach is also an integral part of the general obligation of due diligence of sponsoring States'.[170] The link between the precautionary principle and the obligation of due diligence means that sponsoring States would be required to consider preventative measures not only when the risks of harm are apparent, but also when there are only plausible indications of potential risks.[171]

[165] Ibid [135].
[166] Ibid [128].
[167] Ibid [129].
[168] Ibid [161].
[169] Philippe Cullet, 'Common but Differentiated Responsibility' in Viñuales, *The Rio Declaration* (n 132) 229.
[170] *Advisory Opinion on Activities in the Area* (n 45) [131].
[171] Ibid.

5.4.2 *Appraisal of UNCLOS Tribunals' Decisions on the Precautionary Principle*

A perusal of ITLOS's cases shows that ITLOS was the first tribunal to have applied the precautionary principle in *Southern Bluefin Tuna* in 1999, albeit without calling it by name. It should be noted that the precautionary principle is recognised in almost all fisheries instruments post-UNCLOS, which prompted the argument that even though precaution in fisheries management has yet to reach the status of customary international law, a new norm of marine living resources management is emerging.[172] Such widespread recognition perhaps gave ITLOS the incentive to be more readily accepting of the precautionary principle in fisheries conservation cases, such as *Southern Bluefin Tuna,* as compared to marine pollution cases, such as *MOX Plant* or *Land Reclamation.* Even though ITLOS did not extend the strong support that it had shown for the precautionary principle in *Southern Bluefin Tuna* to these two subsequent cases when there was arguably room for the application of the principle, it seems that the principle was never completely dismissed. Some have argued that the Provisional Measures Orders in *MOX Plant* and *Land Reclamation* had a certain precautionary character as they were premised on considerations of 'prudence and caution.'[173] In his statement to the UN General Assembly, former ITLOS President Golitsyn remarked that the term 'prudence and caution' was 'equivalent to acting by applying a precautionary approach'.[174]

The *Advisory Opinion on Activities in the Area* came closest to endorsing the customary status of the precautionary principle seen in any international decisions. The SDC's view that there was now a trend towards making this approach part of customary law was the boldest acknowledgement of the principle by any international tribunal. This was also the first time an international tribunal analysed the structure and meaning of the precautionary principle as contained in Principle 15 of the Rio Declaration in any detail, providing an important clarification of the meaning and application of this principle. ITLOS, therefore, can be said to be the forerunner in the adoption of the precautionary principle.

[172] See: Kaye (n 60) 261.

[173] Sands and Peel (n 134) 225.

[174] Vladimir Golitsyn, 'Agenda Item 74(a) "Oceans and The Law Of The Sea"' (9 December 2014) at the Plenary of the Sixty-Ninth Session of the United Nations General Assembly, [22] www.itlos.org/fileadmin/itlos/documents/statements_of_president/Golitsyn/Statement_GA_09122014_FINAL_EN.pdf accessed 25 January 2022.

ITLOS's treatment of the precautionary principle can be contrasted with the approach of other international courts and tribunals when faced with this principle. In cases such as *Gabcikovo/Nagymaros*,[175] or *Whaling*,[176] the ICJ did not once endorse or apply the principle. In *Pulp Mills* in 2010, the Court only engaged in a brief discussion of the precautionary principle, acknowledging that 'a precautionary approach may be relevant in the interpretation and application of the provisions of the Statute'.[177] This statement notwithstanding, the ICJ still required Argentina, who was opposed to the operation of the *Pulp Mills*, to show clear evidence for the existence of harmful substance to the factory.[178] One can only find references to the principle in the dissenting or separate opinions of the judges, most noticeably those of Judge Weeramantry in *Nuclear Tests*,[179] Judge Cançado Trindade in *Pulp Mills*,[180] and Judge Charlesworth in *Whaling*.[181] The World Trade Organization (WTO) Appellate Body has likewise been rather cautious whenever the precautionary principle arose in its case law. So far, it has not recognised the principle as a customary rule, calling the status of the principle as 'less than clear'.[182] The WTO Appellate Body in the *EC–Hormones* only acknowledged that the precautionary principle had been 'incorporated and given a specific meaning in article 5.7 of the SPS Agreement'[183] but declined to comment on the question of the status of the principle, opining that such a question was 'important' but 'abstract'.[184]

Notwithstanding ITLOS's acknowledgment of the precautionary principle, as the principle has been dealt with only in the provisional measure and advisory proceedings, the Tribunal's contribution to the development of the normative content of the principle has been rather limited. However, ITLOS

[175] *Gabcikovo-Nagymaros Project (Hungary/Slovakia)* [1997] ICJ Rep 7 [112].

[176] *Whaling* (n 64). Smith argues, however, that the *Whaling* decision still advances the precautionary approach. See: Jeffrey J Smith, 'Evolving to Conservation? The International Court's Decision in the Australia/Japan Whaling Case' (2014) 45(4) ODIL 301, 318.

[177] *Pulp Mills* (n 98) [257].

[178] Ibid [164].

[179] *Request for an Examination of the Situation in Accordance with Paragraph 63 of the Court's Judgement of 20 December 1974 in the Nuclear Tests (New Zealand v France) Case* (Request for an examination of the situation – Request for the Indication of Provisional Measures, Dis Op Weeramantry) [1995] ICJ Rep 1995, 288, 342.

[180] *Pulp Mills on the River Uruguay (Argentina v Uruguay)* [2010] ICJ Rep 14 (Judgment, Sep Op Cancado Trindande) [62]–[92].

[181] *Whaling in the Antarctic*, Separate Opinion of Judge ad hoc Charlesworth (n 64) [6]–[9].

[182] *European Communities – Measures Concerning Meat and Meat Products (Hormones)*, WT/DS26/AB/R (16 January 1998).

[183] Ibid [120].

[184] Ibid [123].

still managed to clarify some points that were still unclear regarding the application of the precautionary principle. In terms of the threshold for the severity of harm, in *Southern Bluefin Tuna*, ITLOS read the gravity of harm contained in Article 290, that is, 'serious harm', as the triggering point for the application of the precautionary principle. In *MOX Plant* and *Land Reclamation*, whether 'serious harm' occurred to the marine environment was also examined, interchangeably with 'irreversible harm' or 'significant impact'. However, as ITLOS did not invoke the precautionary principle as the basis for its provisional measures in these later cases, it seems that the discussion on the level harm was part of the examination of Article 290(5), not of the precautionary principle.

With regards to the burden of proof, the provisional measures cases all seem to indicate that ITLOS did not reverse the burden of proof. The applicants still bore the obligation to prove 'serious harm' to the environment when requesting precautionary measures from the respondents. However, it is arguable that, as Judge Wolfrum acknowledged in *MOX Plant*,[185] the reversal of the burden of proof was not undertaken in the case because ITLOS was only required to establish prima facie jurisdiction in provisional measures. Therefore, the refusal to reverse the burden of proof in ITLOS case law was dictated by the exceptional nature of provisional proceedings.[186] It is not possible, therefore, to draw a definitive conclusion from ITLOS's decisions regarding the impact of the precautionary principle on the reversal of the burden of proof in other contexts beyond provisional measure.

Even though ITLOS was prepared to apply the precautionary principle in *Southern Bluefin Tuna*, it is worth asking whether Judge Treves' statement that 'the precautionary principle is inherent in provisional measure' holds true, particularly in the context of fisheries conservation. Article 290(5) requires that provisional measures could be prescribed only when 'the urgency of the situation so requires'. This means that the party requesting the provisional measure must show that damage would occur in the limited window of time, although ITLOS's decisions are inconsistent as to whether this limited time is between the provisional measure proceedings and the constitution of the arbitral tribunal,[187] or between the provisional measure proceedings and consideration of the merits of the case by the Annex VII arbitral tribunal.[188]

185 *MOX Plant Order*, Separate Opinion of Judge Wolfrum (n 81) 3.

186 A refusal to reverse the burden of proof could also be seen in the *Pulp Mills* case by the ICJ in the context of a contentious proceeding. See *Pulp Mills* (n 98) [164].

187 *Southern Bluefin Tuna Order* (n 5) [81].

188 *Land Reclamation Order* (n 86) [72].

This requirement, if read into the precautionary principle, would seem to add an extra temporal element to the threshold for the application of the precautionary principle. This may create a situation of dilemma where on the one hand, the precautionary principle encourages environmental-friendly actions even in the face of scientific uncertainty; and on the other hand, the lack of scientific certainty regarding the possible harm to the environment may make it impossible to predict urgency of the situation. This scenario is especially prone to happen in cases involving the protection of marine living resources where it is inherently difficult to be certain of the level of stocks that is available or depleted.[189] One scholar has argued that '[s]cientific uncertainty is normally the rule in fisheries management and a straightforward application of the precautionary principle would have resulted in the impossibility of proceeding with any activity relating to marine fisheries'.[190]

In the context of an advisory proceeding, the *Advisory Opinion on Activities in the Area* was the first to clarify the link between precautionary principle and several other environmental obligations. In earlier cases, namely *MOX Plant* and *Land Reclamation*, ITLOS already hinted at the link between the precautionary principle and the procedural obligations, using 'prudence and caution' as the basis for prescribing provisional measures which were of a procedural nature, such as the duty to cooperate.[191] The SDC, however, expanded the relationship between the precautionary principle not only to the duty to cooperate, but also to the principle of 'common but differentiated responsibility' and due diligence. As ITLOS was only required to examine the precautionary principle in the abstract in an advisory proceeding, it did not elaborate more on the peculiarities of these links.

In short, ITLOS's decisions have added an authoritative voice to endorsing the status and applicability of the precautionary principle to marine environment protection under UNCLOS. ITLOS has also contributed to clarifying certain elements of the principle's normative content, although

189 Simon Marr, 'The Southern Bluefin Tuna Cases: The Precautionary Approach and Conservation and Management of Fish Resources' (2000) 11(4) EJIL 815, 822.

190 Francisco Orrego Vicuña, *The Changing International Law of High Seas Fisheries* (CUP 1999) 157.

191 Note, however, that ITLOS's prescription of procedural measures not requested by the applicants was not without criticism, both by the individual judges and by some commentators. See Donald L Morgan, 'A Practitioner's Critique of the Order Granting Provisional Measures in the Southern Bluefin Tuna Case' in John Norton Moore and Myron H Nordquist (eds), *Current Marine Environmental Issues and the International Tribunal for the Law of the Sea* (Martinus Nijhoff 2001) 182.

the contribution was limited by the nature of the proceedings in which the principle was examined.

5.5 CONCLUDING REMARKS

UNCLOS tribunals' contributions to the law concerning the protection of the marine environment initially came from ITLOS but in recent years, the Annex VII arbitral tribunals have also managed to add their voices. These contributions are most evident in two respects.

First, UNCLOS tribunals have adopted a holistic and integrated understanding of 'marine environmental protection', which, as observed by one commentator, 'emphasises an integrated, rather than a zonal, approach'.[192] More importantly, UNCLOS tribunals have also adopted an evolutionary interpretation of the general obligation to protect and preserve the marine environment found in Article 192 UNCLOS. In the aftermath of *South China Sea*, this general obligation can no longer be seen merely hortatory. Instead, it has now been interpreted as an obligation of due diligence, whose content assumes a dynamic character to be determined with reference to not only other provisions of Part XII but also the wider corpus of international environmental law. UNCLOS tribunals' interpretative approach clearly shows that they view Part XII and UNCLOS more generally as a living instrument, subject to new developments in international law.

Second, UNCLOS tribunals confirmed the status of important principles of environmental law. In particular, the duty to cooperate, the obligation of due diligence and the obligation to conduct an EIA are now all part of general international law. It is not immediately clear whether the tribunals' use of the term 'general international law' implied customary international law. Opinions differ as to what sources of law are encompassed in this term. Although UNCLOS tribunals did not specify which sources of law they intended to refer to with the use of the term 'general international law', it is clear that in the view of the tribunals, these principles also exist independently of UNCLOS. With regard to the controversial precautionary principle, while not explicitly acknowledging its customary status, ITLOS is the only international tribunal to date which has given a green light to the precautionary principle belonging to the corpus of general international law, as demonstrated in the *Advisory Opinion on Activities in the Area*. It is important to note that not all of these environmental principles can be found under UNCLOS;

[192] Ibid 104.

in fact only the obligation to cooperate and the obligation to conduct EIA are expressly provided for under the Convention. The keenness of UNCLOS bodies to accept emerging principles which are either still controversial or vague in their content and bring them into the corpus of UNCLOS shows that the tribunals were open to treating the Convention as having an evolving nature, and that they are willing to interpret UNCLOS in line with new developments in the field. This approach is highly welcome and reasonable, for UNCLOS came into being at a time when international environmental law was not yet fully developed and had only started to gather attention.

However, the fact that international courts and tribunals acknowledge and confirm the existence of environmental principles may not necessarily mean they have meaningfully shed light on normative content of these principles.[193] The contributions of UNCLOS tribunals to clarifying the normative content of the principles have been of varying specificity.

ITLOS's application of the precautionary principle in *Southern Bluefin Tuna*, albeit not by name, and the examination of the precautionary principle under Principle 15 of the Rio Declaration dealt with aspects of the precautionary principle which had not been discussed in international jurisprudence before and thus, mark an important contribution of ITLOS to the development of the principle. However, in *Southern Bluefin Tuna*, the precautionary principle was applied in a provisional measure proceeding, thus its normative content, such as the threshold to trigger the application of the precautionary principle under UNCLOS, was informed by Article 290. This may restrict the applicability of the conclusions to other cases. In respect of the obligation to cooperate, while the contours of the duty to cooperate in preventing marine pollution has been clarified, UNCLOS tribunals remain overly coy when it comes to specifying concrete measures for States to fulfil the duty to cooperate in the conservation of marine living resources. With regards to the obligation to conduct EIA, while UNCLOS managed to establish a clear link between EIA and the duty to consult and notify relevant stakeholders, they have not shed much light on the normative content of the obligation to conduct EIA under Article 206.

Finally, a few observations are in order regarding the procedural aspect of cases relating to the protection of the marine environment. Although Article 290(1) allows ITLOS to prescribe provisional measures to prevent serious harm to the marine environment, it has been argued that it is the States that bring the cases, not the marine environment; therefore, there is no guarantee that

[193] Daniel M Bodansky, 'Customary (and Not So Customary) International Environmental Law' (1995) 3(1) Ind J Global Legal Stud 105, 116.

the marine environment may benefit from the measures prescribed or that the development of principles of marine environment protection may occur during the process of dispute resolution.[194] As *Land Reclamation* shows, provisional measures requiring serious and meaningful cooperation played an important role in not only resolving disputes between the parties but also in the protection of the marine environment in the Straits of Johor.[195] It follows that the protection of the parties' interests and the goal of protecting the marine environment are not mutually exclusive. Provisional measures ordering the disputing parties to undertake a joint monitoring or EIA or requiring the parties to cooperate to ensure conservation and optimum utilisation of a fish stock and to devise measures to prevent land-based marine pollution 'can contribute to enforce community interests regarding marine environmental protection',[196] while at the same time, serve to protect the rights of the parties. ITLOS's decisions, therefore have shown that, despite their limitations, provisional measures proceedings can still play an important role in advancing environmental interests.

[194] Gwenaele Rashbrooke, 'The International Tribunal for the Law of the Sea: A Forum for the Development of Principles of International Environmental Law?' (2004) 19(4) IJMCL 515.

[195] Tullio Treves, 'A System for Law of the Sea Dispute Settlement' in Richard Barnes, David Freestone and David Ong, *The Law of the Sea: Progress and Prospects* (OUP 2006).

[196] Yoshifumi Tanaka, 'Provisional Measures Prescribed by ITLOS and Marine Environmental Protection' (2014) 108 Proceedings of the Annual Meeting of the American Society of International Law 365, 367.

6

Procedural Rules on Dispute Settlement

The procedural rules on dispute settlement are primarily contained in Part XV of the United Nations Convention on the Law of the Sea (UNCLOS). These rules set out the conditions for UNCLOS tribunals to establish and exercise their compulsory jurisdiction to hear contentious disputes. In addition to disputes between States, UNCLOS also grants the Seabed Disputes Chamber (SDC) of the International Tribunal for the Law of the Sea (ITLOS) advisory jurisdiction pursuant to Article 191 UNCLOS. ITLOS, however, has found that as a full tribunal it may also exercise advisory jurisdiction despite the absence of an explicit provision to that effect under UNCLOS and the ITLOS Statute. This chapter examines UNCLOS tribunals' decisions relating the conditions for the establishment of compulsory jurisdiction in contentious proceedings under Part XV and the establishment of advisory jurisdiction of both the SDC and the ITLOS as a full tribunal, in order to determine the extent to which UNCLOS tribunals have clarified the procedural law under the Convention.

In addition to contentious disputes, UNCLOS also provides for provisional measures proceedings and prompt release proceedings under Articles 290 and 292, respectively. This chapter, however, does not examine procedural issues pertaining to these two types of incidental proceedings. While not exhaustive, procedural issues pertaining to these proceedings have been addressed to in Chapters 1–5, such as nationality of ships or reasonable bonds in prompt release proceedings, or prima facie jurisdiction or urgency in the context of marine environmental protection in provisional measures proceedings. The focus on this chapter is therefore on procedural issues relating to contentious jurisdiction and advisory jurisdiction.

6.1 JURISDICTION IN CONTENTIOUS PROCEEDINGS

The conditions for UNCLOS tribunals to exercise jurisdiction to hear contentious cases can be categorised into three main groups, corresponding to the three sections under Part XV UNCLOS. The conditions found in the three sections of Part XV are both vague and complex, requiring further guidance for implementation. First, under Section 1, UNCLOS tribunals can hear a dispute only when the parties have not chosen another means to settle their dispute, be they negotiations or through bilateral, regional or general agreements. Under Section 2, Article 288(1) makes clear that UNCLOS tribunals only have jurisdiction 'over the interpretation and application of the Convention'. Finally under section 3, Articles 297 and 298 contain the lists of disputes that are excluded from the jurisdiction of UNCLOS tribunals. Each of these conditions are examined in turn.

6.1.1 *General Provisions under Section 1*

Section 1 acknowledges that the dispute settlement system of Part XV is merely one of the choices available to States to resolve their disputes. The three most important provisions of Section 1 include Articles 281, 282 and 283, each of which sets out a scenario allowing State parties to UNCLOS to have recourse to procedures other than Part XV to settle their disputes. These articles concretise the normative policy principle contained in Article 280 that gives priority to the forms of dispute settlement agreed upon by the parties.[1] UNCLOS tribunals have had the opportunity to interpret and apply these three provisions in several cases.

6.1.1.1 Article 281

Article 281 essentially provides that when the parties to the case have agreed to an alternative means of dispute settlement, UNCLOS tribunals can only exercise jurisdiction if the parties have not been able to settle the dispute between them using the means agreed *and* if the parties have not agreed to exclude further procedures, including recourse to the UNCLOS dispute settlement procedures. While, as mentioned, the parties' agreed means of

[1] Rüdiger Wolfrum, 'Conciliation under the UN Convention on the Law of the Sea' in Christian Tomuschat and others (eds), *Conciliation in International Law: The OSCE Court of Conciliation and Arbitration* (Brill 2016) 177.

settlement is given priority, two questions remain unclear: (i) what constitutes 'an agreed means' by the parties within the meaning of Article 281, and (ii) what is the nature of the alternative means of settlement that takes priority over Part XV procedures?

With regards to the first question, in *Barbados v Trinidad and Tobago*, the arbitral tribunal considered that the nature of the means agreed was the factor that distinguished Articles 281 and 282. In particular, the tribunal held that Article 281 'is intended primarily to cover the situation where the Parties have come to an ad hoc agreement as to the means to be adopted to settle the particular dispute which has arisen', which differs to 'a standing bilateral or multilateral dispute settlement agreement which could cover the UNCLOS dispute which has arisen' under Article 282.[2] The tribunal did not provide any explanation for such a finding and it is in any case difficult to see on what basis Article 281 is limited to ad hoc arrangements.[3] In subsequent cases in which Article 281 was invoked, UNCLOS tribunals have in fact included within their scope of examination standing bilateral and multilateral agreements.

As regards the nature of the alternative 'procedure', the *South China Sea* tribunal made clear that the agreements containing the alternative procedure need to be of a legally binding nature.[4] However, this does not mean that the alternative means contained in these agreements necessarily need to lead to a binding decision. The means of settlement under examination in both *Southern Bluefin Tuna* and *South China Sea* included the means those of a diplomatic nature, such as negotiation or conciliation, which did not result in a binding outcome. This strongly indicates that the alternative 'procedures' under Article 281 are not limited to those that entail a binding decision.[5]

The second requirement under Article 281, namely the agreement to exclude further procedures, has perhaps been the most controversial element of this article, and has been subjected to contrasting interpretations by different tribunals. In *Southern Bluefin Tuna* in 2001, Japan had argued that Article

2 *Arbitration between Barbados and the Republic of Trinidad and Tobago, Relating to the Delimitation of the Exclusive Economic Zone and the Continental Shelf Between Them (Barbados v Trinidad and Tobago)* (11 April 2006) RIAA Volume XXVII 147–251 [200(ii)].

3 Natalie Klein, 'The Vicissitudes of Dispute Settlement under the Law of the Sea Convention' (2017) 32 IJMCL 332, 337.

4 *South China Sea Arbitration (Philippines v China)*, Award on Jurisdiction and Admissibility (2015) RIAA XXXIII 1 [219].

5 Bjørn Kunoy, 'The Scope of Compulsory Jurisdiction and Exceptions Thereto under the United Nations Convention on the Law of the Sea' (2020) 58 Canadian Yearbook of International Law 78, 91. See also: Bernard Oxman, 'Courts and Tribunals: The ICJ, ITLOS, and Arbitral Tribunals' in Donald R Rothwell and others (eds), *The Oxford Handbook of the Law of the Sea* (OUP 2015) 401.

16 of the Convention on Conservation of Southern Bluefin Tuna (CCSBT)[6] excluded recourse to UNCLOS dispute settlement procedures.[7] In the provisional measures phase of the case, ITLOS, having to establish only prima facie jurisdiction, simply found that 'the fact that the Convention of 1993 applies between the parties does not preclude recourse to the procedures in Part XV, section 2, of the Convention on the Law of the Sea'.[8] When the case proceeded to the merits stage, the Annex VII arbitral tribunal however agreed with Japan, stating that although Article 16 of the CCSBT did not expressly exclude the applicability of the procedures of Section 2 Part XV of UNCLOS, 'the absence of an express exclusion of any procedures in Article 16 is not decisive'.[9] What was important was that paragraph (2) of Article 16 provided for an express obligation to continue to seek resolution of the dispute by the means listed in paragraph (1).[10] The express 'obligation to continue to seek resolution' in the tribunal's view was tantamount to an exclusion of further judicial measures. *Southern Bluefin Tuna* thus implies that the existence of any list of dispute settlement methods and a commitment to resolving the dispute by peaceful means would suffice as an implicit exclusion of UNCLOS procedures.[11]

This interpretation was heavily criticised by Judge Keith in his Separate Opinion, in which he argued that the wording of Article 281, the structure of Part XV UNCLOS, and the object and purpose of UNCLOS as a whole pointed to the conclusion that 'strong and particular wording' would have to be included in Article 16 CCSBT to prevent the arbitral tribunal from exercising jurisdiction.[12] Several scholars subsequently endorsed Judge Keith's interpretation of Article 281 instead of that of the majority.[13] As a result,

6 Convention for the Conservation of Southern Bluefin Tuna, 819 UNTS 360 (10 May 1993).

7 *Southern Bluefin Tuna Case (Australia and New Zealand v Japan)*, Award on Jurisdiction and Admissibility (4 August 2000) 39 ILM 1359, [34]. [Southern Bluefin Tuna Award].

8 *Southern Bluefin Tuna (New Zealand v Japan; Australia v Japan)* (Provisional Measures, Order of 27 August 1999) ITLOS Reports 1999, 280 [55] [Southern Bluefin Tuna Order].

9 Ibid [57].

10 Ibid.

11 Robin Churchill, 'Some Reflections on the Operation of the Dispute Settlement System of the UN Convention on the Law of the Sea During Its First Decade' in David Freestone, Richard Barnes, and David Ong (eds), *The Law of the Sea: Progress and Prospects* (OUP 206) 403.

12 *Southern Bluefin Tuna Award*, Separate Opinion of Judge Kenneth Keith (n 7) [18], [19].

13 Deborah Horowitz, 'The Catch of Poseidon's Trident: The Fate of High Seas Fisheries in the Southern Bluefin Tuna Case' (2001) 25 Melbourne University Law Review 810; Alan Boyle, 'The Southern Bluefin Tuna Arbitration' (2001) 50 ICLQ 447; David A Colson and Peggy Hoyle, 'Satisfying the Procedural Prerequisites to the Compulsory Dispute Settlement Mechanisms of the 1982 Law of the Sea Convention: Did the Southern Bluefin Tuna Tribunal Get It Right?' (2003) 34 ODIL 59; Bernard Oxman, 'Complementary Agreements and Compulsory Jurisdiction' (2001) 95 AJIL 277, 277, 304; Igor V Karaman, *Dispute Resolution in Law of the Sea* (Brill 2012) 260. But see also: Natalie Klein, *Dispute Settlement in the UN*

there remained serious uncertainty regarding the scope of Article 281 in the aftermath of *Southern Bluefin Tuna*, despite it being the only judicial authority on the matter for a long period of time.[14]

In *South China Sea* in 2016, the tribunal had to decide whether Article 281 applied to exclude the tribunal's jurisdiction to hear the dispute brought by the Philippines against China concerning the South China Sea, given that there were several instruments containing the parties' agreement to settle their disputes by a variety of peaceful means.[15] Even though some of these instruments were found to be nonbinding, thus condition (i) as specified above was not met, the tribunal still felt the need to address the remaining elements of Article 281, including the question as to whether an implicit or explicit exclusion is needed to deprive the tribunal of its jurisdiction under Article 281. On this point, the tribunal rejected the *Southern Bluefin Tuna* tribunal's interpretation of Article 281. Sharing the view of Judge Keith in *Southern Bluefin Tuna*, the tribunal concluded that 'the better view is that Article 281 requires some clear statement of exclusion of further procedures'.[16] This interpretation was based on the wording of Article 281 as well as object and purpose of the Convention as construed from the negotiating history.[17] This has been one of the few instances to date in which an UNCLOS tribunal explicitly rejected the interpretation adopted by a previous tribunal on the same UNCLOS provision.

The *South China Sea* tribunal's decision to embrace the approach of Judge Keith in interpreting Article 281 is arguably more nuanced in at least two ways. First, the broad and loose interpretation of what constitutes an agreement to exclude recourse to UNCLOS dispute settlement procedures adopted by the majority in the *Southern Bluefin Tuna* would render Article 281 a near impossible obstacle to overcome given the prevalence of provisions containing a list of peaceful dispute settlement means in international agreements. Second, the *Southern Bluefin Tuna* tribunal's interpretation of Article 281 as allowing parties to 'confine the applicability of compulsory procedures of section 2 of Part XV to cases where all parties to the dispute

Convention on the Law of the Sea (CUP 2005) 35–43; Barbara Kwiatkowska, 'The Southern Bluefin Tuna Arbitral Tribunal Did Get It Right: A Commentary and Reply to the Article by David A. Colson and Dr. Peggy Hoyle' (2003) 34 ODIL 369.

14 Md. Saiful Karim, 'Litigating Law of the Sea Disputes Using the UNCLOS Dispute Settlement System' in Natalie Klein (ed), *Litigating International Law Disputes: Weighing the Options* (CUP 2014) 270.

15 *South China Sea Arbitration* (Jurisdiction and Admissibility) (n 4) [196].

16 Ibid [223].

17 Ibid [224], [225].

have agreed upon submission of their dispute to such compulsory procedures' introduced an additional step for the establishment of compulsory jurisdiction of UNCLOS tribunals not found under Part XV. Taken together, the tribunal's interpretation would defeat the purpose of a compulsory dispute settlement system under UNCLOS. While the *South China Sea* tribunal's decision seems to have imposed a higher bar for the invocation of Article 281 to exclude the jurisdiction of UNCLOS tribunals as compared to that of *Southern Bluefin Tuna*, it still pays respect to the choice of procedure given to States in settling their disputes, thus in line with the purpose of Section 1.

Given the lack of hierarchy between international courts and tribunals, it is unclear which of the two interpretations of Article 281 prevails. Therefore, while Article 281 has been clarified, UNCLOS tribunals' contrasting approaches have created uncertainty in the interpretation of this article.

6.1.1.2 Article 282

Article 282 is narrower than Article 281 in two main respects. The first lies in the nature of the alternative procedure that takes precedence over Part XV procedures. Unlike Article 281 which only envisages in general 'a peaceful means of [the parties'] own choice', Article 282 specifies that Part XV procedures should only give way to a compulsory procedure 'that entails a binding decision' which are found in 'general, regional or bilateral agreements or otherwise'. As such, Article 282 has been viewed not as an exception to compulsory procedures under Part XV but as a choice of forum since it 'simply expresses a preference for a forum outside of those prescribed by Part XV, section 2'.[18] Second, whereas Article 281 requires an 'opting out' of Part XV procedures, the *South China Sea* tribunal clarified that as 'Part XV procedures are excluded by the alternative compulsory binding procedure', Article 282 required the parties to 'opt back in' to using UNCLOS procedures 'by "agreeing otherwise"'.[19] However, as the tribunal did not need to consider this point, it remains open to question what language would be required to demonstrate the parties' intention to 'opt back in', and whether the 'opt-in' could be implied or explicit as in the case of Article 281.

According to the *South China Sea* tribunal, Article 282 can only be invoked when four requirements are met, namely: (a) that the parties have agreed

[18] Nigel Bankes, 'Precluding the Applicability of Section 2 of Part XV of the Law of the Sea Convention' (2017) 48(3–4) ODIL 239, 253.

[19] *South China Sea Arbitration* (Award on Jurisdiction and Admissibility (n 4) [224].

through a 'general, regional or bilateral agreement or otherwise' (b) at the request of any party to the dispute, (c) the dispute be submitted to a procedure 'that entails a binding decision' and (d) the parties have not otherwise agreed to retain access (i.e., to opt back in) to the Part XV, Section 2 procedures.[20] Condition (c) demonstrates the difference between Article 282 and 281 as explained above.

With respect to the other three conditions, the tribunal found that the nature of the agreement in condition (a) for the purposes of Article 282 is the same as that for Article 281, that is, they must be legally binding.[21] Although this article specifies that the agreement could be multilateral, regional or bilateral, it does not articulate whether the alternative agreement should cover the same field or subject matter as UNCLOS in order to fall within the meaning of Article 282. In *MOX Plant* provisional measure proceedings, the UK seemed to have answered this question in the negative when it argued that 'the main elements of the dispute submitted to the Annex VII arbitral tribunal are governed by the compulsory dispute settlement procedures of the Convention for the Protection of the Marine Environment of the North-East Atlantic (OSPAR Convention) or the EC Treaty or the Euratom Treaty'[22] thus the Annex VII arbitral tribunal to be constituted would not have *prima facie* jurisdiction. ITLOS, however, confirmed that the general, regional or bilateral agreements within the meaning of Article 282 can only be invoked if they 'provide for the settlement of disputes concerning ... "the interpretation or application of this Convention"'.[23] ITLOS then found that the treaties invoked by the UK 'deal with disputes concerning the interpretation or application of those agreements, and not with disputes arising under the Convention'.[24] More importantly, the tribunal remarked that even if the external agreements contain 'rights or obligations similar to or identical with the rights or obligations set out in the Convention, the rights and obligations under those agreements have a separate existence from those under the Convention'.[25] ITLOS thus adopted the view that regardless of whether the external agreement and UNCLOS have the same regulatory scope, disputes that concerned both UNCLOS and this external agreement remain two distinct disputes. As such, each should be resolved using the dispute

20 Ibid [291].
21 Ibid [299].
22 *MOX Plant (Ireland v United Kingdom)* (Provisional Measures, Order of 3 December 2001) ITLOS Reports 2001, 95 [43]. [*MOX Plant Order*]
23 Ibid [48].
24 Ibid [49].
25 Ibid [50].

resolution mechanism of the relevant treaties. This interpretation has set a high threshold for an external agreement to fall within the meaning of Article 282 as even those having the same or even identical regulatory scope with UNCLOS would not qualify. The Annex VII arbitral tribunal in the provisional measure phase of *MOX Plant* took a more nuanced approach. Although it agreed with ITLOS that the disputes before it was one that concerned UNCLOS, this was primarily because the OSPAR Convention did not 'substantially covers the field of the present dispute so as to trigger the application of articles 281 or 282 of the Convention'.[26] This statement suggests that the test for an agreement to fall under Article 282 then depends on the extent to which this agreement and UNCLOS overlap with regard to the subject matter of the dispute. Given the inconsistent interpretation of this requirement in existing decisions, the question regarding the nature and scope of the external agreement remains unclear.

The question as to what is encompassed in the category of 'otherwise' has not to date come before an UNCLOS tribunal. It has, however, arisen in *Somalia v Kenya*, in which the ICJ had to consider whether an optional clause declarations pursuant to Article 36(2) of the ICJ Statute containing a reservation excluding '[d]isputes in regard to which the parties to the dispute have agreed or shall agree to have recourse to some other method or methods of settlement' falls within the scope of Article 282. The ICJ concluded that Article 282 should be interpreted 'so that an agreement to the Court's jurisdiction through optional clause declarations falls within the scope of that Article and applies "in lieu" of procedures provided for in Section 2 of Part XV, even when such declarations contain a reservation to the same effect as that of Kenya'.[27]

Condition (c) is for its part closely connected with condition (a), and as mentioned above, constitutes the distinguishing feature between Article 282 and Article 281. While the *South China Sea* tribunal did not explain what is meant by 'entailing a binding decision', its examination of the relevant

[26] *MOX Plant (Ireland v United Kingdom)*, Order No. 3 of 24 June 2003 [18] https://pcacases.com/web/sendAttach/867 accessed 25 January 2022.

[27] *Maritime Delimitation in the Indian Ocean (Somalia v Kenya)* (Preliminary Objections) [2017] ICJ Rep 2017, 3 [130]. Judge Robinson, however, argued that 'by reason of Kenya's reservation, the optional clause declarations of the Parties do not constitute an agreed procedure under Article 282 of UNCLOS'. *Somalia v Kenya*, Dissenting Opinion of Judge Robinson, [38]. For a critical comment on the implication of the ICJ's conclusion: Marco Benatar and Erik Franckx, 'The ICJ's Preliminary Objections Judgement in Somalia v. Kenya: Causing Ripples in Law of the Sea Dispute Settlement?' EJIL Talk! (22 February 2017) www.ejiltalk.org/the-icjs-preliminary-objections-judgment-in-somalia-v-kenya-causing-ripples-in-law-of-the-sea-dispute-settlement/ accessed 25 January 2022.

instruments showed that it did not consider measures such as negotiation, good offices, mediation, inquiry or conciliation to meet this requirement.[28] By contrast, the tribunal considered procedures such as arbitration or international courts, as provided for under Article 27(3) of the Convention on Biological Diversity (CBD), for example, to entail a binding decision. The tribunal's interpretation confirmed that Article 282 only envisions recourse to judicial and arbitral means of settlement. Further, in examining Article 27(4) of the CBD which requires that the dispute be submitted to conciliation, the tribunal concluded that this requirement rendered the conciliation procedure compulsory but not binding.[29] Thus, a distinction should be made between a mechanism that is compulsory and one that is binding, with only the latter falling within the scope of Article 282.

Even if procedures that entail a binding decision exist, condition (b) still needs to be satisfied in order for Article 282 to come into play, meaning that one of the parties to the case has invoked the binding procedure to exclude the jurisdiction of the tribunal under Article 282. The *South China Sea* tribunal seems to have attached particular weight to the term 'of *any* party' by interpreting this requirement to mean a unilateral invocation of the dispute by either of the parties. Thus when an alternative procedure can only be applied with the agreement of all the parties to the dispute, as was the case with dispute resolution mechanisms contained in Articles 13, 14 and 15 of the Treaty of Amity, the tribunal found that Article 282 could not be invoked.[30] Further, the invocation of the alternative procedure has to be manifested by concrete actions. For example, as mentioned, Article 27(3) of the CBD allows State parties to accept arbitration of the ICJ but only by a written declaration lodged with the Depositary. The *South China Sea* tribunal found that as no such declarations had been deposited by either the Philippines or China, the procedures contemplated under Article 27(3) of the CBD could not be available 'at the request of any party'.[31] What is clear then is that under Article 282, the jurisdiction of UNCLOS tribunals is not automatically excluded by virtue of the mere existence of other compulsory dispute settlement procedures. Instead, a specific act of the parties to invoke them is further required.

[28] *The South China Sea Arbitration between the Republic of the Philippines and the People's Republic of China (Philippines v China)* (2016) RIAA XXXIII 153 [309].

[29] Ibid [320].

[30] Ibid [308].

[31] Ibid [320].

6.1.1.3 Article 283

Article 283 which imposes on State parties an obligation to 'proceed expeditiously to an exchange of views regarding its settlement by negotiation or other peaceful means' has been the most frequently invoked article in Section 1 for the purposes of objecting to UNCLOS tribunals' jurisdiction. As a result, UNCLOS tribunals have had ample opportunity to shed light on the requirements contained in this article.

First, it should be noted that Article 283 provides for an obligation to exchange views, not an obligation to negotiate. As the *Chagos MPA* tribunal made clear, Article 283 'requires the Parties to exchange views regarding the means for resolving their dispute; it does not require the Parties to in fact engage in negotiations or other forms of peaceful dispute resolution'.[32] As such, Article 283 is 'distinct from a requirement that parties engage in negotiations prior to resorting to arbitration'.[33] Article 283 thus does not impose an obligation to negotiate the substance of a dispute as a precondition that needs to be satisfied before UNCLOS tribunals could exercise jurisdiction pursuant to Part XV. It follows, therefore, that as long as the parties expeditiously conduct an exchange of views on the means to resolve the dispute, Article 283 has been satisfied. The parties do not need to comprehensively canvas the means for the peaceful settlement of disputes set out in either the UN Charter or UNCLOS, to discuss the possibility of compulsory settlement, or to warn the other party regarding the possibility of litigation, before resorting to compulsory jurisdiction.[34]

The distinction discussed above has been blurred in the context of the settlement of a maritime delimitation dispute in *Barbados v Trinidad and Tobago*. More specifically, paragraphs (1) and (2) of Articles 74 and 83 require the delimitation of the exclusive economic zone (EEZ) and continental shelf, respectively, to be effected by agreement and if no agreement can be reached within a reasonable period of time the parties should resort to the procedures in Part XV. The arbitral tribunal found that 'the requirement of Article 283(1) for settlement by negotiation is, in relation to Articles 74 and 83, subsumed within the negotiations which those Articles require to have already taken place'[35] and that when negotiations have failed to result in an agreement on delimitation, the parties would not need to separately exchange views under

[32] *Chagos Marine Protected Area Arbitration (Mauritius v United Kingdom)* (2015) RIAA XXI 359 [378] [Chagos MPA]

[33] Ibid [378].

[34] Ibid [385].

[35] Ibid [202].

Article 283 because 'the required exchange of views is also inherent in the (failed) negotiations'.[36] These statements seem to have been premised on an understanding of Article 283 as containing an obligation to settle the dispute by negotiation. In the light of the *Chagos MPA* tribunal's narrower interpretation, the conclusion reached in *Barbados v Trinidad and Tobago* that the obligation under Article 283 is subsumed within the obligation to negotiate a maritime boundary under Articles 74 and 83 may no longer be tenable. In the more recent *Mauritius v Maldives* case before ITLOS Special Chamber, the Maldives maintained the distinction between the obligation under Article 283 and the obligation to negotiate under Articles 74 and 83.[37] The Special Chamber, however, neither addressed this point nor did it discuss Article 283.

Second, with regards to the manner in which the exchange of views should take place, ITLOS has clarified that 'a State Party is not obliged to continue with an exchange of views when it concludes that the possibilities of reaching an agreement have been exhausted'.[38] The Annex VII arbitral tribunal in *Southern Bluefin Tuna* further observed that the obligation under Article 283 would be fulfilled by virtue of 'prolonged, serious and intense' negotiation.[39] It can be seen that earlier cases on Article 283 did not pay much attention to whether 'the communications that were considered sufficient for the purposes of Article 283 were substantive or procedural in nature' as lamented by the *Chagos MPA* tribunal.[40] While acknowledging that '[i]n practice, substantive negotiations concerning the parties' dispute are not neatly separated from exchanges of views on the preferred means of settling a dispute',[41] the *Chagos MPA* tribunal held that Article 283 should be applied 'without an undue formalism as to the manner and precision with which views were exchanged and understood', meaning that 'Article 283 requires that a dispute have arisen with sufficient clarity that the Parties were aware of the issues in respect of which they disagreed.'[42] It follows that existing jurisprudence accords States large discretion to decide how and until when the exchange of views is to be conducted.

36 Ibid [203].

37 *Dispute concerning delimitation of the maritime boundary between Mauritius and Maldives in the Indian Ocean (Mauritius/Maldives)* (Preliminary Objections, Order of 28 January 2021) ITLOS Reports 2021, 28 [261].

38 *Southern Bluefin Tuna Order* (n 8); *MOX Plant Order* (n 22) [60].

39 *Southern Bluefin Tuna Award* (n 7) [55].

40 *Chagos MPA* (n 32) [381].

41 Ibid.

42 Ibid [382].

In this connection, UNCLOS tribunals have also taken a lenient approach to what constitutes an exchange of views within the meaning of Article 283. In *M/V Louisa*, ITLOS was satisfied that the obligation under Article 283 was discharged based on requests for more information regarding the detention of M/V Louisa sent by the maritime administration of Saint Vincent and the Grenadines – the flag State – to the port authorities of Spain[43] and a Note Verbale sent by the former's Permanent Mission to the UN to the latter's, both of which did not receive a reply from the relevant Spanish authorities.[44] Thus the obligation under Article 283 can be met even when the respondent failed to respond to the communications sent by the applicant. This interpretation turned the obligation to exchange views under Article 283 into an obligation of conduct, and not one of result. ITLOS in support of this finding placed particular emphasis on the conclusion in its earlier cases that a party is not obliged to continue with exchanging views if it has concluded that the possibilities of reaching an agreement has been exhausted. While the silence on the part of the respondent on numerous occasions may relieve Saint Vincent and the Grenadines of the obligation to continue communications with Spain, it is worth noting that ITLOS paid little attention to the content of the communications between the parties in considering whether they meet the requirements of Article 283. In this case, the communications only mentioned the detention of the ship and the applicant's objection thereto, instead of how to settle the dispute between the parties.[45] Thus even the low threshold regarding the content of the exchange set out in *Chagos MPA* appeared to not have been met here. Given the silence of the respondent, it would seem that ITLOS in this case was keen to follow the jurisprudence to not require the exchange of views to continue indefinitely, enabling the respondent to frustrate the fulfilment of Article 283 by refusing to respond in good faith.[46] Such an interpretation seems reasonable given that Article 283(3) requires the exchange of views to 'proceed expeditiously'.

The importance attached to the requirement of expeditious exchange of views was explicitly confirmed by the *Arctic Sunrise* arbitral tribunal, in which the tribunal held that Article 283(1) 'was intended to facilitate recourse to peaceful dispute settlement (including compulsory procedures) by encouraging parties to consider different procedures as soon as a dispute arises, and

[43] *The M/V 'Louisa' Case (Saint Vincent and the Grenadines v Kingdom of Spain)* (Provisional Measures, Order of 23 December 2010) ITLOS Reports 2010, 18 [59].

[44] Ibid [60].

[45] See also: *The M/V 'Louisa' Case (Saint Vincent and the Grenadines v Kingdom of Spain)* (Provisional Measures, Order of 23 December 2010, Dis Op Treves) [11].

[46] Bankes, (n 18) 258.

not to preclude or unduly delay the resolution of the dispute'.[47] In this case, the tribunal paid closer attention to the content of the communications between the parties and followed the approach of *Chagos MPA* to consider only the communication which 'specifically pertained to the means by which their dispute might be resolved'.[48] While acknowledging that this communication was sent to Russia only one day before the Netherlands initiated the case,[49] the tribunal found that in light of the purpose of Article 283 to unduly delay the resolution of the dispute as mentioned above and the urgency of the situation, the obligation to exchange views was satisfied. While a window of merely one day is hardly sufficient to reach the conclusion that 'the possibilities of reaching an agreement have been exhausted', the *Arctic Sunrise* tribunal did highlight the unique factual circumstances of the case before it to justify its decision.[50] Consequently, the question regarding the time frame in which the exchange of views is to take place remains unclear, although there are indications that UNCLOS tribunals would likely adopt a less than stringent approach to this requirement.[51]

The preceding discussion shows that UNCLOS tribunals have adopted a relatively low threshold for meeting the requirement of Article 283. This was achieved by requiring the parties only to exchange views on the method of dispute settlement, not the substance of the dispute, by giving the parties large discretion in determining how and for how long the exchange of views should proceed and by examining in a cursory manner the evidence of communications of the parties. As a result of all these factors, no States have ever successfully invoked Article 283 before an UNCLOS tribunal.

6.1.2 *Scope of Jurisdiction* Ratione Materiae

The jurisdiction *ratione materiae* of UNCLOS tribunals is established under Article 288(1), which states that UNCLOS tribunals have jurisdiction over disputes concerning the 'interpretation and application of the Convention'. Article 288(1) thus sets the parameters in terms of the subject matter within

47 *'Arctic Sunrise' (Kingdom of the Netherlands v Russian Federation)*, Award on the Merits [154] https://pcacases.com/web/sendAttach/1438 accessed 25 January 2022.

48 Ibid [153].

49 Ibid.

50 Ibid [155].

51 In *M/V Louisa*, Saint Vincent and the Grenadines' Note Verbale to Spain was sent after the former's communication to ITLOS registry nominating its agent for the purposes of initiating a dispute before ITLOS. Yet, ITLOS did not comment on this nor found it to bar the fulfilment of Article 283. *M/V Louisa* (n 43) [3].

which UNCLOS tribunals are to operate and confirms the specialised nature of UNCLOS tribunals. Being specialised, however, does not necessarily mean being self-contained. In several cases to date, UNCLOS tribunals have been requested to deal with issues which are not regulated under the Convention, such as the use of force, territorial sovereignty, human rights or State immunity. UNCLOS tribunals have therefore had the opportunity to examine the extent to which they can extend their jurisdiction to questions beyond UNCLOS. This section first analyses UNCLOS tribunals' interpretation of the scope of jurisdiction under Article 288(1), before turning to discuss whether and how UNCLOS tribunals have extended their jurisdictional ambit through Article 293(1), the concept of 'incidental' jurisdiction and Article 297(1).

6.1.2.1 Article 288(1)

Article 288(1) contains two requirements, namely that a dispute exists and that the dispute concerns the interpretation and application of the Convention. While UNCLOS tribunals in some cases dealt with these two tests separately,[52] in the majority of cases, the first requirement is merely presumed to exist and focus is thus directed to the second.

Regarding the second requirement, ITLOS in *M/V Louisa* held that in order for a dispute to fall within the jurisdiction of an UNCLOS tribunal, it was necessary to 'establish a link between the facts advanced by [the Applicant] and the provisions of the Convention referred to by it and show that such provisions can sustain the claim or claims submitted by [the Applicant]'.[53] On that basis, ITLOS found that it lacked jurisdiction under Article 288(1) due to the fact that the UNCLOS provisions invoked by Saint Vincent and the Grenadines either 'could not serve as a basis for the claims submitted'[54] or 'were not relevant'.[55] It follows that the mere invocation of UNCLOS provisions is not sufficient to establish jurisdiction, the parties would need to prove the link between these provisions and the facts or claims advanced. This view has found support in subsequent decisions.[56] Going even further, in their Joint Separate Opinion to the *ARA Libertad* Provisional Measure Order, Judges Wolfrum and Cot require the Applicant 'to invoke

[52] *The M/V 'Norstar' Case (Panama v Italy)* (Preliminary Objections, Judgment) ITLOS Reports 2016, 44 [62].

[53] *The M/V 'Louisa' Case (Saint Vincent and the Grenadines v Kingdom of Spain)* (Judgment) ITLOS Reports 2013, 4 [99].

[54] Ibid [105], [109], [113], [117].

[55] Ibid [119].

[56] See, for example, M/V Norstar (n 52) [109].

and argue particular provisions of the Convention which plausibly support its claim and to show that the views on the interpretation of these provisions are positively opposed by the Respondent'.[57] Even though in this instance ITLOS only had to find that the Annex VII arbitral tribunal to be constituted had prima facie jurisdiction,[58] this statement seems to go further than the finding of ITLOS in *M/V Louisa* mentioned above, in that it does not only require a link between UNCLOS provisions and claims but also proof of different views on the interpretation of the relevant UNCLOS provisions.

While requiring the link between an UNCLOS provision and the claims advanced, UNCLOS tribunals have not always been very clear regarding the test to establish this link. In *M/V Norstar*, ITLOS found that only Article 87 on the freedoms of the high seas was relevant to the claims advanced by Panama because '[t]he Decree of Seizure by the Public Prosecutor at the Court of Savona against the M/V "Norstar" with regard to activities conducted by that vessel on the high seas and the request for its execution by the Prosecutor at the Court of Savona may be viewed as an infringement of the rights of Panama under article 87 as the flag State of the vessel'.[59] ITLOS, however, reached such a conclusion without much examination or explanation. As analysed in Chapter 3, ITLOS in the merits phase found that Article 87 was applicable and breached using the same facts without much distinction, even when it initially acknowledged that these were two separate issues. It is unclear from *M/V Norstar* what standards should be applied to find that an UNCLOS is relevant or applicable to the facts,[60] or how they differ to finding a breach of the same provision.

The *South China Sea* tribunal offered a different way altogether to determine the existence of a dispute concerning the interpretation and application of UNCLOS. In examining whether it had jurisdiction to entertain the Philippines' Submissions 1 and 2 concerning China's maritime entitlements and its claim to the nine-dash line in the South China Sea, the tribunal interpreted China's entitlements in the South China Sea to have been based on an understanding of 'historic rights existing independently of, and allegedly preserved by, the Convention'.[61] The tribunal then held that:

57 *The 'ARA Libertad' Case (Argentina v Ghana)* (Provisional Measures, Order of 15 December 2012, Joint Sep Op Wolfrum and Cot) ITLOS Reports 2012, 363 [35].

58 The establishment of prima facie jurisdiction requires a lower threshold than the finding of jurisdiction *in merito*. See: *M/V Louisa*, Declaration of Judge Paik (n 53) [18].

59 *M/V Norstar* (n 56) [122].

60 James Harrison, 'Defining Disputes and Characterizing Claims: Subject-Matter Jurisdiction in Law of the Sea Convention Litigation' (2017) 48 ODIL 269, 275.

61 *South China Sea Arbitration* (Jurisdiction and Admissibility) (n 4) [168].

> This is ... not a dispute about the existence of specific historic rights, but rather a dispute about historic rights in the framework of the Convention. A dispute concerning the interaction of the Convention with another instrument or body of law, including the question of whether rights arising under another body of law were or were not preserved by the Convention, is unequivocally a dispute concerning the interpretation and application of the Convention.[62]

On the one hand, it could be argued that this approach has widened the jurisdictional scope of UNCLOS tribunals as it allowed the tribunal to look at issues not specifically regulated under UNCLOS, namely historic rights. On the other hand, what the tribunal seemed to be saying was that the determination of whether historic rights were preserved under the Convention necessarily entailed the interpretation of the content and scope of relevant UNCLOS provisions concerning the extent of coastal States' maritime entitlements under the Convention. In essence, therefore, the tribunal would still be required to interpret particular provisions of UNCLOS as required under Article 288(1). In the Award on the Merits, as analysed in Chapter 2, the tribunal indeed focused on examining Articles 56, 58 and 77 in order to determine the scope and exclusivity of coastal States' sovereign rights in the EEZ and continental shelf and how coastal States' exclusive sovereign rights under UNCLOS interacted with historic rights.

6.1.2.2 Relationship between Articles 288(1) and 293(1)

While Article 288(1) confines UNCLOS tribunals' jurisdiction to disputes concerning the Convention, Article 293 on Applicable Law allows UNCLOS tribunals in the course of settling disputes concerning the interpretation and application of the Convention to 'apply this Convention and other rules of international law not incompatible with this Convention'. The relationship between Articles 288(1) and 293, particularly the question as to whether Article 293 could be used to expand the scope of UNCLOS tribunals' jurisdiction, has been subjected to contrasting interpretation by different UNCLOS tribunals.

In *M/V Saiga (No 2)*, ITLOS acknowledged that UNCLOS did not contain 'express provisions on the use of force in the arrest of ships', but nevertheless asserted that it had jurisdiction to consider whether Guinea had used excessive

62 Ibid.

and unreasonable force in stopping and arresting the Saiga because 'international law, which is applicable by virtue of Article 293 of the Convention, requires that the use of force must be avoided as far as possible and, where force is unavoidable, it must not go beyond what is reasonable and necessary in the circumstances'.[63] ITLOS thus used Article 293 on applicable law to expand its jurisdictional scope to include issues which were not provided for under UNCLOS. Similarly, in *Guyana v Suriname*, the Annex VII tribunal, recalling ITLOS's above statement, held that it had the competence, under Article 293, to decide on matters that concerned the UN Charter and general international law on the use of force.[64] The question of whether a State has resorted to the use of force in violation of general international law is, however, in itself a stand-alone dispute that neither required the interpretation of the Convention, nor was it necessary for ITLOS or the Annex VII arbitral tribunal in the abovementioned cases to consider this question of the use of force before it could settle a dispute concerning the Convention.

By contrast, the arbitral tribunal in *MOX Plant* in 2003 adopted a completely opposite interpretation of the relationship between Articles 288(1) and 293. In addressing the parties' arguments relating to the scope of Ireland's claims arising under other treaties and instruments, including the OSPAR Convention, the tribunal held that 'there is a cardinal distinction between the scope of its jurisdiction under Article 288, paragraph 1 of the Convention, on the one hand, and the law to be applied by the Tribunal under Article 293 of the Convention on the other hand'.[65] It held further that to the extent that any aspects of Ireland's claims arose directly under legal instruments other than the Convention, such claims would be inadmissible.[66] Taking the same approach as *MOX Plant*, the arbitral tribunal in *Arctic Sunrise* in 2015 rejected the Netherlands' claims on breaches of Articles 9 and 12(2) of the International Covenant on Civil and Political Rights (ICCPR). Instead, the tribunal took the view that:

> [I]t may have regard to general international law in relation to human rights in order to determine whether law enforcement action such as the boarding, seizure, and detention of the Arctic Sunrise and the arrest and detention of those on board was reasonable and proportionate. This would be to interpret the relevant Convention provisions by reference to relevant context. This is

63 *M/V 'SAIGA' (No. 2) (Saint Vincent and the Grenadines v Guinea)* (Judgment) ITLOS Reports 1999, 10 [155].

64 *Arbitration between Guyana and Suriname (Guyana v Suriname)* (2007) RIAA XXX 1 [406].

65 *MOX Plant*, Order No. 3 (n 26) [19].

66 Ibid.

> not, however, the same as, nor does it require, a determination of whether there has been a breach of Articles 9 and 12(2) of the ICCPR as such.[67]

More recent arbitrations seem to follow this approach and strictly confine their jurisdiction to deciding on violations of UNCLOS. For example, in *Duzgit Integrity*, the tribunal held that it 'is not competent to determine if fundamental human rights obligations were violated by São Tomé, or if São Tomé applied its own laws correctly'.[68]

What has become clear is that, notwithstanding the few contradictory earlier cases, UNCLOS tribunals have taken a more stringent approach in deciding which issues may fall within their competence. UNCLOS tribunals have established that they cannot entertain claims relating to violations of external sources independently from claims based on UNCLOS. This approach is surely more reasonable. Although Article 293 allows judges or arbitrators to resort to legal rules and principles contained under general international law to settle a dispute, such use should be strictly limited to assisting them to decide a dispute that arises under the Convention, not as the basis for jurisdiction to hear that dispute.[69]

6.1.2.3 'Ancillary' or 'Incidental' Jurisdiction

While UNCLOS tribunals do not have the jurisdiction to hear disputes concerning violation of external sources, this does not mean that they are altogether barred from considering legal issues regulated beyond UNCLOS. Two such issues have arisen before UNCLOS tribunals, namely territorial sovereignty and State immunity. In order to determine whether they have jurisdiction to entertain these issues, UNCLOS tribunals have developed the so-called test of 'ancillary' or 'incidental' jurisdiction. This test was first adopted by the arbitral tribunal in *Chagos MPA* and subsequently followed, either explicitly or implicitly, by other tribunals.

In *Chagos MPA*, the tribunal found that an examination of Mauritius' Submissions 1 and 2 concerning the status of the UK and Mauritius as the 'coastal State' with regard to the Chagos Archipelago would require it to

67 *Award in the Arbitration regarding the Arctic Sunrise (Kingdom of the Netherlands v Russian Federation)*, Award on Jurisdiction (2014) RIAA XXXII 183 [197].

68 *The Duzgit Integrity Arbitration (Malta v São Tomé and Príncipe)*, Arbitral Award of 5 September 2016 [210] https://pcacases.com/web/sendAttach/1915 accessed 25 January 2022.

69 Michael Wood, 'The International Tribunal for the Law of the Sea and General International Law' (2007) IJMCL 351, 353.

engage with a dispute over the territorial sovereignty of the Chagos Archipelago.[70] In order to determine whether it would have the jurisdiction to do so, the tribunal set out a two-tier test. The first step involved the characterisation of the dispute in order to identify 'the real issue' and the 'object of the claim'.[71] In the second step, the tribunal had to consider whether the real dispute concerned the interpretation or application of the Convention. These two steps seem to correspond to the two requirements of Article 288(1) as alluded to above. If the answer to the second step is in the positive, the jurisdiction of a court or tribunal pursuant to Article 288(1) could extend to 'ancillary determinations of law' – which in this case was territorial sovereignty over the Chagos Archipelago – that are necessary to resolve the dispute.[72] The tribunal observed that 'in some instances a minor issue of territorial sovereignty could indeed be ancillary to a dispute concerning the interpretation or application of the Convention'.[73] If, on the other hand, the real dispute did not relate to the interpretation or application of the Convention, 'an incidental connection between the dispute and some matter regulated by the Convention is insufficient to bring the dispute, as a whole, within the ambit of Article 288(1)'.[74] The tribunal eventually found that the real dispute between the parties in relation to Mauritius' Submission 1 and 2 was that concerning territorial sovereignty over the Chagos Archipelago, thus declining to exercise jurisdiction over these two claims. The tribunal's approach in *Chagos MPA* made clear that there are instances in which UNCLOS tribunals may exercise jurisdiction over territorial sovereignty as an incidental or ancillary issue, provided that the real issue before them concerns UNCLOS.

In *South China Sea*, the parties as well as the tribunal also acknowledged the existence of a sovereignty dispute concerning different insular features in the South China Sea between the Philippines and China.[75] However, unlike Mauritius in *Chagos MPA*, the Philippines did not request the tribunal to deal with sovereignty questions. The tribunal, however, still found it necessary to

70 Whether disputes concerning territorial sovereignty fall within the jurisdiction of UNCLOS tribunals has been one of the most longstanding issues concerning UNCLOS tribunals' scope of jurisdiction. See, for example, Irina Buga, 'Territorial Sovereignty Issues in Maritime Disputes: A Jurisdictional Dilemma for Law of the Sea Tribunals' (2012) 27 IJMCL 59; Robert W Smith and Bradford L Thomas, 'Island Disputes and the Law of the Sea: An Examination of Sovereignty and Delimitation Disputes' in Myron H Norquist and John Norton Moore (eds), *Security Flashpoints: Oil, Islands, Sea Access and Military Confrontation* (Brill 1998).

71 *Chagos MPA* (n 32) [206].

72 Ibid [220].

73 Ibid [221].

74 Ibid [220].

75 *South China Sea Arbitration* (Jurisdiction and Admissibility) (n 4) [152].

determine whether the Philippines' submissions were related to sovereignty. It held that:

> The Tribunal might consider that the Philippines' Submissions could be understood to relate to sovereignty if it were convinced that either (a) the resolution of the Philippines' claims would require the Tribunal to first render a decision on sovereignty, either expressly or implicitly; or (b) the actual objective of the Philippines' claims was to advance its position in the Parties' dispute over sovereignty. Neither of these situations, however, is the case.[76]

This statement seems to contain two different tests. On the one hand, test (a) concerns whether a prior decision on sovereignty needs to be made. Thus even if the real dispute is one that concerns the interpretation and application of UNCLOS, the tribunal would still not have jurisdiction if the first step to be taken in resolving that dispute requires a decision on territorial sovereignty. This test seems to differ from the ancillary test set out by the *Chagos MPA* tribunal above. On the other hand, test (b) seems to follow the dispute's relative weight approach of *Chagos MPA*, the 'actual objective' of the claim bears much resemblance to the test of real dispute in that case. It is arguable, therefore, that South China Sea has introduced yet another test to determine whether an UNCLOS tribunal has jurisdiction over an issue implicated in the dispute but beyond the scope of UNCLOS.

In *Coastal State Rights* between Ukraine and Russia, the Annex VII arbitral tribunal also had to consider whether it had jurisdiction to decide on a sovereignty dispute relating to Crimea that formed part of a broader dispute over coastal state rights in the Black Sea, Sea of Azov and Kerch Strait. In examining this question, the arbitral tribunal recalled and followed the *Chagos MPA* tribunal's approach of identifying the relative weight of the dispute and whether 'a sovereignty dispute over Crimea in the present case is an issue ancillary to a dispute concerning the interpretation or application of the Convention'.[77] However, unlike *Chagos MPA* and *South China Sea* in which all relevant parties acknowledged the existence of a sovereignty dispute, Ukraine in *Coastal State Rights* had argued that no sovereignty dispute existed between the parties.[78] This prompted the tribunal to conduct a separate examination of whether a sovereignty dispute indeed existed. Only when the

[76] Ibid [153].

[77] *Dispute Concerning Coastal State Rights in the Black Sea, Sea of Azov, and Kerch Strait (Ukraine v the Russian Federation)*, Award on Preliminary Objections [194] https://pcacases.com/web/sendAttach/9272 accessed 25 January 2022 [*Coastal State Rights*].

[78] Ibid [162].

answer to this question was in the positive would the tribunal then proceed to the question of ancillary jurisdiction.

In its examination, the tribunal paid particular attention to Ukraine's arguments that Russia's sovereignty claims were inadmissible and implausible. Two points in the tribunal's examination of these claims merit mentioning. Ukraine's arguments relating to admissibility revolved around the resolutions of United Nations General Assembly (UNGA) which in its view 'reflect the consensus of the international community regarding the territorial status of Crimea, to which the Arbitral Tribunal operating under the Convention must defer'.[79] The tribunal however, found that it could not accept Ukraine's interpretation of the UNGA resolutions, as that would 'imply that the Arbitral Tribunal finds that Crimea is part of Ukraine's territory' which the tribunal had no jurisdiction to do.[80] Given that the tribunal also held in the same breath that 'it has the power to interpret the texts of documents of international organisations, including the resolutions of the UNGA',[81] one may be tempted to inquire why the tribunal only considered the possibility of accepting Ukraine's interpretation but not that of conducting its own interpretation of the UNGA resolution in question. The implication of the tribunal's approach seems to be that any act of interpretation of the UNGA resolution would require the tribunal to take a view on a sovereignty dispute which is beyond its jurisdictional scope.

As for implausibility, the tribunal took the view that could not 'engage in a full evaluation of the sovereignty claims of the Parties, as it has no such competence'.[82] For jurisdictional purposes, its power 'should be limited to assessing the Russian Federation's claim of sovereignty for the sole purpose of verifying whether there exists a dispute as to which State has sovereignty over Crimea'.[83] The tribunal then found that Russia's claim of sovereignty was not a mere assertion fabricated solely to defeat jurisdiction, thus it was satisfied of the existence of a sovereignty dispute between the two parties.[84]

Ultimately, based on the classic definition of a dispute being 'a disagreement on a point of law or fact' and evidence showing that 'the Parties are in disagreement on various points of law and facts relating to the question as to which State is sovereign over Crimea',[85] the tribunal found that a dispute

79 Ibid [176]
80 Ibid.
81 Ibid.
82 Ibid [186].
83 Ibid.
84 Ibid [189].
85 Ibid [165].

indeed existed. The tribunal then found that the sovereignty dispute was not a 'minor issue ancillary to the dispute concerning the interpretation or application of the Convention'[86] but rather 'a prerequisite to the Arbitral Tribunal's decision on a number of claims submitted by Ukraine under the Convention'.[87] As a result, it concluded that it 'lacks jurisdiction over the dispute as submitted by Ukraine to the extent that a ruling of the Arbitral Tribunal on the merits of Ukraine's claims necessarily requires it to decide, expressly or implicitly, on the sovereignty of either Party over Crimea'.[88] In both *Chagos MPA* and *Coastal State Rights*, therefore, the respective tribunals did not extend their jurisdiction to territorial sovereignty issues.

In *Mauritius v Maldives*, the existence or otherwise of a territorial sovereignty dispute also formed part of the ITLOS Special Chamber's examination of whether it had jurisdiction over the dispute.[89] However, the Special Chamber's approach to dealing with this question drastically differed from that of the Annex VII tribunal in *Coastal State Rights*. While the Special Chamber agreed that disputes which require the determination of a question of territorial sovereignty did not fall within the meaning of Article 288(1),[90] it found that no such dispute existed.[91] In reaching this conclusion, the Special Chamber did not follow the *Coastal State Rights* tribunal's approach to determine whether Mauritius and the UK were in disagreement on fact and law regarding the status of the Chagos Archipelago. Rather, in view of the fact that 'the questions relating to the legal status of the Chagos Archipelago had been considered' by other courts and tribunals,[92] the Chamber then proceed to examine whether this jurisprudence had resolved the legal status of the Chagos Archipelago. The Chamber found *Chagos MPA* Award did not discuss sovereignty, but the ICJ *Advisory Opinion on the Chagos Archipelago* provided the Chamber with a 'prior authoritative determination' on sovereignty to Chagos.

It is worth noting, however, that the ICJ Advisory Opinion did not directly address the question of whether Mauritius or the UK had sovereignty over the

86 Ibid [195].
87 Ibid.
88 Ibid [197].
89 *Mauritius v Maldives* concerned maritime delimitation, in which the Maldives argued that only opposite or adjacent state may bring disputes concerning maritime delimitation under Articles 74 and 83 UNCLOS. As a preliminary objection, the Maldives contended that the Chamber did not have jurisdiction to consider whether Mauritius was a State with opposite or adjacent coast to the Maldives because this would require a determination of territorial sovereignty over the Chagos Archipelago which was in dispute between Mauritius and the UK.
90 *Mauritius/Maldives*, Preliminary Objections (n 37) [110].
91 Ibid [245].
92 Ibid [128].

Chagos Archipelago, rather it revolved around the UK's decolonisation obligations vis-à-vis Chagos under international law. As a result, the Chamber had to engage in a process of interpreting the Advisory Opinion in order to examine whether 'the advisory opinion has, expressly or implicitly, addressed the sovereignty dispute over the Chagos Archipelago'.[93] By engaging in the interpretation the ICJ Advisory Opinion,[94] it would seem that the Chamber in effect took upon itself the task of evaluating and pronouncing on the sovereignty claims of Mauritius – the very task that the tribunal in *Coastal State Rights* declined to do due to the restrictions of Article 288(1). In that sense, ITLOS Special Chamber seems to have agreed with the plausibility test put forward by Ukraine but was subsequently rejected by that Annex VII tribunal in that case.

The preceding discussion demonstrates that UNCLOS tribunals have adopted different approaches to determining whether a sovereignty dispute exists for the purposes of determining their jurisdiction. Whereas the *Coastal State Rights* tribunal opted for an objective test of assessing whether there exists a disagreement between the parties concerned regarding which State has sovereignty, ITLOS Special Chamber took a step further to assess the sovereignty claims of the States concerned. On the one hand, the objective approach allows a tribunal to stay within its jurisdictional limit. However, it may be prone to abuse by one party fabricating claims for the purposes of creating a dispute, even though the tribunal seems to have introduced the abuse of rights test as a safeguard. On the other hand, the assessment of a sovereignty claim by relying on a prior determination of a point of law, particularly when this prior determination requires a further subjective assessment of its findings, raises the question regarding the extent to which an UNCLOS tribunal can interpret decisions of other institutions while remaining their jurisdictional limits. In any event, if the key question that an UNCLOS tribunal needs to answer under Article 288(1) is whether it can exercise jurisdiction over a sovereignty claim in the course of deciding a dispute concerning UNCLOS, it is worth asking whether it would even need to engage with the question as to whether a dispute over sovereignty (still) exists between the parties. Once it has established that the relative weight of the dispute before it lies with the interpretation and application of UNCLOS, following the approach of *Chagos MPA*, the tribunal's jurisdiction would extend to making

93 Ibid [167].

94 For a commentary on ITLOS Special Chamber's interpretation of the ICJ Advisory Opinion, see: Fabian Simon Eichberger, 'The Legal Effect of ICJ Advisory Opinions Redefined? The Mauritius/Maldives Delimitation Case – Judgment on Preliminary Objections' (2021) 22(2) Melbourne Journal of International Law 1, 16.

ancillary determination on the question of sovereignty. Whether there exists a dispute between the parties on this question should thus not be the decisive factor.

Apart from territorial sovereignty, another issue of general international law that has arisen before an UNCLOS tribunal is State immunity. In *Enrica Lexie*, the arbitral tribunal found that the dispute between India and Italy was one relating to jurisdiction arising under UNCLOS and it 'may raise, but is not limited to, the question of immunity of the Marines'.[95] However, the tribunal found that it 'could not provide a complete answer to the question as to which Party may exercise jurisdiction without incidentally examining whether the Marines enjoy immunity'.[96] While the tribunal made no mention of *Chagos MPA* or *Coastal States Rights*, it seemed to have followed these tribunals' approach concerning ancillary jurisdiction. The tribunal held that 'while the Convention may not provide a basis for entertaining an independent immunity claim under general international law, the Arbitral Tribunal's competence extends to the determination of the issue of immunity of the Marines that necessarily arises as an incidental question in the application of the Convention'.[97] The *Enrica Lexie* case marked the first time an UNCLOS tribunal decided to examine an external issue based on its characterisation as an incidental issue within a dispute concerning UNCLOS.

Even though the incidental nature of an issue plays a central role in the establishment of UNCLOS tribunals' jurisdiction, none of the tribunals in the cases mentioned above shed much light on how to determine what constitutes an incidental issue. The tribunals in *Chagos MPA* and *Coastal States Right*, having found that territorial sovereignty constituted the real dispute between the parties, did not need to go into further detail on the issue of incidental question. The tribunal in *Enrica Lexie*, in contrast, found that the real dispute concerned UNCLOS but did not explain further how immunity was incidental, other than saying that:

> [I]mmunity from jurisdiction, by definition, operates as an exception to an otherwise-existing right to exercise jurisdiction. Whether that exception applies in the present case is a question that forms an integral part of the Arbitral Tribunal's task to determine which Party may exercise jurisdiction over the Marines.[98]

95 *The 'Enrica Lexie' Incident (Italy v India)*, Arbitral Award of 21 May 2021 [243] https://pcacases.com/web/sendAttach/16500 accessed 25 January 2022 [*Enrica Lexie*].

96 Ibid [808].

97 Ibid [809].

98 Ibid [808].

This would suggest that an incidental issue must be one that forms an integral part of the examination of a dispute concerning UNCLOS falling under the tribunal. However, two questions remain.

First, the tribunal did not identify the dispute concerning UNCLOS of which immunity formed an integral part. The tribunal stated that the dispute was one relating to which state could exercise jurisdiction over the Enrica Lexie and the two Marines, however it did not explain how this dispute regarding jurisdiction fell within the ambit of UNCLOS. Following the approach in *M/V Louisa* discussed above, the tribunal should have made clear which UNCLOS provisions were at stake and how they were linked to the facts of the case. This should have been made clear because only if the dispute concerning the State's exercise of jurisdiction over the Enrica Lexie fell within the tribunal's jurisdiction under Article 288(1) would it have been able to extend jurisdiction over the incidental question of immunity. In the Dispositif, the conclusion regarding the Marines' immunity was placed as an independent conclusion, on the same footing as other conclusions relating to UNCLOS, rather than an incidental question to a claim relating to UNCLOS.[99]

Second, if an issue is considered an 'integral' part of a tribunal's examination, does it then become 'the real issue' of the case or can it remain an incident issue? As argued by Judge Robinson in his Dissenting Opinion in *Enrica Lexie*, the issue of immunity of the Marines 'is a core element of the dispute dividing the Parties'.[100] According to Judge Robinson, '[a] claim to immunity is . . . definitionally incapable of being independent. It will always relate to jurisdiction (and in some cases to enforcement).'[101]. Therefore, '[t]here is no main issue in this case; there is no incidental issue in this case. Rather, there is one issue: the question of the Indian exercise of criminal jurisdiction over the marines in the face of their claim to immunity therefrom.'[102] If the approach of *Chagos MPA* and *Coastal State Rights* were to be followed, as the real issue of the case falls beyond the scope of UNCLOS, the tribunal would not have had jurisdiction to entertain the claim of immunity.

To summarise, the preceding discussions show that UNCLOS tribunals are not automatically barred from considering a claim involving issues not

99 Ibid [1094(B)(2)].
100 *The 'Enrica Lexie' Incident (Italy v India)*, Dissenting Opinion of Judge Patrick Robinson [39] https://pcacases.com/web/sendAttach/16774 accessed 25 January 2022.
101 Ibid [34].
102 Ibid [41].

regulated under UNCLOS. The key requirement for an UNCLOS tribunal to examine such a claim is that it has to be incidental to a dispute concerning the interpretation and application of UNCLOS. The incidental nature of the issue is therefore key in the establishment of UNCLOS tribunals' jurisdiction. However, UNCLOS tribunals have not provided a clear definition of what constitutes an 'ancillary' or 'incidental' issue or how to determine if one exists.[103]

6.1.2.4 Expansion of Jurisdiction under Article 297(1)

The structure and content of Article 297 are rather convoluted and confusing. Although paragraph (1) of Article 297 is situated within an article which provides for limitations on the applicability of compulsory settlement procedures under Section 2 of Part XV, this paragraph contains a list of disputes which nonetheless 'shall be subject to the procedures provided for under section 2'. Given the existence of Article 288(1) establishing the jurisdiction of UNCLOS tribunals, the question is whether Article 297(1) provides yet another basis for UNCLOS tribunals to establish their jurisdiction and if so, what is the relationship between Articles 288(1) and 297(1).

The *Southern Bluefin Tuna* arbitral tribunal viewed Article 297(1) as providing for a jurisdictional limitation, not jurisdictional affirmation. The tribunal interpreted Article 297(1) as limiting the application of compulsory procedures 'to disputes concerning the exercise by a coastal State of its sovereign rights or jurisdiction in certain identified cases *only*' as enumerated in subparagraphs (a)–(c).[104] The tribunal provided no basis to explain why the term 'only' was inserted even though the wording of Article 297(1) does not contain this term. It is worth noting that the tribunal in this case did not seek to shed light on Article 297(1) per se; instead it was merely highlighting the existence of Article 297 as 'providing significant limitations on the applicability of compulsory procedures insofar as coastal States are concerned'[105] to support

[103] Elsewhere, an incidental issue has been defined as 'an issue that a court or tribunal has to decide for it to be able to rule on a claim within its jurisdiction'. See: Callista Harris, 'Incidental Determinations in Proceedings under Compromissory Clauses' (2021) 70(2) ICLQ 417, 433.

[104] *Southern Bluefin Tuna Award* (n 7) [61] (emphasis added). Note that Suriname also adopted a similar interpretation when raising a jurisdictional objection in *Guyana v Suriname*, arguing that 'Article 297 says that section 2, compulsory dispute settlement, is only available for certain kinds of disputes that relate to the exercise by a coastal state of its sovereign rights or jurisdiction'. The tribunal, however, did not examine Article 297(1) but only Article 297(3). See *Guyana v Suriname* (n 64) [411].

[105] Ibid.

its conclusion that 'UNCLOS falls significantly short of establishing a truly comprehensive regime of compulsory jurisdiction entailing binding decisions.'[106] Based on this conclusion, it is not difficult to see why the tribunal read Article 297(1) as restricting the scope of compulsory jurisdiction.

While this interpretation also has support in numerous scholarly writings,[107] it seemed to have been implicitly rejected by the arbitral tribunal in *Guyana v Suriname*. Suriname in this case objected to the tribunal exercising jurisdiction over a dispute concerning a coastal State's enforcement of sovereign rights over non-living resources. To support this argument, Suriname construed Article 297(1) as limiting compulsory jurisdiction over disputes concerning coastal States' exercise of sovereign rights only to instances specified under subparagraphs (a)–(c).[108] According to Suriname, since a dispute concerning coastal States' enforcement power over non-living resources was not found under subparagraphs (a)–(c), it fell beyond the tribunal's compulsory jurisdiction. In response, the tribunal relied on Article 297(3) to find that only disputes concerning coastal States' sovereign rights over living resources are excepted and thus disputes concerning sovereign rights over non-living resources cannot be excluded from compulsory jurisdiction.[109] While not addressing Article 297(1) as such, the approach of the tribunal in this case sent a clear message that the limitations to compulsory jurisdiction under Article 297 are not found under paragraph (1) but in the other two paragraphs of this article. As a result, paragraph (1) cannot be considered as providing a limitation to jurisdiction.

Such an approach was explicitly spelled out by the *Chagos MPA* tribunal. The tribunal explained, based on a lengthy examination of the negotiating history of UNCLOS, that the placement of paragraph (1) is a relic of history and a reflection of UNCLOS drafter' endeavour to balance the contrasting interests of States parties.[110] The tribunal did not only interpret Article 297(1) as reaffirming an UNCLOS tribunal's jurisdiction pursuant to Article 288(1),[111] but also most strikingly went further to hold that:

[106] Ibid [62].

[107] Stephen Allen, 'Article 297 of the United Nations Convention on the Law of the Sea and the Scope of Mandatory Jurisdiction' (2017) 48(3–4) ODIL 313, citing Robin Churchill and Vaughan Lowe, *The Law of the Sea* (3rd ed, Manchester University Press 1999) 455; Oxman (n 5) 404.

[108] *Guyana v Suriname* (n 64) [411]–[412].

[109] Ibid [415].

[110] *Chagos MPA* (n 32) [314]–[315]

[111] Ibid [308].

> Article 297(1) expands the jurisdiction of a Tribunal over the enumerated cases beyond that which would follow from the application of Article 288(1) alone. In addition to describing disputes relating to the interpretation and application of the Convention itself, each of the three specified cases in Article 297(1) includes a renvoi to sources of law beyond the Convention itself.[112]

Related to rules concerning the protection and preservation of the marine environment, the tribunal specified further that the reference to 'international rules and standards' contained in Article 297(1)(c) did not only include those of a substantive nature but also procedural rules existing elsewhere in international environmental law.[113]

The existence of two opposing views on the interpretation of Article 297(1) was acknowledged by the *South China Sea* arbitral tribunal in its Award on Jurisdiction and Admissibility in 2015.[114] The tribunal in this case nonetheless did not provide its own view on the matter,[115] so it remains open as to which approach will prevail. On the one hand, the interpretation adopted by *Southern Bluefin Tuna* at first sight makes the placement of paragraph (1) in Article 297 more logical, as it implies a limitation on the jurisdiction of compulsory procedures in keeping with the overall purpose of Article 297. On the other hand, the interpretation adopted by the *Chagos MPA* tribunal is arguably preferable as it is more in line with the overall structure and nature of the dispute settlement system established under Part XV. As the tribunal's review of the negotiating history of Article 297(1) indicated, the disappearance of the word 'only' included in earlier drafts of what eventually became paragraph (1) suggests that states agreed to expand the scope of compulsory dispute settlement under UNCLOS beyond what was initially envisioned. To balance out this expansion, the limitations to this compulsory jurisdiction have to be made explicit in paragraphs (2) and (3) – and further optionally under Article 298. Reading limitations that were not explicitly made into Article 297 risks upsetting this delicate balance that the drafters strived to maintain within Art 297 and the whole of Part XV.

[112] Ibid [316].
[113] Ibid [322].
[114] *South China Sea Arbitration* (Jurisdiction and Admissibility) (n 4) [359].
[115] The *South China Sea* tribunal's holding in para 359 has been interpreted to be in line with the *Southern Bluefin Tuna*. However, there does not appear to be any basis to argue that the *South China Sea* tribunal preferred one view over the other. See: Erietta Scalieri, 'Discretionary Power of Coastal States and the Control of Its Compliance with International Law by International Tribunals' in Angela Del Vecchio and Roberto Virzo (eds), *Interpretations of the United Nations Convention on the Law of the Sea by International Courts and Tribunals* (Springer 2019) 390.

While Article 297(1) should not be construed as limiting UNCLOS tribunals' compulsory jurisdiction, it does not readily follow that, as the *Chagos MPA* tribunal concluded, this paragraph expands the tribunal's jurisdiction to disputes involving the contravention of not only UNCLOS but also other legal instruments, and thus serves as a renvoi to the sources of law beyond UNCLOS itself.[116] The tribunal offered no basis to support such an expansive reading, which, as one commentator argues, brings within the jurisdictional scope of UNCLOS tribunals 'disputes concerning the interpretation or application of international agreements that do not expressly refer to the UNCLOS'.[117]

The tribunal's interpretation goes much further than merely allowing UNCLOS courts or tribunals to invoke external sources to interpret provisions of UNCLOS similar to Article 293 as analysed above. By interpreting Article 297(1) as a jurisdiction-affirming provision and as 'a renvoi to sources of law beyond the Convention', the arbitral tribunal effectively expanded UNCLOS tribunals' jurisdiction to 'certain disputes involving the contravention of legal instruments beyond the four corners of the Convention itself',[118] therefore giving UNCLOS tribunals a scope of jurisdiction that is even broader than Article 288(1).[119] As observed by another scholar, the tribunal's interpretation of Article 297(1)(c) means that 'cases addressing environmental issues may well find their way into compulsory adjudication, where courts and tribunals will be called upon to also apply such generally accepted standards enshrined in instruments that are as yet not subject to compulsory jurisdiction'.[120] However, as implied by the tribunal in *Enrica Lexie*, there may be limits as to how far an UNCLOS tribunal's jurisdiction extends under Article 297(1). In *Enrica Lexie*, the tribunal required the applicability of Article 297(1)(a) and (b) to pertain to the exercise of freedoms, rights and uses of the seas.[121] Thus, a contravention of external sources that fall within the ambit of Article 297(1) still needs to be tied to UNCLOS, particularly to the exercise of coastal States' exercise of rights.

[116] *Chagos MPA* (n 32) [316].

[117] Stefan Talmon, 'The Chagos Marine Protected Area Arbitration: Expansion of the Jurisdiction of UNCLOS Part XV Courts And Tribunals' (2016) 65 ICLQ 927, 936.

[118] *Chagos MPA* (n 32) [316].

[119] Ibid.

[120] Maria Gavouneli, 'Protection Standards for the Marine Environment: Updating Part XII of the Law of the Sea Convention?' in Stephen Minas and Jordan Diamond (eds), *Stress Testing the Law of the Sea: Dispute Resolution, Disasters and Emerging Challenges* (Brill 2018) 259.

[121] *Enrica Lexie* (n 95) [802].

6.1.3 *Limitations and Exceptions under Section 3*

Section 3 contains two important articles, namely Articles 297 and 298 which respsectively set out the limitations and exceptions to compulsory jurisdiction. This means that UNCLOS tribunals cannot exercise jurisdiction over the categories of disputes contained in these two articles. The main difference between the two is that the limitations under Article 297 are automatically applicable,[122] while those contained under Article 298 are optional. This means that the categories of disputes contained in Article 298 are excluded from compulsory jurisdiction only when the States concerned have made a declaration to that effect.[123] This section analyses the decisions relating to the interpretation and application of Articles 297 and 298 in order to understand how UNCLOS tribunals have determined the scope of the limitations and exceptions to compulsory jurisdiction.

6.1.3.1 Article 297(3)

Article 297 contains two express limitations in paragraphs (2) and (3) pertaining to disputes concerning marine scientific research and disputes concerning fisheries, respectively.[124] To date no cases concerning the applicability of Article 297(2) have been brought before UNCLOS tribunals. The analysis in this section focuses on the limitation under Article 297(3).

The complicated design of the Convention regarding fisheries competences means that the scope of application of Article 297(3) is not at all clear. The first part of Article 297(3)(a) confirms that fisheries disputes arising under UNCLOS are subject to compulsory jurisdiction, it is only the second part of this paragraph that excludes 'dispute relating to its sovereign rights with respect to the living resources in the [EEZ] or their exercise, including its discretionary powers for determining the allowable catch, its harvesting capacity, the allocation of surpluses to other States and the terms and conditions established in its conservation and management laws and regulations'. As judges Kateka and Wolfrum correctly pointed out, Article 297(3)(a) cannot, therefore, be used as a

[122] Note, however, that Wolfrum has argued that even though the limitations under Article 297 'work automatically which means they do not have to be declared', the limited jurisprudence on this article shows that 'such exceptions have to be invoked'. See: Wolfrum (n 1) 174.

[123] For a list of declarations that have been made under Article 298, see: www.itlos.org/en/main/jurisdiction/declarations-of-states-parties/declarations-made-by-states-parties-under-article-298/#:~:text=Pursuant%20to%20article%20298%20de,provided%20for%20in%20section%202 accessed 25 January 2022.

[124] Paragraph (1) of Article 297 has been analysed above.

blanket limitation to exclude all fisheries disputes.[125] While the wording of this paragraph suggests that only a specific subset of these disputes falls beyond the scope of compulsory jurisdiction, the exact scope of this specific subset is not entirely clear. UNCLOS tribunals' decisions have offered some guidance on the question of which fisheries disputes fall within the scope of Article 297(3)(a) and which do not. Each of these categories is examined in turn.

DISPUTES FALLING WITHIN THE SCOPE OF ARTICLE 297(3)(A). The decisions of UNCLOS tribunals to date have confirmed that three types of disputes fall within the scope of Article 297(3)(a) and are thus excluded from the compulsory jurisdiction of UNCLOS tribunals.

First, the tribunal in *Chagos MPA* confirmed that the limitation contained in Article 297(3) applies to the straddling fish stocks and highly migratory species under Articles 63 and 64 to the extent that they are found in the EEZ of the coastal State although the wording of this article only explicitly excludes disputes relating coastal States' exercise of sovereign rights *in* the EEZ.[126] While the tribunal acknowledged the shortcomings of a jurisdictional separation of disputes relating to fisheries in the EEZ and those in the high seas, it stated that States preferred and continued to endorse such an approach, to which the tribunal stayed faithful.[127]

Further, as Articles 63 and 64 provide for procedural obligations, the arbitral tribunal in *Chagos MPA* confirmed that the exclusion in Article 297(3) also applies to procedural obligations.[128] The tribunal provided no legal grounds to support the extension of Article 297(3) to procedural obligations, other than the general statement that 'Articles 63 and 64 (as well as the UNFSA) are, on their face, measures in respect of fisheries and in their application in the [EEZ] are subject to the exclusion in Article 297(3)(a)'[129] and the reference to previous cases including *Barbados v Trinidad and Tobago* and *Southern Bluefin Tuna*. However, neither of these cases lent support to the tribunal's conclusion. As the tribunal acknowledged itself, the *Southern Bluefin Tuna* tribunal did not 'make any suggestion that the jurisdictional exclusion in the [EEZ] pursuant to Article 297(3) was potentially applicable'[130] thus the reference to this case was in fact pointless. *Barbados v Trinidad and Tobago* was a

[125] *Chagos Marine Protected Area Arbitration (Mauritius v United Kingdom)*, Dissenting and Concurring Opinions of Judges Kateka and Wolfrum [58].
[126] *Chagos MPA* (n 32) [300].
[127] Ibid [301].
[128] Ibid [300].
[129] Ibid.
[130] Ibid.

maritime delimitation case in which Barbados requested the tribunal, in case it did not adjust the equidistance line, to grant Barbadian fishermen 'access to the stocks of flying fish while they are within the waters of Trinidad and Tobago'.[131] The tribunal, in response, held that it did not 'have the jurisdiction to make an award establishing a right of access for Barbadian fishermen to flying fish within the EEZ of Trinidad and Tobago, because that award is outside its jurisdiction by virtue of the limitation set out in UNCLOS Article 297(3)(a)'.[132] As this statement made clear, the question at stake in this case was the establishment of Barbados' right of access to the fish stocks found in Trinidad and Tobago's EEZ, and as such would trigger an examination of Trinidad and Tobago's exercise of exclusive sovereign rights over its fisheries resources in its EEZ. This was the reason why Article 297(3)(a) was applicable, not because of Article 63. In fact, Article 63(1) was mentioned to highlight the need for cooperation between the parties and the commitment made by the parties to comply with this article.[133] It is therefore difficult to see how an exclusion containing procedural obligations under Article 297(3)(a) could be implied as it was plain that no connection was made between procedural obligations under Article 63 and Article 297(3) in this case.[134]

By contrast, in *Chagos MPA*, the question presented before the tribunal was of a different nature. Mauritius claimed that the UK had failed to seek agreement on the measures necessary to coordinate the conservation and development of stocks of tuna under Article 63(1), or to cooperate directly with Mauritius and other States with regards to highly migratory species under Article 64(1). An analogy cannot be made between the right to access fish stocks in the EEZ and the obligation to seek to agree and to cooperate, as the latter does not prejudice or compromise the exercise of sovereign rights of the UK over the fish stocks in the EEZ of the Chagos Archipelago. In fact, this point was explicitly made by Judge Paik in his Separate Opinion to ITLOS's *Advisory Opinion on IUU Fishing*. Judge Paik pointed out that Article 63(1) made clear that the obligation to seek to agree under this article was 'without prejudice to the other the provisions of Part V',[135] meaning that 'the failure to comply with an obligation to cooperate under article 63, paragraph 1, of the Convention does not entail any constraint or restriction on the exercise of the sovereign rights of the SRFC Member State to conserve and manage the

[131] *Barbados v Trinidad and Tobago* (n 2) [273].
[132] Ibid [283].
[133] Ibid [285]–[287].
[134] See also: Kunoy (n 5) 114.
[135] *Request for Advisory Opinion submitted by the Sub-Regional Fisheries Commission* (Advisory Opinion, Sep Op Paik) ITLOS Reports 2015, 4 [33].

transboundary stocks within its EEZ'.[136] In the event that any Member State refuses to cooperate in good faith, he argued that other States may 'invoke the liability of that State for the breach of obligations under article 63, paragraph 1, of the Convention, but not to try to restrict the exercise of its sovereign rights in the EEZ'.[137] Procedural obligations such as the duty to cooperate are, therefore, distinct from the coastal State's exercise of sovereign rights. It is therefore arguable that the tribunal wrongly narrowed the scope of its compulsory jurisdiction by expanding the applicability of Article 297(3) to include procedural obligations.

Second, the tribunal in *Chagos MPA* confirmed that Article 297(3) excludes measures that relate to coastal States' exercise of sovereign rights in the EEZ even when such measures are aimed at the conservation and management of living resources, thus having an environmental purpose. This conclusion also shed light on the relationship between paragraphs (1) and (3) of Article 297. In this case, Mauritius contended that if a dispute fell within the scope of Article 297(1), it could not be excluded from compulsory jurisdiction of the tribunal even when this dispute also concerned a coastal State's sovereign rights over the living resources of the EEZ or their exercise.[138] Mauritius thus viewed the relationship between the two paragraphs of Article 297 as being 'independent of one another'. The UK, on the other hand, argued that even if the ban on fishing was characterised as having an environmental purpose, it did not cease to be about conservation and management of living resources. Consequently, the purpose of environmental protection could not prevail over conservation and management for jurisdictional purposes.[139] This approach treated the two paragraphs (1) and (3) as not being independent, but having the relationship of the general rule and the exception.

The tribunal sided with the UK on this matter and clarified that even when a dispute was deemed to fall under Article 297(1), the limitations under Article 297(3) would not cease to apply. This meant that any aspects of the dispute pertaining to fisheries in the EEZ would still be excluded from the jurisdiction of the tribunal.[140] Although, as discussed in Chapter 5, the scope of the protection and preservation of the marine environment under UNCLOS has been broadened to include the conservation of marine living resources,

[136] Ibid [38].
[137] Ibid.
[138] *Chagos MPA* (n 32) [243].
[139] *Chagos MPA* (n 32) [248].
[140] Ibid [97], [300].

this expansion still does not allow for disputes concerning the marine environment to subsume those concerning coastal States' conservation of living resources. As argued by one commentator, '[a]n evolutionary and environmental interpretation of article 297 designed to bring conservation of living resources within Part XV jurisdiction would overturn a clear policy preference of the negotiating states at UNCLOS III, a preference reiterated and endorsed in 1995 when the UN Fish Stocks Agreement adopted exactly the same dispute settlement provisions, mutatis mutandis.'[141]

Third, in *South China Sea*, the arbitral tribunal found that 'Article 297(3) could potentially bar the Tribunal's jurisdiction over the Philippines claims in relation to fisheries, to the extent that the events in question took place in China's exclusive economic zone or an area of overlapping entitlements.'[142] The tribunal did not eventually find any areas of overlapping entitlements, this point was not explained in more detail. It is worth asking, however, whether the tribunal's expansion of the scope of application of Article 297(3) to an area of overlapping entitlements is tenable. The answer would likely be in the negative. The wording of Article 297(3)(a) is clear, it does not exclude all disputes concerning fisheries from UNCLOS tribunals' compulsory jurisdiction, only those relating to coastal States' sovereign rights over living resources in the EEZ. In areas of overlapping entitlements, it is difficult to determine which disputing States would be considered the coastal State entitled to exercise its sovereign rights and consequently, whose EEZ it is that is in question.[143] It follows that in areas of overlapping entitlements to the EEZ pending delimitation, the coastal State's sovereign rights cannot have been definitively established so as to give rise to a dispute relating to its exercise of sovereign rights triggering the application of Article 297(3). In fact, the arbitral tribunal in *Coastal State Rights* rejected the applicability of Article 297(3)(a) to fisheries claims because 'the interference by the Russian Federation with fisheries activities alleged by Ukraine occurred within an area that cannot be determined to constitute the exclusive economic zone of the Russian

[141] Alan Boyle, 'UNCLOS Dispute Settlement and the Uses and Abuses of Part XV' (2014) 47 Revue Belge De Droit International 182, 193.

[142] *South China Sea Arbitration* (Jurisdiction and Admissibility) (n 4) [359].

[143] As the Special Chamber held in *Ghana/Côte d'Ivoire* in relation to overlapping continental shelf entitlements, '[o]nly a decision on delimitation establishes which part of the continental shelf under dispute appertains to which of the claiming States'. *Delimitation of the Maritime Boundary in the Atlantic Ocean (Ghana/Côte* d'Ivoire) ITLOS Reports 2017, 4 [591]. Note that this holding has been subject to much criticism, due to its view of a delimitation decision as constitutive of coastal States' rights.

Federation or Ukraine'.[144] While not referring to *South China Sea*, it clearly took the opposite approach.

In any case, it would seem that in areas of overlapping EEZ pending delimitation, a fisheries measure such as a fishing ban should be more properly seen as a unilateral act in disputed maritime zones falling under Article 74(3), rather than a measure that is part of a coastal State's exercise of sovereign rights under Article 56. A dispute concerning a violation of the obligation stipulated under Article 74(3) is distinct from a dispute concerning a State's sovereign rights. There is arguably little basis to conclude that a dispute concerning a unilateral measure in overlapping EEZ under Article 74(3) would fall under the ambit of Article 297(3).

DISPUTES FALLING BEYOND THE SCOPE OF ARTICLE 297(3)(A). In addition to clarifying disputes that *do* fall within the scope of Article 297(3), UNCLOS tribunals have also thrown light on disputes which are not encompassed within the scope of Article 297(3). Two such categories of disputes have been identified.

First, the arbitral tribunal in *Guyana v Suriname* confirmed that Article 297 (3) only excludes disputes relating to sovereign rights over living resources in the EEZ. Disputes relating to coastal States' exercise of sovereign rights over non-living resource thus do not fall within the ambit of Article 297(3) and are still subject to compulsory jurisdiction.[145]

Second, in *South China Sea*, in examining whether China had interfered with the Philippines' petroleum exploration, seismic surveys, and fishing in the latter's EEZ, the arbitral tribunal held that Article 297(3) 'do[es] not apply where a State is alleged to have violated the Convention in respect of the [EEZ] of another State'.[146] This statement seems at first glance to contradict the *Chagos MPA* tribunal's interpretation of Article 297(3). In this case, the tribunal rejected Mauritius' contention that Article 297(3) only excludes disputes concerning coastal States' sovereign rights over living resources in the EEZ, but not those involving the rights of other States in the EEZ. As stated by this tribunal, these two categories of rights are deeply intertwined, making such a distinction artificial and as such, 'a dispute regarding Mauritius' claimed fishing rights in the exclusive economic zone cannot be separated from the exercise of the United Kingdom's sovereign rights with

[144] *Coastal State Rights* (n 77) [402].
[145] *Guyana v Suriname* (n 64) [415].
[146] *South China Sea Arbitration* (Merits) (n 28) [695].

respect to living resources'.[147] However, a closer examination of the two arbitral tribunals' seemingly contrasting statements reveals that they may each be justified on account of the specific circumstances of each case. In *South China Sea*, the challenge was brought by the Philippines against China, that is, the coastal state against the non-coastal State, regarding the non-coastal State's violation of its obligations under UNCLOS in the EEZ of the coastal State. The coastal State's exercise of sovereign rights in the EEZ and non-coastal States' obligation in another State's EEZ are two separate legal issues under UNCLOS, with only the former captured within the scope of Article 297(3). As the tribunal made clear, Article 297(3) 'serve[s] to limit compulsory dispute settlement where a claim is brought against a State's exercise of its sovereign rights in respect of living resources in its own [EEZ]'.[148] This was the exact scenario in *Chagos MPA*, in which the UK was assumed to be the coastal State insofar as submission 4 was concerned, and the challenge was brought by Mauritius against the UK, that is, the non-coastal State against the coastal State, concerning the latter's failure to fulfil its undertakings with regards to living resources in its EEZ. Moreover, Mauritius' claimed fishing rights in the Chagos Archipelago's EEZ were unique in that they were based upon the UK's previous undertakings given to Mauritius, creating the intertwining relationship as described by the tribunal. As a result, Mauritius' claimed fishing rights could not be separated from the coastal State's exercise of sovereign rights over living resources in the EEZ. While envisaging different scenarios, combined implication of the *Chagos MPA* and *South China Sea* arbitral tribunals' approaches is that coastal States' sovereign rights in the EEZ are 'firmly insulated' from compulsory jurisdiction.[149] Other States cannot challenge the coastal State's exercise of sovereign rights before an UNCLOS tribunal, but the coastal State can challenge violations of those other States in the EEZ.

6.1.3.2 Article 298(1)

The exceptions to compulsory jurisdiction under Article 298 are found under subparagraphs (a)–(c) of Article 298(1). UNCLOS tribunals have not heard any disputes relating to the exceptions under (c) relating to 'disputes in respect of which the Security Council of the United Nations is exercising the

[147] *Chagos MPA* (n 32) [297].
[148] *South China Sea* (Merits) (n 28) [695].
[149] Klein, 'The Vicissitudes of Dispute Settlement under the Law of the Sea Convention' (n 3) 351.

functions assigned to it by the Charter of the United Nations'. This section therefore only deals with the exceptions under paragraphs (a) and (b).

EXCEPTIONS UNDER SUBPARAGRAPH (A). Paragraph (a) contains two categories of disputes, namely 'disputes concerning the interpretation or application of articles 15, 74 and 83 relating to sea boundary delimitation' and 'those involving historic bays or titles'.

The exception concerning disputes concerning maritime delimitation has only been examined in detail in one case, namely *South China Sea*. In this case, while China did not participate in the proceedings of this case, it had issued a Position Paper setting out its view that the Philippines' submissions concerning the existence and extent of China's maritime entitlements in the South China Sea were 'actually a request for maritime delimitation by the Arbitral Tribunal in disguise. The Philippines' claim have in effect covered the main aspects and steps in maritime delimitation.'[150] As noted by the tribunal, China thus viewed maritime delimitation as 'an integral and systemic process' encompassing any issues which might arise in the process of delimitation. The tribunal was thus presented with the opportunity to consider what issues would be integral to maritime delimitation.

The tribunal disagreed with China and found that 'a dispute concerning the existence of an entitlement to maritime zones is distinct from a dispute concerning the delimitation of those zones in an area where the entitlements of parties overlap'.[151] It agreed that the 'fixing the extent of parties' entitlements and the area in which they overlap will commonly be one of the first matters to be addressed in the delimitation of a maritime boundary',[152] but that '[w]hile all sea boundary delimitations will concern entitlements, the converse is not the case: all disputes over entitlements do not concern delimitation.'[153] On this basis, the tribunal concluded that Article 298(1)(a) excluding disputes concerning maritime delimitation 'does not reach so far as to capture a dispute over the existence of entitlements that may – or may not – ultimately require delimitation'.[154] The tribunal thus adopted a narrow understanding of the term 'disputes concerning maritime delimitation' for the purposes of Article 298(1).

150 Position Paper of the Government of the People's Republic of China on the Matter of Jurisdiction in the South China Sea Arbitration Initiated by the Republic of the Philippines (7 December 2014) www.fmprc.gov.cn/mfa_eng/zxxx_662805/t1217147.shtml accessed 25 January 2022.

151 *South China Sea Arbitration* (Jurisdiction and Admissibility) (n 4) [156].

152 Ibid.

153 *South China Sea Arbitration* (Merits) (n 28) [204].

154 Ibid.

This interpretation has not been without controversy. Some scholars have critiqued the tribunal for essentially 'salami-slicing'[155] one big dispute into isolated issues for the purposes of exercising jurisdiction[156] and for failing to have regard to the term 'concerning' which requires a non-restrictive interpretation of the exception.[157] It is submitted, however, that a narrow approach to interpreting the scope of exception under Article 298(1) is indeed warranted. An examination of the drafting history of Convention during UNCLOS III shows that as a compromise for excluding highly sensitive disputes from compulsory jurisdiction,[158] States also agreed to limit to the maximum extent possible these exceptions.[159] As a result, the exclusions in Article 298 should be construed narrowly to include only the three categories of disputes specified therein.[160] Therefore a broad interpretation of Article 298 to cover issues that are not explicitly stipulated but only potentially related to the exceptions would not seem to be consistent with the intention of the drafters.

The *South China Sea* tribunal's narrow interpretation as discussed above seems to be in contrast with the interpretation of Article 298(1)(a)(i) in two other instances. The first instance was before Conciliation Commission in the *Conciliation between Timor-Leste and Australia*. The Commission found that the question of transitional period and provisional arrangements of practical nature pending delimitation fell within the scope of Article 298(1)(a) and were thus excluded from compulsory jurisdiction.[161] While such an interpretation at first glance suggests a broad reading of the scope of Article 298(1)(a) beyond

[155] This term is borrowed from Boyle, 'UNCLOS Dispute Settlement' (n 141) 184.

[156] See, for example, Stefan Talmon, 'The South China Sea Arbitration: Is There a Case to Answer?' in Stefan Talmon and Bing Bing Jia (eds), *The South China Sea Arbitration: A Chinese Perspective* (Hart Publishing 2014) 56; Sienhoo Yee, 'The South China Sea Arbitration (The Philippines v. China): Potential Jurisdictional Obstacles or Objections' (2014) 13 CJIL 708; Klein, 'The Vicissitudes of Dispute Settlement under the Law of the Sea Convention' (n 3) 355.

[157] Keyuan Zou and Qing Ye, 'Interpretation and Application of Article 298 of the Law of the Sea Convention in Recent Annex VII Arbitrations: An Appraisal' (2017) 48(3–4) ODIL 331, 335.

[158] Myron H. Nordquist (eds),*United Nations Convention on the Law of the Sea, 1982: A commentary* (Martinus Nijhoff 1985)110

[159] Ibid.

[160] P. Chandrasekhara Rao, 'Delimitation Disputes under the United Nations Convention on the Law of the Sea: Settlement Procedures' in Tafsir Malick Ndiaye and Rüdiger Wolfrum (eds), *Law of the Sea, Environmental Law and Settlement of Disputes: Liber Amicorum Judge Thomas A. Mensah* (Martinus Nijhoff 2007).

[161] See: Conciliation between the Democratic Republic of Timor-Leste and the Commonwealth of Australia, Decision on Australia's Objection to Competence (19 September 2016) [97] https://pcacases.com/web/sendAttach/1921 accessed 25 January 2022.

maritime boundary delimitation itself,[162] it should be pointed out that the question excluded is still regulated under Articles 74 and 83. The wording of Article 298(1)(a) envisions the exclusion of disputes relating to these articles, which extend to the issues found in their paragraphs (3). Such an extension cannot readily be made to legal issues which are not regulated under these provisions.

Second, in *Coastal State Rights*, the Annex VII arbitral tribunal in examining the maritime delimitation exception under Article 298(1)(a) held that:

> [F]or the purpose of determining the applicability of the delimitation exception under Article 298, paragraph 1, subparagraph (a), of the Convention, one of the key questions is whether there are entitlements and whether there is an area of overlapping maritime entitlements. If such area exists, the question of delimitation inevitably arises and the delimitation exception may be triggered.[163]

Due to the way it was phrased, this statement could be understood in two ways. On the one hand, it can be inferred from this statement that maritime delimitation necessarily includes the determination of entitlements and identification of overlapping entitlements, thus the maritime delimitation exception under Article 298(1)(a) would extend to the question of maritime entitlement. Interpreted as such, the approaches of the *South China Sea* and *Coastal State Rights* tribunals would be inconsistent with one another. On the other hand, by virtue of the phrase '[if] such area exists', the tribunal could also be understood as saying that only when the entitlements overlap does the delimitation exception apply, meaning that the step of determining entitlement is not excepted from the jurisdiction of an UNCLOS tribunal. This interpretation would then be consistent with that of the *South China Sea* tribunal.

In any case, the *Coastal State Rights* tribunal rejected the application of Article 298(1)(a) because it found that it did not have jurisdiction to determine 'whether there are entitlements of either Party to the maritime areas around Crimea, let alone whether such entitlements overlap' due to the fact that it could not decide on the sovereignty of either party over Crimea.[164] In this regard, the *Coastal State Rights* tribunal's approach clearly differed from that of the *South China Sea* tribunal. The latter found that the determination of entitlement of insular features can be made independently from the question

[162] Zou and Ye (n 157) 336.
[163] *Coastal State Rights* (n 77) [381].
[164] Ibid [383].

of who had sovereignty over the features. In the end, while the result of the two arbitration was the same, that is, Article 298(1)(a) was not applicable, the reasoning process was vastly different.

Turning to disputes concerning historic bays and historic titles, the *South China Sea* tribunal found that the term 'those' following 'or' in Article 298(1)(a) refers to 'disputes' and not only 'delimitation disputes'. Consequently, contrary to the Philippines' assertion, Article 298(1)(a) excludes 'disputes … involving historic bays or titles' more broadly, not only delimitation disputes 'involving historic bays or titles'.[165] In order to determine whether the exclusion involving historic titles was applicable to the Philippines' claims concerning China's historic rights in the South China Sea, the tribunal then conducted a detailed examination of the scope and meaning of the term 'historic title' under Article 298(1)(a). As analysed in Chapter 2, the tribunal found that 'the reference to "historic titles" in Article 298(1)(a)(i) of the Convention is … a reference to claims of sovereignty over maritime areas derived from historical circumstances'.[166] It was not intended to exclude jurisdiction over 'a broad and unspecified category of possible claims to historic rights falling short of sovereignty'.[167] As the tribunal found that China's claims to historic rights in the South China Sea did not amount to 'historic title to the waters of South China Sea, but rather a constellation of historic rights short of title', the exception in Article 298(1)(a) did not apply.

EXCEPTIONS UNDER SUBPARAGRAPH (B). Article 298(1)(b) contains two exceptions, namely 'disputes concerning military activities, including military activities by government vessels and aircraft engaged in non-commercial service', and 'disputes concerning law enforcement activities in regard to the exercise of sovereign rights or jurisdiction excluded from the jurisdiction of a court or tribunal under article 297, paragraph 2 or 3'.

The second group of disputes, namely those concerning law-enforcement activities came under scrutiny in *Arctic Sunrise* between Netherlands and Russia which involved the latter's boarding, arrest and detention of a vessel flying the Dutch flag and its crew.[168] In this case, the arbitral tribunal had to consider whether the Russian declaration which excluded all 'disputes

[165] *South China Sea Arbitration (Merits)* (n 28) [215].

[166] Ibid [226].

[167] Ibid.

[168] Article 298 first came up in *Chagos MPA*. However, Article 298 was examined in order to shed light on the question regarding whether the arbitral tribunal had jurisdiction to entertain territorial sovereignty disputes under Article 288(1). The tribunal did not scrutinise any of the exceptions contained in this article.

concerning law-enforcement activities in regard to the exercise of sovereign rights or jurisdiction"[169] was permissible under Article 298. The arbitral tribunal's response was in the negative.[170] It held that States cannot 'exclude from the jurisdiction of the procedures in Section 2 of Part XV of the Convention "every dispute" that concerns "law-enforcement activities in regard to the exercise of sovereign rights or jurisdiction"'.[171] Instead, 'the only areas in which the jurisdiction of a court or tribunal can validly be excluded pursuant to Articles 297(2) and 297(3) read with 298(1)(b) of the Convention' were disputes concerning enforcement activities in relation to marine scientific research or fisheries.[172] The *Arctic Sunrise* arbitral tribunal thus confirmed that scope of Article 298(1)(b) was to be determined with reference to the exceptions under Article 297,[173] which allowed it to reject an expansive interpretation of the Article 298(1)(b) to include all disputes relating to law enforcement activities. The *South China Sea* tribunal also recognised close link between the exclusion contained in Article 298(1)(b) concerning law enforcement activities and Article 297. This means that for law enforcement activities in relation to fisheries in the EEZ, similar to Article 297(3) as discussed above, the exclusion under Article 298(1)(b) does not 'apply where a State is alleged to have violated the Convention in respect of the exclusive economic zone of another State'.[174]

Finally, the exception concerning disputes over military activities has been brought before UNCLOS tribunals in three cases to date. This exception was discussed for the first time in *South China Sea* in relation to two separate submissions brought by the Philippines, one concerning Chinese land reclamation activities at seven reefs in the South China Sea, and the other concerning China's activities in and around Second Thomas Shoal and China's interaction with the Philippine military forces stationed on the Shoal. With regards to the first submission, the tribunal found that Article 298(1)(b) was not applicable but based simply on the fact that 'the Tribunal accepts China's repeatedly affirmed position that civilian use comprises the primary (if not the only) motivation underlying the extensive construction activities on the seven reefs in the Spratly Islands'.[175] In examining the second

169 *Arctic Sunrise* (Award on Jurisdiction) (n 67) [51].
170 Ibid [69].
171 Ibid.
172 Ibid [76].
173 ITLOS in the provisional measure phase also noted this connection between the two articles. *The 'Arctic Sunrise' Case (Kingdom of the Netherlands v Russian Federation)* (Provisional Measures, Order of 22 November 2013) ITLOS Reports 2013, 230 [45].
174 *South China Sea Arbitration* (Merits) (n 28) [695].
175 Ibid [938].

claim relating to activities around Second Thomas Shoal, the tribunal held that 'Article 298(1)(b) applies to "disputes concerning military activities" and not to "military activities" as such.' As a result, what is pertinent for the purposes of Article 298(1)(b) is 'whether the dispute itself concerns military activities, rather than whether a party has employed its military in some manner in relation to the dispute'.[176] The tribunal put great emphasis on the need for an existence of a dispute that concerns military activities, further stressing that '[w]here a State Party has initiated compulsory dispute settlement under the Convention in respect of a dispute that does not concern military activities, Article 298(1)(b) would not come into play if the other Party were later to begin employing its military in relation to the dispute in the course of proceedings.'[177] However, when applying this test to the facts of the case, the tribunal particularly noted 'the deployment of a detachment of the Philippines' armed forces that is engaged in a standoff with a combination of ships from China's Navy and from China's Coast Guard and other government agencies' and that 'China's military vessels have been reported to have been in the vicinity'.[178] In the view of the tribunal, 'this represents a quintessentially military situation, involving the military forces of one side and a combination of military and paramilitary forces on the other, arrayed in opposition to one another' [179] It would seem that the tribunal, contrary to the test that it set out, attached more weight to the presence of military forces in the situation before it rather than whether there was any dispute concerning military activities. As a result, the threshold set by the *South China Sea* tribunal for the application of Article 298(1)(b) was quite low.

In the *Ukrainian Naval Vessels* the provisional measures phase between Ukraine and Russia, ITLOS in determining whether the Annex VII arbitral tribunal to be constituted to hear the merits of the case would have prima facie jurisdiction also had to consider whether the exception concerning military activities was applicable due to Russia's declaration under Article 298. ITLOS's approach, however, drastically differed to that of South China Sea in two important respects. First, ITLOS did not focus on either of the questions raised by the tribunal in *South China Sea*, namely whether the dispute concerned military activities or whether the military was employed in relation to the dispute. Instead, ITLOS's entire analysis rest upon the distinction between military activities and enforcement activities, and as such,

[176] Ibid [1158].
[177] Ibid [1168].
[178] Ibid [1161].
[179] Ibid.

upon the question as to whether Russia's arrest and detention of the three Ukrainian vessels 'took place in the context of a military operation or a law enforcement operation'.[180] Second, unlike the *South China Sea* tribunal, in the process of identifying the nature of Russia's actions, ITLOS held that the characterisation of the relevant activities could not be 'based solely on the characterization of the activities in question by the parties to a dispute . . . such characterization may be subjective and at variance with the actual conduct'.[181] As a result, ITLOS disregarded the evidence presented by each party holding the other party to the characterisation that it had made prior to the case,[182] stating that 'the distinction between military and law enforcement activities must be based primarily on an objective evaluation of the nature of the activities in question'.[183]

In order to conduct its 'objective evaluation', ITLOS examined the sequence of events leading to the arrest of detention. In its view, the underlying dispute leading to the arrest concerned the passage of the Ukrainian naval vessels through the Kerch Strait,[184] and so 'the core of the dispute was the Parties' differing interpretation of the regime of passage through the Kerch Strait'.[185] While force was used by the Russian Coast Guard, the use of force was in ITLOS's view 'in the context of a law enforcement operation rather than a military operation'.[186] ITLOS thus concluded that 'the arrest and detention of the Ukrainian naval vessels by the Russian Federation took place in the context of a law enforcement operation'[187] thus Article 298(1)(b) was not applicable.

In *Coastal State Rights*, another case initiated by Ukraine against Russia concerning the latter's alleged interference with the former's access to gas fields and fisheries in several different maritime zones, the Annex VII arbitral tribunal provided a more detailed analysis of the wording of Article 298(1)(b). Noting that Article 298(1)(b) employs the term 'concerning' as opposed to more expansive terms such as 'arising out of', 'arising from' or 'involving', the tribunal held that 'the term "concerning" circumscribes the military activities exception by limiting it to those disputes whose subject matter is military

[180] *Case concerning the detention of three Ukrainian naval vessels (Ukraine v Russian Federation)* (Provisional Measures, Order of 25 May 2019) ITLOS Reports 2019, 283 [67].

[181] Ibid [65].

[182] Ukraine in fact referred to the *South China Sea* tribunal's deference to China's characterisation of its land reclamation activities as non-military in nature to support its argument. Ibid [56].

[183] Ibid [66].

[184] Ibid [68].

[185] Ibid [72].

[186] Ibid [74].

[187] Ibid [75].

activities'.[188] As a result, 'a mere "causal" or historical link between certain alleged military activities and the activities in dispute cannot be sufficient to bar an arbitral tribunal's jurisdiction'[189] In the case at hand, the tribunal considered that the origin or the background of a broader alleged armed conflict was immaterial to trigger Article 298(1)(b), rather 'the relevant question is whether "certain specific acts subject of Ukraine's complaints" "constitute military activities"'.[190] In order to qualify as 'military activities', the tribunal found that the mere involvement or presence of military vessels is in and by itself not sufficient[191] and similarly, 'the alleged use of physical force is insufficient to conclude that an activity is military in nature'.[192] Applying these criteria to the facts of the case, the tribunal found that while Russia's military were involved in many of the activities complained by Ukraine and that there was even the alleged use of physical, these facts could not trigger the application of Article 298(1)(b). As the tribunal explained, not only did the involvement or presence of the military insufficient to trigger this exception but also the actions taken by the Russian military personnel, including the detention or harassment of Ukrainian fishing boat and the alleged use of force either took place within a law enforcement context[193] or was aimed at maintaining civilian activities.[194]

The preceding discussion shows that, despite being the key term of the exception under Article 298(1)(b), no UNCLOS tribunal has explained what the term 'military activities' encompasses. However, what is clear is that ITLOS and the Annex VII arbitral tribunal in the two cases involving Ukraine and Russia adopted a higher threshold for the application of the military exception in Article 298(1)(b) than the *South China Sea* tribunal. The mere presence of military forces or even the use of force by military forces in itself is not sufficient to trigger this exception. In both cases, the tribunals' analysis revolved around the question as to whether they were by nature military and enforcement activities. As has been noted, the line between military and enforcement activities is not always crystal clear.[195] The approach

[188] *Coastal State Rights* (n 77) [330].
[189] Ibid.
[190] Ibid [331].
[191] Ibid [334].
[192] Ibid [336].
[193] Ibid [338].
[194] Ibid [336].
[195] See, for example, *Case Concerning the Detention of Three Ukrainian Naval Vessels (Ukraine v Russian Federation)* (Provisional Measures, Declaration of Judge Kittichaisaree) ITLOS Reports 2019, 345 [4];

of the tribunals to not characterise a dispute as one or the other based merely on the presence of military forces or the use of force, but rather paying attention to the context in which military forces were involved and the reason for the use of force, seems reasonable.[196]

In that light, it is difficult to disagree with the *Coastal State Rights* tribunal's classification of the activities conducted by Russian military forces as law enforcement activities, given that the context in which the activities complained of took place and the purposes of the activities were purely civilian. The same conclusion reached by ITLOS in *Ukrainian Naval Vessels* has, however, been more controversial even though admittedly, the threshold to finding jurisdiction was less stringent as ITLOS only had to establish prima facie in the provisional measure phase. The distinction between military and enforcement activities in this case was more muddled due to the involvement of naval vessels on both sides and the wider context of an ongoing conflict between the two States. Judge Gao in his Separate Opinion to *Ukrainian Naval Vessels* argued while the incident might have started as a law enforcement operation, 'the firing of target shots against a naval vessel is tantamount to the use of force against the State whose flag the vessel flies' and thus turned it into a military activity triggering the application of Article 298(1)(b).[197] This interpretation is reminiscent of the *South China Sea* tribunal's approach, classifying a standoff between military forces of the parties involved as 'quintessentially a military situation' as mentioned above. However, an argument could be made that whether or not there existed a military standoff which cannot in itself be the decisive factor. As held by the *Coastal State Rights* tribunal, what matters should be whether there is a dispute 'whose subject matter is military activities'. Attention should thus be paid to the subject matter of the dispute brought before the UNCLOS tribunal. In *Ukrainian Naval Vessels*, the subject matter of Ukraine's claims was the breach of immunity accorded to the vessels and its crew members. The Annex VII arbitral tribunal constituted to hear the merits of the case will thus need to consider whether a dispute concerning the breach of immunity of a warship is one that concerns military activities

David Letts, Rob McLaughlin and Hitoshi Nasu, 'Maritime Law Enforcement and the Aggravation of the South China Sea Dispute: Implications for Australia' (17) 34 Australian Year Book of International Law 53, 61.

196 The tribunal in *Guyana v Suriname* held that: 'the Tribunal accepts the argument that in international law force may be used in law enforcement activities provided that such force is unavoidable, reasonable and necessary'. *Guyana v Suriname* (n 64) [445].

197 *Case concerning the detention of three Ukrainian naval vessels (Ukraine v Russian Federation)* (Provisional Measures, Sep Op Gao) ITLOS Reports 2019, 345 [33].

and in that regard provide a clarification of what constitutes 'military activities' within the meaning of Article 298(1)(b).[198]

6.2 ADVISORY JURISDICTION

Under UNCLOS, advisory jurisdiction is not explicitly conferred upon ITLOS as a whole but only on the SDC. The SDC is established in accordance with Part XI, Section 5 of the Convention, and comprises of eleven judges selected from the judges of ITLOS.[199] According to Article 191 UNCLOS, the SDC is mandated to 'give advisory opinions at the request of the Assembly or the Council on legal questions arising within the scope of their activities'. As ITLOS made clear in the *Advisory Opinion on Activities in the Area*, three conditions need to be met for the SDC to exercise its jurisdiction under Article 191, namely, '(a) that there is a request from the Council [or the Assembly]; (b) that the request concerns legal questions; and (c) that these legal questions have arisen within the scope of the Council's activities'.[200] Given the clear legal basis, the jurisdiction of the SDC to render an advisory opinion does not cause much controversy.

The more controversial question relates to the advisory jurisdiction of ITLOS as a full tribunal. An explicit provision under UNCLOS and ITLOS Statute conferring advisory jurisdiction to ITLOS as a full tribunal is absent, giving rise to much debate regarding the full ITLOS's advisory jurisdiction.[201] ITLOS finally resolved this issue in the *Advisory Opinion on IUU Fishing* in 2015, in which it found that the full tribunal indeed has the jurisdiction to render advisory opinions.

198 Yurika Ishii, 'Introductory Note to Case Concerning the Detention of Three Ukrainian Naval Vessels (Ukraine v. Russian Federation): Provisional Measures Order (ITLOS)' (2019) 58 American Society of International Law, 1148.

199 Article 35 of the Statute of the International Tribunal of the Law of the Sea.

200 *Responsibilities and obligations of States with respect to Activities in the Area* (Advisory Opinion, 1 February 2011) ITLOS Reports 2011, 10 [32].

201 See, for example, Doo-yong Kim, 'Advisory Proceedings before the International Tribunal for the Law of the Sea as an Alternative Procedure to Supplement the Dispute-Settlement Mechanism under Part XV of the United Nations Convention on the Law of the Sea' (2010) 11 issues in Legal Scholarship 1; JL Jesus, 'Commentary on Article 138 of the Rules of the Tribunal' in P Chandrasekhara Rao and Philippe Gautier, *The Rules of the International Tribunal for the Law of the Sea: A Commentary* (Martinus Nijhoff 2006) 39; Shabtai Rosenne, 'International Tribunal for the Law of the Sea: 1996–97 Survey' (1998) 13 IJMCL 487; Ki-Jun You, 'Advisory Opinions of the International Tribunal for the Law of the Sea: Article 138 of the Rules of the Tribunal, Revisited' (2008) 39 ODIL 360; Tafsir Malick Ndiaye, 'The Advisory Function of the International Tribunal for the Law of the Sea' (2010) 9 CJIL 565.

ITLOS founded its advisory jurisdiction on the basis of a combined reading of Article 21 of ITLOS Statute and Article 138 of the Rules of Procedure of ITLOS.[202] More specifically, ITLOS held that Article 21 of ITLOS Statute, which 'stands on its own footing and should not be read as being subject to article 288 of the Convention',[203] allows the tribunals to exercise jurisdiction over not only 'disputes' and 'applications' but also 'all matters provided for in any other agreement which confers jurisdiction on the Tribunal'.[204] The words 'all matters' in ITLOS's view, 'must mean something more than only "disputes"' and 'that something more must include advisory opinions if specifically provided for in any other agreement'.[205] The Tribunal emphasised that Article 21 in itself does not establish its advisory jurisdiction, rather 'it is the "other agreement" which confers such jurisdiction on the Tribunal'.[206] It thus concluded that the basis of the advisory jurisdiction of ITLOS comprises 'Article 21 and the "other agreement" conferring jurisdiction on the Tribunal'.[207] In this connection, ITLOS rejected the contention that Article 138 of the ITLOS Rules formed the basis for the advisory jurisdiction of the Tribunal, rather it 'furnishes the prerequisites that need to be satisfied before the Tribunal can exercise its advisory jurisdiction.[208] Based on the wording of Article 138, the tribunal then held that these prerequisites include:

> [A]n international agreement related to the purposes of the Convention specifically provides for the submission to the Tribunal of a request for an advisory opinion; the request must be transmitted to the Tribunal by a body authorized by or in accordance with the agreement mentioned above; and such an opinion may be given on 'a legal question'[209]

202 Article 21 of ITLOS Statute provides that: 'The jurisdiction of the Tribunal comprises all disputes and all applications submitted to it in accordance with this Convention and all matters specifically provided for in any other agreement which confers jurisdiction on the Tribunal'.
Article 138 of the ITLOS rules provides:
1. The Tribunal may give an advisory opinion on a legal question if an international agreement related to the purposes of the Convention specifically provides for the submission to the Tribunal of a request for such an opinion.
2. A request for an advisory opinion shall be transmitted to the Tribunal by whatever body is authorized by or in accordance with the agreement to make the request to the Tribunal.

203 *Request for Advisory Opinion submitted by the Sub-Regional Fisheries Commission* (Advisory Opinion, 2 April 2015) ITLOS Reports 2015, 4 [52] [Advisory Opinion on IUU Fishing].

204 Ibid [54].

205 Ibid [56].

206 Ibid [58].

207 Ibid.

208 Ibid [59].

209 Ibid [60].

Applying these prerequisites to the request made by the SRFC, ITLOS found that they were all satisfied thanks to the existence of the MCA Convention which is closely related to the purposes of UNCLOS,[210] the fact that the Conference of Ministers of the SRFC had authorised the Permanent Secretary of the Commission to request an advisory opinion to the Tribunal, and the fact that the questions asked of ITLOS were 'framed in terms of law', requiring the Tribunal to 'interpret relevant provisions of the Convention and of the MCA Convention and to identify other relevant rules of international law'.[211] ITLOS thus concluded that it had jurisdiction to render an advisory opinion on the questions raised by the SRFC.

Given the highly controversial nature of the topic it was addressing and the strong objection to ITLOS's advisory jurisdiction of by large number of States in both the written and oral phases of the proceedings,[212] one would have expected ITLOS to have provided a much more detailed and thorough explanation of its decision to establish advisory jurisdiction particularly in the absence of an of expressed conferral of such jurisdiction under both the UNCLOS and the ITLOS Statute.[213] Instead, it dealt with this issue in fewer than ten paragraphs in its Advisory Opinion. More importantly, ITLOS did not invoke or apply any of the rules of treaty interpretation found in the Vienna Convention on the Law of Treaties (VCLT). It merely recalled the wording of the relevant provisions before offering its interpretation of the crucial terms contained in these provisions, albeit without sufficiently explaining how it reached such an interpretation. This simple reliance on the wording of the provision was most apparent with the interpretation of that the term 'all matters' in Article 21 of ITLOS Statute, which was perhaps the key finding for the establishment of its advisory jurisdiction. The Tribunal neither took into account into account the context of this provision or object and purpose of the Convention as required under Article 31(1) VCLT, nor did it refer to subsequent conduct of the parties under Article 31(3), the drafting history of the relevant provisions under Article 32 VLCT. While mentioning the French text of Article 21, ITLOS also did not see the need to apply Article 33(4) VLCT to seek a clarification of the meaning of this provision in another

[210] Ibid [62]–[63].

[211] Ibid [65].

[212] Judge Lucky considered these arguments to be 'cogent, clear and articulate, as well as considerably persuasive'. See *Request for Advisory Opinion submitted by the Sub-Regional Fisheries Commission* (Advisory Opinion, Sep Op Lucky) ITLOS Reports 2015, 88 [1].

[213] Tom Ruys and Anemoon Soete, 'Creeping' Advisory Jurisdiction of International Courts and Tribunals? The Case of the International Tribunal for the Law of the Sea' (2016) 29 LJIL 155, 162.

authentic language. Furthermore, ITLOS also did not meaningfully engage with the arguments put forward by States in the course of the proceedings to reject the advisory jurisdiction, such as the inapplicability of the doctrine of implied powers, the fact that Article 138 was ultra vires, or even those that supported advisory jurisdiction, such as the arguments regarding the Tribunal as a living institution, suggesting that an evolutionary interpretation of its scope of jurisdiction should be permitted.[214] The regrettable lack of reasoning provided by ITLOS as discussed above has left its decision to establish advisory jurisdiction less than convincing and as such, has invited much criticism.[215]

Not only did the advisory jurisdiction rest upon a fragile legal basis, the requirements for the exercise of such jurisdiction – which as held by the Tribunal are found under Article 138 of the ITLOS Rules – also remain extremely vague.[216] ITLOS did not clarify who could qualify as a 'body' within the meaning of Article 138 of ITLOS Rules to request an advisory opinion. It also adopted a broad interpretation of the scope of matters to which the advisory extends, stating that 'there is no reason why the words "all matters specifically provided for in any other agreement" in article 21 of the Statute should be interpreted restrictively' to include only those concerning the interpretation or application of specific provisions of the agreement conferring it advisory jurisdiction.[217] The unidentified scope of the term 'body' combined with the lax interpretation of the questions that could be requested of the Tribunal give States large discretion to invoke the advisory function of the full Tribunal. This has raised concerns regarding abuse and manipulation as States might be encouraged 'to enter into new agreements, the sole purpose of which is to request for a conferral of an advisory jurisdiction on the full Tribunal over a matter under another agreement that does not confer such jurisdiction'.[218]

[214] Judge Lucky argued that UNCLOS and ITLOS Statute should be considered as 'living instruments' that can 'grow' and 'adapt' in light of changing circumstances and advances in technology. *Advisory Opinion on IUU Fishing*, Separate Opinion of Judge Paik (n 212) [18]–[19]. See also: Miguel García García-Revillo, 'The Jurisdictional Debate in the Request for an Advisory Opinion Submitted by the Sub-Regional Fisheries Commission (SRFC) to the International Tribunal for the Law of the Sea' in Del Vecchio and Virzo (n 115) 135.

[215] See, for example, Massimo Lando, 'The Advisory Jurisdiction of the International Tribunal for the Law of the Sea: Comments on the Request for an Advisory Opinion Submitted by the Sub-Regional Fisheries Commission' (2016) 29(2) LJIL 460; Ruys and Soete (n 213) 161; Yoshifumi Tanaka, 'Reflections on the Advisory Jurisdiction of ITLOS as a Full Court: The ITLOS Advisory Opinion of 2015' (2015) 14 The Law and Practice of International Courts and Tribunals 318, 333.

[216] Ruys and Soete (n 213) 164.

[217] *Advisory Opinion on IUU Fishing* (n 203) [68].

[218] Tanaka (n 215) 338. See also: *Request for Advisory Opinion Submitted by the Sub-Regional Fisheries Commission* (Advisory Opinion, Declaration Cot) ITLOS Reports 2015, 73 [9].

As the basis for ITLOS's advisory jurisdiction is Article 21 ITLOS Statute and 'any other agreement', it is also open to question as to whether this 'other agreement' could authorise ITLOS to address questions which go beyond the scope of UNCLOS. This, in turn, begs the question as to how far ITLOS is willing to interpret the term 'related to the purposes of the Convention' under Article 138 ITLOS Rules. It is worth noting that on 31 October 2021, Antigua and Barbuda and Tuvalu announced that they had signed an agreement which establishes a Commission of Small Island Developing States on Climate Change and International Law, which has been authorised to request an advisory opinion from ITLOS on the legal responsibility of States for carbon emissions, marine pollution, and rising sea levels.[219] It is yet unclear how the specific questions will be formulated at the time of writing; however, the first issue indicated, namely the legal responsibility of States for carbon emissions, may well touch upon legal questions that are beyond the scope of UNCLOS. It remains to be seen whether and how ITLOS may exercise advisory jurisdiction over such issues.

Whatever criticism there may be in the aftermath of the advisory opinion, it seems clear that the advisory jurisdiction of ITLOS as a full tribunal has been established and States are now beginning to make use of this advisory function. As a result, it would seem unlikely that ITLOS will retreat on the question of advisory jurisdiction in the future.

6.3 CONCLUSION

The inclusion of a comprehensive and compulsory dispute settlement system is one of the major novelties of UNCLOS. However, the complicated structure of Part XV as well as the general and ambiguous wording of the provisions contained therein has resulted in uncertainties regarding the conditions for the establishment of jurisdiction and the scope of compulsory jurisdiction. In almost every case brought under the auspices of Part XV, States have raised jurisdictional objections, thus giving UNCLOS tribunals ample opportunity to engage with the interpretation and application of the procedural rules under Part XV.

The picture that has emerged from the case law on Part XV is not one of great coherence. While the decisions relating to Article 283 have provided a

[219] The Gleaner, 'Antigua, Tuvalu to Seek Justice over Climate Change Damage' (31 October 2021) https://jamaica-gleaner.com/article/world-news/20211031/antigua-tuvalu-seek-justice-over-climate-change-damage accessed 25 January 2022.

more or less consistent interpretation of this article and has imposed a low bar for the fulfilment of the requirements therein, a coherent understanding of Articles 281 and 282 has yet to crystallise due to the conflicting interpretation of the specific elements of these articles. Similarly, in determining the scope of their jurisdiction, UNCLOS tribunals have increasingly taken stringent approach to interpreting Article 288(1) and its relationship of Article 293 to ground compulsory jurisdiction on disputes arising from UNCLOS. At the same time, the tribunals have used other bases to expand the scope of their jurisdiction, namely by developing the test of 'ancillary' or 'incidental' jurisdiction and by adopting an expansive interpretation of Article 297(1). As a result, UNCLOS tribunals have the competence to not only deal with law of the sea disputes but also other questions beyond UNCLOS. Even though there still seems be the requirement that these external issues need to be connected with the law of the sea issue for the tribunals to exercise jurisdiction, what this connection should look like remains unclear. Finally, with regards to the limitations and exceptions contained under Articles 297 and 298, due to the different, even contrasting views on the interpretation of these two articles by different tribunals, there also exists great uncertainty regarding the 'right' approach to understanding the limitations and exceptions to compulsory jurisdiction. In the interpretation of all these articles, the tribunals seemed to have been guided predominantly by the intention of the drafters. This is perhaps not surprising as jurisdiction of international courts and tribunals is still strongly rooted in state consent. Even though in the case of UNCLOS, consent has been given by virtue of the States becoming a party to the Convention, the scope of that consent still needs to be determined.

Notwithstanding the inconsistencies in the interpretation of the relevant provisions, a general trend can be discerned in the approach of UNCLOS tribunals to establishing compulsory jurisdiction. In particular, UNCLOS tribunals have had a tendency to confirm rather than decline jurisdiction[220] by adopting a restrictive interpretation of the exceptions to jurisdiction, expanding the scope of the subject matter that can fall within jurisdiction

[220] ITLOS has only declined jurisdiction over an entire case in *M/V Louisa*. The Annex VII arbitral tribunal has only found it lacked jurisdiction in *Southern Bluefin Tuna* and the arbitral tribunal in *MOX Plant* decided to stay the proceedings pending a case between the UK and Ireland. Note, however, that UNCLOS tribunals have more frequently found that they lacked jurisdiction over one or two submissions of the case, but still retained jurisdiction for other submissions. See, for example, *Chagos MPA* (n 21), *South China Sea Arbitration*, Award on Jurisdiction and Admissibility (n 26), *Coastal State's Rights* (n 21).

and establishing a high threshold for the invocation of other dispute settlement procedures. The reinforcement of compulsory jurisdiction has enabled UNCLOS tribunals to hear the majority of cases brought by States, thereby increasing the opportunity to develop the law. In a similar vein, the fact that ITLOS has confirmed that it too can exercise advisory jurisdiction has certainly opened a wider door for the Tribunal to add its voice to questions of law of the sea.

7

Contribution of UNCLOS Tribunals to the Development of the Law of the Sea

7.1 TAKING STOCK OF UNCLOS TRIBUNALS' CONTRIBUTION TO THE DEVELOPMENT OF THE LAW OF THE SEA

Chapters 2–6 have examined in detail the United Nations Convention on the Law of the Sea (UNCLOS) tribunals' clarification of the rules and principles of the law of the sea in various areas. Based on the analysis in these chapters, this section takes stock of the contribution of UNCLOS tribunals to the development of the law of sea, specifically looking into the areas of the law of the sea in which the contribution has been most prominent (Section 7.1.1) and the types of contribution that have been made (Section 7.1.2). As analysed in Chapter 1, the contribution of a court or tribunal to the development of the law does not only depend on the answer given but also on the legal reasoning that accompanies it. Section 7.1.3 thus examines the interpretative methods that UNCLOS tribunals have employed in the course of deciding their disputes or rendering advisory opinions.

7.1.1 *Types of Contribution*

The types of contributions made by international courts or tribunals to the development of the law, as mentioned in Chapter 1, can take three main forms, namely (i) defining the scope of rights and obligations under UNCLOS, (ii) giving meaning to vague terms under the Convention and (iii) confirming a rule of customary international law. The following summarises the contribution of UNCLOS tribunals made in each of these categories.

7.1.1.1 Defining the Scope and Content of Rights and Obligations under UNCLOS

First, UNCLOS tribunals have helped to define the nature and the extent of coastal States' and flag States' rights and obligations in the exclusive economic zone (EEZ) and continental shelf.

With regards to coastal States, the *South China Sea* tribunal not only confirmed the exclusive nature of coastal States' sovereign rights in the EEZ but also adopted a broad understanding of this exclusivity. In particular, coastal States' exclusive sovereign rights both require non-coastal States' compliance with the coastal State's fishing laws and preclude any laws or regulations by non-coastal States which purport to have a deterring effect on the coastal States' exercise of sovereign rights in the EEZ, even when those laws and regulations are not effectively enforced on the ground.[1] The exclusive nature of coastal States' sovereign rights in the EEZ is further reinforced by the finding in *South China Sea* that sovereign rights in the EEZ under UNCLOS supersede any claims to historic fishing rights that may exist under customary international law.[2]

In the exercise of its sovereign rights, ITLOS clarified that the scope of coastal States' regulatory power extends to any activity which has a direct connection with fishing, such as bunkering of fishing vessels as seen in *Virginia G*. Coastal States' regulatory power has thus been given a broad scope, particularly as compared to previous case law, beyond the specified list found under UNCLOS. Furthermore, coastal States' enforcement power with regards to both living and non-living resources in the EEZ has also been elucidated, albeit not to the same degree of clarity as with the regulatory power. By examining the permissibility of the confiscation of vessels as an enforcement measure regarding alleged violations of fisheries law its EEZ, ITLOS made clear in *Virginia G* that coastal States' enforcement measures could go beyond those explicitly provided for under Article 73(1), but only insofar as it is 'necessary' to enforce their rules and regulations. Regrettably, ITLOS failed to provide guidance on how to determine 'necessity' or the standards by which international tribunals may assess necessity, leaving the term which is perhaps the most important in Article 73(1) open-ended. The arbitral tribunal in *Arctic Sunrise* for its part confirmed that coastal States have the power to take enforcement measures with regards to non-living resources in the EEZ despite the absence of a

[1] See Section 2.1.1.1.
[2] See Section 2.2.3.

provision under UNCLOS to that effect but did not shed light on the scope of this enforcement jurisdiction.[3]

With respect to coastal States' scope of jurisdiction over artificial islands, installations and structures as specified in Articles 56(1)(b)(i) and 60 UNCLOS, only one particular aspect of this jurisdiction has been brought before an UNCLOS tribunal. This concerns the scope of measures that coastal States may take with regards to safety zones established around installations and structures. The Annex VII arbitral tribunal in *Arctic Sunrise* clarified that under Article 60(4), coastal States are entitled to exercise both prescriptive and enforcement jurisdiction over activities in the safety zone but that the scope of both these types of jurisdiction is limited. In particular, legislative and enforcement measures adopted by the coastal States must be aimed at ensuring the safety of navigation and the installations themselves, and enforcement measures must be taken within – not beyond – the safety zone established.

Turning to flag States' rights, UNCLOS tribunals have made important findings regarding the scope of two key principles, namely flag States' exclusive jurisdiction under Article 92 and freedom of the high seas under Article 87. ITLOS in *M/V Norstar* and the Annex VII arbitral tribunal in *Enrica Lexie* both found that the freedom of the high seas entitles the flag State to be free not only from the physical interference or enforcement on the high seas, but also from the application of a non-flag State's criminal and customs laws to the high seas as well as its criminalisation of activities carried out by foreign ships. The broad scope of freedom of navigation also resulted in a broad scope of flag State exclusive jurisdiction due to the close relationship between the two principles. Both tribunals interpreted the scope of flag State exclusive jurisdiction to include not only exclusive enforcement jurisdiction as has long been assumed but also exclusive prescriptive jurisdiction. The tribunals' expansive interpretation of the scope of flag State exclusive jurisdiction and freedom of navigation has undoubtedly bolstered the primacy of flag State in the high seas and, albeit to a more limited extent, in the EEZ.[4]

With respect to flag States' obligations, UNCLOS tribunals have contributed to clarifying the scope of flag States' obligation to ensure safety at sea and the obligation to ensure that vessels flying their flags do not engage in IUU fishing in the EEZ of another States. The *South China Sea* tribunal confirmed that the scope of flag States' obligation to 'ensure safety at sea' is informed by 'generally accepted' external regulations, procedures and

[3] See Section 2.1.1.2.

[4] See Section 3.2.

practices as stipulated under Article 94(5) and shed light on the threshold for international regulations, procedures and practices to be considered 'generally accepted'. Further, notwithstanding the absence of such an obligation under UNCLOS, ITLOS in the *Advisory Opinion on IUU Fishing* confirmed that flag States have an 'obligation to ensure' that vessels flying their flags do not conduct IUU fishing activities in the EEZ of another State.

UNCLOS tribunals have also clarified the scope of the obligation to protect and preserve the marine environment under UNCLOS. In particular, ITLOS in *Southern Bluefin Tuna* or the Annex VII arbitral tribunals in *Chagos MPA* and *South China Sea* found that in addition to the prevention of marine pollution – the main focus of Part XII – the protection and preservation of the marine environment under UNCLOS also includes the conservation of marine living resources, the preservation of biodiversity and protection of the ecosystem. More significantly, UNCLOS tribunals have read the obligation to protect and preserve the marine environment found in Article 192 as one of due diligence whose content is informed by other provisions of Part XII as well as specific obligations set out in other international agreements. As a result, the scope of the obligation to protect and preserve the marine environment under Article 192 has greatly expanded. Beyond this general obligation, ITLOS also managed to clarify the content of the obligation to cooperate, albeit mostly in the prevention of marine pollution, and the obligation to conduct environmental impact assessments (EIAs).

7.1.1.2 Giving Substance to General or Undefined Concepts

Defining the scope of rights and obligations and giving substance to vague concepts are not always distinct exercises. Through the clarification of vague concepts, UNCLOS tribunals also clarify the scope of certain rights and obligations. For example, as discussed above, the interpretation of the scope of coastal States' enforcement power centres on the term 'necessary'. At the same time, UNCLOS is replete with terms and concepts which are either undefined and thus entirely open-ended or whose definition remains vague.[5] Many of these terms are key to effective implementation of the Convention. This section thus proceeds on the premise that giving substance to vague terms constitutes a separate contribution worthy of scrutiny in its own right.

Some of the key terms and concepts which UNCLOS tribunals have been asked to examine include, in no order of importance: the concepts of 'coastal

5 For a non-exhaustive list of undefined terms under UNCLOS, see: George K Walker, *Definitions for the Law of the Sea: Terms Not Defined by the 1982 Convention* (Brill 2011).

State' and 'flag State', 'reasonable bond', 'due regard', 'responsibility to ensure', 'natural prolongation', 'historic rights', 'rocks'. In so doing, UNLOS tribunals have also contributed to distinguishing concepts falling within a certain category, such as the category insular features (islands, rocks, artificial islands, installations, and structures) or historic claims (historic bays, historic title, historic waters and historic rights). The tribunals have also contributed to clarifying the relationship between terms which are closely related ('entitlement' and 'outer limits of the continental shelf') or are often confusingly used in an interchangeable manner ('delimitation' and 'delineation').

UNCLOS tribunals have not to date interpreted the term 'coastal State'. While the applicants in *Chagos MPA* and *Coastal State Rights* had directly requested the Annex VII arbitral tribunals to do so, both tribunals found that the task of interpretating the term 'coastal State' essentially amounted to deciding on a territorial sovereignty dispute which fell beyond their scope of jurisdiction.[6] However, the *Chagos MPA* tribunal made a brief observation that the term 'coastal State' 'is not defined in the Convention, although its usage in the text makes evident that it was intended to denote a State having a sea coast, as distinct from a land-locked State'.[7] Similarly, UNCLOS tribunals have not defined the term 'flag State'. However, they have shed light on this concept through the clarification of the concept 'nationality of the ship' which establishes the link between the State and the flag under Article 91. In *M/V Saiga*, ITLOS made clear that the determination of the nationality of the ship is entirely based on whether the ship has been complied with domestic law regulating the granting of nationality to ships, including ship registration. In this connection, ITLOS has clarified that the requirement of a 'genuine link' between the State and the ship does not constitute a condition or a prerequisite for a vessel to fly the flag of a State. Instead, 'genuine link' has been interpreted as the State's exercise of effective jurisdiction and control over that ship in order to ensure that it operates in accordance with international standards.

'Reasonable bond' is without a doubt the most important term in Article 73(2) which provides for the prompt release procedure under UNCLOS. If one envisages the prompt release procedure as a scale to balance the rights of coastal States and flag States, 'reasonable bond' is the fulcrum on which this scale operates. The clarification of what is considered 'reasonable' and what constitutes a 'bond' is therefore crucial in the operation of prompt release

6 See Section 6.1.2.3.

7 *Chagos Marine Protected Area Arbitration (Mauritius v United Kingdom)* (2015) RIAA XXI 359 [203].

proceedings. ITLOS has developed a list of relevant factors to assess the reasonableness of the bond imposed by the coastal State. This list has seen little change since the first cases and contains mostly quantifiable factors. However, the assessment of one of these factors, namely the gravity of the offence, has evolved over time. While the gravity of the offence was only based on the penalty imposed under the coastal State's domestic law in earlier cases, ITLOS gradually started to show willingness to also consider coastal States' international commitments in the conservation of marine resources. This progress clearly demonstrated ITLOS's increased awareness of the significance of sustainable fishing.

The obligation of 'due regard' found under Articles 56(2) and 58(3) symbolises the mutuality in the relationship of the coastal State and other States and the balance to be struck between the rights and the duties of the coastal State and those of other States in the EEZ. The arbitral tribunals in *Chagos MPA*, *South China Sea* and *Arctic Sunrise* have interpreted the obligation of due regard to contain both the procedural component– requiring consultation between coastal States and other States – and the substantive component requiring a balancing exercise between the rights and the interests of those involved. The relevant decisions have shown that the balancing exercise does not require that the two sets of rights at stake be given equal weight, but that the significance of the rights in question should inform the decision as to which set of rights prevails in the balancing exercise.

Turning to 'natural prolongation', this term has long held a special position in the legal regime for the continental shelf as it forms the basis of a coastal State's entitlement to a continental shelf as defined under Article 76(1). However, this term had never been properly defined either under UNCLOS or by international courts. ITLOS in *Bangladesh/Myanmar*, followed by the Annex VII tribunal in *Bangladesh/India*, were the first tribunals to spell out the meaning of 'natural prolongation' under UNCLOS. They clarified that the term 'natural prolongation' contained in Article 76(1) refers to the seabed that extends from the coastal State's land territory to the outer edge of its continental margin. This means that 'natural prolongation' is to be determined by the formulae that UNCLOS provides under Article 76(4) to identify the outer edge of the continental margin. In clarifying the basis of entitlement to the outer continental shelf, UNCLOS tribunals have also clarified the relationship between the concepts of 'entitlement' and the 'outer limits of the continental shelf' and between 'delineation' and 'delimitation'. ITLOS and the Annex VII tribunal in the *Bay of Bengal* and *Ghana/Côte d'Ivoire* cases made clear that 'delineation' – which refers to the establishment of the limits of the continental shelf, a process involving the Commission on the Limits of the Continental Shelf (CLCS or 'the Commission') – is independent from 'delimitation' – which refers to the establishment of a boundary that divides overlapping entitlements lying beyond 200 nm. The independent relationship of these two processes also informs the interaction between UNCLOS tribunals and the CLCS in performing their respective tasks of delimitation and delineation.[8]

One of the unique features of the mining regime in the Area is that non-State actors have the right under UNCLOS to participate in the exploration and exploitation activities in the deep seabed, but they could only do so if they are sponsored by a State party to UNCLOS.[9] The sponsoring State, for its part, bears the 'responsibility to ensure' that activities carried out in the in Area are in conformity with Part XI pursuant to Article 139. UNCLOS, however, does not specify the nature of the 'responsibility to ensure' or what it requires on the part of the sponsoring State. ITLOS provided answers to both these questions in the *Advisory Opinion on Activities in the Area* and clarified that this 'obligation to ensure' is an obligation of due diligence and an obligation of conduct. This also provided ITLOS with the opportunity to for the first time elucidate the meaning of the standard of due diligence, particularly in the context of areas beyond national jurisdiction and the types of measure required of the sponsoring State to comply with this obligation.[10]

UNCLOS tribunals have also made important contribution to distinguishing the different insular features found under the Convention, namely islands, rocks, artificial islands, installations, and structures. Broadly speaking, they can be categories into two groups: natural features, including islands, rocks and low-tide elevations and man-made features, including artificial islands, installations and structures. The distinction between the two categories hinges upon whether they are 'naturally formed' which the *South China Sea* tribunal interpreted to mean 'natural condition, prior to the onset of significant human modification'. This clarification, however, still requires a determination of what constitutes 'significant' human modification and a critical date on which to evaluate the status of the feature, on both of which the tribunal was not entirely clear. Within the category of man-made features, Article 60 UNCLOS does not offer any guidance to distinguish artificial islands, installations and structures. While not directly addressing the differences between them, the *South China Sea* tribunal suggested that installations and structures are submerged at high tide and more closely linked to economic purposes

8 See Section 4.2.2.1.
9 Article 153 UNCLOS.
10 See Section 3.3.2.

than artificial islands. Within the category of natural features, there also exists a distinction between high-tide features which includes islands and rocks under Article 121 and low-tide features which include low-tide elevations under Article 13. This distinction, in turn, rests upon the feature's height relative to high tide, requiring a clarification on how to determine 'high tide'. On this point, *South China Sea* tribunal clarified that States retain wide discretion to choose high-water datum in order to determine whether the feature is above water at high tide. Further, within the category of high-tide features, Article 121 makes a distinction between the entitlements of islands and rocks in its paragraphs (1) and (3), respectively. Article 121(3) contains notoriously vague terms and conditions, whose detailed interpretation has been provided only by one tribunal to date, namely the *South China Sea* tribunal. The tribunal in this case adopted a high threshold in the interpretation and strict application of the terms found in Article 121(3).[11]

Finally, the *South China Sea* tribunal was the first to spell out the relationship between different terms originating from historical processes, namely 'historic bays', 'historic title' – which are found under Articles 10, 15 and 298 (1)(a)(a) of UNCLOS – 'historic rights' and 'historic waters' – which are not provided under the Convention. The tribunal found that historic rights encompass historic bays, historic title and historic waters, all three of which imply a claim of sovereignty, but historic rights could also include non-exclusive rights falling short of sovereignty such as fishing rights. The *South China Sea* tribunal also shed important light on the nature and requirements for existence of nonexclusive historic fishing rights. The tribunal highlighted the exceptional nature of historic rights, emphasising on the requirement of a right being at variance with the Convention and on the role of acquiescence in the formation of historic rights.[12]

7.1.1.3 Confirmation of Customary International Law

In the course of hearing cases concerning UNCLOS, UNCLOS tribunals are at times faced with issues arising under customary international law. UNCLOS tribunals do not have the jurisdiction to settle a dispute concerning customary international law due to the scope of their jurisdiction *ratione materiae* under Article 288(1) being limited to settling 'dispute concerning the interpretation and application of the Convention'. Under Article 293,

[11] See Section 4.1.2.

[12] See Section 4.2.1.

however, UNCLOS tribunals have the power to resort to customary rules to resolve a dispute concerning the Convention. As analysed in Chapter 6, while the line between jurisdiction and applicable might have been blurred in some earlier decisions, UNCLOS tribunals have now adopted a more stringent approach to distinguishing jurisdiction and applicable law, and confined its jurisdiction to disputes arising under the Convention. As a result, UNCLOS tribunals would not be the appropriate fora in which a detailed discussion or the development of customary rules can be expected.

Having said that, the decisions of UNCLOS tribunals have not been devoid of consideration of customary international law. UNCLOS tribunals' reference to customary international law has taken different forms. In some cases, UNCLOS tribunals have acknowledged the existence of relevant customary rules and examined their interaction with rights and obligations under UNCLOS. This was, for example, the case with the interaction between historic rights and exclusive sovereign rights in the EEZ as discussed in *South China Sea*. In other cases, UNCLOS tribunals have acknowledged that customary rules apply and inform the interpretation of UNCLOS provisions, without specifying what those customary rules are. An example in this regard can be seen in delimitation cases. ITLOS in *Bangladesh/Myanmar*, for example, found that customary rules are applicable to the delimitation of the EEZ and continental shelf under Articles 74 and 83.[13] Similarly, the arbitral tribunal in *Barbados v Trinidad and Tobago* held that customary law helps to shape the considerations that apply to the process of delimitation under these two articles.[14]

The most noteworthy contribution of UNCLOS tribunals in relation to customary international law has perhaps been their confirmation and endorsement of the customary status of certain rules and principles. ITLOS held in *MOX Plant*, *Land Reclamation* and the *Advisory Opinion on IUU Fishing* that the duty to cooperate had become part of general international law, and in the *Advisory Opinion on Activities in the Area* that the obligation to conduct EIA was an obligation under customary international law. AS UNCLOS already provides for both obligations, it was not strictly necessary for the tribunal to

[13] *Dispute concerning delimitation of the maritime boundary between Bangladesh and Myanmar in the Bay of Bengal (Bangladesh/Myanmar)* (Judgment) ITLOS Reports 2012, 4 [183] [Bangladesh/Myanmar].

[14] *Arbitration between Barbados and the Republic of Trinidad and Tobago, Relating to the Delimitation of the Exclusive Economic Zone and the Continental Shelf Between Them* (2006) RIAA XXVII 147 [223] [*Barbados v Trinidad and Tobago*].

have taken the extra step to confirm the customary nature of these principles. The willingness of ITLOS to do so was nonetheless a welcome contribution to reinforcing the importance of these principles beyond the confines of the Convention. By contrast, UNCLOS does not provide for the precautionary principle. The fact that ITLOS still relied on the precautionary principle to prescribe provisional measures in *Southern Bluefin Tuna* – albeit without referring to the principle by name – thus lent support to the customary status of this principle. ITLOS's statement in the *Advisory Opinion on Activities in the Area* that 'there is now a trend towards making this approach part of customary law' further indicated endorsement of the customary nature of the precautionary principle. ITLOS's decisions, therefore, added authoritative weight to affirming the customary status of this principle, or at least, gave it a much-needed push towards attaining this status.

As is clear, UNCLOS tribunals' confirmation of the existence of customary rules has mainly been in the area of marine environment protection.[15] This is particularly important as UNCLOS was negotiated at a time when international environmental law was still in its infancy. Thus despite their efforts to embrace a more environment-friendly approach to managing the oceans than that in previous law of the sea instruments, the drafters of the Convention could not have foreseen the significant efforts that have been made in the protection of the environment in more recent times.[16] By confirming the status of these important environmental principles and reading them into the Convention, the tribunals have helped ensure that UNCLOS develops in keeping with the important progress that been made in international environmental law since 1982.

7.1.2 *Areas of Contribution*

As dispute settlement bodies, UNCLOS tribunals can only examine legal issues that have been brought to them in contentious or advisory proceedings.

[15] Note that UNCLOS tribunals have also confirmed the customary status of general rules of international law such as Article 31 VCLT or Articles 1 and 31(1) of the ILC Articles on State Responsibility. See, for example, *M/V 'Virginia G' (Panama/Guinea-Bissau)* (Judgment) ITLOS Reports 2014, 4 [430]; *Responsibilities and obligations of States with respect to Activities in the Area* (Advisory Opinion, 1 February 2011) ITLOS Reports 2011, 10 [194].

[16] See, for example, Peter H Sand, 'The Evolution of International Environmental Law' in Daniel Bodansky, Jutta Brunnée and Ellen Hey (eds), *The Oxford Handbook of International Environmental Law* (OUP 2008) 29; Edith Brown Weiss, 'The Evolution of International Environmental Law' (2011) 54 JYBIL 1.

As discussed in Chapter 1, the most important innovations include the introduction of two new maritime zones, namely: the EEZ and the Area, the concept of the continental shelf beyond 200 nm, the regime of islands and rocks, a dedicated Part XII on the protection and preservation of the marine environment and a compulsory dispute settlement system. The contribution of UNCLOS tribunals can be seen in all these novel areas of the Convention.

Looking at the list of ITLOS cases, one can see that the majority of its cases was initiated by flag States concerning the arrest and detention of vessels flying their flags.[17] This has given the Tribunal the opportunity to clarify important issues pertaining to flag States, such as the right to grant ships their nationality and the scope of flag State exclusive jurisdiction. Moreover, most of the cases pertaining to arrest and detention of vessels revolved around the coastal State's interference of the vessel's activities in the EEZ,[18] thus further allowing the Tribunal to discuss coastal States' rights and obligations in the EEZ. As for Annex VII arbitral tribunals, of the ten cases in which the tribunals proceeded to the merits,[19] four

[17] Of the twenty-eight disputes listed on ITLOS official website, seventeen cases concerned the arrest and detention of vessels and their crew. Among these, nine were prompt release cases, four were provisional measures order and four cases concerning the merits. (*M/V 'Saiga' (No. 2)) (Saint Vincent and the Grenadines v Guinea)* (Judgment) ITLOS Reports 1999, 10; *The 'ARA Libertad' Case (Argentina v Ghana)* (Provisional Measures, Order of 20 November 2012) ITLOS Reports 2012, 326; *M/V 'Virginia G' (Panama/Guinea-Bissau)* (Judgment) ITLOS Reports 2014, 4; *The M/V 'Louisa' Case (Saint Vincent and the Grenadines v Kingdom of Spain)* ITLOS Reports 2013, 4; *Award in the Arbitration regarding the Arctic Sunrise (Kingdom of the Netherlands v Russian Federation)* (Provisional Measures, Order of 25 October 2013) ITLOS Reports 2013, 224; *The M/V 'Norstar' Case (Panama v Italy)* (Judgment) ITLOS Reports 2019; *The 'Enrica Lexie' Incident (Italy v India)*, (Provisional Measures, Order of 24 July 2015) ITLOS Reports 2015, 176; *Case concerning the detention of three Ukrainian naval vessels (Ukraine v Russian Federation)* (Provisional Measures, Order of 25 May 2019) ITLOS Reports 2019, 283; *The M/T 'San Padre Pio' Case (Switzerland v Nigeria)* (Provisional Measures, Order of 6 July 2019) ITLOS Reports 2019, 375.

[18] All prompt release cases concerned requests for prompt release of vessels alleged to have violated the coastal State's domestic fisheries legislation in the EEZ. Amongst the nine non-prompt release cases, only four cases (*ARA Libertad, Norstar and Ukrainian Naval Vessels*) did not concern activities in the EEZ.

[19] As of January 2022, fifteen cases have been initiated before Annex VII arbitral tribunals, of which four were terminated by agreement between the parties before the tribunal rendered a decision (*MOX Plant (Ireland v United Kingdom)* Order No 3 Suspension of Proceedings on Jurisdiction and Merits, and Request for Further Provisional Measures; *Case concerning Land Reclamation by Singapore in and around the Straits of Johor (Malaysia v Singapore)* (2005) RIAA XVII 133; *The Atlanto-Scandian Herring Arbitration (The Kingdom of Denmark in respect of the Faroe Islands v The European Union)*, Termination Order https://pcacases.com/web/sendAttach/781 accessed 25 January 2022; *ARA Libertad* Termination Order, https://pcacases.com/web/sendAttach/432 accessed 25 January 2022). One case saw the tribunal declining

cases concerned the arrest and detention of vessels including two cases involving activities in the EEZ, and three cases pertained to different aspects of coastal States' rights in the EEZ.[20] The predominance of disputes relating to coastal States' and flag States' rights and obligations in the EEZ means that UNCLOS tribunals have been given ample opportunity to clarify the scope of coastal States' rights and obligations in the EEZ, such as the scope of coastal States' regulatory and enforcement jurisdiction in the EEZ or the obligation to have due regard. By identifying the scope of coastal States and flag States' rights and obligations in the EEZ, UNCLOS tribunals also provide guidance on the balance to be struck in the EEZ between coastal States and flag States' rights and obligations, particularly in light of new activities taking place at sea as well new challenges facing the oceans.

The second area in which UNCLOS tribunals have left a strong footprint is in the development of procedural rules. This is unsurprising as procedural issues arise in every case brought before the tribunals, usually when preliminary objections are raised by the parties but even by the tribunals themselves in cases on nonappearance in order to fulfil its obligation that the case is 'well-founded in law and fact'. As a result, UNCLOS tribunals have had ample opportunity to examine key provisions under Part XX. However, due to the conflicting interpretation of these key procedural rules, particularly those relating to the general conditions to establishing jurisdiction, such as Articles 281 and 282, and the limitations and exceptions to jurisdiction, such as Articles 297, 298, the contribution of UNCLOS tribunals to the clarification of the procedural rules has thus been more limited than its potential. This conclusion thus challenges the assumption that the more cases (relating to a particular issue) a court or tribunal hear, the greater its contribution is. The larger number of cases presents the court or

jurisdiction (*Southern Bluefin Tuna (New Zealand v Japan; Australia v Japan)* Award on Jurisdiction and Admissibility (4 August 2000) 39 ILM 1359.

20 *Chagos MPA* (n 7); *The South China Sea Arbitration between the Republic of the Philippines and the People's Republic of China (Philippines v China)* (2016) RIAA XXXIII 153; *Dispute Concerning Coastal State Rights in the Black Sea, Sea of Azov, and Kerch Strait (Ukraine v the Russian Federation)*, Award on Preliminary Objections https://pcacases.com/web/sendAttach/9272 accessed 25 January 2022 [Coastal State Rights]. Note that in all these three cases, there was disagreement to different extents and in different forms regarding which State could be regarded as the coastal State. In *Chagos MPA* and *South China Sea*, the tribunals did not address the question of which State was the coastal State, but it still proceeded to examine various coastal States' obligations under UNCLOS on the assumption that one of the disputing parties was the coastal State for the purposes of the case.

tribunal with the opportunity to contribute – and thus in itself a necessary factor – but is by no means sufficient. The jurisprudence produced must also be considered to assess the contribution.

With regards to the other areas of novelty such as the regime of the continental shelf beyond 200 nm, the Area, and the protection of the marine environment, the number of cases touching upon these issues has been relatively low.[21] The low number of cases pertaining to these issues means that UNCLOS tribunals have not been able to establish a *jurisprudence constante*, thus creating a certain degree of uncertainty or unpredictability in the understanding of the relevant legal rules. However the decisions of UNCLOS tribunals offered the first authoritative interpretation for some of these issues. This can be seen, for example, with the interpretation of the relationship between delimitation and delineation of the continental shelf, the delimitation method for the continental shelf beyond 200 nm, the interpretation of 'rocks' under Article 121(3), the interpretation of environmental protection principles in the Area or the interpretation of the general obligation to protect and preserve the marine environment under Article 192. The tribunals' approach to some of these issues, such as the relationship between delineation and delimitation and the delimitation method for the outer continental shelf, has been accepted by States and other courts over time. Others, such as the strict interpretation of Article 121 or the expansive interpretation of Article 192, still need to stand the test of time. The role of UNCLOS tribunals in this regard should perhaps be more properly seen as that of pioneers or trailblazers, kick-starting a slow and steady process of law-development.

[21] Issues relating to the continental shelf beyond 200 nm arose in the three delimitation cases before ITLOS (*Bangladesh/Myanmar* (n 13); *Delimitation of the Maritime Boundary in the Atlantic Ocean (Ghana/Côte* d'Ivoire) ITLOS Reports 2017, 4; *Dispute concerning delimitation of the maritime boundary between Mauritius and Maldives in the Indian Ocean (Mauritius/Maldives)* (Preliminary Objections, Order of 28 January 2021) ITLOS Reports 2021, 28) and one delimitation case before the Annex VII arbitral tribunal (*The Bay of Bengal Maritime Boundary Arbitration between the People's Republic of Bangladesh and the Republic of India (Bangladesh v India)* (2014) RIAA XXXII 1. The protection of the marine environment arose in three provisional measure orders by ITLOS (*Southern Bluefin Tuna* (Provisional Measures, Order of 27 August 1999) ITLOS Reports 1999, 280, *MOX Plant* (Provisional Measures, Order of 3 December 2001) ITLOS Reports 2001, 95, *Land Reclamation* (Provisional Measures, Order of 8 October 2003) ITLOS Reports 2003, 4), one advisory opinion (*Advisory Opinion on Activities in the Area* (n 15) and one case before the Annex VII arbitral tribunal (*South China Sea* (n 21)). Issues relating to the Area arose in one advisory opinion, namely the *Advisory Opinion on Activities in the Area* (n 15).

7.1.3 *Interpretative Method Employed by UNCLOS Tribunal*

The development of the law of sea by UNCLOS tribunals is brought about through the interpretation and application of the legal rules relevant to the case before them. Thus, if we were to accept that interpretation is the principal way in which international courts and tribunals develop the law, then at first glance, the interpretative method that the court or tribunal uses is of limited significance. As long as the law is interpreted and thus clarified, it has been developed. However, the question as to whether the law has been clarified, as argued in Chapter 1, cannot be assessed based only on whether an answer has been provided by the court or tribunal on a point of law. Instead, such an assessment also needs to be take into account on the justification and reasoning accompanying such an answer. The latter prompts an inquiry into the interpretative approaches adopted by a court or tribunal. Accordingly, this section examines the interpretative approaches that have been used by UNCLOS tribunals in deciding the cases.

The departure point for any treaty interpretation exercise would be the principles of treaty interpretation contained in Articles 31–33 of the Vienna Convention on the Law of Treaties (VCLT). The ways in which and the extent to which UNCLOS tribunals have engaged with these provisions vastly differ. In some cases, UNCLOS tribunals explicitly mentioned Article 31 and applied each of the elements of this article in a systematic manner to interpret the term before it. This was seen, for example, in *South China Sea* where the arbitral tribunal explicitly stated that 'the Tribunal must apply the provisions of the [VCLT]',[22] particularly Articles 31 and 32 in interpreting the term 'rock' under Article 121(3). It then conducted a detailed examination of the meaning of the terms contained in this article, its context, the object and purpose of the Convention, and the *travaux préparatoires* of the Convention.[23] In other cases, UNCLOS tribunals cited Article 31 VCLT but would only apply one or two elements of this article. For example, in *Coastal State Rights*, the arbitral tribunal referred to Art 31 VCLT in the interpretation of the scope of jurisdiction over law enforcement activities under Article 298(1)(b), but in fact only examined the wording of this article and not other elements. Yet in other cases, UNCLOS tribunals cited rules of interpretation found in the VCLT and

[22] *South China Sea Arbitration* (Merits) (n 21) [476].
[23] Ibid [477].

held that they were applicable to the case, but subsequently it was not at all clear how those rules of interpretation were applied. Examples of this approach could be found in *Bangladesh/Myanmar* when ITLOS had to consider whether to proceed with the delimitation of the continental shelf beyond 200 nm. The Tribunal cited Article 31 VCLT in full,[24] but it did not apply the elements of this article to the examination of Article 76(8) UNCLOS and Article 2 of Annex II to UNCLOS. Similarly, in the *South China Sea* Jurisdiction and Admissibility Award, the arbitral tribunal cited Article 31(3) VCLT, along with Article 293(1) UNCLOS, as the basis for its resort to the Convention on Biological Diversity (CBD) and the Convention on International Trade in Endangered Species (CITES) for the purposes of interpreting Articles 192 and 194 UNCLOS.[25] Yet again, the tribunal did not engage with this article, it did not explain whether the CBD and CITES qualified as subsequent agreement, subsequent practice or simply relevant rules applicable between the parties for the purposes of interpreting UNCLOS.

Apart from these cases, UNCLOS tribunals have sparingly referred to the VCLT. This does not mean, however, that they have completely ignored the relevant articles of the VCLT. UNCLOS tribunals still resorted to the interpretative principles found in the VCLT, but in an implicit manner. In some cases, for example in *Chagos MPA*, the Annex VII tribunal despite not referring to Article 31, applied all the elements of this article including the 'ordinary meaning' of the terms, the 'context', 'object and purpose' as well as the negotiating history of the article in the course of interpreting Article 2(3) UNCLOS.[26] In most other cases, UNCLOS tribunals have haphazardly applied the principles of the VCLT. They would pick and choose certain elements from Articles 31–33 VCLT and apply them to the case without referring to the VCLT or sufficiently explaining why only those elements were relevant to the interpretation exercise. Three examples illustrate this point. A prominent example of reliance on the wording of relevant UNCLOS provisions can be seen in the *Advisory Opinion on IUU Fishing*, in which ITLOS restricted itself to relying solely on the wording of relevant UNCLOS provisions to establish flag States' due diligence obligation over vessels and insisted that the wording of relevant UNCLOS provisions provided the basis for different the flag State obligations enumerated in the Advisory Opinion.

[24] *Bangladesh/Myanmar* (n 22) [372].

[25] *South China Sea Arbitration (Philippines v China)*, Award on Jurisdiction and Admissibility (2015) RIAA XXXIII 1 [176].

[26] *Chagos MPA* (n 7) [499]–[504].

The second example concerns UNCLOS tribunals' reference to subsequent practice or subsequent developments as recorded in domestic legislation or international instruments to assist them in giving meaning to certain terms used under UNCLOS or in determining whether certain activities or principles are compatible with UNCLOS. For instance, in *M/V Saiga*, ITLOS referred to the 1986 Convention on the Conditions for the Registration of Ships, the 1993 Food and Agriculture Organization (FAO) Compliance Agreement and the UNFSA to interpret the requirement of 'genuine link' between a ship and a flag state in establishing the nationality of ship under Article 94.[27] In *Virginia G*, ITLOS took into account the definitions of 'fishing' and 'fishing-related' activities in several international agreements, most of which came into force after UNCLOS, which establish the close connection between fishing and bunkering activities.[28] It also referred to national legislation which recognises the right of the coastal State to regulate bunkering activities.[29] However, ITLOS did not make clear what the legal basis for relying on subsequent practice was, and more specifically, whether it was invoking Article 31(3) to interpret relevant UNCLOS provisions. By contrast, the *South China Sea* tribunal was more explicit in acknowledging Article 31(3)(b) in interpreting Article 121(3) UNCLOS. Nevertheless, even then, the tribunal did not engage a detailed examination of either this subparagraph or a survey of relevant State practice. In general, UNCLOS tribunals have tended to refrain from discussing whether the certain conduct qualified as subsequent agreements or subsequent practice, or from examining whether the instruments or conduct relied upon for interpretative purposes meet the requirements under subparagraphs (a) and (b) of Article 31(3).

The third example concerns recourse to the preparatory work of the treaty and is found in *Chagos MPA*. In this case, the tribunal directed its attention exclusively to the negotiating records of Article 298(1)(a)(i) to determine whether it had jurisdiction to hear a territorial sovereignty dispute.[30] The tribunal resorted to this supplementary means of interpretation under Article 32 VCLT even when the general rules found under Article 31 have not been applied or, if applied, have not led to an outcome that met the requirements under Article 32(a) and (b). In this case, the tribunal's focus on the negotiating history was understandable in light of the parties' focus to the drafters' intention behind Article 298(1)(a)(i) in their arguments. It should be noted that

[27] *'Saiga' (No. 2)* (n 18) [85].
[28] *Virginia* G (n 18) [216].
[29] Ibid [218].
[30] Ibid [214]–[217].

while the reliance on the intent of the parties to the treaty and he identification of the underlying objective of a treaty or particular provision can be seen as two separate interpretative approaches,[31] UNCLOS tribunals have in some cases combined these two together by using the examination of the drafters' intention to identify the objective of the particular provision. This approach was not only evident in the *South China Sea* tribunal's interpretation of Article 121(3), but also in its examination of the preservation of historic rights in the EEZ.

As discussed in Section 7.1, UNCLOS tribunals have in certain cases interpreted relevant provisions so as to incorporate into the Convention developments that have taken place and to reflect current trends in the law of the sea. In that sense, UNCLOS tribunals have developed the law in line with evolving circumstances, thereby maintaining the relevance and applicability of the Convention in the regulation of current activities at sea. In this light, it is worth asking whether UNCLOS tribunals have employed a particular interpretative method to assist them, through interpretation, in developing UNCLOS in line with new developments. Apart from resort to subsequent agreements and conduct as mentioned above, the evolutionary interpretative method is an interpretative tool used by international courts to establish the meaning of a treaty term in the light of the circumstances at the time of its application.[32] Evolutionary interpretation has been used particularly when the treaty subject to interpretation is considered 'a living treaty',[33] which normally includes human rights treaties as well as constitutive instruments of international organisations, such as the UN Charter, and law-making treaties such as those in the field of humanitarian law or

[31] See: Joost Pauwelyn and Manfred Elsig, 'The Politics of Treaty Interpretation. Variations and Explanations across International Tribunals' in Jeffrey L Dunoff and Mark A Pollack (eds), *Interdisciplinary Perspectives on International Law and International Relations. The State of the Art* (CUP 2013) 450.

[32] Evolutionary interpretation has been employed by several courts such as the ICJ, the Appellate Body of the WTO and the European Court of Human Rights (ECtHR). See, for example, *Case Concerning Rights of Nationals of the United States of America in Morocco (France v US)* [1952] ICJ Rep 189; *Legal Consequences for States of the Continued Presence of South Africa in Namibia (South West Africa) Notwithstanding Security Council Resolution 276 (1970)*, Advisory Opinion, [1971] ICJ Rep 16; *Dispute regarding Navigational and Related Rights (Costa Rica v Nicaragua)* [2009] ICJ Rep 243 [63]; *Tyrer v the United Kingdom*, Application No. 5856/72, Judgment of 25 April 1978; *Marckx v Belgium*, Application no. 6833/74, Judgment of 13 June 1979. *United States-Shrimps*.

[33] See Alastair Mowbray, 'The Creativity of the European Court of Human Rights' (2005) 5(1) Human Rights Law Review 57; George Letsas, 'The ECHR as a Living Instrument in Andreas Føllesdal, Birgit Peters and Geir Ulfstein (eds), *Constituting Europe: The European Court of Human Rights in a National, European and Global Context* (CUP 2003) 106.

environmental law.[34] As mentioned in Chapter 1, UNCLOS serves as a 'Constitution for the oceans' and a framework Convention for all uses of the sea. Moreover, it is also a law-making treaty as it sets up a new legal regime for ocean governance and has an integral dispute settlement system of its own. A recent study in fact concluded that UNCLOS has all the characteristics of a living treat due to the 'structure and substance, and the complex legal networks it generates and is situated within' which 'enable it to adopt to changing realities'.[35]

Despite all these characteristics, UNCLOS tribunals have never acknowledged that evolutionary interpretation had a role to play in their decision-making process. There was some vague hint in the *Advisory Opinion on Activities in the Area*, in which the SDC stated that the concept of the 'obligation to ensure', as an obligation of due diligence, 'may change over time as measures considered sufficiently diligent at a certain moment may become not diligent enough in light, for instance, of new scientific or technological knowledge'.[36] However, the SDC did not take this matter further. In contentious cases, some States parties appearing before UNCLOS tribunals have called on the tribunals to adopt an evolutionary interpretation of UNCLOS provisions. However, UNCLOS tribunals have all rejected such an invitation. For example, in *Virginia G*, Guinea-Bissau advocated for 'an evolutionary interpretation of the Convention' to recognise the regulation of bunkering of fishing vessels in the EEZ as falling under the sovereign rights and jurisdiction of the coastal State.[37] ITLOS did not respond to this argument in its judgment. In *Chagos MPA*, Mauritius, in arguing for the tribunal's jurisdiction over territorial sovereignty, called for 'an evolutionary process in the application of compulsory dispute settlement under the Convention'.[38] The Annex VII tribunal, however, rejected this evolutionary approach for several reasons, one of which being that an expansion of jurisdiction to cover matters of land sovereignty 'would do violence to the intent of the drafters of the Convention'.[39]

In the same vein, UNCLOS tribunals have not expressly acknowledged that the Convention is a 'living treaty'. An examination of the case law of both

[34] Daniel Moeckli and Nigel D White, 'Treaties as "Living Instruments"' in Dino Kritsiotis and Michael Bowman (eds), *Conceptual and Contextual Perspectives on the Modern Law of Treaties* (CUP, forthcoming).

[35] Richard Barnes, 'The Continuing Vitality of UNCLOS' in Jill Barrett and Richard Barnes (eds), *Law of the Sea: UNCLOS as a Living Treaty* (British Institute of International and Comparative Law 2017) 487.

[36] *Advisory Opinion on Activities in the Area* (n 15) [117].

[37] *Virginia G* (n 18) [187].

[38] *Chagos MPA* (n 7) [200].

[39] Ibid [219].

ITLOS and Annex VII arbitral tribunals shows that the notion of 'living treaty' never appeared in the decisions of these bodies. This term only appeared once in the *Advisory Opinion on IUU Fishing*. But even then, ITLOS was merely recalling the argument made by some States,[40] and it did not address this argument in its examination of Article 21 of the Statute. In fact, the only instance in which this term was used was in the Separate Opinion of Judge Lucky in the *Advisory Opinion on IUU Fishing*, in which he argued that UNCLOS, as well as the Statute of ITLOS, were 'living instruments' which '"grow" and adapt to changing circumstances'.[41] As 'the law of the sea is not static' and it is 'dynamic', Judge Lucky argued that 'through the interpretation and construction of the relevant Articles a court or tribunal can adhere and give positive effect to this dynamism'.[42] It follows, therefore, that UNCLOS tribunals have not acknowledged the use of evolutionary interpretation, even though it is arguable that their treaty interpretation exercises in many cases produced results that were evolutionary in nature.

Finally, there have been instances in which UNCLOS tribunals simply provided answers with little to no justification. While courts may deliberately choose to abstain from explaining how their decision was driven by interpretation,[43] the absence of legal justification should in the first place be avoided. The lack of reasoning casts doubts over the quality and persuasiveness of the answer provided, thus creating uncertainty and unclarity in the understanding of the rule under interpretation. The lack of reasoning becomes even more problematic when the tribunal's findings raise controversial issues, as was the case with ITLOS's conclusion on flag State exclusive prescriptive jurisdiction in *Norstar*, or its decision to establish advisory jurisdiction for the full tribunal in the *Advisory Opinion in IUU Fishing*.

In conclusion, while it has been contended that most international courts have central tendencies or to generally prefer certain types of interpretation over others,[44] the preceding discussion suggests that there is no clear pattern in

40 *Request for Advisory Opinion submitted by the Sub-Regional Fisheries Commission* (Advisory Opinion, 2 April 2015) ITLOS Reports 2015, 4 [49] [Advisory Opinion on IUU Fishing].

41 *Request for Advisory Opinion Submitted by the Sub-Regional Fisheries Commission* (Advisory Opinion, Sep Op Lucky) ITLOS Reports 2015, 4 [18].

42 Ibid.

43 Pauwelyn and Elsig (n 32) 499.

44 See: Pauwelyn and Elsig (n 32) 450; Claus-Dieter Ehlermann, 'Experiences from the WTO Appellate Body' (2005) 38(3) Texas Journal of International Law 469, 481 (arguing that the Appellate Body of the WTO also has the tendency to rely on the ordinary meaning of the terms of the treaty which has 'protected the Appellate Body from criticism that its reports have added to or diminished the rights and obligations provided in the covered agreements').

the interpretative method employed by UNCLOS tribunals. UNCLOS tribunals have generally refrained from explaining interpretative method adopted. While there is some reference to the interpretation principles in the VCLT, UNCLOS tribunals have not applied them in a systematic manner but instead have tended to give one or more of these means more weight than others in different cases. While the lack of systematic use of interpretative methods does not automatically render the clarification provided by UNCLOS tribunals untenable, it may lead to the impression that the answers were contrived and predetermined and thus more prone to criticism. That said, certain UNCLOS tribunals' findings have found subsequent support and endorsement despite the initial criticism directed at the quality of their reasoning. In the interest of building confidence in the tribunals and to ensure that the contribution is properly recognised, it is suggested that UNCLOS tribunals should not overlook the importance of well-explained and methodologically sound decisions.

7.2 UNDERSTANDING UNCLOS TRIBUNALS' CONTRIBUTION TO THE DEVELOPMENT OF THE LAW OF THE SEA

The judges of ITLOS and arbitrators of Annex VII tribunals, similar to those of any other international court and tribunal, are not 'free agents with unfettered discretion to weigh into all aspects of international law'.[45] These tribunals operate within a legal framework with constraints and limitations which impact the way they decide cases and thus the extent to which they can contribute to developing the law. In order to understand the contribution of UNCLOS tribunals to the development of the law of the sea, this section seeks to examine the factors that may explain the decision-making process of UNCLOS tribunals and thus the room available for UNCLOS tribunals to take on the role of developing the law. These factors include the scope of jurisdiction that UNCLOS confers on the tribunals (Section 7.2.1), the institutional structure of UNCLOS (Section 7.2.2) and the expected and self-perceived roles of UNCLOS tribunals (Section 7.2.3). It is not argued that the abovementioned factors provide an exhaustive account of the contribution of UNCLOS tribunals. However, they can go some way into providing insights on what can be expected from UNCLOS tribunals in terms of their law-development role and thus on the contribution that they have made.

[45] Rosa Aloisi and James Meernik, *Judgment Day: Judicial Decision Making at the International Criminal Tribunals* (CUP 2017) 21.

Finally, while this book uses the term 'UNCLOS tribunals' to collectively refer to both ITLOS and Annex VII arbitral tribunals, scepticism still exists regarding whether they could be viewed as having the same level of authority and impact on the development of the law of the sea.[46] Section 7.2.4 thus offers some observations on whether there are major differences in the contribution of ITLOS and Annex VII tribunals to the development of the law of the sea.

7.2.1 *Jurisdictional Scope of UNCLOS Tribunals*

The contribution of UNCLOS tribunals to the development of the law transpires through the decisions rendered in the course of settling disputes or issuing advisory opinions. The decision to bring cases or advisory requests to UNCLOS tribunals – or to international courts more generally – rests entirely with States. It is impossible to predict with any degree of certainty when States would be willing to do so or what motivates them.[47] However, even when States are able to reach an agreement to settle their disputes before UNCLOS tribunals, the extent to which UNCLOS tribunals could engage in the development of the law is still informed by the tribunals' jurisdictional scope in these proceedings. The scope of UNCLOS tribunals' compulsory jurisdiction has been analysed in Chapter 6. A few remarks are offered below regarding the impact of the jurisdictional scope on the contribution of UNCLOS tribunals to the development of the law.

First, in contentious proceedings, the fact that UNCLOS tribunals have been given compulsory jurisdiction has undoubtedly paved the way for States to unilaterally make use of the procedures provided under Part XV, particularly in long-standing cases involving parties not in favour of third-party settlement.[48] As analysed in Chapter 6, while the interpretation of

46 See, for example, Zhang Hua, 'The Development of International Law of the Sea by International Courts and Tribunals: A Case Study of Due Diligence Obligation' (2021) 9(1) The Korean Journal of International and Comparative Law 132, 152; Peter Tomka, 'The Contribution of the International Tribunal for the Law of the Sea to the Progressive Development of International Law' in *The Contribution of the International Tribunal for the Law of the Sea to the Rule of Law: 1996–2016* (Brill 2017) 192.

47 See: Md. Saiful Karim, 'Litigating Law of the Sea Disputes Using the UNCLOS Dispute Settlement System' in Nathalie Klein (ed), *Litigating International Law Disputes. Weighing the Options* (CUP 2014).

48 For example, before *Chagos MPA* was initiated before the Annex VII tribunal, Mauritius had reportedly contemplated taking the Chagos issues against the UK before the ICJ but was prevented from doing so due to the UK's amendment to its declaration under Article 36(2) of the ICJ Statute, allegedly to preempt Mauritius's intention. See: Kaiyan Kaikobad and others,

the specific provisions in Part XV may not have always been entirely consistent, the fact is that UNCLOS tribunals have rarely declined to exercise their jurisdiction. The tribunals' willingness to exercise jurisdiction has certainly increased the likelihood for them to examine and clarify relevant legal issues and enhanced their ability to contribute to developing the law of the sea.

Second, it might be reasonable to assume that the contribution of UNCLOS tribunals to the development of the law would be more limited in areas which are excluded from the compulsory jurisdiction of the tribunals, such as coastal States' fisheries and marine scientific research in the EEZ by virtue of Article 297, as well as law enforcement with regard to fisheries in the EEZ, military activities and maritime delimitation by virtue of Article 298. However, the exceptions in Article 298 are optional. Not all states have made a declaration under Article 298, and not all declarations have excluded all the categories contained therein.[49] Therefore, the possibility of Article 298 to restrict the jurisdiction of UNCLOS tribunals is already more limited than it might seem. In practice, the only limitation which has successfully been invoked is that relating to fisheries in the EEZ under Article 297(3). But as has been shown, the extent to which UNCLOS tribunals have contributed to the rules regarding fisheries in the EEZ is quite significant. This seemingly contradictory reality reminds us that the limitation under Article 297(3) does not cover *all* fisheries-related disputes, only subcategories of it. Admittedly, this limitatin has impeded UNCLOS tribunals from considering issues concerning sovereign rights of coastal States over fisheries resources in the EEZ, even in a transboundary context in cases like *Barbados v Trinidad and Tobago*, *Chagos MPA* or in the *Advisory Opinion on IUU Fishing*. However, there is still room for UNCLOS tribunals to contribute to clarifying other aspects of fisheries disputes such as the coastal State's regulatory enforcement power, the flag State's obligations in respect of fisheries in the EEZ, or the law regulating high seas fisheries.

'United Kingdom Materials on International Law 2004' (2004) 75(1) British Yearbook of International Law 595, 804; Anthony Aust, *Handbook of International Law* (2nd ed, CUP 2010) 419. Stephen Allen, *The Chagos Islanders and International Law* (Hart Publishing 2014) 284.

49 As of January 2022, around forty declarations have been appended under Article 298, the majority of which do not exclude all the categories of disputes provided under Article 298. See Declarations and Statements under Articles 287, 298 and 310 of the Convention https://treaties.un.org/Pages/ViewDetailsIII.aspx?src=TREATY&mtdsg_no=XXI-6&chapter=21&Temp=mtdsg3&clang=_en accessed 25 January 2022.

Third, the contribution of UNCLOS tribunals does not seem to depend on whether the legal findings were made in a contentious or advisory proceedings. While ITLOS has only rendered two advisory opinions to date, the pronouncements made in these advisory opinions carry important weight in clarifying the pertinent legal issues. In fact, it has been argued that advisory proceedings are more likely to give international courts and tribunals leeway to develop the law.[50] As the legal questions submitted for advisory opinions are usually formulated in a more abstract and general manner, and not confined to the facts of the case, the interpretation and clarification of the law in advisory proceedings have the potential to transcend the particular instance and have wider applicability. This is certainly true for ITLOS advisory opinions Various tribunals have adopted and followed the interpretation provided in the two ITLOS advisory opinions, for example, in relation to the nature and meaning of due diligence, the responsibility of flag States for fishing vessels – proving their impact despite the non-binding nature of the advisory opinions.[51]

7.2.2 *Position of UNCLOS Tribunals within the Institutional Architecture of the Law of the Sea*

UNCLOS, whilst termed the 'Constitutions for the Oceans', is but one component of international legal framework regulating uses of the oceans. From an institutional perspective, the framework for ocean governance 'has a complex, multi-level structure, involving global, regional, national and sub-national institutions'.[52] At the global level, UNCLOS itself acknowledges the existence of other international organisation by referring to them as 'the competent organization' and deferring to their expertise for certain substantive

[50] Manfred Lachs, 'Some Reflections on the Contribution of the International Court of Justice to the Development of International Law' (1983) 10 Syracuse Journal of International Law and Commerce 239, 249; James L Kateka, 'Advisory Proceedings before the Seabed Disputes Chamber and before the ITLOS as a Full Court' (2013) 17(1) Max Planck Yearbook of United Nations Law Online 159, 161; Kerin Oellers-Frahm, 'Lawmaking Through Advisory Opinions?' in Armin von Bogdandy and Ingo Venzke (eds), *International Judicial Lawmaking: On Public Authority and Democratic Legitimation in Global Governance* (Springer 2012) 86.

[51] Robin Churchill, while critical of the extent to which UNCLOS tribunals have contributed to the development of the law, acknowledged that the development of the sea by UNCLOS tribunals has been greater in the two advisory opinions. See: Robin Churchill, '"Compulsory" Dispute Settlement under the United Nations Convention on the Law of the Sea – How Has It Operated?' (Dispute Settlement in the Law of the Sea and Beyond, University of Tromsø, 26–28 May 2016) www.jus.uio.no/pluricourts/english/blog/guests/2016-06-09-churchill-unclos-pt-2.html accessed 25 January 2022.

[52] Donald R Rothwell and Tim Stephens, *The International Law of the Sea* (2nd ed, Hart Publishing 2016) 525.

issues, such as the International Maritime Organization (IMO) with regards to navigation, shipping and marine pollution or the FAO in the field of fisheries. At the same time, UNCLOS also contributes to the institutional architecture of the law of the sea by creating new institutions, namely dispute settlement bodies, including ITLOS as a permanent tribunal, the CLCS and the International Seabed Authority (ISA). However, unlike other framework conventions,[53] UNCLOS does not establish a new treaty body or organisation of general competence to oversee the implementation of the Convention.[54] Instead, Article 319(2)(a) entrusts the UN Secretary General with the mandate to report to all the parties on issues of a general nature that have arisen with respect to the Convention while Article 319(2)(e) requires the Secretary General to 'convene necessary meetings of States Parties in accordance with this Convention'.

What has become clear from this brief introduction is that UNCLOS tribunals do not operate in a vacuum but alongside other international institutions and organisations, each equipped with the competence to develop rules and regulations within its sphere of expertise in the law of the sea. Accordingly, this section briefly surveys the tasks assumed by institutions involved in the law of the sea and how UNCLOS tribunals have interacted with the work of these institutions, with a view to understanding whether and how they may help understand the contributions of UNCLOs tribunals to the development of the law of the sea.

7.2.2.1 Institutions Established under UNCLOS

Alongside dispute settlement bodies, UNCLOS also established the CLCS and the ISA. The former is a technical body responsible for considering data and other material submitted by coastal States and for making recommendations regarding where the outer limits of the continental shelf are located.[55] The latter is tasked with managing the Area and giving effect to

[53] Such as the World Trade Organization, or other multilateral environmental agreements such as the United Nations Framework Convention on Climate Change (9 May 1992) 1771 UNTS 107 or the Convention on Biological Diversity (5 June 1992) 1760 UNTS 79.

[54] This has prompted the observation that UNCLOS is a constitution that lacks a strong organisational structure. See: Niels M Blokker, 'Governance of the International Tribunal of the Law of the Sea: The Role of the Meeting of States Parties to the Law of the Sea Convention' in Angela Del Vecchio and Roberto Virzo (eds), *Interpretations of the United Nations Convention on the Law of the Sea by International Courts and Tribunals* (Springer 2019) 85.

[55] Article 76(8) UNCLOS.

the principle of common heritage of humankind under Part XI of the Convention.[56] In addition, the Meeting of the State Parties to the Law of the Sea Convention (SPLOS) , despite not being an institution established by UNCLOS in a strict sense, is also given limited functions primarily of an administrative and financial nature. The functions of these institutions are now examined in turn.

As discussed in Chapter 4, in *Bangladesh/Myanmar*, ITLOS determined that the CLCS has technical and scientific expertise while its function extends to examining 'issues that are predominantly legal in nature'.[57] ITLOS thus acknowledged the distinction between the function of the CLCS as a scientific body and that of its own as a dispute settlement body by drawing the line between technical and legal issues. While this seemed to suggest that UNCLOS tribunals would not have the power to engage with technical and scientific issues, is the reverse also true? In other words, does the CLCS have the power to provide legal interpretation of the Convention? This question is pertinent as it means that with regards to issues relating to the continental shelf legal regime, there may be an overlap in the functions of the CLCS and the UNCLOS tribunals. This then raises questions regarding how this overlap might impact UNCLOS tribunals' handling of the relevant issues.

The answer to the question as to whether the CLCS have the power to provide legal interpretation of the Convention seems to be in the positive if one looks at its Scientific and Technical Guidelines. These Guidelines state that one of their purposes is 'to clarify its interpretation of scientific, technical and *legal terms* contained in the Convention',[58] and further provide the reasons to explain why such a clarification of legal terms is a necessary part of its functions.[59] Moreover, the mandate of the CLCS is to consider State parties' submissions and to provide recommendation regarding the outer limits of the continental shelf 'in accordance with Article 76'.[60] The concept of 'continental shelf' under Article 76 is not only purely scientific but is also of a juridical nature. Law and science are thus deeply intertwined. It would not be difficult, therefore, to envision a situation in which '[w]hile one interpretation of a provision of Article 76 may lead to the conclusion that specific data proves that the requirements of the Article are met, under another interpretation the same data might not provide sufficient proof in this

56 Articles 156, 157 UNCLOS.
57 *Bangladesh/Myanmar* (n 22) [413].
58 CLCS, 'Scientific and Technical Guidelines of the Commission on the Limits of the Continental Shelf' (13 May 1999) CLCS/11.
59 Ibid, 7.
60 Article 3(1)(a) of Annex II to UNCLOS.

respect.'[61] In the course of assessing scientific information in the submissions, the CLCS may thus have to undertake the task of interpreting legal terms under Article 76 in order to decide whether the submissions have met the technical requirements of this article.[62] As a result, the International Law Association noted that:

> The Convention does not charge the Commission to consider and make recommendations on legal matters. However, the Commission has to be presumed to be competent to deal with issues concerning the interpretation or application of Article 76 or other relevant Articles of the Convention to the extent this is required to carry out the functions which are explicitly assigned to it.[63]

It follows that the line between what could be considered a scientific and what is a legal interpretation of Article 76 may not be as clear cut as UNCLOS tribunals made it out to be in the *Bay of Bengal* cases. As a result, there is an overlap in the functions of the two as far as the application of Article 76 is concerned. In practice, in assessing the submissions of State parties regarding the outer limits of the continental shelf, the CLCS's interpretation of the terms contained under Article 76 also contributes to interpreting this article by introducing new requirements to Article 76 or new rules to Annex II.[64] For example, ITLOS in *Bangladesh/Myanmar* referred to the 'test of appurtenance' contained in the CLCS' Scientific and Technical Guidelines – a concept which is not found under Article 76 – to assist it in interpreting the meaning of the term 'natural prolongation'. Although this was just one example, this case suggests that the work of the CLCS, while

61 First Report of the Committee, 'Legal Issues of the Outer Continental Shelf' in International Law Association Report of the Seventy-Second Conference (International Law Association, Berlin 2004) 3.

62 Bjorn Kunoy, 'The Terms of Reference of the Commission on the Limits of the Continental Shelf: A Creeping Legal Mandate' (2012) 25 LJIL109, 110; Rudiger Wolfrum, 'The Role of International Dispute Settlement Institutions in the Delimitation of the Outer Continental Shelf' in Rainer Lagoni and Daniel Vignes (eds), *Maritime Delimitation* (Martinus Nijhoff 2006) 24; LDM Nelson, 'The Continental Shelf: Interplay of Law and Science' in Nisuke Ando and others (eds), *Liber Amicorum Judge Shigeru Oda*, vol 2 (Kluwer Law International 2002) 1238.

63 First Report of the Committee, 'Legal Issues of the Outer Continental Shelf' in *International Law Association Report of the Seventy-Second Conference* (International Law Association, Berlin 2004) 5.

64 See Kunoy, 'The Terms of Reference' (n 63) 118, 119; Andrew Serdy, 'The Commission on the Limits of the Continental Shelf and Its Disturbing Propensity to Legislate' (2011) 26 IJCML 355; Øystein Jensen, *The Commission on the Limits of the Continental Shelf: Law and Legitimacy* (Brill 2014) 47–92.

primarily of a technical and scientific nature, may have an impact on the judicial function of UNCLOS tribunals. Consequently, although UNCLOS tribunals are not deterred from hearing a case when the question before them may implicate the function of the CLCS, they may still need to take into account the interpretation as well as the recommendations provided by CLCS in settling disputes concerning the continental shelf in order to ensure a uniform implementation of the Convention.

Turning to the ISA, the ISA is an international organisation 'through which States Parties shall ... organize and control activities in the Area, particularly with a view to administering the resources in the Area'.[65] The core function of the ISA is to encourage the development of deep seabed mining, but it is also entrusted with other important tasks, such as the transfer of technology to developing States, the protection of human life with respect to activities in the Area, and the protection of the environment from harmful effects that may arise from such activities. In fulfilling its core function, the ISA has to date adopted three Exploration Regulations which have allowed for the exploration of deep seabed resources beyond those initially discussed during UNCLOS III.[66] These Regulations are thus evidence that the ISA has a critical role to play in developing the legal regime of the Area.

Disputes relating to the Area fall under the jurisdiction of the SDC pursuant to Article 187. One of the reasons for the existence of the SDC was the uncertainties regarding the manner in which the ISA might carry out its responsibilities, prompting the view during UNCLOS III that a tribunal should be established to serve as a check on the ISA's actions.[67] However, Article 189 makes clear that the SDC has 'no jurisdiction with regard to the exercise by the Authority of its discretionary powers' under Part XI of the Convention and 'in no case shall it substitute its discretion for that of the ISA'. This article thus prevents the SDC from venturing into areas which are under the exclusive regulatory power of the ISA. The SDC was very much aware of this limitation itself. In the *Advisory Opinion on Activities in the Area*, the SDC found that the Authority has only dealt with the sponsoring State's liability with respect to prospecting and exploration, but not liability arising from

65 Article 157 UNCLOS.

66 Helmut Tuerk, 'UNCLOS Institutions and Their Roles', Maritime Issues (28 February 2017) www.maritimeissues.com/uploaded/HTBD8/UNLCOS%20institutions%20and%20their%20role.pdf accessed 25 January 2022.

67 John E Noyes, 'Compulsory Third-Party Adjudication and the 1982 United Nations Convention on the Law of the Sea' (1989) 4 Connecticut Journal of International Law 675, 677.

exploitation.[68] It however stated that 'it does not consider itself to be called upon to lay down such future rules on liability'. Article 187 further confirms this distinction between the legislative role of the ISA and the judicial role of the SDC. Apart from contentious proceedings, the SDC also has the exclusive power to render advisory opinions on legal questions arising within the scope of the activities of the Assembly and Council of the ISA. The SDC made use of this jurisdiction in the *Advisory Opinion on Activities in the Area* to elucidate an important obligation relating deep seabed mining under UNCLOS – the obligations of sponsoring States in the Area. In this Advisory Opinion, the two Regulations of the ISA played an important part in guiding the SDC in the interpretation of the 'obligation to ensure'. It is clear, therefore, that the discretionary power of the ISA, resulting in specific rules and regulations, facilitated the capacity of SDC to interpret the Convention.

The SPLOS is not an institution established by UNCLOS; instead it is convened by the UN Secretary-General pursuant to Article 319(2)(a). According to its Rules of Procedure,[69] the functions of the Meeting of State Parties only include electing the members of ITLOS and of the CLCS, considering the annual report of ITLOS and dealing with budgetary and administrative matters. While this means that SPLOS is 'the main forum to which ITLOS is accountable', it is also important to remember that the Tribunal remains independent from SPLOS. ITLOS's judgments are not subject to review or voting by the SPLOS. State parties, however, have the opportunity to comment on the decisions taken by ITLOS each year when the President of ITLOS presents an annual report to the SPLOS.[70] This reporting system establishes a clear link between ITLOS and States which 'helps to guarantee that international judges remain responsive to State interests, thus ensuring that States continue to trust these judicial institutions'.[71] As its functions mainly involve issues of procedural nature, there still exists uncertainty regarding whether the SPLOS also has the mandate to review the developments in the law of the sea or to take decisions on substantive issues relating to the implementation of the Convention.[72] Even though in practice,

68 *Advisory Opinion on Activities in the Area* (n 15) [168].

69 Rules of Procedure for Meetings of States Parties (24 January 2005), SPLOS/2/Rev.4.

70 Blokker (n 55) 88–89.

71 James Harrison, 'The Law of the Sea Convention Institutions' in Donald R Rothwell and others (eds), *The Oxford Handbook of the Law of the Sea* (OUP 2015) 382.

72 See Irina Buga, 'Between Stability and Change in the Law of the Sea Convention: Subsequent Practice, Treaty Modification, and Regime Interaction' in Rothwell and others (n 72) 54; Tullio Treves, 'The General Assembly and the Meeting of States Parties in the Implementation

the SPLOS has taken a number of decisions that in effect amended the Convention, thus going beyond its explicit mandate,[73] there are also examples indicating that the SPLOS does not consider itself having a role to play in interpreting provisions of UNCLOS.[74]

In sum, UNCLOS clearly envisions separate roles for the different institutions that it establishes and to a certain extent their relationship. On the one hand, the relationship between the ITLOS and the SPLOS is mainly that of procedural oversight rather than substantive interaction, thus the impact of SPLOS functions on the task of ITLOS to interpret and apply the Convention may be limited. On the other hand, UNCLOS tribunals and the CLCS are placed on equal footing, each vested with the power to provide legal and technical interpretation and application of Article 76. The ISA, for its part, assumes a different kind of role in insofar as deep seabed mining is concerned, as it is empowered to adopt rules and regulations concerning activities in the Area. The limited practice to date suggests that UNCLOS tribunals have been mindful of the roles of the other two institutions, as well as the distinction between their roles and the tribunals' judicial function. When it was called on to pronounce on new legal rules, ITLOS acknowledged and showed deference to the legislative power of the ISA as seen in the *Advisory Opinion on Activities in the Area*. By contrast, when the task concerned the interpretation and application of the Convention, UNCLOS tribunals did not refrain performing their task, which could potentially overlap with the competence of the other institutions. Furthermore, the *Bay of Bengal* cases and the *Advisory Opinion on Activities in the Area* demonstrated that UNCLOS tribunals have harnessed the expertise that the Convention confers on these institutions to assist them in clarifying relevant UNCLOS provisions.

7.2.2.2 International Bodies beyond UNCLOS

Beyond UNCLOS, a number of global institutions, including several of UN specialised bodies, and regional organisations are involved in the regulation of ocean issues. It would be impossible within the limited space of this chapter to examine all these organisations. Attention will thus be directed to two

of the LOS Convention' in Alex G Oude Elferink (ed), *Stability and Change in the Law of the Sea: The Role of the LOS Convention* (Martinus Nijhoff 2005) 55.

73 Alex G. Oude Elferink, Reviewing the Implementation of the LOS Convention: The Role of the United Nations General Assembly and the Meeting of States Parties' in Alex G Oude Elferink and Donald R Rothwell, *Oceans Management in the 21st Century: Institutional Frameworks and Responses* (Brill 2004) 309.

74 Ibid 209.

international organisations to which UNCLOS refers: namely the IMO and FAO, and the UN General Assembly.

The IMO has competence in the regulation of international shipping and navigation for safety, vessel-source pollution, and maritime security.[75] The IMO plays a particularly important role in developing UNCLOS as it provides 'substantive content to the jurisdictional schemes and prescriptions for cooperation on navigation and shipping matters in the [UNCLOS]'.[76] When UNCLOS refers to the 'competent international organization' in provisions relating to shipping, prevention and control of marine pollution vessels, it is widely accepted that 'the competent organisation' is the IMO.[77] UNCLOS defers to the expertise of the IMO in two ways, either by assigning the task of developing the rules under UNCLOS to States acting through the IMO, or by making implicit reference to IMO's own competence.[78] Moreover, as mentioned in Chapter 3, many UNCLOS provisions uses the rule of reference which refers to rules and standards usually found in IMO conventions adopted before UNCLOS or those amended and further developed under the auspices of the IMO.[79] The *South China Sea* tribunal, for example, recognised the Convention on the International Regulations for Preventing of Collisions at Sea (COLREGS)[80] – a Convention adopted under the auspices of the IMO – as 'generally accepted international regulations' in order to determine the scope of flag States' duties under Article 94(5).[81]

The close connection between various UNCLOS provisions and the IMO thus gives the IMO a unique place within the UNCLOS legal framework. On the one hand, as the IMO serves as the source of rules and standards to which many UNCLOS provisions refer, it plays an important role in interpreting and clarifying those provisions. As remarked by one author, 'if the member States of the organization have diverging views on the implication of a specific

75 IMO, 'Introduction to IMO' www.imo.org/en/About/Pages/Default.aspx accessed 25 January 2022.

76 Aldo Chircop, 'The International Maritime Organization' in Donald R Rothwell et al (eds), *The Oxford Handbook of the Law of the Sea* (OUP 2015) 418.

77 Myron H Nordquist (eds), *United Nations Convention on the Law of the Sea, 1982: A Commentary*, Vol IV (Martinus Nijhoff 1985) 201 [Virginia Commentary, vol IV]; Implications of the United Nations Convention on the Law of the Sea for the International Maritime Organization, Document LEG/MISC/6, September 10, 2008, 7.

78 Chircop (n 77) 431.

79 Robert Beckman and Zhen Sun, 'The Relationship between UNCLOS and IMO instruments' (2017) 2 Asia-Pacific Journal of Ocean Law and Policy 201, 221.

80 Convention on the International Regulations for Preventing Collisions at Sea (20 October 1972) 1050 UNTS 16.

81 *South China Sea Arbitration* (Merits) (n 21) [1083].

wording contained in the Convention the outcome of the deliberations in the IMO can be critical to the further elaboration of its regime'.[82] On the other hand, the IMO has in practice employed terms which do not squarely fit within the UNCLOS framework but which may potentially have an impact on the jurisdictional framework of UNCLOS.[83] It follows that while not explicitly conferred the power to interpret UNCLOS, the ways in which UNCLOS defers to the IMO and the practice of the latter show that the work of this international organisation may have an important impact on the interpretation and application of relevant UNCLOS provisions.

With regards to FAO, this organisation has an important role in the field of fisheries and aquaculture, especially in promoting responsible and sustainable use of fisheries resources. As such, FAO 'provides, both at global and regional levels, an institutional framework within which, … rules and standards may be negotiated but also political commitments adopted as well as concrete measures'.[84] In particular, FAO adopted in 1995 the Code of Conduct for Responsible Fisheries and several other important international instruments in the form of plans of actions, strategies, guidelines and agreements, with varying degrees of bindingness, aimed at strengthening the mechanisms to combat harmful fishing practices.[85] In addition, FAO has regional fisheries management organisations (RFMOs) present in all regions of the world, which are a key component of the international institutional framework for fisheries governance.[86] Given the emphasis under UNCLOS on the conservation and management of marine resources, as well as the need for cooperation between States in this regard, it is not difficult to see the important role that FAO plays and the impact that the instruments adopted under its auspices have on the development of the law relating to sustainable fisheries. In the

[82] David Freestone and Alex Oude Elferink, 'Flexibility and Innovation in the Law of the Sea – Will the LOS Convention Amendment Procedures Ever Be Used?' in Oude Elferink, *Stability and Change* (n 73) 214.

[83] Ibid., 216 (giving the example of the concept of 'particularly sensitive sea areas').

[84] Jean-François Pulvenis, 'FAO, Ocean Governance, and the Law of the Sea' in Harry N Scheiber and Jin-Hyun Paik (eds), *Regions, Institutions and the Law of the Sea* (Brill 2013) 123.

[85] See, for example, The United Nations Agreement for the Implementation of the Provisions of the United Nations Convention on the Law of the Sea of 10 December 1982 relating to the Conservation and Management of Straddling Fish Stocks and Highly Migratory Fish Stocks, 2167 UNTS 3 (4 August 1995); FAO, International Plan of Action to Prevent, Deter and Eliminate Illegal, Unreported and Unregulated Fishing (23 June 2001) [FAO IPOA–IUU]; FAO, Agreement on Port State Measures to Prevent, Deter and Eliminate Illegal, Unreported and Unregulated Fishing (22 November 2009).

[86] For a list of regional fisheries bodies, see FAO website: www.fao.org/fishery/rfb/search/en accessed 25 January 2022.

Advisory Opinion on IUU Fishing, the fisheries agreements that FAO had adopted, in addition to the UNFSA, provided the basis for ITLOS to read into UNCLOS the flag State's obligations regarding fishing vessels and States' obligation for sustainable development of fisheries resources, albeit without any such acknowledgement. Many of the instruments adopted by these bodies are nonbinding in nature, thus by themselves, they have little normative force to compel action by States. However, by incorporating them into UNCLOS, the tribunals endowed authority on them and strengthened their normative value. In that sense, UNCLOS tribunals and the FAO enjoy a mutually reinforcing relationship.

Finally, Article 319 grants the UN Secretary General a review function. However, in practice, the UN Secretary General performs the task of preparing a report on oceans and law of the sea, on the basis of which the United Nations General Assembly (UNGA) conducts its annual discussion on these issues and passes a resolution on the law of the sea. The UNGA has in fact assumed the responsibility to conduct annual consideration, review and evaluation of developments relating to the implementation of the Convention and developments relating to ocean affairs and the law of the sea in general.[87] In reviewing and evaluating the implementation of UNCLOS, the UNGA also addresses the conformity of State practice with UNCLOS. Due to the general manner in which such an assessment is conducted, however, the review 'provides little guidance on the specific interpretations of the Convention'.[88]

Apart from reviewing the UNGA also has the responsibility to '[encourage] the progressive development of international and its codification'.[89] In the law of the sea, the seabed regime under UNCLOS, for example, originated from the concept of 'common heritage of mankind' first introduced by the UNGA Resolution 2749 in 1970. In the past decades, the UNGA has been the forum at which States discuss emerging issues in the law of the sea which are not currently regulated, either under UNCLOS or customary law. For example, in 2015 the UNGA adopted Resolution 6/292 which decided to develop an international legally binding instrument under UNCLOS on the conservation and sustainable use of marine biological diversity of areas beyond national

87 The decision to undertake this role was taken in Resolution 49/28 of 6 December 1994. See also: Hans Corell, 'Oversight of the Implementation of the Global Ocean Regime: The Role of the United Nations' in Davoe Vidas and Willy Onstreng (eds), *Orders for the Oceans at the Turn of the Century* (Kluwer Law International 1999) 340.

88 Oude Elferink and Rothwell (n 74) 305.

89 Charter of the United Nations, 1 UNTS XVI, Article 13.

jurisdiction (ABNJ).[90] Since then, intergovernmental conferences dealing with this topic have taken place at the UNGA, discussing various issues relating to the legal framework that governs ABNJ. UNGA resolutions, as well as conferences taking place under the auspices of the UNGA, furnish the tribunals with evidence regarding where States stand on emerging issues and the path towards which the law regulating these issues is heading. At the same time, the fact that States are still negotiating these issues means that their legal regime is yet to be settled. This may restrain the discretion of the tribunals when requested to pronounce on certain issues, as they should be mindful not to prematurely decide what the law should be before States, the law-makers under international law, could reach an agreement.

7.2.2.3 State Practice

States are the main actors behind the creation of new rules under international law, and thus they have the power to change and develop the law. As alluded to above, States influence the development of the law through collective State actions in international organisations or at multilateral conferences. Apart from that, the unilateral practice of State also contributes to the development of the law. By engaging in a wide range of practice, such as making unilateral statements, enacting and enforcing domestic legislation on the ground, protesting against other States' activities, States generate practice that reflects their understanding of the scope, content and application of the rules and principles contained in UNCLOS. State practice thus provides important material for the interpretation of UNCLOS. As held by ITLOS in the *Advisory Opinion on IUU Fishing*, the laws and regulations of States parties in conformity with UNCLOS, constitute 'part of the legal order for the seas and oceans established by the Convention'.[91] The importance of State practice as an element in treaty interpretation is recognised in Article 31(3) VCLT. In addition, State practice is inherently dynamic, embodying and reflecting new developments and contemporary uses of the oceans. UNCLOS is a product of the negotiations that took place in the 1970s. As a result, in order to remain a relevant 'Constitution for the Oceans', UNCLOS

90 UNGA, Development of an International Legally Binding Instrument under the United Nations Convention on the Law of the Sea on the Conservation and Sustainable Use of Marine Biological Diversity of Areas Beyond National Jurisdiction' (19 June 2015) UN Doc A/RES/69/292.

91 *Advisory Opinion on IUU Fishing* (n 41) [102].

needs to grow and evolve in light of State practice.[92] In this sense, State practice provides important guidance for an evolutionary interpretation of the Convention.

In conclusion, as mentioned in Chapter 1, UNCLOS tribunals are not the only driving force behind the development of the law of the sea. They are merely one amongst the many 'agents of development'. The brief overview of the main global institutions involved in the law of the sea and their functions confirms that the process of normative development in the law of the sea is one that involves a variety of nonhierarchically related actors,[93] each of whom assumes a different kind of task and thus plays a different role in the development of the law. There are the actors who make the law or set out the legal framework for the conduct of activities, such as States or the ISA in the case of the Area. Then there are bodies and institutions of a more specialised character that provide technical and scientific standards and regulations in order to implement the broader principles contained under UNCLOS such as the CLCS, IMO and FAO. Finally, there are institutions such as SPLOS or the UNGA which mainly perform administrative and reviewing tasks. Such broad categorisation does not mean that the division of the tasks of these institutions is fixed or that each actor can assume one role.[94] As discussed, the UNGA as a form of State collective action may have an important role in law-making; the IMO or the CLCS are involved not only in setting out technical standards and regulations but also in the interpretation of legal terms under UNCLOS. The point, however, is that UNCLOS tribunals operate within a wider network of actors. Thus the contribution of UNCLOS tribunals to the development of the law of the sea needs to be appreciated in light of their position in the overall structure of the law of the sea.

More specifically, UNCLOS tribunals cannot be expected to create new rules or principles – a domain already reserved for other actors. As a result, it would not be reasonable to expect UNCLOS tribunals to introduce groundbreaking developments or devise a new direction for the development of the law. Through the settlement of disputes or rendering of advisory opinions, the

[92] Donald R Rothwell, 'The Impact of State Practice on the Jurisdictional Framework Contained in the LOS Convention: A Commentary' in Oude Elferink, *Stability and Change* (n 73) 148.

[93] Ellen Hey, 'Reviewing Implementation of the LOS Convention and Emerging International Public Law' in Oude Elferink, *Stability and Change* (n 73) 83.

[94] In the context of the ICJ, Lowe and Tzanakopoulos have classified the actors involved in the development of the law of the sea into '"codifier", "regulators" and "adjudicators"'. See Vaughan Lowe and Antonios Tzanakopoulos, 'The Development of the Law of the Sea by the International Court of Justice' in Christian J Tams and James Sloan (eds), *The Development of International law by the International Court of Justice* (OUP 2013).

contribution of UNCLOS tribunals will be built upon already existing rules and principles, and thus will mainly take the form of clarifying or refining the scope and content of these rules and principles. The significance of UNCLOS decisions seems to be at a micro rather than macro level: they have mostly been in the form of fine-tuning the provisions of UNCLOS by fleshing out the details of the vague provisions and defining the scope of the relevant principles. In the course of doing so, however, UNCLOS tribunals should not similarly be expected to shape the content of the law by providing technical or scientific standards, as this role is already undertaken by other institutions. What UNCLOS tribunals can do, and have in fact done, is to harness the wisdom and utilise the work of these specialised bodies to help interpret relevant UNCLOS provisions.

Being one component of the network also means that the interpretation of UNCLOS provisions provided by UNCLOS tribunals should be appraised within a broader context of the legal issue in question, taking into account the developments that have taken place in other fora and the need for coherence in the application of the law. This need for coherence on the one hand explains the approach of UNCLOS tribunals in some cases to situate their decisions within the existing corpus of law relating to the issue in question, and on the other hand, provides an angle by which to assess the cogency of the tribunals' findings. For example, as analysed in Chapter 3, one of the reasons why ITLOS's finding that the scope of flag State exclusive jurisdiction to include exclusive both prescriptive jurisdiction has attracted much criticism is that it is at odds with developments taking place at FAO and State practice. In other words, a proper acknowledgement of the contribution of UNCLOS tribunals as but one element of a broader systemic process of change is crucial to both understand and manage expectations of the kind of contribution that UNCLOS tribunals can make.

7.2.3 *Expected and Self-Perceived Roles of UNCLOS Tribunals*

The past decades have witnessed the emergence of a large number of international dispute settlement mechanisms, many of which entrusted with the compulsory jurisdiction to settle disputes in specific areas of law – the so-called new style international courts.[95] For specialised courts and tribunals

[95] Cesare P R Romano, 'The Shift from the Consensual to the Compulsory Paradigm in International Adjudication: Elements for a Theory of Consent' (2007) 39 New York University Journal of International Law and Policy 4; Alter points out that: 'Of the twenty-five permanent ICs operational as of 2006, twenty-one (84 per cent) have at least partial compulsory jurisdiction, thirteen (52 per cent) allow international institutional actors to initiate binding litigation, and sixteen (64 per cent) have provisions that allow private actors to initiate litigation.

which are embedded in a multilateral convention and given compulsory jurisdiction, the assumption seem to be that they are inherently better positioned to assume the role of developing the law.[96] In the particular case of UNCLOS, the compulsory jurisdiction of UNCLOS tribunals is believed to '[make] judicial interpretation a potentially important mode of change of UNCLOS'.[97] This section revisits this assumption by examining two issues: (i) whether the drafters expected the UNCLOS dispute settlement bodies to perform a law-development function when endowing them with compulsory jurisdiction and (ii) whether the UNCLOS tribunals see themselves as having such a function. This exercise does not seem strictly necessary as international courts and tribunals in practice contribute to the development of the law through the very act of rendering decisions, even in the absence of any explicit acknowledgement or conferral of such competence.[98] However, an understanding of the expectation of the drafters and the perception of the judges and tribunals of their roles may help explain whether UNCLOS tribunals have made a conscious endeavour to contribute to the development of the law of the sea.

7.2.3.1 Expected Role of UNCLOS Tribunals

UNCLOS is commonly referred to as 'the Constitution for the Ocean' – a term used by Ambassador Tommy Koh, the President of the UNCLOS III in

These design features explain, in part, why IC usage has also increased.' Karen J Alter, 'The Multiple Roles of International Courts and Tribunals: Enforcement, Dispute Settlement, Constitutional and Administrative Review' (2012) Faculty Working Papers 212, 348 https://scholarlycommons.law.northwestern.edu/cgi/viewcontent.cgi?article=1211&context=facultyworkingpapers accessed 25 January 2022.

96 See, for example, von Bogdandy and Venzke, 'The Spell of Precedents: Lawmaking by International Court and Tribunals' in Cesare Romano, Karen Alter and Yuval Shany (eds), *Oxford Handbook of International Adjudication* (OUP 2013)516 (arguing that '[i]nternational judicial lawmaking is above all a phenomenon of younger and revived judicial institutions that often have compulsory jurisdiction'); Jochen von Bernstorff, 'Specialized Courts and Tribunals as the Guardians of International Law? The Nature and Function of Judicial Interpretation in Kelsen and Schmitt' in Andreas Follesdal and Geir Ulfstein (eds), *The Judicialization of International Law: A Mixed Blessing?* (OUP 2018) 22 ('courts with compulsory jurisdiction have a central law-making function for any legal system').

97 Jill Barrett, 'The UN Convention on the Law of the Sea: A Living Treaty?' in Jill Barrett and Richard Barnes (eds), *Law of the Sea: UNCLOS as a Living Treaty* (British Institute of International and Comparative Law 2017) 27.

98 Christopher G. Weeramantry, 'Constitutional and Institutional Developments: The Function of the International Court of Justice in the Development of International Law' (1997) 10(2) LJIL 309, 312 (arguing that judges 'may be told that they are not making law. They may believe that they are not making law. Yet, in fact, they are making law'.)

his statement during its final session in 1982.[99] This constitutional nature of UNCLOS is evident from the goal set out in its Preamble to set up 'a legal order for the seas and oceans'[100] and 'to govern all aspects of the resources and uses of the oceans'.[101] As a result of the goal to 'govern all aspects' of the oceans in one single convention, UNCLOS became extremely broad and comprehensive.[102] The large number of issues that eventually made their way into UNCLOS meant that it was impossible for UNCLOS to regulate every legal issue with depth or specificity. The Convention instead aimed to provide a normative framework for the regulation of activities at sea.[103] Consequently, the provisions of UNCLOS 'are of varying normative strengths',[104] often containing general principles without specific normative content or ambiguous terms and phrases.[105] UNCLOS thus provides for a

99 Tommy Koh, 'A Constitution for the Oceans' (Third United Nations Conference on the Law of the Sea, Montego Bay, December 1982) www.un.org/depts/los/convention_agreements/texts/koh_english.pdf accessed 25 January 2022. Note, however, that Scott remarked that Koh was not the first to refer to UNCLOS as a 'constitution for the oceans'. This reference was already mentioned by scholars in 1975 and in other government documents in 1976. See Shirley V Scott, 'The LOS Convention as Constitutional Regime for the Oceans' in Alex G Oude Elferink (ed), *Stability and Change in the Law of the Sea: The Role of the LOS Convention* (Martinus Nijhoff 2005) 12.

100 Myron H Nordquist (ed), *United Nations Convention on the Law of the Sea 1982: A Commentary*, Vol I (Martinus Nijhoff 1985) 461 [Virginia Commentary, vol I]. For an analysis of the validity of references to UNCLOS as 'Constitution for the Oceans', see, for example, Scott (n 100); Oran R Young, 'Commentary on Shirley V. Scott "The LOS Convention as Constitutional Regime for the Oceans"' in Oude Elferink (n 100); Ronald Macdonald, 'The Charter of the United Nations in Constitutional Perspective' (1999) 20 Australian Year Book of International Law 205, 220; Rudiger Wolfrum, 'The Legal Order for the Seas and Oceans' in Myron H Nordquist and John Norton Moore (eds), *Entry into Force of the Law of the Sea Convention* (Martinus Nijhoff 1995) 161–185; Robin Churchill, 'The 1982 United Nations Convention on the Law of the Sea' in Donald Rothwell and others (eds), *The Oxford Handbook of the Law of the Sea* (OUP 2018) 45; Scott (n 100) 18–20.

101 Tommy Koh, 'UNCLOS at 30: Some Reflections' in Lilian de Castillo (ed), *Law of the Sea: From Grotius to the International Tribunal for the Law of the Sea, Liber Amicorum Judge Hugo Caminos* (Brill 2015) 107.

102 Rothwell and Stephens (n 53) 14; Philip Allott, 'Power Sharing in the Law of the Sea' (1983) 77 (1) AJIL 1, 8; Arvid Pardo, 'The New Law of the Sea and Some of Its Implications' (1987) 4 J L & Env't 1, 12.

103 Richard Barnes, David Freestone and David Ong, 'The Law of the Sea: Progress and Prospects' in Richard Barnes, David Freestone and David Ong (eds), *The Law of the Sea: Progress and Prospects* (OUP 2006) 3; Scott (n 100) 24.

104 Churchill (n 101) 30.

105 Pardo (n 103) 12 (going so far as to consider 'vagueness, ambiguity [and] silence' one of the major shortcomings of UNCLOS); Bernard H Oxman, 'The Rule of Law and the United Nations Convention on the Law of the Sea' (1996) 7 EJIL 353, 357 (remarking that UNCLOS 'is amply endowed with indeterminate principles, mind-numbing cross-references, institutional redundancies, exasperating opacity and inelegant drafting'.)

'system of governance' in which to address substantive issues rather than dealing with all substantive matters.[106]

Apart from its constitutional and framework nature, UNCLOS is also characterised as a 'package deal'. During the negotiations, the 'package deal' manifested itself both in terms of the inclusion of a wide range of issues, which were of different levels of importance to different negotiating States, as well in the negotiating technique adopted that followed the approach of 'nothing is agreed until everything is agreed'.[107] The package deal was further reinforced by the consensus procedure in adopting the Convention.[108] The consensus approach meant that, as decided by the UNGA, 'the Conference should make every effort to reach agreement on substantive matters by way of consensus and there should be no voting on such matters until all efforts at consensus have been exhausted'.[109]

The combination of the package deal and the consensus approach meant that UNCLOS had to be able, to the greatest extent possible, to accommodate all the demands of 160 States present during a negotiation process that lasted for nearly a decade. This inevitably resulted in a final Convention which was hinged upon extremely delicate compromises. These compromises were evident in the large number of UNCLOS provisions which were either deliberately kept vague or ambiguous so as to cater for the interests of as many

[106] Scott (n 100) 24.

[107] UN Doc A/Conf. 62/WP.10/Rev. 2 (1980). See also: Hugo Caminos and Michael R Molitor, 'Progressive Development of International Law and the Package Deal' (1985) 79(4) AJIL 871; Xuexia Liao, 'The LOSC as a Package Deal and Its Implications for Determination of Customary International Law' (2020) 35 IJMCL 704, 712; Sienho Yee, 'En Route to the Final Shape of the UNCLOS Dispute Settlement System: Some Pivotal Negotiating Procedural Steps Worthy of Consideration by Future Treaty-makers and Leaders in Treaty-making' (2014) 13 CJIL 185.

[108] See: Louis B Sohn, 'Voting Procedures in United Nations Conferences for the Codification of International Law' (1975) 69(2) AJIL 310, 324–52; Barry Buzan, 'Negotiating by Consensus: Developments in Technique at the United Nations Conference on the Law of the Sea' (1981) 75(2) AJIL 324; Wybo P Heere (ed), *International Law and Its Sources: Liber Amicorum Maarten Bos* (Kluwer Law International 1989) 27–28.

[109] Decision made by the UNGA at the 2169th meeting in 1973, 28 GAOR, 24 (Item 40), on the proposal of the First Committee, in A/9278, [16]. Note, however, that in April 1982, the Conference determined that all efforts at reaching consensus had been exhausted. At the end of that session, at the request of the United States of America, a recorded vote on the draft convention and resolutions took place. See also: Albert W Koers, 'The Third United Nations Conference on the Law of The Sea – Some Remarks on Its Contribution Towards the Making of International Law' in Heere and Bos (n 109) 28; Alan Boyle and Christine Chinkin, 'UNCLOS III and the Process of International Law-Making' in Tafsir Malick Ndiaye and Rüdiger Wolfrum (eds), *Law of the Sea, Environmental Law and Settlement of Disputes: Liber Amicorum Judge Thomas A. Mensah* (Martinus Nijhoff 2007).

States as possible, or worded in general terms due to States' inability to reach an agreement on the matter.[110]

It follows from the preceding discussion that, in terms of substance, the Convention excels in breadth but lacks in depth. As a combined consequence of the attempt to regulate all activities in the ocean space and to accommodate the interests of the negotiating States, the drafters of the Convention were plainly aware of the gaps and uncertainties scattered throughout the Convention. However, they accepted them as a necessary outcome of the bargaining process that took place during UNCLOS III.

In order to ensure that the hard-fought compromises would not be tampered with and reduced to empty black letters, the drafters agreed to include a compulsory dispute settlement system as an integral part of UNCLOS. The rationale for the establishment of a compulsory dispute settlement system is captured by the following statement made by the President of the Conference:

> Dispute settlement procedures will be the pivot upon which the delicate equilibrium of the compromise must be balanced. Otherwise, the compromise will disintegrate rapidly and permanently .... Effective dispute settlement would also be the guarantee that the substance and intention within the legislative and language of the convention will be interpreted both consistently and equitably.[111]

As is clear from this statement, the dispute settlement system was put in place with the primary aim to resolve any dispute that might arise between the parties in the implementation of the Convention. However, it is equally clear that UNCLOS dispute settlement bodies were expected to also (i) safeguard the delicate balance of rights and interests of States parties as recorded in the Convention and (ii) provide authoritative, consistent and equitable interpretation of the law contained in the Convention. These two tasks show that, within the framework of the Convention, UNCLOS tribunals were expected to assume roles that transcend the confines of settling concrete disputes. More specifically, the tribunals, as the 'pivot upon which the delicate equilibrium of the compromise must be balanced', were expected to protect the integrity of the Convention as a whole. Put another way, UNCLOS tribunals should not

[110] Pardo (n 103) 13 (remarking that 'there are strong grounds for believing that representatives at the Conference, having ascertained the difficulty of reaching agreement on the substance of an issue, searched for a formula sufficiently vague or sufficiently ambiguous so as not to arouse strong opposition'.)

[111] Myron H Nordquist (ed), *United Nations Convention on the Law of the Sea 1982: A Commentary*, Vol V (Martinus Nijhoff, 1985) 10.

interpret the law under UNCLOS merely to dispose a disagreement between the parties to the dispute. Instead, UNCLOS tribunals were expected to provide normative guidance to States in implementing the Convention in order to safeguard the uniformity and integrity of the Convention.

While UNCLOS tribunals' role was expected to go beyond settling bilateral disputes, the drafters of the Convention did not explicitly assign a particular role of developing the law for the tribunals. The function that UNCLOS dispute settlement bodies were set up to perform bore more resemblance to that of governance.[112] As mentioned above, UNCLOS dispute settlement bodies were expected to provide consistent and authoritative interpretation to safeguard the balance of rights and obligations in the Convention, thereby ensuring uniform implementation of the Convention and endorsing order and stability in ocean spaces. By discharging these tasks, UNCLOS dispute settlement bodies are clearly expected to go beyond the mere interests of the parties before them in order to 'endorse' and protect the legal order that has been set up by the Convention. In a sense, they become the institutional guardians of the UNCLOS legal regime.

Still, the governance function is not the same as the law-development function. That UNCLOS dispute settlement bodies are endowed with the governance function does not automatically translate to them having a law-development role. But can one in fact give rise to other? The governance function is served through the clarification of law and fact that 'reduce uncertainty within distinct regimes as well as within states'.[113] While the goal of interpretation as part of the governance function is to reduce uncertainty within the regime as opposed to interpretation to clarify the law per se, there seems to be an overlap in the two functions. In the case of UNCLOS, while the Convention sets out a framework for regulating activities at sea, it is also repleted with ambiguous or generally worded provisions. By providing authoritative interpretation to safeguard the uniformity of the Convention – the governance function – UNCLOS dispute settlement bodies at the same time fill in the gaps, as well as shape the meaning of treaty terms and scope of the rights and obligations under the Convention to provide authoritative reference points in the legal discourse, thus assuming the law-development function.

[112] The governance function anticipates that the judges and arbitrators 'consider the impact of their rulings on states, persons, or entities not directly represented in the case before them' in order to 'give meaning to or endorse public values. See: José E Álvarez, 'What Are International Judges for? The Main Functions of International Adjudication' in Cesare Romano, Karen Alter and Yuval Shany (eds), *Oxford Handbook of International Adjudication* (OUP 2013) 158.

[113] Ibid 177.

In short, the UNCLOS dispute settlement system was set up to provide uniform and consistent interpretation of the Convention, with a view to protecting the legal order set up by UNCLOS. The drafters of the Convention thus seemed to have entrusted UNCLOS dispute settlement bodies with the governance function, akin to that of an institutional guardian. However, in light of the fact that UNCLOS is repleted with general provisions or nebulous terms whose meaning was deliberately left open as a result of the framework and package deal nature of the Convention, UNCLOS dispute settlement bodies in interpreting UNCLOS provisions would also assume the task of clarifying the legal rules and filling in the gaps in the Convention. It may be argued, therefore, that in performing their governance function, UNCLOS tribunals also perform the law-development function even though this may not have been explicitly endowed upon them.

7.2.3.2 Perception of UNCLOS Tribunals of Their Roles

This section examines whether ITLOS and the Annex VII arbitral tribunals explicitly or implicitly through their decisions acknowledge that they have a role to play beyond dealing with the disputes or requests brought to them and if so, what impact, if any, it has on the way in which the tribunals decided the cases?

ITLOS'S PERCEPTION. A perusal of the judgments rendered by ITLOS shows that it has not once explicitly acknowledged that it does or should undertake the role of developing the law of the sea.

In the two advisory proceedings, the type of proceedings which, as argued above,[114] is normally considered to give international courts and tribunals more leeway to develop the law, ITLOS was still careful to avoid portraying its role as that of a law-maker, emphasising that this task belonged to the States, or the Authority in the case the Area.[115] Instead, ITLOS stated that its role in advisory proceedings was two-fold. First, it assisted the requesting body – the Council of the ISA and the SRFC, respectively – in the performance of its function. Second, the Advisory Opinions would 'contribute to the implementation of the Convention' through the interpretation of the rules pertinent to the issue in question. This second role was further specified by the

[114] See Section 7.2.1.
[115] *Advisory Opinion on Activities in the Area* (n 15) [168]; *Advisory Opinion on IUU Fishing* (n 41) [74].

suggestion in the *Advisory Opinion on Activities in the Area* that the members of the ISA might take some 'guidance' from the interpretation in the Advisory Opinion of the pertinent rules on the liability of the sponsoring States in the Convention,[116] and that '[t]he functions of the Chamber ... are relevant for the good governance of the Area'.[117] In the *Advisory Opinion on IUU Fishing*, ITLOS took the same approach by affirming that 'by answering the questions it will assist the SRFC in the performance of its activities *and* contribute to the implementation of the Convention'.[118]

The first role identified above, that of assisting the requesting body in the performance of its function, is nothing out of the ordinary for an international tribunal when rendering an advisory opinion.[119] However, the second role of 'contribut[ing] to the implementation of the Convention' is particularly noteworthy as it extended to an acknowledgement of a role pertaining to ensuring the effective implementation of UNCLOS legal regimes.

Beside advisory proceedings, the only contentious case in which ITLOS acknowledged that it had role broader than dispute settlement was *Bangladesh/Myanmar*. As analysed in Chapter 4, ITLOS in this case for the first time dealt with the highly controversial question regarding the relationship between itself and the CLCS in cases involving delimitation of the outer continental shelf in the absence of a recommendation regarding the outer limits of the shelf by the CLCS. ITLOS held that '[a] decision by the Tribunal not to exercise its jurisdiction over the dispute relating to the continental shelf beyond 200 nm would not only fail to resolve a long-standing dispute, but also would not be conducive to the efficient operation of the Convention.'[120] It further said that if it did not resolve the case, the parties 'would be left in a position where they may be unable to benefit fully from their rights over the continental shelf'.[121] These statements indicate that in the view of ITLOS, its task was not only to resolve the dispute before it but also to safeguard the system of rights and obligations that UNCLOS conferred upon State parties.

116 *Advisory Opinion on Activities in the Area* (n 15) [168].
117 Ibid [29]
118 *Advisory Opinion on IUU Fishing* (n 41) [77]. (emphasis added)
119 Oellers-Frahm, after surveying the advisory function of several international courts such as the ICJ, the Inter-American Court of Human Rights, the European Court of Human Rights (ECtHR), the Court of Justice of the EU (CJEU), concluded that 'the advisory function is conceived, or at least presented, by the courts themselves as a means of merely giving guidance to the requesting organ in the particular circumstance on the basis of the existing law'. See: Oellers-Frahm (n 51) 90.
120 *Bangladesh/Myanmar* (n 22) [391].
121 Ibid [392].

In addition to express statements, one could arguably seek to determine whether ITLOS views itself as having a broader role beyond dispute settlement by asking whether the Tribunal has been willing to pronounce on issues which were not strictly necessary to resolve the dispute before it. This inquiry is premised on the argument that, 'courts and tribunals tend to decide on the narrowest available bases and if possible to avoid fundamental questions about the legal order . . .. They focus on the narrower function of deciding particular disputes . . . rather than seeing themselves overtly responsible for developing the legal regime.'[122] It follows that, as an *a contrario* argument, an endeavour on the part of ITLOS to discuss or decide on questions beyond what was needed to provide an answer to the questions posed to it would signal that, notwithstanding the lack of an explicit acknowledgement of a law-development role in its decisions, ITLOS does embrace such a role.

A survey of ITLOS's decisions in contentious proceedings, however, provides little evidence of such practice. In advisory proceedings, as discussed in Chapter 5, the SDC proceeded to comment on the status of the precautionary principle under customary international law, even though the precautionary principle was already provided for in the two Regulations, and hence there was no need to determine whether the precautionary principle existed as a rule of customary rule in order for it to be applicable to the case. On the one hand, given the controversial status of the precautionary principle, one could reasonably construe the SDC's attempt to endorse the customary status of the precautionary principle as an endeavour to contribute to the development of this rule under international law. On the other hand, in the same advisory proceeding, the SDC was faced with an argument that, the SDC, unlike the ICJ, did not have the discretionary power to decline a request for advisory opinion pursuant to Article 191.[123] In response to this question, the SDC simply said that 'the Chamber does not consider it necessary to pronounce on the consequences of that difference with respect to admissibility in the present case'.[124] The SDC thus forewent an opportunity to expound on the contour of its advisory jurisdiction under the Convention.

[122] The exceptions are tribunals such as the CJEU and ECtHR, and increasingly the WTO Appellate Body, which see themselves as responsible for the development of their 'sectoral' legal regime. See Lowe and Tzanakopoulos (n 95) 186.

[123] *Advisory Opinion on Activities in the Area* (n 22) [48].

[124] Ibid [48].

The preceding discussion shows that ITLOS has only explicitly recognised its role in contributing to the implementation of the Convention by ensuring the enjoyment of the rights and obligations under the Convention. While not going so far as acknowledging that it has a role to play in the development of the law of the sea, at least such a recognition indicates that ITLOS sees itself as having a role that is not merely confined to responding to the questions put to it, either by international organisations in advisory proceedings or by States in contentious proceedings. Instead, there seems to be an understanding on the part of ITLOS that its answers have a broader significance, in that they contribute to protecting the legal regime created by the Convention and further enabling its effective implementation. These functions are arguably the essence of that of an institutional guardian, aligning ITLOS's perception of its role with the expectation of the drafters as mentioned above.

Even though ITLOS as the full tribunal has been quite reserved, individual ITLOS judges have been much more willing to advocate or acknowledge a creative role for the tribunal. In their separate and dissenting opinions, one can find strong and explicit endorsement for ITLOS to undertake a broader function that mere dispute settlement. For example, in *Bangladesh/Myanmar*, Judge Treves contended that:

> All courts and tribunals called to decide on the interpretation and application of the Convention, including its provisions on delimitation, should consider themselves as parts of a collective interpretative endeavour, in which, while keeping in mind the need to ensure consistency and coherence, each contributes its grain of wisdom and particular outlook.[125]

The call for all courts and tribunals to be part of 'a collective interpretative endeavour' clearly show an understanding of a broader more systemic role for the tribunal than settling concrete disputes. Several judges have even called for an outright recognition of the role of the tribunal in developing the law. Judge Wolfrum explicitly stated that ITLOS is expected to have a 'law-making function' in the context of maritime delimitation. He argued that 'Article 287 of the Convention entrusts three institutions with the tasks and responsibility of interpreting the Convention, and within its framework, to progressively develop it.'[126] In perhaps the strongest endorsement of the role of ITLOS to develop the law, he stated that:

[125] *Delimitation of the Maritime Boundary in the Bay of Bengal (Bangladesh/Myanmar)* (Judgment, Decl. Treves) ITLOS Reports 2012, 141, [2].

[126] *Delimitation of the Maritime Boundary in the Bay of Bengal (Bangladesh/Myanmar)* (Judgment, Decl. Wolfrum) ITLOS Reports 2012, 137.

> It is the responsibility of these courts and tribunals not only to decide delimitation cases while remaining within the framework of such *acquis judiciaire* but also to provide for the progressive development of the latter. They are called upon in further developing this *acquis judiciaire* to take into account new scientific findings.[127]

In the *Advisory Opinion on IUU Fishing*, several judges took the opportunity to voice their opinion regarding the role of the Tribunal. In Judge Ndiyae's view, where there is no law, 'the judge, acting in keeping with the principle of the "court's duty to decide", interprets so as to avoid a non liquet',[128] that is to avoid uncertainty or gaps in the law. The development of the law in this sense takes the form of filling in the gaps in the law. Similarly, Judge Lucky strongly endorsed the power of judges to develop the law by stating that 'judges do not make law, but they can point out deficiencies or ambiguities in the law or give a wide interpretation to an Article or section of a treaty or convention to assist in the development of the jurisprudence of international law'.[129] When Russia declined to participate in the proceedings in the *Arctic Sunrise* provisional measure phase, ITLOS was faced for the first time with a case of non-appearance, a situation envisioned by Article 28 of the ITLOS Statute. However, when examining the consequences of non-appearance on the proceedings within the framework of UNCLOS, ITLOS did not once refer to this Article 28, but instead extensively relied on the jurisprudence of the ICJ on the issue of non-appearance. Several judges were critical of the Tribunal's approach, for they felt that ITLOS had missed an important opportunity to clarify and develop the legal regime provided under UNCLOS. Judge Paik, for example, contended that:

> [T]he legal regime based on a statute and the jurisprudence of the tribunal entrusted to safeguard that regime cannot be expected to develop unless serious efforts are made to clarify some inevitable uncertainties or ambiguities lurking in many statutory provisions.[130]

The first sentence of this statement clearly indicates that Judge Paik saw a role of developing the law through interpretation for the tribunal, albeit in this case for a procedural issue. Beyond the confines of their individual opinions, various judges have also expressed their view, rather firmly, that ITLOS has

[127] Ibid.

[128] *Request for Advisory Opinion submitted by the Sub-Regional Fisheries Commission* (Advisory Opinion, Sep. Op. Ndiyae) ITLOS Reports 2015, 4 [5].

[129] Separate Opinion of Judge Lucky (n 42) [10].

[130] *'Arctic Sunrise' (Kingdom of the Netherlands v Russian Federation)* (Provisional Measures, Order of 22 November 2013, Sep. Op. Paik) ITLOS Reports 2013, 230 [6].

a role to play in developing the law of the sea in various different fora,[131] as well as in their extrajudicial writings.[132]

In short, several ITLOS judges have expressed the view that the tribunal's role should include developing the law by clarifying the content of the rules pertinent to the case, filling in the gaps and stating what the law is when there are no relevant rules to regulate the issue. The question that arises is then: when ITLOS in its decisions does not set out its perception of its own role, what can the views of individual judges tell us about the tribunal's perception? These individual opinions are not, of course, representative of the view of the whole tribunal. Yet they still arguably carry some weight.[133] As commented by one author, the Separate and Dissenting Opinions of ITLOS judges do not only critique substantive legal issues but also 'how the Tribunal applies its decision-making powers'. She further observed that '[t]he effort Judges put into drafting their Separate Opinions and Dissenting Opinions reflects keenly a desire by some judges to focus on institution building that imparts an internal value to the court independent of the opinion of UNCLOS state

[131] See Vladimir Golitsyn, 'The Report of the Tribunal', (20 June 2016) at the Twenty-Sixth Meeting of States Parties to the United Nations Convention on the Law of the Sea, 3 www.itlos.org/fileadmin/itlos/documents/statements_of_president/Golitsyn/MSP_Statement_English_June_20_2016.pdf accessed 25 January 2022; Vladimir Golitsyn, , 'Agenda Item 74(a) "Oceans and The Law Of The Sea"' (9 December 2014) at the Plenary of the Sixty-Ninth Session of the United Nations General Assembly, para 16 www.itlos.org/fileadmin/itlos/documents/statements_of_president/Golitsyn/Statement_GA_09122014_FINAL_EN.pdf accessed 25 January 2022; Rüdiger Wolfrum, 'Agenda Item 71(a)' (8 December 2014) at the Plenary of the Sixty-First Session of the United Nations General Assembly www.itlos.org/fileadmin/itlos/documents/statements_of_president/wolfrum/ga_081206_eng.pdf accessed 25 January 2022; Helmut Tuerk, 'Presentation to the Seminar on Exploration and Exploitation of Deep Seabed Mineral Resources in the Area: Challenges for Africa, and Opportunities for Collaborative Research in the South Atlantic Ocean' (24 March 2009), Abuja, Nigeria www.itlos.org/fileadmin/itlos/documents/statements_of_president/jesus/tuerk_nigeria_240309__eng.pdf accessed 25 January 2022.

[132] Tullio Treves 'Judicial Lawmaking in an Era of "Proliferation" of International Courts and Tribunals: Development or Fragmentation of International Law?' in Rudiger Wolfrum and V Röben (eds), *Developments of International Law in Treaty Making* (Springer Berlin 2005) 587; David H Anderson, 'Some Aspects of the Use of Force in Maritime Law Enforcement' in Nerina Boschiero and others (eds), *International Courts and the Development of International Law: Essays in Honour of Tullio Treves* (Springer 2013) 241.

[133] Note, however, that the discussion relating to the value of individual opinions of judges to date mostly concerns their potential impact on substantive issues of law. See, for example, Manley O Hudson, 'The Twenty-Eighth Year of the World Court' (1950) 44 AJIL 20; R P Anand, 'The Role of Individual and Dissenting Opinions in International Adjudication' (1965) 13(3) ICLQ 788; Robert Y Jennings, 'The Internal Judicial Practice of the ICJ' (1988) LIX BYBIL 31; Gleider Hernandez, *The International Court of Justice and the Judicial Function* (OUP 2014) 119.

members.'[134] The fact that such views repeatedly surfaced in the opinions of different judges, in more than just one case, signals that an understanding of the law development existed, at least in the minds of some of the judges. It arguably indicates that the lack of pronouncement on law development does not necessarily mean that the tribunal was not aware of this role, merely that it was being cautious about acknowledging such a creative role.

ANNEX VII ARBITRAL TRIBUNALS' PERCEPTION. Similar to ITLOS, no Annex VII arbitral tribunals have acknowledged that they should or do have a role to play in the development of the law of the sea. In fact, a perusal of the fourteen awards rendered by Annex VII arbitral tribunals to date shows that a discussion regarding the role that they should play is largely missing. Only in *Bangladesh/India* did the arbitral tribunal allude to the fact that its decision would allow States to benefit fully from their rights in the continental in line with object and purpose of the Convention.[135] This pronouncement is reminiscent of ITLOS's statement in *Bangladesh/Myanmar*, signifying the tribunal's appreciation of its role to ensure the effective implementation of the Convention.

Further, in relation to maritime delimitation, the tribunal added that 'transparency and the predictability of the delimitation process as a whole are additional objectives to be achieved in the process'.[136] This statement suggests that the tribunal was conscious that it had a broader role than merely drawing a boundary line as requested by the parties, and instead should also contribute to developing the law on maritime delimitation. More interestingly, the tribunal held that:

> [T]he ensuing—and still developing—international case law constitutes, in the view of the Tribunal, an *acquis judiciaire*, a source of international law under Article 38(1)(d) of the Statute of the International Court of Justice, and should be read into Articles 74 and 83 of the Convention.[137]

Here, the tribunal, while seemingly just accepting that under Article 38(1)(d) judicial decisions are merely a supplementary source of law, actually gives judicial decisions a much more significant role. By saying that the case law should be read into Articles 74 and 83, the tribunal was acknowledging that it

[134] Anastasia Telesetsky, 'The International Tribunal for the Law of the Sea: Seeking the Legitimacy of State Consent' in Nienke Grossman, Harlan Grant Cohen, Andreas Follesdal, Geir Ulfstein, *Legitimacy and International Courts* (CUP 2018) 187.

[135] *Bangladesh/India* (n 22) [82].

[136] Ibid [339].

[137] Ibid.

is the judicial decisions that provides the normative content and scope of the rules on maritime delimitation. This statement thus implicitly admits that judicial decisions have an important role in developing the law, at least in the context of maritime delimitation. That international courts and tribunals play a law-making role in the delimitation of the EEZ and continental shelf due to the nature of Articles 74 and 83 has widely been recognised.[138] The above-mentioned statement by the Annex VII arbitral tribunal, therefore, is not unsurprising and is hardly representative of the arbitral tribunals' perception of its role on a more general basis.

Other than this one example, the idea that their decisions should have a larger role to play, even if held by the arbitrators, was not expressed in any of the arbitral awards that have been rendered by Annex VII tribunals. One could argue that such a lack of discussion regarding a systemic role on the part of the arbitral tribunals or even the arbitrators reflects the commonly held belief that ad hoc arbitral tribunals are only concerned with settling the specific disputes before them. As noted by one commentator, 'judges who are not out for hire on a case-by-case basis are more likely than politicians or non-judicial decision-makers (e.g. mediators or arbitrators) to consider the long term consequences of their decisions'.[139] What is noteworthy, however, is that the Annex VII tribunals in several cases showed willingness to go beyond what was necessary to deal with the questions brought to them by the parties. For example, in *Arctic Sunrise*, the tribunal examined whether coastal States are entitled to take enforcement measures over non-living resources in the EEZ even when it acknowledged that this issue was neither raised by the parties nor was it necessary for the tribunal to do so.[140] Similarly, in *Enrica Lexie*, the arbitral tribunal also recalled and reaffirmed the finding made by ITLOS in *M/V Norstar* that flag State exclusive jurisdiction included exclusive prescriptive jurisdiction even though this was not strictly necessary as the tribunal was dealing in that case with only enforcement jurisdiction. As mentioned above, the tribunals' willingness to address issues beyond what was necessary to resolve the dispute may indicate a willingness to use the dispute settlement role as a vehicle to contribute to the broader development of international law.

In conclusion, UNCLOS tribunals have not acknowledged that they were consciously taking on the role of developing the law, despite the fact that the drafters of the Convention arguably gave the tribunals a broader role than

[138] See Massimo Lando, *Maritime Delimitation as a Judicial Process* (CUP 2020) 291–308.

[139] Karen J Alter, 'Agents or Trustees? International Courts in their Political Context' (2008) 14(1) European Journal of International Relations 33, 45.

[140] See Section 2.1.2.2.

dispute settlement under the Convention and that individual judges have called on ITLOS to decide the cases in a way that contributes to the development of the law of sea. Nevertheless, for ITLOS, there are certain signs indicating that it sees itself as having a role that extends beyond just settling the disputes brought before it, to that of an institutional guardian. The general lack of pronouncement on a law development role, however, should perhaps not come as a surprise, given the prevalence of the conventional view regarding the judicial function of international courts and tribunals. While UNCLOS tribunals do seem to be guided by the need to fulfil their law-development role, the lack of explicit acknowledgement of a law-development role appears to have little impact on the ability of UNCLOS tribunals to develop the law in practice.

7.2.4 *Ad Hoc Tribunal v Permanent Tribunal: Is There a Difference in Their Contribution?*

ITLOS as a permanent court and Annex VII arbitral tribunals as ad hoc arbitral tribunals differ in several fundamental aspects. As is well known, ad hoc arbitral tribunals are constituted to settle the single dispute brought before them. Arbitrators are selected by the parties to the disputes, with a specified rule of procedure and a set of applicable law to decide the dispute.[141] As a result, the conventional wisdom is that international arbitral tribunals would be more focused on settling the dispute before them and in a way that is most acceptable to the parties to the case, and that arbitrators are less inclined to address issues that go beyond what is needed to settle the dispute. Moreover, as they operate on an ad hoc basis and thus there is no continuity in the decisions rendered, it is often assumed that it would be impossible to speak of a consistent arbitral case law.[142] Ad hoc arbitral tribunals are, therefore, considered to be less likely to have an impact on the development of international law compared to permanent courts.[143] Following this logic, the contribution of Annex VII arbitral tribunals to the development of the law of the sea would also be limited, or as least more limited than ITLOS as a permanent tribunal.

Given the prevalence of international arbitral tribunals in many areas of international law today, the distinction between permanent courts and ad hoc

[141] See generally John G Merrills, *International Dispute Settlement* (6th ed, CUP 2017) 88–95.

[142] See, for example, Gabrielle Kaufmann-Kohler, 'Arbitral Precedent: Dream, Necessity or Excuse?' (2007) 3(1) Arbitration International 357.

[143] John G Merrills, 'The Place of International Litigation in International Law' in Natalie Klein (ed), *Litigating International Law Disputes: Weighing the Options* (CUP 2014) 11.

tribunals may in general need to be reconsidered.[144] The presumed differences between standing courts and ad hoc arbitral tribunals are even less pronounced in the case of ITLOS and Annex VII arbitral tribunals. Admittedly, the design and composition of the two tribunals remain different, reflected in the different procedural rules and the flexibility that is usually associated with arbitration in the case of Annex VII arbitration under UNCLOS. Nevertheless, as Article 4 of Annex VII makes clear, an arbitral tribunal constituted under Annex VII 'shall function in accordance with this Annex and the other provisions of this Convention'. ITLOS and Annex VII arbitral tribunals are thus conferred the same scope of jurisdiction over 'disputes concerning the interpretation and application of the Convention' as specified under Article 288(1) UNCLOS and are subject to the same jurisdictional conditions under Part XV. In other words, when ITLOS and Annex VII arbitral tribunals decide cases brought to them under the Convention, they operate under the same jurisdictional framework, dealing with disputes arising out of the same convention and applying the same body of law – law of the sea and other relevant general rules of international law – as provided under Article 293. It follows that the disparities between these two bodies from a procedural perspective may be more apparent than real.

Furthermore, Annex VII arbitral tribunals are part of the dispute settlement system of UNCLOS. Thus, as noted by one commentator, '[u]nder Part XV of UNCLOS, arbitration and a permanent court may be mutually reinforcing; a permanent court may act in support of an arbitral process pending establishment of the tribunal, thus removing one disadvantage of ad hoc arbitration.'[145] For instance, according to Article 3(c), (d) and (e) of Annex VII, when the respondent fails to appoint its arbitrator or when the two parties are unable to agree on the remaining three arbitrators, the appointment of these arbitrators is made by the President or Vice-President of ITLOS. In practice, many Annex VII arbitrators is or has been ITLOS judges. All of this not only highlights the close relationship between these two bodies but also the fact that Annex VII arbitral tribunals are deeply embedded in and assisted by the framework of UNCLOS. The mutually reinforcing relationship between ITLOS and Annex VII arbitral tribunals further manifests itself in the fact

[144] See Christine Gray and Benedict Kingsbury, 'Developments in Dispute Settlement: Inter-State Arbitration Since 1945' (1993) 63(1) BYBIL 97; Clovis J Trevino, 'State-to-State Investment Treaty Arbitration and the Interplay with Investor–State Arbitration Under the Same Treaty' (2014) 5 JIDS 199; Tamar Meshel, 'The Evolution of Interstate Arbitration and the Peaceful Resolution of Transboundary Freshwater Disputes' (2016) 1 JIDS 361.

[145] Michael Wood, 'Choosing between Arbitration and a Permanent Court: Lessons from Inter-State Cases' (2017) 32(1) ICSID Review 1, 8.

that, as apparent in the previous chapters, these two bodies frequently refer to and cite each other's decisions in deciding their cases. This practice suggests that in their view there is little difference between the value of an ITLOS judgment and an Annex VII arbitral award, and that they 'see themselves as serving the same international legal system'.[146]

Admittedly, there remain some differences between ITLOS and Annex VII arbitral tribunals. For example, as mentioned above, ITLOS and its judges have shown a clearer acknowledgement of their systemic role as expanding beyond settling disputes – something that is missing when it comes to Annex VII arbitral tribunals. Further, the analysis in Chapter 6 shows that the inconsistencies in the interpretation of the procedural rules in Part XV have mainly come from the decisions of Annex VII arbitral tribunals. In other words, Annex VII arbitral tribunals have more frequently contradicted earlier decisions of other arbitral tribunals, either explicitly or implicitly, than ITLOS – at least when it comes to jurisdictional issues. Both observations may thus reinforce the impression that ad hoc tribunals are not overly concerned with the need to maintain a consistent jurisprudence or with the broader impact of their decisions. However, by and large, the preceding chapters shows that the decisions of ITLOS and Annex VII arbitral tribunals have made equally significant contribution to the development of the law of the sea. ITLOS might have had more cases, but the number of cases is of course not determinative of the impact on the development of the law. The cases before Annex VII arbitral tribunals have touched upon some key issues under UNCLOS, such as due regard, historic rights, maritime entitlement, and the arbitral tribunals accordingly have managed to elucidate and provide guidance for the development of these issues in the law of the sea. Consequently, it is difficult to maintain that there the contribution of Annex VII arbitral tribunals to the development of the law of the sea has been more limited than that of UNCLOS.

7.3 UNCLOS TRIBUNALS AND THE DEVELOPMENT OF THE LAW OF THE SEA

Despite earlier criticism and scepticism,[147] the UNCLOS dispute settlement bodies continue to receive and settle cases, thereby contributing to the

146 Ibid 9.

147 See, for example, Shigeru Oda, 'Dispute Settlement Prospects in the Law of the Sea' (1995) 44 (04) ICLQ 863; Rosemary Rayfuse, 'The Future of Compulsory Dispute Settlement under the Law of the Sea Convention' (2005) 36 Victoria University of Wellington Law Review 683.

development of the law of the sea and strengthening their position within the institutional architecture of the law of the sea. Admittedly, the number of cases received and the number of decisions (and advisory opinions) rendered by UNCLOS tribunals pale in comparison to those of other specialised dispute settlement systems.[148] The low number of cases should, however, be understood in the broader context. States do not always prefer to bring their maritime disputes to international courts and tribunals for different reasons,[149] one of which being that some contested or emerging issues are more suitably dealt with in other fora than international courts. While the low number of cases may limit the potential of UNCLOS tribunals to make pronouncements on certain areas or issues, this number in itself should not be determinative in the assessment of the contribution made by the tribunals.

Furthermore, the cases received by the UNCLOS tribunals have not only increased in number but also diversified in terms of the legal issues raised over the past three decades. The decisions rendered by UNCLOS tribunals in these cases therefore provide sufficient material to gain a better picture of the role that UNCLOS tribunals have played in developing the law of the sea. It seems clear that for the most part, UNCLOS tribunals have managed to establish an authoritative pattern in their interpretation and application of the applicable rules and principles, thus settling previously debated questions and creating some degree of certainty for States in implementing the relevant rules.[150] However, there remain certain issues for which UNCLOS tribunals have failed to provide a consistent jurisprudence or whose interpretation have been faced with objections from States and the scholarly community. The legal regime regulating these issues thus remains in a state of flux, awaiting further clarification which may or may not come from UNCLOS tribunals themselves. These decisions may give rise to inquiries into the authority or legitimacy of UNCLOS tribunal,[151] or fragmentation of international law caused by UNCLOS tribunals. A separate study would need to be conducted to do these questions justice.

Within the scope of this book, it suffices to say that the existence of certain level of inconsistency in the way UNCLOS tribunals interpret certain issues of

[148] Since 1995, 607 disputes have been brought to the WTO and over 350 rulings have been issued. See: WTO, 'Dispute Settlement' www.wto.org/english/tratop_e/dispu_e/dispu_e.htm accessed 25 January 2022.

[149] Karim (n 48) 266–283.

[150] Øystein Jensen, 'Reflections' in Øystein Jensen (ed), *The Development of the Law of the Sea Convention: The Role of International Courts and Tribunals* (Edward Elgar Publishing 2020) 265.

[151] See: Telesetsky (n 135).

the law of the sea should not diminish the role that UNCLOS tribunals have played in developing the law of the sea. While the contribution of the tribunals may not be considered ground-breaking and UNCLOS tribunals cannot be viewed as having single-handedly shaped the law of the sea, the discussion in Section 7.2 shows that such expectations are unrealistic in the first place. By contributing at a micro rather than macro level, UNCLOS tribunals have fine-tuned the provisions of UNCLOS and thus at least fulfilled the role of providing normative guidance to States in implementing UNCLOS. Moreover, while the 'internal' inconsistencies between decisions of UNCLOS tribunals themselves certainly ought to be fleshed out in order to provide more legal certainty, it is difficult to generalise that UNCLOS tribunals have created or contributed to the fragmentation of international law as initially feared. UNCLOS tribunals have to a large extent endeavoured to ensure that their decisions are properly situated within the existing corpus of international, and vice versa, other courts and tribunals have also taken into account the decisions of UNCLOS tribunals. As a result, the law of the sea taken as whole as interpreted by UNCLOS tribunals has generally developed in harmony with the developments taking in other fora. In short, the case law produced by UNCLOS tribunals has shown that when given the opportunity, they are able contribute to the development of the law of the sea. While it is impossible to predict with any certainty to what extent States will continue to turn to UNCLOS tribunals for their disputes or what types of issues will come before the tribunals, there is no reason to doubt that UNCLOS tribunals will continue to be important players in the ocean legal order and one of the driving forces behind the development of the law of the sea.

Bibliography

Adede AO, *The System for Settlement of Disputes under the United Nations Convention on the Law of the Sea: A Drafting History and a Commentary* (Martinus Nijhoff 1987).

Akehurst MB, A *Modern Introduction to International Law* (Unwin Hyman 1988).

Allen S, 'Article 297 of the United Nations Convention on the Law of the Sea and the Scope of Mandatory Jurisdiction' (2017) 48(3–4) *ODIL* 313.

The Chagos Islanders and International Law (Hart 2014).

Allott O, 'Power Sharing in the Law of the Sea' (1983) 77(1) *AJIL* 1.

Aloisi R and Meernik J, *Judgment Day: Judicial Decision Making at the International Criminal Tribunals* (CUP 2017).

Alter K, *The New Terrain of International Law: Courts, Politics, Rights* (Princeton University Press 2014).

Álvarez J, 'What Are International Judges for? The Main Functions of International Adjudication' in Cesare Romano, Karen Alter and Yuval Shany (eds), *Oxford Handbook of International Adjudication* (OUP 2013).

Anand RP, 'The Role of Individual and Dissenting Opinions in International Adjudication' (1965) 13(3) ICLQ 788.

Anderson D, 'Developments in Maritime Boundary Law and Practice' in David A Colson and Robert W Smith (eds), *International Maritime Boundaries*, vol V (Brill Nijhoff 2005).

'Islands and Rocks in the Modern Law of the Sea' in Myron H Nordquist (ed), *The Law of the Sea: US Accession and Globalisation* (Martinus Nijhoff 2012).

Anderson DH, 'Some Aspects of the Use of Force in Maritime Law Enforcement' in Nerina Boschiero and others (eds), *International Courts and the Development of International Law: Essays in Honour of Tullio Treves* (Springer 2011).

Andreone G, 'The Exclusive Economic Zone' in Donald R Rothwell and others (eds), *The Oxford Handbook of the Law of the Sea* (OUP 2015).

Antunes NM and Becker-Weinberg V, 'Entitlement to Maritime Zones and Their Delimitation: In the Doldrums of Uncertainty and Unpredictability' in Alex G Oude Elferink, Tore Henriksen and Signe Veierud Busch (eds), *Maritime Boundary Delimitation: The Case Law – Is It Consistent and Predictable?* (CUP 2018).

Attard DJ, *The Exclusive Economic Zone in International Law* (Clarendon Press 1987).

Aust A, *Handbook of International Law* (2nd ed, CUP 2010).

Bankes N, 'Precluding the Applicability of Section 2 of Part XV of the Law of the Sea Convention' (2017) 48(3–4) ODIL 239.

Barnes RA, 'Flag States' in Donald R Rothwell and others (eds), *Oxford Handbook on Law of the Sea* (OUP 2015).

'The Continuing Vitality of UNCLOS' in Jill Barrett and Richard Barnes (eds), *Law of the Sea: UNCLOS as a Living Treaty* (British Institute of International and Comparative Law 2017).

Barnes RA, Freestone D and Ong D, 'The Law of the Sea: Progress and Prospects' in Richard Barnes, David Freestone and David Ong (eds), *The Law of the Sea: Progress and Prospects* (OUP 2006).

Barrett J, 'The UN Convention on the Law of the Sea: A Living Treaty?' in Jill Barrett and Richard Barnes (eds), *Law of the Sea: UNCLOS as a Living Treaty* (British Institute of International and Comparative Law 2017).

Becker MA, 'Request for an Advisory Opinion Submitted by the Sub-Regional Fisheries Commission (SRFC)' (2015) 109(4) AJIL 851.

Becker-Weinberg V, 'The Interpretation and Application of the Freedom of Navigation and Flag State Jurisdiction in the M/V "Norstar" and the M/T "San Padre Pio" Cases' (2021) 9 Korean Journal of International and Comparative Law 108.

Beckman R and Sun Z, 'The Relationship between UNCLOS and IMO Instruments' (2017) 2 Asia-Pacific Journal of Ocean Law and Policy 201.

Bencze M and Yein Ng G, 'Measuring the Unmeasurable?' in Mátyás Bencze and Gar Yein Ng (eds), *How to Measure the Quality of Judicial Reasoning* (Springer 2018).

Berman F, 'The International Court of Justice as an "Agent" of Legal Development?' in Christian J Tams and James Sloan (eds), *The Development of International Law by the International Court of Justice* (OUP 2013).

Bernard L, 'Historic Rights and the Exclusive Economic Zone' (2021) 18 Indonesian J Int'L 161.

'The Effect of Historic Fishing Rights in Maritime Boundaries Delimitation' in Harry N. Scheiber and Moon Sang Kwon (eds), *Securing the Ocean for the Next Generation* (Berkeley Law School 2013).

Birnie P, Boyle A and Redgwell C, *International Law and the Environment* (3rd ed, OUP 2009).

Bjorke E, 'The Vienna Rules, Evolutionary Interpretation and the Intention of the Parties' in Andrea Bianchi, Daniel Peat and Matthew Windsor (eds), *Interpretation of International Law* (OUP 2015).

Blitza E, 'Article 206' in Alexander Proelss (ed), *United Nations Convention on the Law of the Sea: A Commentary* (CH Beck, Hart, Nomos 2017).

Blokker NM, 'Governance of the International Tribunal of the Law of the Sea: The Role of the Meeting of States Parties to the Law of the Sea Convention' in Angela Del Vecchio and Roberto Virzo (eds), *Interpretations of the United Nations Convention on the Law of the Sea by International Courts and Tribunals* (Springer 2019).

Bodansky DM, 'Customary (and Not So Customary) International Environmental Law' (1995) 3(1) IJGLS 105.

Boyle A, 'Developments in the International Law of Environmental Impact Assessments and Their Relation to the Espoo Convention' (2011) 20(3) RECIEL 227.

'The Environmental Jurisprudence of the ITLOS (2007) 22 IJMCL 369.
'The Southern Bluefin Tuna Arbitration' (2001) 50 ICLQ 447.
'UNCLOS Dispute Settlement and the Uses and Abuses of Part XV' (2014) 47 Revue Belge De Droit International 182.
Boyle A and Chinkin C, *The Making of International Law* (OUP 2007).
'UNCLOS III and the Process of International Law-Making' in Tafsir Malick Ndiaye and Rüdiger Wolfrum (eds), *Law of the Sea, Environmental Law and Settlement of Disputes: Liber Amicorum Judge Thomas A. Mensah* (Martinus Nijhoff 2007).
Brown ED, 'Rockall and the Limits of National Jurisdiction of the UK' (1978) 2 Marine Policy 181.
Buergenthal T, 'Lawmaking by the ICJ and Other International Courts' (2009) 103 Proceedings of the American Society of International Law 403.
Buga I, 'Between Stability and Change in the Law of the Sea Convention: Subsequent Practice, Treaty Modification, and Regime Interaction' in Donald R Rothwell and others (eds), *The Oxford Handbook of the Law of the Sea* (OUP 2015).
'Territorial Sovereignty Issues in Maritime Disputes: A Jurisdictional Dilemma for Law of the Sea Tribunals' (2012) 27 IJMCL 59.
Buzan B, 'Negotiating by Consensus: Developments in Technique at the United Nations Conference on the Law of the Sea' (1981) 75(2) *AJIL* 324.
Caddell R, 'Platforms, Protestors and Provisional Measures: The Arctic Sunrise Dispute and Environmental Activism at Sea' in Mónika Ambrus and Ramses A Wessel (eds), *Netherlands Yearbook of International Law* (T.M.C. Asser Press 2014).
Caminos H and Molitor MR, 'Progressive Development of International Law and the Package Deal' (1985) 79(4) AJIL 871.
Cançado Trindade AA, 'Precaution' in Jorge E. Viñuales (ed), *The Rio Declaration on Environment and Development: A Commentary* (OUP 2015).
Chinkin C, 'Dispute Resolution and the Law of the Sea: Regional Problems and Prospects' in James Crawford and Donald Rothwell (eds), *The Law of the Sea in the Asian Pacific Region: Developments and Prospects* (Martinus Nijhoff 2012).
Chircop A, 'The International Maritime Organization' in Donald R Rothwell and others (eds), *The Oxford Handbook of the Law of the Sea* (OUP 2015).
Christie DR, 'The Conservation and Management of Stocks Located Solely within the Exclusive Economic Zone' in Ellen Hey (ed), *Developments in International Fisheries Law* (Kluwer Law International 1999).
Churchill R, 'Dispute Settlement in the Law of the Sea: Survey for 2015 – Part I' (2016) 31(4) IJMCL 555.
'Revealing a Mosaic: International Jurisprudence concerning the Non-Fisheries Elements of the Exclusive Economic Zone Regime' in Øystein Jensen (ed), *The Development of the Law of the Sea Convention* (Edward Elgar 2020).
'Some Reflections on the Operation of the Dispute Settlement System of the UN Convention on the Law of the Sea During Its First Decade' in David Freestone, Richard Barnes, and David Ong (eds), *The Law of the Sea: Progress and Prospects* (OUP 206).
'The 1982 United Nations Convention on the Law of the Sea' in Donald Rothwell and others (eds), *The Oxford Handbook of the Law of the Sea* (OUP 2018).

'The *Bangladesh/Myanmar* Case: Continuity and Novelty in the Law of Maritime Boundary Delimitation' (2012) 1(1) Cambridge Journal of International and Comparative Law 137.

'The Jurisprudence of the International Tribunal for the Law of the Sea Relating to Fisheries: Is There Much in the Net?' (2007) 22 IJMCL 383.

'The LOSC Regime for Protection of the Marine Environment – Fit for the Twenty-First Century?' in Rosemary Gail Rayfuse (ed), Research *Handbook on International Marine Environmental Law* (Edward Elgar 2015).

Churchill R and Lowe V, *The Law of the Sea* (3rd ed, Manchester University Press 1999).

Cogliati-Bantz VP, 'International Tribunal for the Law of the Sea, Hoshinmaru (Japan v Russian Federation) and Tomimaru (Japan v Russian Federation), Prompt Release Judgments of 6 August 2007' (2009) 58(1) ICLQ 241.

'Introductory Note to The M/V 'Virginia G' Case (Panama/Guinea-Bissau) (ITLOS)' (2014) 53(6) ILM 1161.

Colson DA, 'The Delimitation of the Outer Continental Shelf between Neighboring States' (2003) 97 AJIL 91.

Colson DA and Hoyle P, 'Satisfying the Procedural Prerequisites to the Compulsory Dispute Settlement Mechanisms of the 1982 Law of the Sea Convention: Did the Southern Bluefin Tuna Tribunal get it Right?' (2003) 34 ODIL 59.

Corell H, 'Oversight of the Implementation of the Global Ocean Regime: The Role of the United Nations' in Davoe Vidas and Willy Onstreng (eds), *Orders for the Oceans at the Turn of the Century* (Kluwer Law International 1999).

Craik N, *The International Law of Environmental Impact Assessment: Process, Substance and Integration* (CUP 2008).

Crawford J, *Chance, Order, Change: The Course of International Law, General Course on Public International Law* (Hague Academy of International Law 2014).

Cullet P, 'Common but Differentiated Responsibility' in Jorge E. Viñuales (ed), *The Rio Declaration on Environment and Development: A Commentary* (OUP 2015).

Czybulka D, 'Article 192' in Alexander Proelss (ed), *United Nations Convention on the Law of the Sea: A Commentary* (CH Beck, Hart, Nomos 2017).

'Article 237' in Alexander Proelss (ed), *United Nations Convention on the Law of the Sea: A Commentary* (CH Beck, Hart, Nomos 2017).

Danilenko GM, *Law-making in the International Community* (Brill 1992).

De Baere G, Chane AL and Wouters J, 'The Contributions of International and Supranational Courts to the Rule of Law: A Framework for Analysis' in De Baere G and Wouters J (eds), *Contribution of International and Supranational Courts to the Rule of Law* (Edward Elgar 2015).

de Sadeleer N, *Environmental Principles: From Political Slogans to Legal Rules* (OUP 2002).

Devaney JG and Tams CJ, 'In Re Arbitration Between the Italian Republic and the Republic of India Concerning the 'Enrica Lexie' Incident' (2021) 115 AJIL 513.

Del Vecchio A and Virzo R (eds), *Interpretations of the United Nations Convention on the Law of the Sea by International Courts and Tribunals* (Springer 2019).

Djalal H, '"Due Regards" and "Abuse of Rights" in UNCLOS' in Shicun Wu, Mark Valencia and Nong Hong (eds), *UN Convention on the Law of the Sea and the South China Sea* (Routledge 2015).

Dupuy F and Dupuy P-M, 'A Legal Analysis of China's Historic Claims in the South China Sea' (2013) 107 American Journal of International Law 124.
Dupuy P-M and Vinuales JE, *International Environmental Law* (CUP 2015).
Ehlermann C-D, 'Experiences from the WTO Appellate Body' (2005) 38(3) TJIL 469.
Eichberger FS, 'The Legal Effect of ICJ Advisory Opinions Redefined? The Mauritius/Maldives Delimitation Case – Judgment on Preliminary Objections' (2021) 22(2) Melbourne Journal of International Law 1.
Evans MD, 'Maritime Boundary Delimitation' in Donald R Rothwell and others (eds), *The Oxford Handbook of the Law of the Sea* (OUP 2015).
'Maritime Boundary Delimitation: Whatever Next?' in Jill Barrett and Richard Barnes (eds) *Law of the Sea: UNCLOs as a Living Treaty* (British Institute of International and Comparative Law 2017).
Relevant Circumstances and Maritime Delimitation (Clarendon Press 1989).
'Relevant Circumstances' in Alex G Oude Elferink, Tore Henriksen and Signe Veierud Busch (eds), *Maritime Boundary Delimitation: The Case Law: Is It Consistent and Predictable?* (CUP 2018).
Evans MD and Lewis R, 'The Regime of Islands' in Øystein Jensen (ed), *The Development of the Law of the Sea Convention: The Role of International Courts and Tribunals* (Edward Elgar Publishing 2020).
Faccio S, '"Human Habitation or Economic Life of their Own": The Definition of Features between History, Technology and the Law' (2021) 42 Liverpool Law Review 15.
Ferrell JK, 'Controlling Flags of Convenience: One Measure to Stop Overfishing of Collapsing Fish Stocks', (2005) 35 Envtl L 323.
Fietta S, 'Arbitral Tribunal Decision Guyana v. Suriname' (2008) 46 International Legal Materials 164.
Fitzmaurice G, 'Hersch Lauterpacht – The Scholar as a Judge' (1961) 37 BYBIL 1.
Forteau M, 'The Legal Nature and Content of 'Due Regard' Obligations in Recent International Case Law' (2019) 34 IJMCL 1.
Foster C, *Science and the Precautionary Principle in International Courts and Tribunals: Expert Evidence, Burden of Proof and Finality* (CUP 2013).
Franckx E, 'Reasonable Bond in the Practice of the International Tribunal for the Law of the Sea' (2002) 32(2) CWILJ 303.
'The Regime of Islands and Rocks' in David J Attard, Malgosia Fitzmaurice and Norman A Martínez Gutiérrez (eds), *The IMLI Manual on International Maritime Law*, vol I: *The Law of the Sea* (OUP 2014).
Franckx E and Bernatar M, 'The "Duty" to Co-Operate for States Bordering Enclosed or Semi-Enclosed Seas' (2013) 31 Chinese (Taiwan) Yearbook of International Law and Affairs 66.
Freestone D and Oude Elferink AG, 'Flexibility and Innovation in the Law of the Sea: Will the LOS Convention Amendment Procedures Ever Be Used?' in Alex G Oude Elferink (ed), *Stability and Change in the Law of the Sea: The Role of the LOS Convention* (Martinus Nijhoff 2005).
Friedheim RL, 'Fishing Negotiations at the Third United Nations Conference on the Law of the Sea' (1991) 22 ODIL 209.
Gao J, 'Comments on Guyana v Suriname' (2009) 8 Chinese Journal of International Law 191.

García-Revillo MG, 'The Jurisdictional Debate in the Request for an Advisory Opinion Submitted by the Sub-Regional Fisheries Commission (SRFC) to the International Tribunal for the Law of the Sea' in Del Vecchio A and Virzo R (eds), *Interpretations of the United Nations Convention on the Law of the Sea by International Courts and Tribunals* (Springer 2019).

Gaunce J, 'On the Interpretation of the General Duty of "Due Regard"' (2018) 32 Ocean Yearbook Online 1.

Gautier P, 'The Contribution of the International Tribunal for the Law of the Sea to the Rule of Law' in Geert De De Baere G and Wouters J (eds), *Contribution of International and Supranational Courts to the Rule of Law* (Edward Elgar 2015).

Gavouneli M, 'Protection Standards for the Marine Environment: Updating Part XII of the Law of the Sea Convention?' in Stephen Minas and Jordan Diamond (eds), *Stress Testing the Law of the Sea* (Brill 2018).

Gray C and Kingsbury B, 'Developments in Dispute Settlement: Inter-State Arbitration Since 1945' (1993) 63(1) BYBIL 97.

Greenwood C, 'Sources of International Law: An Introduction' (2008).

'The Development of International Humanitarian Law by the International Criminal Tribunal for the Former Yugoslavia' (1998) 2 Max Planck Yearbook of United Nations Law 97.

Gudlaugsson ST, 'Natural Prolongation and the Concept of the Continental Margin for the Purposes of Article 76' in Myron N Nordquist, John Norton Moore and Tomas H Heidar (eds), *Legal and Scientific Aspects of Continental Shelf Limits* (Martinus Nijhoff 2004).

Guggisberg S, *The Use of CITES for Commercially-Exploited Fish Species: A Solution to Overexploitation and Illegal, Unreported and Unregulated Fishing?* (Springer 2015).

Guilfoyle D, 'Article 87' in Alexander Proelss (ed), *United Nations Convention on the Law of the Sea: A Commentary* (CH Beck, Hart, Nomos 2017).

'Article 91' in Alexander Proelss (ed), *United Nations Convention on the Law of the Sea: A Commentary* (CH Beck, Hart, Nomos 2017).

'Article 92' in Alexander Proelss (ed), *United Nations Convention on the Law of the Sea: A Commentary* (CH Beck, Hart, Nomos 2017).

Gullett W, 'The South China Sea Arbitration's Contribution to the Concept of Juridical Islands' (2018) 47 CIL 5.

Guo J, 'The Developments of Marine Environmental Protection Obligation in Article 192 of UNCLOS and the Operational Impact on China's Marine Policy – A South China Sea Fisheries Perspective' (2020) 120 Marine Policy Journal 1.

Hamamoto S, 'The Genesis of the 'Due Regard' Obligations in the United Nations Convention on the Law of the Sea' (2019) 2019 IJMCL 34.

Harris C, 'Incidental Determinations in Proceedings under Compromissory Clauses' (2021) 70(2) ICLQ 417.

Harrison J, 'Article 73' in Alexander Proelss (ed), *United Nations Convention on the Law of the Sea: A Commentary* (CH Beck, Hart, Nomos 2017).

'Defining Disputes and Characterizing Claims: Subject-Matter Jurisdiction in Law of the Sea Convention Litigation' (2017) 48(3–4) ODIL 269.

Saving the Oceans Through Law: The International Legal Framework for the Protection of the Marine Environment (OUP 2017).

'The Law of the Sea Convention Institutions' in Donald R Rothwell and others (eds), *The Oxford Handbook of the Law of the Sea* (OUP 2015).

Harrison J and Morgera E, 'Article 62' in Alexander Proelss (ed), *United Nations Convention on the Law of the Sea: A Commentary* (CH Beck, Hart, Nomos 2017).

Heere WP (ed), *International Law and Its Sources: Liber Amicorum Maarten Bos* (Kluwer Law International 1989).

Helfer LR, 'The Effectiveness of International Adjudicators' in Cesare Romano, Karen Alter and Yuval Shany (eds), *Oxford Handbook of International Adjudication* (OUP 2013).

Hernandez G, 'International Judicial Lawmaking' in Catherine Brolmann and Yannick Radi (eds), *Research Handbook on the Theory and Practice of International Lawmaking* (Edward Elgar 2016).

'Interpretative Authority and the International Judiciary' in Andrea Bianchi, Daniel Peat and Matthew Windsor (eds), *Interpretation in International Law* (OUP 2015).

The International Court of Justice and the Judicial Function (OUP 2014).

Hey E, 'Reviewing Implementation of the LOS Convention and Emerging International Public Law' in Alex G Oude Elferink (ed), *Stability and Change in the Law of the Sea: The Role of the LOS Convention* (Martinus Nijhoff 2005).

'The Fisheries Provisions of the LOS Convention' in Ellen Hey (ed), *Developments in International Fisheries Law* (Kluwer Law International 1999).

Higgins R, *Problems and Process: International Law and How We Use It* (OUP 1995).

Horowitz D, 'The Catch of Poseidon's Trident: The Fate of High Seas Fisheries in the Southern Bluefin Tuna Case' (2001) 25 MULR 810.

Hudson MO, 'The Twenty-Eighth Year of the World Court' (1950) 44 AJIL 20.

Hua Z, 'The Development of International Law of the Sea by International Courts and Tribunals: A Case Study of Due Diligence Obligation' (2021) 9 Korean Journal of International and Comparative Law 132.

Ikeshima T, 'The "Reasonableness" of Unreasonable Arguments in Prompt Release Cases in the ITLOS' (2010) 6 Waseda Global Forum 107.

Ishii Y, 'Introductory Note to Case Concerning the Detention of Three Ukrainian Naval Vessels (Ukraine v. Russian Federation): Provisional Measures Order (ITLOS)' (2019) 58 International Legal Materials 1147.

Jennings RY, 'The Internal Judicial Practice of the International Court of Justice' (1988) 59 BYBIL 31.

Jensen Ø, 'Maritime Boundary Delimitation beyond 200 Nautical Miles: The International Judiciary and the Commission on the Limits of the Continental Shelf' (2015) 84 NJIL 580.

'Reflections' in Øystein Jensen (ed), *The Development of the Law of the Sea Convention: The Role of International Courts and Tribunals* (Edward Elgar Publishing 2020).

The Commission on the Limits of the Continental Shelf: Law and Legitimacy (Brill 2014).

'The Delimitation of the Continental Shelf beyond 200 nm' in Alex G Oude Elferink, Tore Henriksen and Signe Veierud Busch (eds), *Maritime Boundary Delimitation: The Case Law: Is It Consistent and Predictable?* (CUP 2018).

The Development of the Law of the Sea Convention (Edward Elgar 2020).

Jesus JL, 'Commentary on Article 138 of the Rules of the Tribunal' in P. Chandrasekhara Rao and Ph. Gautier (eds), *The Rules of the International Tribunal for the Law of the Sea : A Commentary* (Martinus Nijhoff 2006).

Jia BB, 'The Notion of Natural Prolongation in the Current Regime of the Continental Shelf: An Afterlife?' (2013) 12(1) CJIL 87.

Kaikobad K, and others, 'United Kingdom Materials on International Law 2004' (2004) 75(1) BYIBL Law 595.

Kammerhofer J, 'Uncertainty in the Formal Sources of International Law: Customary International Law and Some of Its Problems' (2004) 15 EJIL 523.

Karaman, IV, *Dispute Resolution in Law of the Sea* (Brill 2012).

Karim MDS, 'Litigating Law of the Sea Disputes Using the UNCLOS Dispute Settlement System' in Natalie Klein (ed), *Litigating International Law Disputes: Weighing the Options* (CUP 2014).

Kasoulides GC, *Port State Control and Jurisdiction: Evolution of the Port State Regime* (Springer 1993) 75, cited in Rosemary Gail Rayfuse (ed), *Non-Flag State Enforcement in High Seas Fisheries* (Martinus Nijhoff Publishers 2004).

Kateka JL, 'Advisory Proceedings before the Seabed Disputes Chamber and before the ITLOS as a Full Court' (2013) 17(1) MPYBUNLO 159.

Kaye SM, *International Fisheries Management* (Kluwer Law International 2001).

'The Use of Multiple Boundaries in Maritime Boundary Delimitation: Law and Practice' (1998) 19 Aust. YBIL 49.

Kim DY, 'Advisory Proceedings before the International Tribunal for the Law of the Sea as an Alternative Procedure to Supplement the Dispute-Settlement Mechanism under Part XV of the United Nations Convention on the Law of the Sea' (2010) 11 Issues in Legal Scholarship 1.

Kim HJ, 'Natural Prolongation: A Living Myth in the Regime of the Continental Shelf?' (2014) 45 ODIL 374.

Klein N, *Dispute Settlement in the UN Convention on the Law of the Sea* (CUP 2005).

'Islands and Rocks after the South China Sea Arbitration' (2016) 34 Australian Yearbook of International Law 21.

'The Vicissitudes of Dispute Settlement under the Law of the Sea Convention' (2017) 32(2) IJMCL 332.

Knox JH, 'The Myth and Reality of Transboundary Environmental Impact Assessment' (2002) 96 AJIL 291.

Koers AW, 'The Third United Nations Conference on the Law of The Sea – Some Remarks on Its Contribution towards the Making of International Law' in Wybo P Heere and Maarten Bos (eds), *International Law and Its Sources: Liber Amicorum Maarten Bos* (T.M.C. Asser Institute 1989).

Koh T, 'UNCLOS at 30: Some Reflections' in Lilian de Castillo (ed), *Law of the Sea: From Grotius to the International Tribunal for the Law of the Sea , Liber Amicorum Judge Hugo Caminos* (Brill 2015).

Kojima C, 'South China Sea Arbitration and the Protection of the Marine Environment: Evolution of UNCLOS Part XII Through Interpretation and the Duty to Cooperate' (2015) 21 Asian Yearbook of International Law 166.

Kong L, 'Environmental Impact Assessment under the United Nations Convention on the Law of the Sea' (2011) 10 Chinese Journal of International Law 651.

Kopela S, 'Historic Fishing Rights in the Law of the Sea and Brexit' (2019) 32 LJIL 32.

'Historic Titles and Historic Rights in the Law of the Sea in the Light of the South China Sea Arbitration' (2017) 48 ODIL 2.

'Port-state Jurisdiction, Extraterritoriality and the Protection of Global Commons' (2016) 47 Ocean Development and International Law 89.

Kunoy B, 'The Admissibility of a Plea to an International Adjudicative Forum to Delimit the Outer Continental Shelf Prior to the Adoption of Final Recommendations by the Commission on the Limits of the Continental Shelf' (2010) 25 IJMCL 237.

'The Scope of Compulsory Jurisdiction and Exceptions Thereto under the United Nations Convention on the Law of the Sea' (2020) 58 Canadian Yearbook of International Law 78.

'The Terms of Reference of the Commission on the Limits of the Continental Shelf: A Creeping Legal Mandate' (2012) 25 LJIL 109.

Kwiatkowska B, *The 200 Mile Exclusive Economic Zone in the New Law of the Sea* (Martinus Nijhoff 1989).

'The Southern Bluefin Tuna Arbitral Tribunal Did Get It right: A Commentary and Reply to the Article by David A. Colson and Dr. Peggy Hoyle' (2003) 34 *ODIL* 369.

Lachs M, 'Some Reflections on the Contribution of the International Court of Justice to the Development of International Law' (1983) 10 Syracuse Journal of International Law and Commerce 239.

Lagoni R, 'Offshore Bunkering in the Exclusive Economic Zone' in Tafsir Malick Ndiaye and Rüdiger Wolfrum (eds), *Law of the Sea, Environmental Law and Settlement of Disputes: Liber amicorum Judge Thomas A. Mensah* (Martinus Nijhoff 2007).

Laing EA, 'ITLOS Procedures and Practices: Bond' in John Norton Moore and Myron H Nordquist (eds), *Current Marine Environmental Issues and the International Tribunal for the Law of the Sea* (Martinus Nijhoff 2001).

Lando M, 'Judicial Uncertainties Concerning Territorial Sea Delimitation Under Article 15 of the United Nations Convention on the Law of the Sea' (2017) 70 ICLQ 589.

Maritime Delimitation as a Judicial Process (CUP 2019).

'The Advisory Jurisdiction of the International Tribunal for the Law of the Sea: Comments on the Request for an Advisory Opinion Submitted by the Sub-Regional Fisheries Commission' (2016) 29(2) LJIL 441.

Lathrop CG, 'The Provisional Equidistance Line' in Alex G Oude Elferink, Tore Henriksen and Signe Veierud Busch (eds), *Maritime Boundary Delimitation: The Case Law: Is It Consistent and Predictable?* (CUP 2018).

Lauterpacht H, *The Development of International Law by the International Court* (Stevens & Sons 1958).

Leanza U and Caracciolo MC, 'The Exclusive Economic Zone' in David Attard, Malgosia Fitzmaurice and Norman A Martinez Gutierrez (eds) *The IMLI Manual on International Maritime Law*, vol I: *The Law of the Sea* (OUP 2014).

Lee S, 'UNCLOS and the Obligation to Cooperate' in Clive Schofield, Maritime Energy Resources in Asia: Legal Regimes and Cooperation, National Bureau of Asian Research 2012.

Lee S and Bautista L, 'Historic Rights' in Øystein Jensen (ed), *The Development of the Law of the Sea Convention* (Edward Elgar Publishing 2020).

Lepard BD, *Customary International Law: A New Theory with Practical Applications* (CUP 2010).
Letsas G, 'The ECHR as a Living Instrument in A Føllesdal, B Peters and G Ulfstein (eds), *Constituting Europe: The European Court of Human Rights in a National, European and Global Context* (CUP 2003).
Letts D, McLaughlin R and Nasu H, 'Maritime Law Enforcement and the Aggravation of the South China Sea Dispute: Implications for Australia' (2017) 34 Australian Year Book of International Law 53.
Li H, 'Coastal State Jurisdiction in the "Norstar" Case at the ITLOS' (2020) 19 Chinese Journal of International Law 177, 180.
Liao X, *The Continental Shelf Delimitation Beyond 200 Nautical Miles: Towards a Common Approach to Maritime Boundary-Making* (CUP 2021).
'The LOSC as a Package Deal and Its Implications for Determination of Customary International Law' (2020) 35 IJMCL 704.
Liliansa D, 'The Necessity of Indonesia's Measures to Sink Vessels for IUU Fishing in the Exclusive Economic Zone' (2020) 10 Asian J: Int. Law 1.
Lowe V and Tzanakopoulos A, 'The Development of the Law of the Sea by the International Court of Justice' in Christian J Tams and James Sloan (eds), *The Development of International Law by the International Court of Justice* (OUP 2013).
Lucky A, 'The Issues Concerning the Continental Shelf: Reflections' (2015) 17 ICLR 95.
Lyons Y, Luu QH and Tkalich P, 'Determining High-tide Features (or Islands) in the South China Sea under Article 121(1): A Legal and Oceanography Perspective' in S Jayakumar and others (eds), *The South China Sea Arbitration: The Legal Dimension* (Edward Elgar Publishing 2018).
Macdonald R, 'The Charter of the United Nations in Constitutional Perspective' (1999) 20 Australian Year Book of International Law 205.
MacLachlan C, 'The Principle of Systemic Integration and Article 31(3)(c) of the Vienna Convention' (2005) 54 ICLQ 279.
Macnab R, 'The Case for Transparency in the Delimitation of the Outer Continental Shelf in Accordance with UNCLOS Article 76' (2004) 35 ODIL 1.
Magnússon BM, 'Is There a Temporal Relationship between the Delineation and the Delimitation of the Continental Shelf beyond 200 Nautical Miles?' (2013) 28 IJMCL 465.
The Continental Shelf Beyond 200 nm: Delineation, Delimitation and Dispute Settlement (Brill 2016).
Marotta Rangel V, 'Settlement of Disputes Relating to the Delimitation of the Outer Continental Shelf: The Role of International Courts and Arbitral Tribunals' (2006) 21(3) IJMCL 347.
Marr S, 'The Southern Bluefin Tuna Cases: The Precautionary Approach and Conservation and Management of Fish Resources' (2000) 11(4) EJIL 815.
Matland DF, 'Re-evaluating the Status of Flags of Convenience Under International Law' (1990–1991) 23 Vand J Transnat'l L 1017.
Matz-Lück N, 'Final Provisions' in Alexander Proelss (ed), *United Nations Convention on the Law of the Sea: A Commentary* (CH Beck, Hart, Nomos 2017).
Matz-Lück N and Fuchs J, 'Marine Living Resources' in Donald R Rothwell and others (eds), *The Oxford Handbook of the Law of the Sea* (OUP 2015).

Matz-Lück, N and van Doorn E, 'Due Diligence Obligations and the Protection of the Marine Environment' (2017) 42 L'Observateur des Nations Unies 177.
McConnell ML, 'ITLOS and the Tale of the Tenacious 'Genuine Link' in Øystein Jensen (ed), *The Development of the Law of the Sea Convention* (Edward Elgar Publishing 2020).
McDorman T, 'An International Law Perspective on Insular Features (Islands) and Low-tide Elevations in the South China Sea' (2017) 32 The International Journal of Marine and Coastal Law 298.
'International Tribunal for the Law of the Sea' (2001) 21 YIEL 531.
'Rights and Jurisdiction over Resources in the South China Sea: UNCLOS and the 'nine-dash line' in S. Jayakumar, Tommy Koh and Robert Beckman (eds), *The South China Sea Disputes and Law of the Sea* (Edward Elgar 2014).
'The Continental Shelf Regime in the Law of the Sea Convention: A Reflection on the First Thirty Years' in David Freestone (ed), *The 1982 Law of the Sea Convention at 30: Successes, Challenges and New Agendas* (Brill 2013).
McDougal MS, Burke WT and Vlasic IA, 'The Maintenance of Public Order at Sea and the Nationality of Ships' (1960) 54(1) The American Journal of International Law 25.
McRae D, 'The Applicable Law' in Alex G Oude Elferink, Tore Henriksen and Signe Veierud Busch (eds), *Maritime Boundary Delimitation: The Case Law: Is It Consistent and Predictable?* (CUP 2018).
Messenger G, *The Development of World Trade Organization Law* (OUP 2016).
Merrills JG, *International Dispute Settlement* (6th ed, CUP 2017).
'The Place of International Litigation in International Law' in Natalie Klein (ed), *Litigating International Law Disputes: Weighing the Options* (CUP 2014).
Merkouris P, *Article 31(3)(c) VCLT and the Principle of Systemic Integration: Normative Shadows in Plato's Cave* (Brill 2015).
Meshel T, 'The Evolution of Interstate Arbitration and the Peaceful Resolution of Transboundary Freshwater Disputes' (2016) 1 JIDS 361.
Miles C, 'The M/V "Norstar" Case (Panama v Italy)' (2020) 114 American Journal of International Law 116.
Moeckli D and White ND, 'Treaties as 'Living Instruments' in Dino Kritsiotis and Michael Bowman (eds), *Conceptual and Contextual Perspectives on the Modern Law of Treaties* (CUP, 2018).
Morgan DL, 'A Practitioner's Critique of the Order Granting Provisional Measures in the Southern Bluefin Tuna Case' in John Norton Moore and Myron H Nordquist (eds), *Current Marine Environmental Issues and the International Tribunal for the Law of the Sea* (Martinus Nijhoff 2001).
Mossop J, 'The South China Sea Arbitration and New Zealand's Maritime Claims' (2017) 15 New Zealand Journal of Public and International Law 265.
Mowbray A, 'The Creativity of the European Court of Human Rights' (2005) 5(1) Human Rights Law Review 57.
Nagtzaam G and Guilfoyle D, 'Ramming Speed': The Sea Shepherd Conservation Society and the Law of Protest' (2018) 44 Monash University Law Review 360.
Nawab, 'Other Sources of International Law. Are Judicial Decisions of the International Court of Justice a Source of International Law?' (1979) 19 Indian JIL 526.

Ndiaye TM, 'The Advisory Function of the International Tribunal for the Law of the Sea' (2010) 9 CJIL 565.

Nelson LDM, 'The Continental Shelf: Interplay of Law and Science', in Nisuke Ando and others (eds), *Liber Amicorum Judge Shigeru Oda*, vol 2 (Kluwer Law International 2002).

Nguyen LN, 'Expanding the Regulatory Scope of LOSC for Environmental Issues through the Rule of Reference: Potentials and Limits' (2022) 52 Ocean Development & International Law 419.

'Principled Challenges: Between Collective Interest and Individual Freedom' in Vito De Lucia, Alex Oude Elferink and Lan Ngoc Nguyen (eds), *International Law and Marine Areas beyond National Jurisdiction: Reflections on Justice, Space, Knowledge and Power* (Brill 2022).

'UNCLOS Tribunals and the Development of the Outer Continental Shelf Regime' (2018) 67(2) International and Comparative Law Quarterly 425.

Nguyen, LN and Tran YH, 'Coastal States' Enforcement Power over Fishing Activities in the South China Sea: Where is the Line under International Law?' (2019) 37 Chinese (Taiwan) Yearbook of International Law and Affairs 110–145.

Nolte G, *Treaties and Subsequent Practice* (OUP 2013).

Nordquist MH (ed), *United Nations Convention on the Law of the Sea 1982: A Commentary*, vol I (Martinus Nijhoff 1985).

United Nations Convention on the Law of the Sea 1982: A Commentary, vol II (Martinus Nijhoff 1985).

United Nations Convention on the Law of the Sea 1982: A Commentary, vol III (Martinus Nijhoff 1985).

United Nations Convention on the Law of the Sea, 1982: A Commentary, vol IV (Martinus Nijhoff 1985).

United Nations Convention on the Law of the Sea, 1982: A Commentary, vol V (Martinus Nijhoff 1985).

Nordquist MH and Phalen WG, 'Interpretation of UNCLOS Article 121 and Itu Aba (Taiping) in the South China Sea Arbitration Award' in *International Marine Economy* (Brill Nijhoff Publishers 2017).

North R, 'Traditional Fishing Rights in International Law: The South China Sea Arbitration' (2017) 36 UTLR 101.

Noyes JE, 'Compulsory Third-Party Adjudication and the 1982 United Nations Convention on the Law of the Sea' (1989) 4 Conn J Int'l L 675.

O'Connell DP, *The International Law of the Sea*, vol II (Clarendon Press 1984).

Oda S, 'Dispute Settlement Prospects in the Law of the Sea' (1995) 44(4) ICLQ 863.

Oellers-Frahm K, 'Lawmaking Through Advisory Opinions?' in Armin von Bogdandy and Ingo Venzke (eds), *International Judicial Lawmaking: On Public Authority and Democratic Legitimation in Global Governance* (Springer 2012).

Okanawa P, 'Procedural Obligations in International Environmental Agreements' (1997) 67 BYBIL 275.

Oral N, 'The South China Sea Arbitral Award: Casting Light on Article 121 of UNCLOS, Law and Practice of International Courts and Tribunals' (2017) 16(2) *The Law & Practice of International Courts and Tribunals* 354.

Orrego Vicuna F, *The Exclusive Economic Zone* (CUP 1989).

'The Exclusive Economic Zone: Regime and Legal Nature under International Law' (1989), 40 ICLQ 232.
Oude Elferink AG, 'Artificial Islands, Installations and Structures', in *Max Planck Encyclopedia of Public International Law* (Oxford University Press, 2013).
'ITLOS' Approach to the Delimitation of the Continental Shelf Beyond 200 Nautical Miles in the Bangladesh/Myanmar Case: Theoretical and Practical Difficulties' in Rüdiger Wolfrum, Maja Seršić and Trpimir M. Šošić (eds), *Contemporary Developments in International Law: Essays in Honour of Budislav Vukas* (Brill 2016).
Stability and Change in the Law of the Sea: The Role of the LOS Convention (Martinus Nijhoff 2005).
'The Arctic Sunrise Incident: A Multi-faceted Law of the Sea Case with a Human Rights Dimension' (2014) 29 IJMCL 2.
'The Continental Shelf beyond 200 Nautical Miles: The Relationship between the CLCS and Third Party Dispute Settlement' in Alex G Oude Elferink and Donald Rothwell (eds), *Oceans Management in the 21st Century: Institutional Frameworks and Responses* (Brill 2004).
Oude Elferink AG, Henriksen T and Busch SV, 'Conclusions' in Alex G Oude Elferink, Tore Henriksen and Signe Veierud Busch (eds), *Maritime Boundary Delimitation: The Case Law: Is It Consistent and Predictable?* (CUP 2018).
'The Judiciary and the Law of Maritime Delimitation' in Alex G Oude Elferink, Tore Henriksen and Signe Veierud Busch (eds), *Maritime Boundary Delimitation: The Case Law: Is It Consistent and Predictable?* (CUP 2018).
Oxman B, 'Complementary Agreements and Compulsory Jurisdiction' (2001) 95 AJIL 277.
'Courts and Tribunals: The ICJ, ITLOS and Arbitral Tribunals' in Donald R Rothwell and others (eds), *The Oxford Handbook of the Law of the Sea* (OUP 2015).
'The Rule of Law and the United Nations Convention on the Law of the Sea' (1996) 7 EJIL 353.
Pardo A, 'The New Law of the Sea and Some of Its Implications' (1987) 4 J L & Env't 1.
Pauwelyn J and Elsig M, 'The Politics of Treaty Interpretation. Variations and Explanations across International Tribunals' in Jeffrey L Dunoff and Mark A Pollack (eds), *Interdisciplinary Perspectives on International Law and International Relations. The State of the Art* (CUP 2013).
Pellet A, 'Article 38' in Zimmermann et al, *The Statute of the International Court of Justice : A Commentary* (2nd ed, OUP 2012).
Petersen N, 'Lawmaking by the International Court of Justice – Factors of Success' in Armin von Bogdandy and Ingo Venzke (eds), *In Whose Name?: A Public Law Theory of International Adjudication* (OUP 2014).
Pineschi L, 'The Duty of Environmental Impact Assessment in the First ITLOS Chamber's Advisory Opinion: Towards the Supremacy of the General Rule to Protect and Preserve the Marine Environment as a Common Value?' in Nerina Boschiero and others (eds), *International Courts and the Development of International Law* (Springer 2013).
Plakokefalos I, 'Seabed Disputes Chamber of the International Tribunal for the Law of the Sea: Responsibilities and Obligations of States Sponsoring Persons and

Entities with Respect to Activities in the Area Advisory Opinion' (2012) 24(1) Journal of Environmental Law 133.

Prescott V and Schofield C, *The Maritime Political Boundaries of the World* (2nd ed, Martinus Nijhoff 2005).

Proelss A (ed), 'Article 56' in Alexander Proelss (ed), *United Nations Convention on the Law of the Sea: A Commentary* (CH Beck, Hart, Nomos 2017).

'The Contribution of the ITLOS to Strengthening the Regime for the Protection of the Marine Environment' in Angela Del Vecchio and Roberto Virzo (eds), *Interpretations of the United Nations Convention on the Law of the Sea by International Courts and Tribunals* (Springer 2019).

'The Law on the Exclusive Economic Zone in Perspective: Legal Status and Resolution of User Conflicts Revisited' (2012), Ocean Yearbook Online 26.

United Nations Convention on the Law of the Sea: A Commentary (CH Beck, Hart, Nomos 2017).

Pulvenis JF, 'FAO, Ocean Governance, and the Law of the Sea' in Harry N. Scheiber and Jin-Hyun Paik (eds), *Regions, Institutions and the Law of the Sea* (Brill 2013).

Rao PC, 'Delimitation Disputes under the United Nations Convention on the Law of the Sea: Settlement Procedures' in Tafsir Malick Ndiaye and Rüdiger Wolfrum (eds), *Law of the Sea, Environmental Law and Settlement of Disputes: Liber Amicorum Judge Thomas A. Mensah* (Martinus Nijhoff 2007).

Rashbrooke G, 'The International Tribunal for the Law of the Sea: A Forum for the Development of Principles of International Environmental Law?' (2004) 19(4) IJMCL 515.

Rayfuse R, 'The Future of Compulsory Dispute Settlement Under the Law of the Sea Convention' (2005) 36 VUWLR 683.

Rosenne S, 'International Tribunal for the Law of the Sea: 1996–97 Survey' (1998) 13 IJMCL 487.

'Obstacles and Opportunities – Measuring the Quality of Judicial Reasoning' in Mátyás Bencze and Gar Yein Ng (eds), *How to Measure the Quality of Judicial Reasoning* (Springer 2018).

Ringbom H, 'Introduction' in Henrik Ringbom (ed), *Jurisdiction over Ships* (Brill 2014).

'Ships in ABNJ – Broadening Jurisdictional Opportunities for Non-flag States' in Vito De Lucia, Alex Oude Elferink, and Lan Ngoc Nguyen (eds), *International Law and Marine Areas beyond National Jurisdiction* (Brill 2022).

Romano CPR, 'The Shift from the Consensual to the Compulsory Paradigm in International Adjudication: Elements for a Theory of Consent' (2007) 39 NYUJILP 4.

Rothwell D and Stephens T, *The International Law of the Sea* (2nd ed, Hart Publishing 2016).

Ruys T and Soete A, 'Creeping' Advisory Jurisdiction of International Courts and Tribunals? The Case of the International Tribunal for the Law of the Sea' (2016) 29(1) LJIL 155.

Sage-Fuller B, *The Precautionary Principle in Marine Environmental Law: With Special Reference to High Risk Vessels* (Routledge 2013).

Sand PH, 'The Evolution of International Environmental Law' in Daniel Bodansky, Jutta Brunnée and Ellen Hey (eds), *The Oxford Handbook of International Environmental Law* (OUP 2008).

Sands P and Peel J, *Principles of International Environmental Law* (3rd ed, CUP 2012).

Scalieri E, 'Discretionary Power of Coastal States and the Control of Its Compliance with International Law by International Tribunals' in Angela Del Vecchio and Roberto Virzo (eds), *Interpretations of the United Nations Convention on the Law of the Sea by International Courts and Tribunals* (Springer 2019).

Schatz VJ, 'Combating Illegal Fishing in the Exclusive Economic Zone – Flag State Obligations in the Context of the Primary Responsibility of the Coastal State' (2016) 7(2) GJIL 383.

Schofield C, Telesetsky A and Lee S, 'A Tribunal Navigating Complex Waters: Implications of the Bay of Bengal Case' (2013) 444 ODIL 363.

Schofield C and Wang DK-H, 'The Regime of Islands under UNCLOS: Implications for the South China Sea' in Clive Schofield (ed), *Maritime Energy Resources in Asia: Legal Regimes and Cooperation* (National Bureau of Asian Research, Special Report No. 37, February 2012).

Scovazzi T, 'ITLOS and Jurisdiction over Ships' in Henrik Ringbom (ed), *Jurisdiction over Ships* (Brill 2014).

'The Contribution of the Tribunal to the Progressive Development of International Law' in Intl. Tribunal for the Law of the Sea (ed), *The Contribution of the International Tribunal for the Law of the Sea to the Rule of Law: 1996–2016* (Martinus Nijhoff 2017).

'Where the Judge Approaches the Legislator: Some Cases Relating to the Law of the Sea' in Nerina Boschiero and others (eds), *International Courts and the Development of International Law: Essays in Honour of Tullio Treves* (Springer 2013).

Serdy A, 'The Commission on the Limits of the Continental Shelf and Its Disturbing Propensity to Legislate' (2011) 26 IJCML 355.

Serdy A and Bliss M, 'Prompt Release of Fishing Vessels: State Practice in the Light of the Cases before the International Tribunal for the Law of the Sea' in Alex G Oude Elferink and Donald Rothwell (eds), *Oceans Management in the 21st Century: Institutional Frameworks and Responses* (Martinus Nijhoff 2002).

Shany Y, *Assessing the Effectiveness of International Courts* (CUP 2014).

Sharma SP, 'The Single Maritime Boundary Regime and the Relationship between the Continental Shelf and the Exclusive Economic Zone' (1987) 2 Int'l J Estuarine & Coastal L 203.

Smith JJ, 'Evolving to Conservation? The International Court's Decision in the Australia/Japan Whaling Case' (2014) 45(4) ODIL 301.

Smith RW and Thomas BL, 'Island Disputes and the Law of the Sea: An Examination of Sovereignty and Delimitation Disputes' in Myron H Norquist and John Norton Moore (eds), *Security Flashpoints: Oil, Islands, Sea Access and Military Confrontation* (Brill 1998).

Sohn LB, 'Voting Procedures in United Nations Conferences for the Codification of International Law' (1975) 69(2) AJIL 310.

Sohn LB, and others, *Cases and Materials on the Law of the Sea* (2nd ed, Martinus Nijhoff 2014) 79.

Squatrito T, Young OR, Follesdal A and Ulfstein G (eds), *The Performance of International Courts and Tribunals* (CUP 2018).

Stephens T, *International Courts and Environmental Protection* (CUP 2009).

Suarez SV, *The Outer Limits of the Continental Shelf: Legal Aspects of their Establishment* (Springer 2008).

Swan J, 'Fishing Vessels Operating under Open Registers and the Exercise of Flag State Responsibilities: Information and Options 2', FAO, Fisheries Circular No. 980, 2002.

'Port State Measures – From Residual Port State Jurisdiction to Global Standards' (2016) 31 IJMCL 395.

Symmons CR, 'Article 15' in Alexander Proelss (ed), *United Nations Convention on the Law of the Sea: A Commentary* (CH Beck, Hart, Nomos 2017).

'Historic Rights in the Light of the Award in the South China Sea Arbitration: What Remains of the Doctrine Now?' in S. Jayakumar et al. (eds), *The South China Sea Arbitration: The Legal Dimension* (Edward Elgar 2018).

Historic Waters and Historic Rights in the Law of the Sea: A Modern Reappraisal (2nd ed, Martinus Nijhoff 2019) 27.

'Maritime Zones from Islands and rocks' in S Jayakumar, Tommy Koh and Robert Beckman (eds), *The South China Sea Disputes and Law of the Sea* (Edward Elgar Publishing 2014).

Talmon S, 'Article 121' in Alexander Proelss (ed), *United Nations Convention on the Law of the Sea: A Commentary* (CH Beck, Hart, Nomos 2017).

'The Chagos Marine Protected Area Arbitration: Expansion of the Jurisdiction of UNCLOS Part XV Courts and Tribunals' (2016) 65(4) ICLQ 927.

'The South China Sea Arbitration: Is There a Case to Answer?' in Stefan Talmon and Bing Bing Jia (eds), *The South China Sea Arbitration: A Chinese Perspective* (Hart Publishing 2014).

Tams CJ, 'Meta-Custom and the Court: A Study in Judicial Law-Making' (2015) 14 LPICT 51.

'The ICJ as a "Law-Formative Agency": Summary and Synthesis' in Christian J Tams and James Sloan (eds), *The Development of International law by the International Court of Justice* (OUP 2013).

Tams CJ and Tzanakopoulos A, 'Barcelona Traction at 40: The ICJ as an Agent of Legal Development' (2010) 23(4) LJIL 781.

Tanaka Y, *Predictability and Flexibility in the Law of Maritime Delimitation* (2nd ed, Hart 2006).

'Provisional Measures Prescribed by ITLOS and Marine Environmental Protection' (2014) 108 Proceedings of the Annual Meeting of the American Society of International Law 365.

'Reflections on Historic Rights in the South China Sea Arbitration (Merits)' (2017) 32 IJMCL 3.

'Reflections on the Advisory Jurisdiction of ITLOS as a Full Court: The ITLOS Advisory Opinion of 2015' (2015) 14 The Law and Practice of International Courts and Tribunals 318.

The International Law of the Sea (CUP 2012).

The South China Sea Arbitration: Toward an International Legal Order in the Oceans (Hart Publishing 2019).

Telesetsky A, 'The International Tribunal for the Law of the Sea: Seeking the Legitimacy of State Consent' in Nienke Grossman and others (eds), *Legitimacy and International Courts* (CUP 2018).

Tomka P, 'The Contribution of the International Tribunal for the Law of the Sea to the Progressive Development of International Law' in *The Contribution of the International Tribunal for the Law of the Sea to the Rule of Law: 1996–2016* (Brill 2017).

Treves T, 'A System for Law of the Sea Dispute Settlement' in Richard Barnes, David Freestone and David Ong (eds), *The Law of the Sea: Progress and Prospects* (OUP 2006).

'Judicial Lawmaking in an Era of "Proliferation" of International Courts and Tribunals: Development or Fragmentation of International Law?' in Rudiger Wolfrum and V Röben (eds), *Developments of International Law in Treaty Making* (Springer 2005).

'The General Assembly and the Meeting of States Parties in the Implementation of the LOS Convention' in Alex G Oude Elferink (ed), *Stability and Change in the Law of the Sea: The Role of the LOS Convention* (Martinus Nijhoff 2005).

Trevino CJ, 'State-to-State Investment Treaty Arbitration and the Interplay with Investor–State Arbitration Under the Same Treaty' (2014) 5 JIDS 199.

Trevisanut S, 'The Exercise of Administrative Functions by ITLOS: A Comment on Prompt Release Case- Law' in Nerina Boschiero and others (eds), *International Courts and the Development of International Law: Essays in Honour of Tullio Treves* (Springer 2013).

'Twenty Years of Prompt Release of Vessels: Admissibility, Jurisdiction, and Recent Trends' (2017) 48(3–4) ODIL 300.

Trevisanut S, Giannopoulos, N and Roland Holst R, 'Introduction: Regime Interaction in Ocean Governance' in Seline Trevisanut, Nikolaos Giannopoulos and Rozemarijn Roland Holst (eds), *Regime Interaction in Ocean Governance Problems, Theories and Methods* (Brill 2020).

Trouwborst A, *Evolution and Status of the Precautionary Principle in International Law* (Kluwer Law International 2002).

'The Precautionary Principle in General International Law: Combating the Babylonian Confusion' (2007) 16 RECIEL 185.

'The Work of the International Tribunal for the Law of the Sea' (2012) 26 Ocean Yearbook 181.1

Ventura VAMF, 'Tackling Illegal, Unregulated and Unreported Fishing: the ITLOS Advisory Opinion on Flag State Responsibility for IUU fishing and the Principle of Due Diligence', (2015) 12 Braz J Int'l L 50.

Venzke I, *How Interpretation Makes International Law On Semantic Change and Normative Twists* (OUP 2012).

'The Role of International Courts as Interpreters and Developers of the Law: Working out the Jurisgenerative Practice of Interpretation' (2011) 34 LLAICLR 99.

Vicuña FO, *The Changing International Law of High Seas Fisheries* (CUP 1999).

Vidas D, 'The Delimitation of the Territorial Sea, the Continental Shelf, and the EEZ' in Alex G Oude Elferink, Tore Henriksen and Signe Veierud Busch (eds), *Maritime Boundary Delimitation: The Case Law: Is It Consistent and Predictable?* (CUP 2018).

von Bernstorff J, 'Specialized Courts and Tribunals as the Guardians of International Law? The Nature and Function of Judicial Interpretation in Kelsen and Schmitt' in Andreas Follesdal and Geir Ulfstein (eds), *The Judicialization of International Law: A Mixed Blessing?* (OUP 2018).

von Bogdandy A and Jacob M, 'The Judge as Law-Maker: Thoughts on Bruno Simma's Declaration in the Kosovo Opinion' in Ulrich Fastenrath and others (eds), *From Bilateralism to Community Interest: Essays in Honour of Bruno Simma* (OUP 2011).

von Bogdandy A and Venzke I, 'Beyond Disputes: International Judicial Institutions as Lawmakers' in Armin von Bogdandy and Ingo Venzke (eds), *International Judicial Lawmaking: On Public Authority and Democratic Legitimation in Global Governance* (Springer 2012).

International Judicial Lawmaking on Public Authority and Democratic Legitimation in Global Governance (Springer 2012).

In Whose Name?: A Public Law Theory of International Adjudication (OUP 2014).

'The Spell of Precedents: Lawmaking by International Court and Tribunals' in Cesare Romano, Karen Alter and Yuval Shany (eds), *Oxford Handbook of International Adjudication* (OUP 2013).

Vukas B and Vidas D, 'Flags of Convenience and High Seas Fishing: The Emergence of a Legal Framework' in Olav Schram Stokke, *Governing High Seas Fisheries: The Interplay of Global and Regional Regimes* (OUP 2001).

Waldock H, 'The International Court of Justice as Seen from the Bar and the Bench' BYBIL 54 (1983) 4.

Walker GK, *Definitions for the Law of the Sea: Terms Not Defined by the 1982 Convention* (Brill 2011).

Weil P, *The Law of Maritime Delimitation – Reflections* (Maureen MacGlashan tr, Cambridge Grotius Publications Limited 1989).

Weiss EB, 'The Evolution of International Environmental Law' (2011) 54 JYBIL 1.

Winter G (ed), *Towards Sustainable Fisheries Law: A Comparative Analysis* (IUCN 2009).

Wolfrum R, 'Conciliation under the UN Convention on the Law of the Sea' in Christian Tomuschat and others (eds), *Conciliation in International Law: The OSCE Court of Conciliation and Arbitration* (Brill 2016).

'Enforcing Community Interests through International Dispute Settlement: Reality of Utopia' in Ulrich Fastenrath and others (eds), *From Bilateralism to Community Interest: Essays in Honour of Bruno Simma* (OUP 2011).

'The Legal Order for the Seas and Oceans' in Myron H Nordquist and John Norton Moore (eds), *Entry into Force of the Law of the Sea Convention* (Martinus Nijhoff 1995).

'The Role of International Dispute Settlement Institutions in the Delimitation of the Outer Continental Shelf' in Rainer Lagoni and Daniel Vignes (eds), *Maritime Delimitation* (Martinus Nijhoff 2006).

Wood M, 'Choosing between Arbitration and a Permanent Court: Lessons from Inter-State Cases' (2017) 32(1) ICSID Review 1.

'The International Tribunal for the Law of the Sea and General International Law' (2007) 22 IJMCL 351.

'The Law of the Sea Convention and Agenda 21: Marine Environmental Implications' in Alan Boyle and David Freestone (eds) *International Law and Sustainable Development: Past Achievements and Future Challenges* (OUP 1999).

Yao H and Liao X, 'Natural Prolongation and Delimitation of the Continental Shelf beyond 200 nm: Implications of the Bangladesh/Myanmar Case' (2014) 4 Asian Journal of International Law 281.

Yee S, 'En Route to the Final Shape of the UNCLOS Dispute Settlement System: Some Pivotal Negotiating Procedural Steps Worthy of Consideration by Future Treaty-makers and Leaders in Treaty-making' (2014) 13 CJIL 185.

'The South China Sea Arbitration (The Philippines v. China): Potential Jurisdictional Obstacles or Objections' (2014) 13 CJIL 708.

You KJ, 'Advisory Opinions of the International Tribunal for the Law of the Sea: Article 138 of the Rules of the Tribunal, Revisited' (2008) 39 ODIL 360.

Young OR, 'Commentary on Shirley V. Scott "The LOS Convention as Constitutional Regime for the Oceans' in Alex G Oude Elferink (ed), *Stability and Change in the Law of the Sea: The Role of the LOS Convention* (Martinus Nijhoff 2005).

Zimmermann A and others, *The Statute of the International Court of Justice: A Commentary* (2nd ed, OUP 2012).

Zou K and Ye Q, 'Interpretation and Application of Article 298 of the Law of the Sea Convention in Recent Annex VII Arbitrations: An Appraisal' (2017) 48(3–4) ODIL 331.

Zwinge T, 'Duties of Flag States to Implement and Enforce International Standards and Regulations – And Measures to Counter Their Failure to Do So' (2011) 10(2) JIBL 297.

Index

For EU product safety concerns, contact us at Calle de José Abascal, 56–1°,
28003 Madrid, Spain or eugpsr@cambridge.org.

www.ingramcontent.com/pod-product-compliance
Lightning Source LLC
LaVergne TN
LVHW011704200926
848484LV00004B/1064